Helping Grieving People

When tears are not enough

D0108250

The Series in Death, Dying, and Bereavement
Consulting Editor
Robert A. Neimeyer

Beder—*Voices of Bereavement: A Casebook for Grief Counselors*
Davies—*Shadows in the Sun: The Experiences of Sibling Bereavement in Childhood*
Harvey—*Perspectives on Loss: A Sourcebook*
Klass—*The Spiritual Lives of Bereaved Parents*
Jeffreys—*Helping Grieving People—When Tears Are Not Enough: A Handbook for Care Providers*
Leenaars—*Lives and Deaths: Selections from the Works of Edwin S. Shneidman*
Lester—*Katie's Diary: Unlocking the Mystery of a Suicide*
Martin, Doka—*Men Don't Cry ... Women Do: Transcending Gender Stereotypes of Grief*
Morrissette—*The Pain of Helping: Psychological Injury of Helping Professionals*
Nord—*Multiple AIDS-Related Loss: A Handbook for Understanding and Surviving a Perpetual Fall*
Roos—*Chronic Sorrow: A Living Loss*
Rosenblatt—*Parent Grief: Narratives of Loss and Relationship*
Tedeschi & Calhoun—*Helping Bereaved Parents: A Clinician's Guide*
Silverman—*Widow to Widow, Second Edition*
Werth—*Contemporary Perspectives on Rational Suicide*

Formerly the Series in *Death Education, Aging, and Health Care*
Hannelore Wass, Consulting Editor

Bard—*Medical Ethics in Practice*
Benoliel—*Death Education for the Health Professional*
Bertman—*Facing Death: Images, Insights, and Interventions*
Brammer—*How to Cope with Life Transitions: The Challenge of Personal Change*
Cleiren—*Bereavement and Adaptation: A Comparative Study of the Aftermath of Death*
Corless, Pittman-Lindeman—*AIDS: Principles, Practices, and Politics, Abridged Edition*
Corless, Pittman-Lindeman—*AIDS: Principles, Practices, and Politics, Reference Edition*
Curran—*Adolescent Suicidal Behavior*
Davidson—*The Hospice: Development and Administration, Second Edition*
Davidson, Linnolla—*Risk Factors in Youth Suicide*
Degner, Beaton—*Life-Death Decisions in Health Care*
Doka—*AIDS, Fear, and Society: Challenging the Dreaded Disease*
Doty—*Communication and Assertion Skills for Older Persons*
Epting, Neimeyer—*Personal Meanings of Death: Applications for Personal Construct Theory to Clinical Practice*
Haber—*Health Care for an Aging Society: Cost-Conscious Community Care and Self-Care Approaches*
Hughes—*Bereavement and Support: Healing in a Group Environment*
Irish, Lundquist, Nelsen—*Ethnic Variations in Dying, Death, and Grief: Diversity in Universality*
Klass, Silverman, Nickman—*Continuing Bonds: New Understanding of Grief*
Lair—*Counseling the Terminally Ill: Sharing the Journey*
Leenaars, Maltsberger, Neimeyer—*Treatment of Suicidal People*
Leenaars, Wenckstern—*Suicide Prevention in Schools*
Leng—*Psychological Care in Old Age*
Leviton—*Horrendous Death, Health, and Well-Being*
Leviton—*Horrendous Death and Health: Toward Action*
Lindeman, Corby, Downing, Sanborn—*Alzheimer's Day Care: A Basic Guide*
Lund—*Older Bereaved Spouses: Research with Practical Applications*
Neimeyer—*Death Anxiety Handbook: Research, Instrumentation, and Application*
Papadatou, Papadatos—*Children and Death*
Prunkl, Berry—*Death Week: Exploring the Dying Process*
Ricker, Myers—*Retirement Counseling: A Practical Guide for Action*
Samarel—*Caring for Life and Death*
Sherron, Lumsden—*Introduction to Educational Gerontology, Third Edition*
Stillion—*Death and Sexes: An Examination of Differential Longevity Attitudes, Behaviors, and Coping Skills*
Stillion, McDowell, May—*Suicide Across the Life Span—Premature Exits*
Vachon—*Occupational Stress in the Care of the Critically Ill, the Dying, and the Bereaved*
Wass, Corr—*Childhood and Death*
Wass, Corr—*Helping Children Cope with Death: Guidelines and Resource, Second Edition*
Wass, Corr, Pacholski, Forfar—*Death Education II: An Annotated Resource Guide*
Wass, Neimeyer—*Dying: Facing the Facts, Third Edition*
Weenolsen—*Transcendence of Loss over the Life Span*
Werth—*Rational Suicide? Implications for Mental Health Professionals*

Helping Grieving People

When tears are not enough

A HANDBOOK FOR CARE PROVIDERS

J. Shep Jeffreys, Ed.D., C.T.

Brunner-Routledge
Taylor & Francis Group

NEW YORK AND HOVE

Published in 2005 by
Brunner-Routledge
270 Madison Avenue
New York, NY 10016
www.brunner-routledge.com

Published in Great Britain by
Brunner-Routledge
2 Park Square
Milton Park, Abingdon,
Oxon OX14 4RN U.K.
www.brunner-routledge.co.uk

Copyright © 2005 by Taylor & Francis Books, Inc.

Brunner-Routledge is an imprint of the Taylor & Francis Group.

Printed in the United States of America on acid-free paper.

All rights reserved. No part of this book may be reprinted or reproduced or utilized in any form or by any electronic, mechanical, or other means, now known or hereafter invented, including photocopying and recording, or in any information storage or retrieval system, without permission in writing from the publishers.

10 9 8 7 6 5 4 3 2

Library of Congress Cataloging-in-Publication Data

Jeffreys, J. Shep (John Shep)
   Helping grieving people : a handbook for care providers / J. Shep
Jeffreys.
      p. cm. — (Series in death, dying, and bereavement)
   Includes bibliographical references and index.
   ISBN 0-415-94603-4 (pbk.)
   1. Grief.   2. Bereavement--Psychological aspects.   3.
Death—Psychological aspects.   4. Loss (Psychology) I. Title. II.
Series.

   BF575.G7J45 2004
   155.9'37--dc22

2004020090

Dedication

This book is dedicated to the memory of Steven Daniel Jeffreys, who died at age 8 in 1975. His illness and subsequent death have created major and ongoing changes in my family's life and in the development of my own understanding of the human grief response.

These waves of change led me to my focus of working with grieving people and ultimately to the writing of this book. To the extent that my work assists others who are grieving, Steven's illness and death are a gift to their healing process.

In Memorium—Elizabeth Kubler-Ross, M.D. 1926–2004

CONTENTS

SERIES EDITOR'S FOREWORD

"As an 'exquisite witness,'" writes Shep Jeffreys, "we observe more than act, listen more than talk, and follow more than lead. *Witnessing* celebrates the dignity and authority of the grieving person." And indeed, in his book-length elaboration of this theme, Jeffreys exemplifies the sort of witnessing he advocates, offering the reader a handbook for helping professionals that is keenly observant, one that is impressively grounded in his listening to innumerable stories of grief and eventual gain, and one that unflinchingly follows the bereaved into the daunting terrain of a transformed world. What emerges from these pages is not only a keen respect for the authority of the mourner, but also a sense of Jeffreys's own authority, as he winnows the lessons he has learned from his own losses and those of the countless people he has supported in their quest to move beyond the death of a loved one to a life again worth living.

As an appreciative reader, I found the scope of the book remarkable, nearly encyclopedic. Beginning with existential, spiritual, and cultural foundations for an understanding of grief, Jeffreys proceeds to construct a scientific scaffolding for the work to follow. Central to this effort is a consideration of attachment theory and the ways in which various patterns of insecure attachment predispose to complicated bereavement, a discussion that is deepened and broadened by a review of the most progressive contemporary grief theories, focusing on tasks, coping orientations, and processes of meaning reconstruction. Layered onto this primarily individualistic level of analysis, Jeffreys adds a consideration of family structures and transitions that influence the grief of surviving members when a loved one dies. What keeps this from becoming an academic tome is his penchant for distilling relevant procedures for aiding the bereaved person, in the form of loss inventories, family genograms, healing tasks, and a plethora of suggestions for assessing the distressed client or family consulting the professional *witness*.

What follows is in many respects the clinical core of the book: a detailed treatment of the distinctive challenges of various groups of grievers, from children to parents and from bereaved elders to the dying themselves. In every instance, Jeffreys orients the reader to unique factors that exacerbate the distress of the relevant subgroup, condensing his intelligent discussion of illustrative cases into easily assimilated bullet points to remind the helper of the most relevant considerations in working with each. Personally, I found Jeffreys's discussion of the loss of a child especially evocative, perhaps because—as he acknowledges in the book's opening pages—it is a grievous loss that he knows so intimately from personal experience. As he goes on to offer a host of tangible guidelines for responding appropriately to the pain, guilt, and complications of such losses, he weaves consistently between the self and social system, balancing interventions for the individual griever with the facilitation of support on the part of a community of concern. It quickly becomes evident that Jeffreys is equally at home with the psychotherapeutic promotion of forgiveness (of both self and other) and the recruitment of broader supports—sometimes in ritual form—for those most aggrieved by a particular loss. In this respect, this handbook strikes me as equally relevant to the secular and spiritual helper, essentially assisting each to supplement her or his core disciplinary strengths with the complementary resources of other perspectives.

Finally, I would be remiss if I did not draw attention to the style that pervades much of the book. Alternately personal and poetic as well as professional, *Helping Grieving People* draws with equal comfort on the author's own rich trove of experience, on an artistic sensibility for capturing the poignancy of reflective moments, and on a range of contemporary theories that usefully inform our quest to understand bereavement and the needs of those subjected to it. It is a work packed with plenty of practical pointers for professional helpers, and one that is guaranteed to sharpen one's skill as an *exquisite witness* to the anguish and achievements of those whose lives are touched by loss.

Robert A. Neimeyer, Ph.D.
Series Editor
University of Memphis

HOW TO USE THIS BOOK

For many people, tears, prayers, loved ones, friends, and the passage of time will support their grief journey of healing through loss. This book is intended for professional care providers, trained volunteers, and family caregivers who supply varying levels of help for grieving people—the bereaved, the dying, the chronically ill or disabled, and their families—when tears are not enough. This handbook has been written to meet the clinical needs of healthcare professionals, clergy, and other trained individuals as well as the needs of trained volunteers and family caregivers. The chapters follow a pathway to understanding the three aspects of the *exquisite witness*—the "heart" dimension (self-awareness), the "head" dimension (understanding the human grief response), and the "hands" dimension (supportive and clinical interventions).

The "heart" dimension is concerned with the care provider's own unfinished loss material. This is addressed with self-awareness exercises placed in the text as a mechanism to alert you to unfinished personal loss material (Cowbells). I ask you to take these seriously and complete them. They are not clinical assessment tools but rather exercises that can help to stimulate your thinking about your Cowbells. To further assist with the heart dimension, I suggest that you begin a diary or journal of physical and/or emotional reactions to the exercises and any memories that are triggered as you read and reflect. Talk to a trusted friend or colleague, spiritual advisor, or counselor. These reactions are like buried gold. Walking away from this book without examining your feelings can limit the value of the work you can do for grieving people.

The "head" dimension, which is concerned with the understanding of what the complexities of human grief are, is contained in each of the chapters of this book. In chapter 1, we review the cultural and social impacts on how people grieve and the death-related rituals they use. This is followed by a review of theories and explanations of human grief in chapter 2. The role of family in the shaping and healing of human grief follows in chapter 3. The unique needs of three populations of grievers—children, parents, and older adults—are given special attention in chapters 4, 5, and 6 respectively. Chapter 7 is devoted to an understanding of the dying, chronically and terminally ill, and their families.

The "hands" dimension is concerned with care provider interventions. Look for recommendations that have been placed in **care provider boxes** at the end of didactic material in the text. These represent general suggestions regarding a particular issue and should be modified to fit the unique needs of an individual or family. This dimension is further elaborated in chapter 8, where we consider a continuum of supportive and clinical strategies for family caregivers, volunteers, and professional care providers. Chapter 9 reviews complicated grief syndromes as well as associated psychiatric disorders, and includes suggestions for the professional care provider following each description of complicated grief syndrome.

In chapter 10, by way of reviewing the learning experience of readers, seven case studies are presented. Five of the cases are provided with recommendations for initial interventions and two cases have the recommendations omitted for the reader to address.

The epilogue contains a story about people who help others, and who "don't turn their eyes away." It is also a time for saying good-bye, for now.

Appendix A is a list of suggested readings grouped by subject matter; appendix B lists organizational resources, and appendix C is a model of an advanced medical directive.

PREFACE

It was 1972. My wife and I would frequently remark that "our cup runneth over." We had a wonderful marriage, three beautiful children, a new home, a new doctorate, and my recent promotion to head the state education department's program of pupil services—truly we were blessed.

The phone call came late one afternoon from my wife telling me that our pediatrician wanted to see us immediately. Our youngest, 5-year-old Steven, had viral pneumonia, and when it had run its course, a follow-up chest x-ray showed that the original dark patch on his lung had grown twice its size. I knew then that our lives would never be the same; and when the lymph node biopsy indicated lymphosarcoma, "our cup ran dry."

For three years we became part of the pediatric cancer subculture at Johns Hopkins Hospital. We learned about medications, radiation, and about their terrible but necessary side effects and those painful procedures. We learned and lived in the constant nightmarish fear of losing our child. Steven's sister and brother suffered during his illness and after his death from their own grief as well as from our unavailability.

When Steven took his last breath on Sunday night, November 23, 1975, we held him, talked to him, and some hours later, when his body had grown cold, we let go of him physically. We went home and the four of us bundled into bed, wept, and eventually slept.

Thus began a massive rewrite of our lives.

Five years later, as a practicing psychologist preparing a program for parents with children in the pediatric oncology service, I attended a weeklong residential workshop on life, death, and transition given by Elisabeth Kubler-Ross, MD. My unfinished grief emerged like underground waters coming to the surface.

I later became a member of Elisabeth's workshop and training staff. My general practice of psychology transitioned through the years to focus on increasing numbers of bereaved people and those coping with life-threatening and life-limiting medical conditions. In 1990, our family and a group of friends formed The Steven Daniel Jeffreys Foundation, Ltd. Its programs have included grief counseling, "Healing Through Loss" workshops, professional conferences, community education programs, and "Tears and Smiles"—bereavement groups for children and their parents.

In 1988, I began offering seminars and ongoing support groups for the staff of Johns Hopkins' AIDS Service and joined the psychiatry faculty of Johns Hopkins School of Medicine. My work also now includes teaching a course in loss and bereavement in the Pastoral Counseling Department of Loyola College in Maryland. The impetus for this book comes from the need for a resource handbook for my graduate students at Loyola College, the psychiatric residents at Johns Hopkins, and the many professional and volunteer providers and family caregivers who over the years have asked me, "What do I do to help grieving people?"

The effect of Steven's death on my life has moved me into an area that I would likely have never chosen. My work and this book are truly the gift of his loss. His loss makes the blessings we have in our life feel even more precious.

To that extent, "our cup runneth over" again.

ACKNOWLEDGMENTS

Each of us comes to our own self-discovery through life events. I have had the blessing of a wonderful partner in my wife, Helane, who has shared the pain and joy of this life journey and has been at my side throughout this entire project—thank you forever. Our children, Deborah and Ronald, have been an essential part of who we were and became as a family during and after our son Steven's 3-year illness and death. They were gracious enough to provide retrospective commentary in the "Siblings Speak" section of chapter 5.

For an incredible job of editing, I am so happy to thank Roberta Israeloff. Deepest appreciation for the critical reviews and consistent support go to Dr. Grady Dale, Linda Goldman, and Dr. Jay Levinson. To Dr. Ellen Zinner, thank you for your exquisite insights and gracious gift of time. To Ann Rita Zimmerman, eternal gratitude for your exquisite help, and to Sharon Barrett for invaluable help. Very special thanks to Dr. Ron Jeffreys for medical review and suggestions in chapter 7, to colleagues Dr. Gail Walter and Dr. Carol Brothers for psychological content review, and to Patricia Wudel for her valuable inputs and care provider deathbed suggestions in chapter 7. Much appreciation to Phyllis Madachy and the staff of The Howard County (MD) Office of Aging. Thanks also to Richard Yocum, Rev. Janet Buntrock, Mary Cadden, and my sister, Brenda Jeffreys. My grateful appreciation to Dr. John Morgan, Dr. Brad Sachs and Dr. Bob Wicks for their early support and encouragement. Gratitude is also expressed to Margaret and Kent Pendleton and to Stephanie Gianfagna for their generosity of time and information, and to John Hamilton, III, for his recommendations for victims of traumatic brain injury.

Finally, my sincere appreciation goes to Emily Epstein Loeb, and Dana Bliss at Brunner-Routledge for their confidence and helpful guidance.

I would also like to acknowledge the education that I have gained over the years from my private clinical clients, students, and workshop/lecture attendees. I also wish to thank the many bereaved parents I know at the Compassionate Friends, as well as participants in the "Healing Through Loss" workshops of the Steven Daniel Jeffreys Foundation.

My very special appreciation is extended to the late Elisabeth Kubler-Ross, MD, with whom I staffed over 12 years of workshops on life, death, and transition, and from whom I learned much about my own grief and how to help others heal from loss.

J. Shep Jeffreys

INTRODUCTION—THE CARE PROVIDER AS AN EXQUISITE WITNESS

"When you go through the tumbler of life, you can come out crushed or polished."

Elisabeth Kubler-Ross (1981)

You Never Know . . .

What is going on inside someone else's mind—the person walking by you on the street, standing behind you at the checkout stand, waiting at the stop light in the car next to you, smiling hello as you enter the elevator, serving you coffee or sitting across the aisle in the commuter train—what he or she is thinking.

How much pain or rage is tearing at a person's heart or how much an individual is struggling just to make it through another day at work.

Who or what a person has lost and how much that man, woman, or child is obsessing about the loss every waking minute of the day.

How much grief and anguish is being held inside or with how much longing that person wishes that it were just a bad dream.

What else may surface when you are helping a grieving person.

Which of your own losses will be triggered when you help grieving people through their grief, and how this may affect your ability to help.

What another's pain is like even if the loss seems just like your own.

How unprepared you can feel until you experience the sense of, "I don't know what to say or do right now."

How prepared you really are until you relate to the grieving person more as a human soul in pain and less as a diagnosis or the object of a particular clinical skill to be used.

Yet You Can Become . . .

One human soul sitting with another who is suffering the pain of grief.

A care provider who understands that the grief journey is different for each individual.

A care provider who is sensitive to different cultural backgrounds and understands that your function is to support the journey and not control it.

A care provider who learns the "heart, head, and hands" approach to providing care.

A care provider who is an *exquisite witness* for a grieving person—whether you are a trained professional, volunteer, or a family caregiver—this is what so many grieving people hope for.

The goal of this book is to point the way for grief care providers to learn how to become such an exquisite witness using the heart, head, and hands dimensions of care.

Exquisite Witness Defined

The *exquisite witness* is a health care, pastoral, or volunteer care provider who enters the sacred space between two human souls—having the deepest respect for the yearning, seeking, wishful hopes of the other to diminish pain and survive in a new world after a loss.

The term *exquisite witness* encompasses my beliefs regarding the role of anyone who steps forward to help a grieving person. A teacher; funeral director; fire, police, or rescue personnel; employee assistance counselor; a medical receptionist; or a family member who becomes the home caregiver can assume this role. An *exquisite witness* might be a friend, someone from the faith community who comes to visit the family, or the surgeon who stops by the recovery room after removing a tumor and then proceeds to reassure the waiting loved ones. What distinguishes an *exquisite witness* is not one's level of training but one's willingness to approach another human being with compassion and deep respect for that person's needs, fear, and grief.

The *exquisite* nature of the interaction is measured in terms of respect, care, honesty, and the ability to truly hear and understand the grieving person's anger and confusion. It may take very little time. A gifted psychiatrist whom I accompany on rounds for medically ill patients at Johns Hopkins Hospital is able, during a ten-minute conversation, to answer patients' concerns and make them feel cared for, respected, and hopeful. I have also seen a member of the housekeeping staff on an inpatient AIDS unit calm an agitated patient with a smile and casual conversation about the Baltimore Orioles' lineup.

The term *witness* directs the care provider to understand that the grief journey belongs to the grieving person—whether he or she has lost a loved one, has a chronic/terminal illness, has been admitted to the hospital for tests, has a loved one who is ill or dying, or has new job responsibilities in a reorganized workplace. As a witness we *observe more than act, listen more than talk, and follow more than lead. Witnessing* celebrates the dignity and authority of the grieving person.

Characteristics of the Exquisite Witness . . .

Has a commitment to self and is attuned to stored personal loss material. Such a care provider can, therefore, accompany grieving people into painful places on their journey, confident in knowing where his or her limitations in professional and personal availability are. This care provider also knows how to access the professional and spiritual resources available for personal growth.

Is more than a good listener, more than knowledgeable, and more than a skilled intervener. This care provider can join with a person deeply in grief and is generous with time and energy.

Draws from personal life experience to join with grieving people; whose own grief is healed in part through service to others—a "wounded healer."

Has a comfortable command of the psychological and sociological phenomena of human grief and its varied and changing forms.

Has a repertoire of intervention skills, including exquisite listening, to facilitate the healing of grieving people.

Has a commitment to a religious or other spiritual pathway or self-discovery journey that provides continued resources, emotional health, personal growth, and professional development.

Is not simply a matter of "This is what I do because this is what I have trained to do," but rather "This is what I do because this is part of the meaning of who I am and how I choose to live."

The "Heart, Head, and Hands" Dimensions Defined

An *exquisite witness* must address personal loss issues (the heart dimension), is knowledgeable about what to expect from grieving people (the head dimension), and has the skills to respond both usefully and reassuringly (the hands dimension).

The Heart Dimension

The "heart" dimension represents the process whereby old loss material may rise to the surface and interfere with the ability of a care provider to be available to a grieving person. This recall may be triggered by circumstances of the case that are similar to the care provider's current or earlier life grief experiences.

When professional or volunteer care providers do not identify their own personal loss issues, they may consciously or unconsciously avoid areas of interaction that could have been of help to the grieving person. As human beings who attach and bond, we all have loss material, and the grieving person we are working with may trigger some unfinished grief. *No one is untouched.*

The nurse or physician who avoids a particular patient's room—a case worker who limits the depth of information seeking—a counselor who keeps the conversation at a superficial level—or a hospice volunteer who becomes overly involved with one family—may be dealing with old, unfinished loss material.

To be truly available to grieving people, care providers must examine their own unresolved loss and grief. This is the heart dimension of the "heart, head, and hands" approach to *exquisite witness* care providing.

Cowbells

Cowbells—The way unfinished business is stored and its subsequent effects on a provider's own grief experience is illustrated by the following personal story.

When I was 4 years old, I attended a preschool program in a community center just across the street from where my family lived. Each morning the children would line up and get a tablespoon of cod liver oil—all from the same spoon! After some indoor games we were sent outside to the playground. This was an area with a chain link fence separating us from the sidewalk and the street beyond. I could see our home and as soon as we got outside, I would run directly to the fence and stick my little fingers and nose through the fence and look longingly, yearningly toward my home. The image of my "Mommy" was clearly in my mind and I missed her and ached to be back with her.

At that same time every day, a junkman with a pushcart filled with old clothes and items he had been collecting, came by ringing a cowbell roped to the handlebar of the cart, to announce his presence in the neighborhood. The sound of that cowbell and my yearning, grieving feelings became connected.

Throughout my life when I have had aching, grieving feelings come up, the look on my face prompts my wife to ask, Cowbells? And I answer—Cowbells.

Throughout the years, a symphony of Cowbells rings out. We all have our Cowbells.

They accompany us to the bedside of every patient, to our interactions with counseling or pastoral clients, to parishioners, to staff meetings, to treatment planning, and to every human contact we engage in. As care providers, it is our responsibility to be sufficiently aware of them so that our own *Cowbells do not drown out our clients!—ask not for whom the Cowbells toll; they toll for thee . . .* and me!

Personal self-awareness exercises are provided throughout this book and should be part of all provider training and in-service education as well.

The Head Dimension

The "head" dimension refers to knowledge of the phenomenon we know as grief; its many subcategories as well as its dynamic shifts and changes over time. This includes understanding the biological/instinctual basis for grief reactions, the expected feelings and thoughts of grieving, as well as behaviors derived from the social environment over time.

Providers also need to appreciate both the traditional and more recent explanations regarding the nature of grief and its predictable patterns. Knowing what can be expected from grieving people will not only enable care providers to give the highest level of service but will also increase provider comfort.

The Hands Dimension

The "hands" dimension represents what the care provider says and does to help the grieving person engage in the process of mourning in the healthiest way possible. It includes the way providers interact, gather information, make decisions and suggestions, and gauge the level of appropriate intervention. Many grieving people in my clinical practice simply want to tell their story to someone who won't interrupt them or look at their watch or change the subject. A grieving person may need to be heard over and over again without receiving any advice, interpretations, or words of wisdom.

As discussed in chapter 2, the telling and retelling of the story of a grieving person's loss is an important part of his or her healing. In this context the provider agrees to be a nonjudgmental *exquisite witness*. It is more than being a skilled listener. It means hearing with the heart and knowing that you, the *exquisite witness* care provider, are engaged in a healing process with another human being and can feel the joy of this healing. This is sacred ground.

Summary

The "heart, head, and hand" dimensions direct the *exquisite witness* to know his or her own grief issues, to understand the human grief response and its variations, and to have a repertoire of support and/or clinical skills to use for helping grieving people.

When Adam and Eve were sent from the Garden, they were informed that a gift awaited them outside. They wept as they looked back at the sealed gates and were aware after their weeping subsided that they felt comforted. This was their gift—the tears of healing.

But … sometimes *tears are not enough*! That's when grieving people need you.

The Social and Cultural Context of Grief

"We are all tattooed in our cradles with the beliefs of our tribe."

Oliver Wendell Holmes, Sr. (in Fenchuk; 1994, p. 2)

☐ Introduction

The purpose of this chapter is to give the care provider a sense of the social and cultural environment in which grieving people live, and convey the importance of respecting who they are and the societal norms and cultural legacies that influence their grief. Everybody grieves: old—young, incarcerated—free, religious—nonbelievers, foreign born—native born, rich—poor. Death and traumatic loss are part of being alive. Not wanting to talk about it is very human.

We usually associate grief with death and the loss of loved ones. But grief comes from many sources other than illness, death, and the process of dying. The traumatic changes that have been occurring in our world both before and after September 11, 2001, have created ongoing death-like losses for millions of people who have lost jobs, retirement security, and a sense of well-being. Whether a loss is due to death, workplace changes, forest fires, floods, or the loss of a favorite pair of gloves, we each have a reaction called grief.

☐ The Humanness of Avoiding Grief

Let us look for a moment at ways most Western cultures respond to death, loss, and grief. In Western society, we frequently address death, injury, and loss through humor, an approach that enables us to release some of the tension we feel by laughing. Death, loss, and aging make up the material for many stand-up comics, newspaper comic strips, and situation comedies. Humor is a common way to soften, cover up, and avoid the full impact of the reality of our own mortality and that of our loved ones. We see further evidence of our need to avoid the unpleasant reality of death by the wealth of euphemisms we use to refer to it. We say someone "kicked the bucket," "bought the farm," "went to the big ballpark in the sky," "bit the dust," "is pushing up daisies," or "croaked."

Another way to keep the painful reality of death and loss away is simply not to talk about it or avoid the subject. I have heard the following ancient Persian folk tale in many different versions. It illustrates the very human need to run away from death.

> A wealthy prince was preparing for a magnificent banquet and sent a servant out into the garden to gather flowers for the tables. When the young man entered the garden, he shrieked with horror, for there stood Death. It raised its hands. He raced back into the palace and begged his master to save him from Death. The prince said, "Run to the stables and take my fastest horse and flee to Damascus. It is far from this place; you will be safe there!" The prince watched as the servant boy ran to the stables and quickly emerged on a fine racing horse. He soon disappeared in a cloud of dust toward Damascus. The prince angrily strode into the garden where Death stood with its hands still raised and demanded, "How dare you enter my grounds and frighten my servant!" "But Sire," Death replied, "I was only

expressing my surprise at seeing him here, for you see I have an appointment with him tonight—in Damascus."

No matter how far we run away from the inevitability of death and/or other life changes and losses, it happens every day to people in our communities. (See Table 1.1.)

Avoiding Grief

When patients and doctors avoid talking about the gravity of an illness, when families do not want loved ones to know how serious things are, or when death, grief, and painful change are simply avoided topics, we hear the word *denial* used. Some avoidance and use of humor are healthy responses to loss. We need our system of denial to allow ourselves time to get used to the idea that the loss is irreversible—the tumor is malignant, the company has been taken over, or life as we have known it will never be the same. Denial is the shock absorber for painful loss and crisis; it allows us to digest the truth in small bits. But the question remains: How much denial is healthy? When is joking helpful and when is it harmful?

The fact that some have labeled Americans as a "death-denying society" is simply saying that we are a human society that seeks to avoid pain. Who wants pain? No one does. As care providers, we must respect the rights of a grieving person or family or coworkers to formulate some form of a denial system. Denial can be problematic, however, when there is failure to: (a) get medical attention, (b) take needed health or safety precautions, (c) make necessary legal arrangements, (d) follow medical advice, or (e) maintain vigilance against suicidal or other harmful behaviors.

If a person doesn't want to "talk about it" or even have a conversation about advanced directives, these wishes need to be respected. Sensitive caregivers will gently re-introduce the topic during a later conversation. For many in our society, especially health care providers, death represents failure and defeat. It yields guilt and self-reproach as part of the grief response. It is easier simply not to talk about it, distract ourselves, and get to it later. Some people hold on to the hope that a very sick and/or dying person is going to be okay in the face of medical information to the contrary and obvious worsening of the patient's condition.

In a family where a man was rapidly losing ground to cancer, his wife and children were able to continually adjust their expectations about his level of participation in family activities. Yet, his own parents and siblings steadily maintained that he would be fine and that there was no cause for concern. The unfortunate result of this strong resistance to the reality of the man's medical condition was that his wife and children received little or no support from those relatives. The lack of support left this family with continuing major conflicts in the aftermath of this man's death.

In another case, the family was very aware of the rapid deterioration; and it was the patient who was in denial.

A man with advanced cancer came to see me. He was very optimistic about a new chemotherapy treatment his doctor had told him about. His weight had recently dropped drastically, but he remained confident he would be much better after the new treatment began. His wife privately informed me that he was unrealistically positive and had no chance of surviving even if he were able to tolerate the new chemotherapy. She was unable to get him to have a conversation about advanced directives in the event that he would not benefit from the new chemotherapy.

The man came to see me two more times and resisted any discussion of any possibilities other than remission. Before he was able to keep his next appointment, he was hospitalized. When I visited him there, he told me that he and the doctor had agreed that the new chemotherapy would not be useful and he was not going to have any more treatment. He returned home and continued to avoid any discussion of dying or saying good-bye. In a short time he simply lay down in bed, and within an hour, he died. The family was left with much sadness over the absence of any conversation regarding how he felt at the end of life and what he might have said to them before dying.

People who lose a loved one require their own timing as to when and to what extent they accept that the deceased is gone and is not coming back. It is not unusual for a family member to return home after the burial and pick up a ringing phone with the hope that it "might be Mom." ("But we just buried Mom!" "I know, I just thought maybe it was a mistake.") This is not crazy or unusual. The head knows, but the heart is not ready to let go yet.

Holding on in the face of reality may take the form of keeping the room, house, clothing, and other personal effects exactly as they had been. Denial of the terrible truth is what we do. "She's just on a long trip." "He's still away at school." Adults as well as children can engage in "magical thinking," and it serves a useful function by buffering the painful reality. This is made even more difficult when there is no body recovered as in war, explosions, and air and sea disasters. The denial may last a lifetime. The lack of a physical body and the inability to know that life has truly ceased for the loved one leave the survivors with an eternal question that may never be answered.

Here is a personal story of denial before and after the death of our son.

> During the early months of our son Steven's cancer treatment, Elisabeth Kubler-Ross came to my hometown to give a lecture. Our friends all bought her book, *On Death and Dying* (1969), and went to hear her. I did not go. I did not need to go and hear the "death lecture" because Steven was going to get well. We would get him into remission and keep him there until he was "clear of cancer." As each recurrence shattered hopes and plunged us into new panic, I would obtain the new statistics and hold onto the percentage for survival. When the odds for survival dropped from 40% to 10%, I held on to the 10% like a drowning man with a lifeline in 100-foot waves. I did the same when the odds dropped to 1%. Even on the day he died, I hoped that another blood transfusion would create a miracle.
>
> I needed that denial to continue my role in the family, in my work, and just to survive daily caring for and emotionally supporting Steven. Denial didn't end even after the funeral and burial had taken place. I was in such great denial that I needed help from some outside source to help me express the grief locked up within me. I was too busy being a caregiver to the family, maintaining my professional life, and trying to be spiritual in spite of my utter disgust with the notion of a merciful God.
>
> Five years later at a Kubler-Ross workshop, however, I exploded with the stored grief material of Steven's illness and death and also old grief related to the sudden death of my mother when I was 16. I worked to release my pain, anger, and fear of losing anyone else. This eventually gave me much relief and restored enough energy to reclaim life.

Some denial and humor are healthy responses to loss. We need denial to allow us time to get used to the idea that our loved one is gone forever, that the blood test is HIV positive, that the business is bankrupt, that the World Trade Center is gone from the New York skyline, or that prayers were not answered.

☐ Statistical Realities of Death and Illness

In spite of how fast and how far we physically or psychologically flee from the troubling reality of our own mortality and that of loved ones,

TABLE 1.1. U.S. Total All Causes of Death: 2002
Preliminary = 2,447,862

		Total Deaths	
1997 = 2,314,738* 1999 = 2,391,399* 2001 = 2,404,624*			
Total Children Deaths	*2000*	*2001*	*2002* *(Preliminary)*
Under 1	27,983	27,568	27,977
1–4	4,942	5,107	4,862
5–14	7,340	7,095	7,169
15–24	30,959	32,252	33,075
Total	71,230	72,022	73,083
Type of Death	*2000*	*2001*	*2002*
Cardiovascular	709,894	700,141	695,754
Cancer	551,833	553,768	558,847
Cerebrovascular	166,028	163,538	163,010
Pulmonary	123,550	123,013	125,500
All Accidents	93,592	101,537	102,303
Diabetes mellitus	68,662	71,372	73,119
Alzheimer's	49,044	53,852	58,785
Motor Vehicle	41,804		
Septicemia	33,881		
Suicide	28,332	30,646	
Homicide	16,765	20,308**	17,045

*National Vital Statistics Reports 1996, 1997, 2001, 2003, 2004 U.S. Centers For Disease
Control and Prevention
**Includes deaths from 9-11-01

the fact is that the 6 billion people on Earth will die on schedule within their lifetimes. It's estimated that 2,400,000 Americans died in the year 2000. (See Table 1.1.)

The above data have been drawn from several issues of National Vital Statistics Reports (1996, 1997, 2001). Based on the number of deaths for 2000, every year between 14 and 19 million or even more people who are the family and friends of the deceased are estimated to join the ranks of bereaved. Every year roughly 140,000 parents lose a child. Every year over a million and a half people die of illnesses, and many losses occur along the way before the final death. These are the realities, regardless of our use of humor and avoidance.

☐ Cultural Legacies and Societal Values Affecting Grief

Death Happens

Death is a natural part of human life. Through the ages, every society has shaped various cultural behaviors to acknowledge and celebrate the death of one of its members. "We are not born with our attitudes toward dying and bereavement, the way we are born with our needs for food, drink, and sex" (Morgan, 1995, p. 25). We learn these attitudes from the cultural legacies and societal value systems into which we are born. Religious belief systems typically have a set of customary activities—chants, prayers, dance, and ceremonial items related to the death event. Burial sites, tools, and artwork of human cultures as far back as the Ice Age have revealed the variety of human beliefs regarding death and dealing with our bodies when we are no longer alive. This awareness of death and the expectation of a transition to some other existence are shown in the preserved items found in the ground, in caves, and in drawings and writings of earlier civilizations.

The rites and practices surrounding death are largely associated with religious belief systems, although military and other organizational rituals may also be a part of a ceremony. Many religions also specify what are appropriate family practices during the period of active dying, at the time of death, and following death. Varying beliefs in an afterlife are presented in tribal theologies as well as in the more widely practiced faiths of today.

Each civilization provides for this natural part of life. While the behavior of mourners is usually affected by their particular religion or other cultural influences, the outcome of living is the same—*death happens.*

Grief Happens

When death happens, grief happens. But grief does not wait for death to happen in order to make its entrance. Grief gets an early start. It will very likely occur as soon as we form an image of the death that could happen. Grief is an equal opportunity human reaction; grief affects everyone. While there are many similarities in grieving behaviors, there are also many different ways that individuals may show their grief. It is also true that grief does not reserve its presence for death or the threat of death alone. We can have a grief response for losses other than loss of life. Many of these losses have a death-like quality; for example, aging, workplace changes, separation and divorce, and financial insecurity are death-like losses for many people.

Here is a personal story of my own growing awareness of aging as a loss issue:

> When I reached the age of 60, I became aware of an irresistible need to scan the obituary columns every day. What was I looking for? My students typically answer this question with—"Your name?" or "People you know?" What I actually find myself drawn to are the ages of the people who died. When I find an announcement of people who died in their 60s, I quickly turn the page and keep looking. When I see one in which the age is listed as the late 90s, I say, "I'll take that one!"
>
> As a healthy and professionally active person now past the age of 60, I am now aware of all of the changes that are a part of suddenly being eligible for senior citizen benefits! I get discounts and receive lots of retirement news fliers and tips on how to enjoy this time of life. "Huh? What time of life? You mean I am in some new time of life already?" Is this denial on my part or am I simply clueless about having automatically joined the ranks of those older folks? As a member of a society that takes some pride in providing for its elders' financial, social, and health needs, I've always seen these benefits as an important responsibility we have to them. "Now, they are me!"

I also live in a society that places a very high value on youth, physical fitness, sexual attractiveness, and affluence. The shifting picture of myself, as well as the physical, mental, social, and financial limitations of aging, represents specific and highly visible reminders of how I once was and have now changed. For a long time I could win at racquetball when playing with my son. Eventually, we were evenly matched. Then, the time came when I barely offered him competition. As we age, we may be faced with the death of a spouse, friends, and other contemporaries; changes in work status; and altered family roles—resulting in a massive list of losses with which the senior members of our society must cope. Staying alive guarantees multiple losses and grief—*grief happens*.

To help get a sense of the many faces of loss in each of our lives, please complete the following exercise.

Exercise 1: What Do We Lose?

Take a moment to list five types of losses other than death or serious ill-ness (house fire, divorce, workplace change, move to new location, unful-filled dreams, financial crisis, move of a friend, rejection by a friend, being turned down for job or school placement) that have triggered a grief reaction in you or someone else you know.

1.

2.

3.

4.

5.

Review the losses you have listed and note which would seem minor and which have more significant consequences. The traumatic loss expe-rienced by a grieving person will occur against a background of many other losses. Even the flow of time and changes that are expected as well as unexpected contain the potential for grief. I call this "passage-of-time grief." We may find that grieving people become painfully aware of these additional loss factors going on in their lives. Grieving people may have financial, occupational, academic, and/or relational losses occurring as well as the primary loss condition. These other losses each may generate their own grief response; this can add to the intensity of the current grief reaction.

Change causes grief. As we will see in greater detail in chapter 2, *any* change can make us feel a sense of loss with a resulting grief reac-tion—even desired change. The reality is that things are always changing; we are constantly connecting to people, places, routines, objects, and hav-ing to let go of them at some point. When attachments we have made are lost or threatened, the result for most people is the pain of grief. There's no way around it. This is how it is for human beings: *Change = Loss =*

Grief. Whenever there is change, there is loss and when there is loss, there is a grief reaction (Jeffreys, 1995).

Remarkably, although death and other traumatic losses are inextricably bound up with human existence, they continue to be taboo topics in Western society. In spite of the growth of the death education and grief counseling fields, the enormous increase in self-help books dealing with the subject, and hospice and palliative medical care programs, we still *don't want to talk about it!* This view of death as a "failure by those who give care" (Sakalauskas, 1992, p. 84) and grief as a subject to be avoided exists in all components of our society—schools, government, hospitals, religious institutions, and families. As mentioned earlier and as we shall see elaborated in chapter 2, this avoidance is a natural part of the human grief response.

In the same way that societal values impact our reactions to loss, religious and family values substantially shape how we think and feel about life and death, loss and grief. It is also important to note that we who serve as care providers for individuals and families who are grieving bring with us our own personal histories and our own cultural and family influences regarding death and dying. As *exquisite witness* mental health and medical care providers, clergy, hospice volunteers, support group facilitators, employee assistance and human resources personnel, and any other person stepping up to help another who is suffering a grief reaction to loss must be aware of social, cultural, and family differences in order to be able to connect with and be trusted by those grieving.

☐ Cultural Diversity Considerations

"Serving dying and bereaved people from other races and creeds provides us with the privilege of learning from them" (Parkes, Laungani, & Young, 1997, p. 7). Bowlby (1980) views the value of understanding cross-cultural grief reactions as vital to providing help. As care providers, we must grasp the importance of knowing and respecting a family's cultural heritage, mourning rituals, and customs for expressing feelings. The variations affect not only the death-related rituals but also the way that family members communicate to others outside of the family and with each other about the loss and their own feelings. For example, in some Asian cultures, communication by medical and other health care providers may be required to be made to a family member other than the patient. Care providers must be alert to such cultural diversity in the people they are serving.

In some families and ethnic traditions, talking about the deceased is typically not done. I saw a Middle Eastern young man in my practice whose father had been killed. The family was devastated; and he shared with me that, in his family's tradition, feelings about the loss of a loved one were not discussed openly. This prevented me from working with the whole family and helping them to support each other by listening to each other's grief. He sought grief counseling because he had nowhere else to talk about his father and his feelings. I became his only support until we were able to locate a person in his faith community who could also help him. Care providers must be " . . . cautious when relating to people from other ethnic backgrounds than their own, avoiding any advance presumption of what an appropriate response, diagnosis, or treatment might be" (Irish, 1993, p. 10).

A report by the National Caregivers Alliance indicates that "racial and ethnic minority populations are projected to represent 25.4% of the elderly population in 2030, up from 16.4% in 2000" (Talamantes & Aranda, 2004). In the growing multicultural nature of our communities, it is vital that care providers have a good grounding in the unique features of the grieving person's culture. How we view and respond to a family of one tradition may be vastly different from another one (Klass, 1999). Further, studies showing that when clients felt a therapist was not aware of their culture and the issues they confront as members of a minority population, the clients viewed the assistance as not responsive to their needs (Bloombaum, Yamamoto, & James, 1968; Nickerson, Helms, & Terrell, 1994; Sue & Sue, 2003). Other studies find significant differences in the way people of a number of nationalities respond to loss (Klass, 1999). What one culture's tradition considers extreme grief reaction may be quite normal in another. "Grief is expressed so differently from culture to culture that it is absurd to use notions of pathology from one culture to evaluate people from another" (Rosenblatt, 1993, p. 18). It is impossible to include the multitude of cultural variations in one volume. I encourage you to review the readings in appendix A for information beyond that covered in this chapter.

The American Psychological Association's Diversity Guidelines (1993) state that care providers must be responsible and ethical in (a) recognizing cultural diversity, (b) understanding the role that culture and ethnicity/ race play with individuals and groups, and (c) understanding the socio-economic and political factors that impact these groups. Diversity is not only a social issue but a professional issue as well (Hall, 1997, Sue, 2003).

The Spiritual Care Work Group of the International Work Group on Death, Dying, and Bereavement (1990) has developed a series of principles and assumptions regarding the care provider and the grieving individual and family. Several of these, which provide specific direction to providers with regard to the cultural diversity concerns of grieving people, are presented below:

Principles and Assumptions Regarding Cultural Diversity

- Caregivers working with dying and bereaved persons should be sensitive to the interrelationship among spiritual, mental, emotional, and physical aspects of the grief reaction.
- Caregivers should be clear that no single approach to spiritual care is satisfactory for all in a culturally diverse society.
- Caregivers must be sensitive to multicultural differences as well as to the individual's particular interpretation of them.
- Caregivers must be sensitive to the divergent spiritual insights and beliefs that an individual and the family may have.
- Caregivers must be aware that spiritual needs and concerns may change over the course of terminal illness or bereavement.
- No one caregiver should be expected to understand or address the entire spiritual concerns of individuals and families.

  Note: The spiritual case work group uses the term *caregiver* in the same way that *care provider* is used in this book.

Care providers must seek information about and be sensitive to cultural and/or family traditions of populations they serve and adjust care efforts accordingly. This information can be gathered casually by observing and asking questions of the family and friends, by contacting a colleague who has experience with a particular ethnic group, by speaking to a spiritual leader or elder of the family's religious community, or by reviewing the literature on cultural diversity. (See appendix A.)

☐ Psychospiritual Aspects of Healing Grief

"Yea, though I walk through the valley of the shadow of death, I shall fear no evil for Thou art with me."

Psalm 23:4 (King James Version)

Religious belief systems have the potential for diminishing or even replacing the common fear of death. Several studies have shown that mourners who have strong religious belief systems report greater social support, increased ability to find meaning in the loss, continued connection and eventual reunion with the deceased, and less grief distress (Davis, Nolen-Hoeksema, and Larsen, 1998; McIntosh, Silver, and Wortman, 1993).

When we use spiritual explanations to provide meanings for death and other losses in life, we engage in a psychospiritual process for healing our grief. In this process, a belief in a Supreme Being, a Universal Wisdom, serves to explain how our lives and events in the world unfold. The illness, death, or other loss is placed within the context of the spiritual belief system, and this provides meaning and comfort to the grieving person. On the other hand, Doka (2002) points out how loss can challenge the spiritual assumptions of a grieving person to the extent of questioning his or her beliefs.

There are many references in the Bible and Koran on death, the hereafter, mourning behaviors, burial practices, and the raising of the dead (Isaiah 61:13; Samuel 18:13; Matthew 5:4; Ecclesiastes 3:4, 7:2; John 11:1–44; Genesis 23, 37:34, 49:29, 50:22; Holy Koran 6:60, 26:55, 29:57, 40:46). Other references include the Hindu *Upanishads*, the *Egyptian Book of the Dead*, and *The Tibetan Book of the Dead*. (See appendix A.) Many of these scriptures reaffirm that people will suffer less pain from loss as a result of their belief in God. Grievers also find comfort in the belief that those who are deceased will continue to exist in a new place. Many of our current mourning and burial practices have been derived from these Holy Books and other ancient writings.

The support derived from spiritual and religious beliefs throughout life and at the time of death is described by Katherine Neville (2003), author of *The Magic Circle*.

> I had long understood the importance to each individual of connecting the spiritual and material aspects of our lives. Even Socrates speaks of it. But I think what changed as a result of writing *The Magic Circle*, in my attitude toward spirituality, is that I began to realize the extent of the schism we are experiencing in modern times—how much we need to connect these two aspects of ourselves and our reality—as earlier, more agrarian societies were able to do. In ancient times, you were consecrated to the service of a specific god even before you were born, and then trained from the age of 6 in what you were expected to do. Your religion followed you from the cradle to the grave, and all aspects of society helped support you through the difficulties of making each transition in work, marriage—even beyond the grave. We were connected to the cycles of nature, not just the rigors of science, technology, and survival.

For many people who are grieving, feeling empty inside, with no answers for their many questions, their spiritual and religious beliefs assume tremendous importance. Many of the people for whom I have provided care have told me, "When there was nothing else to turn to, there was always their faith to turn to." The rituals and practices that follow a death can provide substantial support and the earliest sense of hope for healing. "The earthquake may be over by the time of burial. But the aftershocks and the survey of destruction have barely begun" (Ashenburg, 2002, p. 50).

Kaddish (the Jewish prayer recited at the grave, and throughout and after the mourning period) has been called one of the earliest forms of bereavement support groups. It is believed to have begun in 12th-century France and Germany (Ashenburg, 2002). Mourners recite a prayer that makes no mention of death but rather is a reaffirmation of faith. The community may stand and join in the prayer or give certain responses as the mourners recite the Kaddish. For many, the process of reciting prayers three times each day with other worshippers during the mourning period supplies a given structure and a healing action to engage in.

In other religious systems, prayers, meditations, or wakes serve a similar function of what to do now that the loved one has been buried or cremated. Additional ways to engage in healing activities are through organized social calls by church members, a schedule of meals brought in, attending special prayer services, meditations, and visiting the grave. Catholic tradition provides for special acknowledgement of a deceased loved one at the celebration of Mass on death anniversaries and at other special times. Such acknowledgment in religious services facilitates the continuing awareness of the loved one in the post-loss life of the family members. Coping with a loss within the context of a religious belief system allows the search for significance or meaning of the death in connection with faith in sacred values (Pargemant, 1997).

A large part of the healing comes not only from having structured actions to take but also from the communal aspect of rituals and prayer services. The ancient procedure of the tribe or clan gathering when one of them has died has its roots in showing visible proof that the community is still intact and will survive. For many mourners, the presence of other people gives a sense of support and the knowledge that they are still part of a larger, protective social group. There is also an expectation by others that when they suffer a loss, there will be similar community support. People who are grieving a socially stigmatized death, such as those that are AIDS or drug related, may not find their faith community welcoming, and must create their own rituals. (See chapter 9 for use of rituals for healing.)

For many, the funeral represents an opportunity for touching the mystery of the unknown. Here is a time when people can be physically close to deceased loved ones, see and/or touch them, and touch the casket. They can assist or observe the deceased being taken out to the burial place or crematorium, completing with the loved one the last steps of his or her transition to the unknown place beyond this earthly life. This may also be a metaphor for the mourner's own transition into the post-loss world.

However, not all individuals follow their own traditional faith beliefs or rituals. They may modify the traditional service or create one that completely departs from their customary rituals. Frequently, the younger, second generation of groups who have recently migrated to North America may reject the "old ways" and create conflicts with more traditionally minded elders. The care provider may serve as a mediator of compromise in such situations.

"There is very little research conclusively demonstrating that one particular mourning practice produces a better outcome than another" (Ashenburg, 2002, p. 17). *It is the availability of structured rituals and the presence of community in support that offers the healing potential of death-related rituals.* Post-funeral rituals, whether pre-existing or created for the occasion, provide an action to take at a time of helplessness and immobility that may emerge after a death, a gradual opportunity to begin to internalize the reality of the loss and start the letting-go process. Nevertheless, as always, we respect the needs of grieving people to engage in as much or as little of ritual practices as fits their own personal circumstances. It is not unusual for some people to desire a brief, simple graveside service and have a member of the family serve as leader. Others create elaborate services with music, readings, prayers, and dancing, and may also include rituals of veterans' organizations or other societies in which the deceased was a member.

☐ Death-Related Rituals: Funerals, Memorials, Burials, and Cremations

Weeks (2004) divides death-associated rituals into three groups: (a) pre-death rituals—prayers, chants, life review, gifting others (giving away belongings), spiritual journeys, and reconnecting with others; (b) immediate post-death rituals—body preparation, wearing certain clothing and accessories (black arm band, cut black ribbon), wakes, body viewing, funerals, burials and cremation, sitting shiva, visitation with mourners; and (c) long-term post-death rituals—visiting the grave; placing flowers, flags, and other items at gravesites and memorials; roadside flower memorials; special sections in prayer services; and acknowledgment at holiday time, birthdays, and/or anniversaries. Rituals enable us "to remain connected with the past, the future, and with each other . . . they also serve to provide us with comfort and security" (p. 114).

If you've attended funeral services outside of your own religious tradition, you've probably noticed, as I have, the wide diversity of observance. At some services, the volume of mourning is loud; at others, you can hear a pin drop.

Some families do not take an active role in the design of the funeral, leaving this entirely in the hands of the clergy and/or funeral director. Others create the service by selecting music and readings, offering eulogies, and encouraging those present to share remembrances. In many funerals, memorials, and cremation services, the clergy and the family will develop and lead services together. There are many funerals that are wholly designed by the faith system the family is connected to; in some memorial services, God is never mentioned.

Some burial rituals end as the casket is lowered into the grave and the family and friends pour symbolic soil into it. Some families (Muslim) wash and prepare the body, dig the grave, lower the coffin, and completely bury the deceased. In other traditions, the coffin is left out above the grave, sitting on the lowering device, with a mound of soil covered with artificial grass to the side. As the family is ushered away from the grave and out of the cemetery, cemetery workers do the actual burial. Several traditions (Hindu, Buddhist) use cremation as an ending ritual. Increasing numbers of people are selecting cremation even though several religions forbid this (Orthodox and Conservative Jews, Muslims). Cremation continues to grow in popularity largely due to its lower cost. Clearly, there is no universal or "right" way for the final arrangements to lay to rest the body of a loved one.

Funerals and the funeral business are sometimes derided in the press (Newman, 2002; Mitford, 1963). However, they provide a very important function for the loved ones of the deceased. Funerals also provide a confrontation with the terrible reality of the loss not only for the family but also for community members. They, too, have an opportunity to express grief, say good-bye, and re-establish a sense of communal support and continuity.

Family members begin the "saying good-bye" process, officially begin their period of mourning, and begin a continuing connection with their deceased loved one during the funeral rites (Bowlby, 1980). Highlighting the need for continuing the bonds with the deceased, many Korean and Chinese American families bring the remains of dead family members from their original overseas burial sites to be reinterred in America. The purpose is to keep the family together and to have the remains available for continued rituals and connection (Fears, 2002).

Care providers may find that conflicts regarding traditional rituals versus newer or more simplified rites arise between older generation and younger family members. This may represent additional loss to those desiring to honor the dead with customs from their cultural background. These time-honored rituals provide a familiar structure for the mourners, guide them through the bereavement period, and even stipulate when the mourning behaviors should come to an end.

It is important for the provider to remember that no two families from the same religious or cultural background will approach the funeral in exactly the same way. Spiritual resources may need to be called in. Be prepared with the information of whom and how to contact such resources and offer this option to a family confused over the nature and format of rituals. The provider must also be aware that there may be several subgroups within any given cultural group, which have their own approach to death-related rituals.

There are many variations within every religious and cultural group. It is impossible to provide a truly comprehensive listing of the different practices within the many subgroups. For example, there is no one Native American, Buddhist, African American, or Asian culture's set of rituals for death. Further, many individual families will adapt their traditions to complement personal preferences and meet their financial needs.

In preparing the list below, I have drawn upon my own personal and clinical experiences, in addition to material from several excellent resources, and direct your attention to appendix A for these reading suggestions. Additionally, clergy and funeral directors are excellent resources for helping a family when the lines to religious and cultural backgrounds are unclear.

Following is a list of funeral practices for several religious/cultural groups. Reading materials that contain more detailed descriptions are provided in appendix A.

Funeral Practices

Buddhist

- Many Asian communities in the United States practice Buddhism.
- Buddhism has over 500 varying schools of thought with a variety of rituals regarding death.
- Buddhists do not believe in one God or Creator; Buddhism resembles a philosophical belief system.

Care providers must learn how to ask questions about a particular ethnic group's death practices as well how members of the group communicate about their reactions to death and dying. In some cultures—for example, Asian, some Latino nations, and Gypsies—the oldest family member is the spokesperson, and the provider must communicate through this person to the family and often to the patient as well.

It remains extremely important for care providers to determine the cultural guidelines as well as the individual person's or family's wishes regarding end-of-life and after-death rituals. For many families, culture serves as a framework, not as a set of restrictions. The care provider must also be aware of how a family expresses itself emotionally regarding death and how its members have coped with and accommodated to past traumatic losses. For some people, certain deaths carry a social stigma, and they may have certain taboos regarding who can and cannot participate during rituals. Gender and age difference may influence these limitations. It is also useful to have a clear sense of the family's need for someone to hear confession at the end of life and to understand the family's ideas regarding afterlife.

When working with individuals who have no religious belief system, a care provider may be able to help them create their own understanding of dying and death that is not based on theology. The provider can offer an opportunity to discuss the individual's philosophy or theories regarding life, end of life, and death, or refer them to another resource person. The provider's own belief system should be kept out of the discussion.

- Buddhists seek increased awareness of all aspects of life to reach a state of enlightenment called Nirvana.
- The Tibetan Buddhist belief in rebirth is widely held.
- Buddhists have special meditations to be used at the time of death; they may request limited morphine dosage for a dying person in order for the person to remain conscious for meditation.
- Cremation is usual, and a family member typically officiates.

Christian

- The concept of an afterlife is widely held as an important goal for the living to attain.
- Mourners can be comforted by the thought that the deceased is being reunited with loved ones and will be in the presence of Jesus Christ in the kingdom of heaven for eternity.

- The time between death and the funeral provides an opportunity for viewing the body, visiting with the family, and giving consolation and social support.
- The casket is typically lowered into the grave after mourners leave.
- Dark clothing is typically worn.

Roman Catholic

- The dying person makes confession to the priest. Last rites performed by a priest are very important; all dying Catholic patients must be given the opportunity to have a priest available to administer the last rites. This serves as a comfort to the family as well.
- The priest officiates at the funeral and burial services.
- Families who have a Catholic heritage but do not have any affiliation to a parish should be given the option of contacting a priest.

Protestant

- Confession and prayer can be made directly to God.
- There is life after death, and the person who has faith will reach eternal life.
- Funeral sermons emphasize the better place the deceased is now in.
- There are many denominations of Protestant churches with varied funeral traditions.

Hindu

- Many gods and goddesses make up the Hindu religion, and they all represent the One God with whom all dead will join.
- Hindus' fate in the next life will depend on how they have lived this life.
- Families will wash the body and prepare it for cremation, which should take place on the day of death. State laws may dictate the length of waiting period before cremation.
- A Hindu priest officiates at the ritual; white is traditionally worn.
- During the 13 days of official mourning, friends visit to offer condolences.
- There are many sects in Hinduism with varying religious practices.

Humanist

- Ethical humanism is a commitment to a way of life that is based on relationship to others.

- Funerals acknowledge loss and celebrate life without the use of religious rituals.
- Funerals are tailored to wishes of the deceased loved one's family.
- Funerals, burials, and cremation memorials may be held in a variety of locations.

Jewish

- Funeral and burial usually occurs within a day or two; cremation is not practiced among Orthodox and most Conservative families.
- Families place symbolic shovels of soil on the lowered casket; a rabbi or cantor officiates.
- A 7-day (or less in some families) period of mourning called "sitting Shiva" is observed. Shiva prayers focus on the sanctification of God's name; talking about the deceased is part of Shiva.
- It is customary to visit and bring food during this period—check the family's kosher food observance before bringing or sending food to the house.
- Sending flowers is not typically a Jewish custom; sympathy cards and charitable donations are the usual practice.
- Jewish theology includes the concept of a hereafter but it is not a primary focus in mourning.
- Attitudes regarding heroic measures and life-support vary among Jewish families: Traditional families generally request that life not be prolonged artificially if there is no possibility of recovery.
- For traditional families, hastening death is typically unacceptable, and a family will seek the presence of a rabbi to hear a special prayer and/or confession at the end of life.
- Forgiveness is an important aspect of saying good-bye to the dying person.

Muslim

- Allah is just. He will judge all people according to their deeds, and they will be either rewarded with heaven or punished with hell.
- Dying is not the end of existence; thus, body preparation is designed for this purpose.
- The mourners carry the coffin to the grave, lower, and bury it.
- Burial takes place as soon as possible.
- Cremation is forbidden, and males do the burials.
- The Imam or Holy Man leads funeral and graveside prayers with the mourners joining in.

- Official mourning lasts for 3 days, 40 days for the surviving spouse.
- Young children are not typically present at the burial rituals.

Native Americans

- Practices vary within individual Nations.
- Some groups avoid contact with the dying.
- Many groups, such as the Hopi culture, adopt a very positive attitude in the presence of the dying person; grieving is done privately, away from the person.
- Some tribal groups include Christian beliefs in their practices.

Summary. Funerals, memorials, burials, cremations, wakes, Shiva, farewell events, and transition ceremonies are all useful rituals that acknowledge the loss of a person or some other significant change in life circumstances. They also bring people together as a supportive community. Even in families where some members are estranged, attendance at funerals usually overrides the conflict—at least temporarily.

The death-related rituals we have each experienced throughout our lives make up our own information base and contribute to our understanding of what grieving people may experience. Some ritual events in our own experience may have been useful, while others may have been lacking in value—or may even have been negative experiences. As a care provider, you may be asked to advise grieving people on the matter of loss rituals. The following exercise, designed to help you recall your own experiences with death-related rituals, will help you advise grieving people.

Now, let yourself reflect back, even to childhood, on past death-associated rituals and recall your impressions and level of participation.

Exercise 2: Death and Loss Rituals Experience

1. What is the earliest memory you have of a death-related ritual? Indicate your age and the setting (home, religious facility, funeral home, graveside, or other). What do you recall that was positive about this experience? What was negative?

2. Very briefly state the elements of your ideal memorial service.

3. How is this information helpful in your work with grieving families?

> *Care providers* may be asked to help a family organize death-associated rituals or obtain resources for the family. Grieving people should be encouraged to participate in memorial events to whatever extent is possible. Funerals, memorial ceremonies, dedications, candle lighting, and even moments of silent reflection provide them with a sense of involvement and an opportunity to say good-bye, reminisce, and digest the reality of the loss.

☐ Conclusions

The *exquisite witness* is a care provider who knows that the grief journey is different for each griever, understands their cultural background, and knows that the function of the provider is to support this journey and not control it. Such a provider guides the client into "the cave of darkness" (Wicks, 1995, p. 127) and accompanies the client on the passage to healing. The care provider must help to equip the grieving person and prepare him or her for this journey of "healing through loss." Ask questions and listen to the answers. Know your client and know your client's culture. The helping behaviors of the care provider as an *exquisite witness* will be explored more fully in chapter 8.

While cultural and religious legacies define the behaviors of grieving people, there are other explanations that underlie the variations in the nature and intensity of the human grief reaction. Chapter 2 will address the psychological ideas which will further reveal how natural and necessary the human grief response is.

CHAPTER

2

The Human Grief Response:
Grief and Its Function

"Should you shield the canyons from the windstorms you would
never see the true beauty of their carvings."

Elisabeth Kubler-Ross (1978, p. 155)

☐ Introduction

Beyond the influence of societal attitudes and cultural environments, we now look at other mechanisms that shape the nature of the human grief response. It is the understanding of the underlying biological and psychosocial basis for human grief that supplies the *exquisite witness* with sensitivity to the normalcy of human grief. This constitutes the "head" dimension of the "heart, head, and hands" approach to helping grieving people.

Knowing the usual and customary patterns of grief over time and being alert to the individual differences among grieving people will give the professional and volunteer care provider a sense of security and clarity in addressing the range of possible grief reactions. We begin with a list of important concepts.

☐ Key Concepts

Listed below are key concepts an *exquisite witness* needs to know before working with grieving people. This listing is followed by an elaboration of each concept.

- Grief is a universal phenomenon among human beings.
- Grief comes from both tangible and intangible losses.
- Grief is a natural reflex that exists to enhance survival.
- Grief is generally an adaptive response, although it may be characterized by temporary disruptions of life.
- Grief is a natural phenomenon, although complications and illness can develop from it.
- Grief is complex and dynamic and varies between individuals and among cultures.
- Avoidance and denial are typical ways people soften or keep out the reality of painful loss.
- Grief has both predictable and unpredictable features.
- Grief support can come from professional care providers, friends, family, and organizational volunteers.

Grief Is a Universal Phenomenon Among Human Beings

A reaction to loss—that is, the breaking of an attachment bond—is common to all peoples. In a world where television brings the tragedies of people of one culture into the living rooms of millions of people of another culture, the similarity of anguished faces of loss is apparent. The skin may be of a different color, the clothing may be unusual to the viewer, the funeral rites may be unfamiliar—but the wailing lament of a mother holding a dead child looks and sounds the same everywhere.

Grief Comes from Both Tangible and Intangible Losses

We usually think of grief as a response to death. Death is only one of many forms of loss. Many other "faces of loss" can trigger a grief reaction. Loss is experienced when anything we have become attached to is no longer there. For example, a friend who moves away, a job that is downsized, a pet, one of a favorite pair of gloves, a credit card, physical functions we can no longer perform, vanished dreams, a loss of our sense of trust and well-being—these and any other loss situations can cause grief.

Change in circumstances creates a loss condition that results in a grief reaction, even when the change is seemingly positive—a promotion, marriage, a new baby. All are positive yet they render the loss of a previous state or life condition, and this carries a grief reaction.

Grief Is a Natural Reflex That Exists to Enhance Survival

At its most primitive level, the human organism acts to reconnect when separated from another upon whom it depends for survival. When this reconnection is not possible, the reaction is grief. Animal offspring who are separated from the mother will utter a cry and seek to restore proximity in order to maintain safety, keep warm, and receive nourishment. Without this natural reflex, the chance for survival would be drastically reduced. The human grief response contains within it the basic drive to restore the attachment to the lost object. Examples of such behavior are: looking in places shared, calling out the name, agitated movement, and sounds of distress. When reattachment is not possible, the individual exhibits despair and associated mourning behaviors—crying, sighing, withdrawal, depression, and, at times, disorganization of usual life activities.

Grief Is Generally an Adaptive Response, Although It May Be Characterized by Temporary Disruptions of Life

Grief reactions may initially appear to be maladaptive—crying, raging, confusion—but they are actually attempts to restore that which is gone and no longer part of the person's world. The grief reaction presents a departure from normal life functioning and may be characterized by some as a form of maladaption. However, in the same way that a physical wound or illness requires a period of reduced function, pain, and change in usual life activity, and perhaps accompanying demoralization, the psychological wound of loss begins a similar period of the individual being "out of commission with life."

Grief Is a Natural Phenomenon, Although Complications and Illness Can Develop from It

While it is expected and important for people who have suffered a terrible loss to grieve, the reactions may become dysfunctional under certain circumstances and require special professional assistance. Natural grieving can go wrong when levels of depression become extreme and prolonged, or when anxiety, rage, and guilt reach proportions that severely limit life activities and place the grieving person at risk for physical and emotional illness.

Grief Is Complex and Dynamic and Varies Between Individuals and Among Cultures

Human grief reactions are varied and contain many subparts. Grief is complex and as such may manifest as physical pain and discomfort, as psychological distress—both emotional and intellectual—as social dysfunction, and spiritual discontinuity. Grief is dynamic because it changes from morning to nighttime, from day to day, or from week to week.

The complexities of an individual's grief are also influenced by the ethnic and cultural traditions associated with death and loss and beliefs about how one is to act as a mourner, speak about the deceased, or express the feelings of grief.

Avoidance and Denial Are Typical Ways People Soften or Keep Out the Reality of Painful Loss

Denial enables us to take in the harsh reality of loss in small doses so that other requirements and obligations can be attended to. The reality of our own mortality is kept at bay by the use of humor and simply "not talking about it." This is a normal and very human characteristic that enables us to go on with living without obsessing over the inevitability of our own death. It is human to push away thoughts that may cause pain. Some people describe this as feeling numb.

Grief Has Both Predictable and Unpredictable Features

While much has been written about the nature and course of human grief, many factors affect the actual resulting feelings, thoughts, and behavior of grieving people. When we look at cross-cultural or universal patterns of grief, we see that most people cry when a loved one dies. The pictures of people around the world burying their dead after natural or human-made disasters look fairly similar. African, Asian, European, and American families who are mourning loved ones look very alike. The faces, sounds, and body language of people in grief around the globe have a uniformity that lets us know that the person is grieving. Yet there are life circumstances that differentiate them from each other. Such determining factors are pre-existing morbidity, personal coping styles, influences of personality type, and social-cultural factors. Such additional influences as nature of loss, age and role of deceased, level of support, and the mental health of the mourner will stamp uniqueness into any one individual's grief reactions.

Grief Support Can Come from Professional Care Providers, Friends, Family, and Organizational Volunteers

Many individuals provide care and comfort to grieving people. Some have medical or nursing backgrounds; others may come from mental health or pastoral care. Still others may be trained volunteers or family caregivers. Funeral directors, school personnel, and community agency outreach staff may also serve grieving people in some capacity. Providers use their own level of knowledge and skills to make their unique contributions to the grief support system.

Grief is a global phenomenon and any person who develops the "heart, head, and hands" dimensions of providing care has the potential to become an *exquisite witness* to the journey of a grieving person.

☐ Defining Grief

The term grief may be used in a variety of ways. Some use grief to mean the behavior seen when people are mourning a death or other tragic loss. *Grief* is also used as a way of indicating that a person is having a hard time—"The umpire is getting a lot of grief from the fans since that last call." Some view the word as a set of internal psychological reactions to loss or the threat of loss. From a theological perspective, grief may be seen as a life condition that has the potential to bring a person closer to his or her faith. Some may see grief as a condition to be cured.

Many intermix the word *grief* with *mourning* and *bereavement*; others distinguish among the three as follows: (a) grief—as internal reactions, (b) mourning—as observable behaviors, and (c) bereavement—as describing the cultural/social role of one who has had a loss. The varied and overlapping uses of the term grief remind me of the five blindfolded men attempting to describe an elephant. Because each of them touched a different part of the elephant—the trunk, the tusk, the ear, the tail—they individually arrived at a different idea of the animal they were experiencing.

Counselors, theologians, experimental psychologists, academic lecturers, cultural anthropologists, and funeral directors all view the concept of grief from their own perspective. Yet each perspective provides a special and useful addition to the understanding of this very complex, dynamic, and human experience known as grief.

In this book, I will use the following definitions:

Grief—A system of feelings, thoughts, and behaviors that are triggered when a person is faced with loss or the threat of loss. Emphasis is on both internal (thoughts and feelings) and external (behavior) reactions.

Mourning—The behaviors that are part of the human grief response and serve to differentiate mourners from others in a person's social network. Emphasis is on external behaviors, expressions of grief, and manner of dress.

Bereavement—A cultural/social role or condition for a person who has experienced a death and engages in cultural rituals and behaviors associated with death. Emphasis is on behaviors or restriction of behaviors dictated by cultural norms.

☐ Common Myths

In my years of clinical practice, teaching, and consulting, I've encountered several myths about grief that people may fall back on when coping with loss or the threat of loss (Jeffreys, 1995, p. ix).

"I can handle this on my own."
"I don't need to talk about it."
"They can't tell how upset I am."
"My pain, anger, and fear will just go away."
"Bad things happen to other people."
"If I don't think about it, nothing happened or will happen."

The first four myths are examples of the human impulse to hold off the pain any way that we can. We tend to bend reality to protect ourselves from the pain of loss. The last two myths are examples of keeping bad news at arm's length to prevent us from experiencing pain.

These and other myths that we tell ourselves are part of the human defense system, which consists of all ideas that a person may use as "trenches [to defend our] existence, or as scarecrows to frighten away reality" (Ortega, 1957, p. 147).

Sometimes we need to hold off the pain any way we can. Making use of these myths is a form of *denial* and is very normal.

☐ Denial

We use denial to keep out or soften terrible news. Too often the use of denial is criticized as "running away from reality"; we are perceived as weak and lacking the ability to face the painful truth of what has or is going to happen. Families with a very sick loved one in the hospital may overhear staff saying, "They really don't get how serious this is; they're in *denial*." However, unless denial creates medical problems or family dysfunction, it serves as a very important and useful shock absorber. Denial allows us to absorb the horrible reality in small doses or push it away, at least for a while. It provides us with the freedom *not to deal* with a grief reaction right away so that we can take care of other needs.

We also use denial when we avoid grieving people. A year after our son Steven had died, my wife and I were approached by a man we knew as we were driving out of a community center parking lot. He told us that he had yet to offer us any condolences about our tragic loss because it was too painful for him to talk about it. While we appreciated his words, I had wondered earlier why he did not approach us sooner.

I was told a story about a man in a bereaved parents support group that demonstrates one way that people react to the grief of a neighbor:

> After his son was killed, he noticed that people he knew in the community would play what he called the "Safeway Samba." When he went shopping, for example, people he recognized would quickly slip into the next aisle. At first, he assumed that they had not seen or heard him, but gradually he realized that they were avoiding him. People in the group nodded, smiled, and recalled similar experiences. This "Safeway Samba" became our code word for being shunned by others who were not able to allow themselves to make contact.

Such avoidance is actually typical and understandable, and people who can't cope with other people's grief aren't "bad." Contact with grieving people can eat away at a person's own denial system, and their avoidance serves the function of keeping a painful reality out of conscious awareness. We flee the horror of tragic circumstances that remind us of what could happen to us. Often, people just don't know what to say. Sadly, this often results in painful isolation for grieving people.

Care providers need to anticipate this avoidance and be prepared to spend time helping the grieving person cope with this sense of isolation when there is a lack of support from friends and family. This lack of support and contact becomes another loss to be grieved. Support groups frequently offer a place for expression of grief and a sense of acceptance as well. (See appendix B.)

☐ The Seven Principles of Human Grief

These principles give care providers an overall blueprint for further understanding grief reactions and what to expect from grieving people.

The Seven Principles of Grief at a Glance

Principle One: You cannot fix or cure grief.
Principle Two: There is no one right way to grieve.
Principle Three: There is no universal timetable for the grief journey.
Principle Four: Every loss is a multiple loss.
Principle Five: Change = Loss = Grief.
Principle Six: We grieve old loss while grieving new loss.
Principle Seven: We grieve when a loss has occurred or is threatened.

Principle One: You Cannot Fix or Cure Grief

While grief is as normal as the common cold, it is not an illness that needs medical attention. You can't scrub it out like a stain on a shirt or fix it like a leaky faucet. The human grief reaction is a combination of thoughts, physical and emotional feelings, and behaviors that enable us to survive. It is, therefore, a normal way of reacting whenever we have already lost or are afraid we will lose someone or something important to us. The losses that create a grief response can be of a person, place, job, work routines, physical objects, dreams, or sense of safety and trust.

Although grief can't be fixed or cured, one thing we can do is listen to it. The *exquisite witness* does not have to say something at every juncture in the conversation. The *exquisite witness* is an "exquisite listener," providing a safe place and the time and permission for the grieving person to express what is going on internally.

Principle Two: There Is No One Right Way to Grieve

Everyone grieves differently. With some, tears are visible; with others, tears are invisible. We must respect the different ways we each grieve. Each culture has its own norms about how grief is expressed; grief reactions also depend upon one's family, personality, and gender. In the cartoon below a little girl explains to her younger brother why they never see Daddy cry.

People's grieving is based on stereotypes of gender, age, and other social-cultural identifications; for example, "men don't cry," "women cry," or "older adults contain their grief." However, lack of crying is not a sign of being disloyal to those who have died. Childhood messages about whether it was acceptable to express sadness, fear, and anger continue to affect how we react to loss and crisis throughout life.

Principle Three: There Is No Universal Timetable for the Grief Journey

The answer to the question, "How long will it take?" is "As long as it takes." We don't heal on anyone else's schedule but our own. Many years after our son Steven's death, my wife and I met an old acquaintance. After the usual small talk, this highly educated individual blurted out, "Are you two *still* grieving over that son of yours?" We were stunned at his harsh and insensitive question. "Yes," I finally said, "and we will, probably for life." People may get impatient with another's grief and after awhile encourage them to be okay, stop crying, and be "happy again."

Principle Four: Every Loss Is a Multiple Loss

When we lose a job by being laid off or by having our job description changed, we lose more than our familiar routine: we lose our social contacts, identity, status, financial security, career dreams, sense of well-being, and dreams for the future.

We incur secondary losses whenever we lose a person or place; loss ripples outward the same way a pond surface does when a stone is dropped into it. We lose not only the body and being of our loved one but also the part of ourselves that was bonded in relationship to the deceased, as well as the various roles he or she played in our life.

We are also affected by the grief of others; when our nation was attacked on September 11, 2001, we lost the sense that we were safe. These layers of secondary loss add to the intensity of the grief reaction as it moves outward from the nuclear family to other relatives, friends, coworkers, and neighbors.

Principle Five: Change = Loss = Grief

Change is a part of life. Our physical and social environments change daily. Whenever there is change, we lose what we left behind and begin to connect with what comes next. Any change—even good change—can bring about a sense of loss and thus a grief reaction. Even happy life cycle transitions—leaving school and being hired for your first job, getting married, having a baby, retiring—can trigger a grief reaction because we left one lifestyle behind as we moved on to another. When the change is death or a serious illness or an unexpected, traumatic, and sudden disaster, the grief reaction may be very intense and painful. As indicated in Principle Four, change in the workplace also creates loss and grief as employees must let go of a familiar work world and adjust to new beginnings. In fact, any notable change in the way things have been results in the loss of how it used to be. Any loss can result in many "spin-off" or secondary losses.

Principle Six: We Grieve Old Loss While Grieving New Loss

As we move through the transitions of life and experience losses, we accumulate the loss material referred to in the introduction as Cowbells. It is not uncommon for us to be reminded of a death that took place years ago when a loved one dies or a significant new loss or trauma occurs. In spite of our previous grieving, some unfinished and unaccommodated grief may remain. When a new loss occurs, the old, stored grief mingles with the new, intensifying the grief reaction.

Principle Seven: We Grieve When a Loss Has Occurred or Is Threatened

We don't need an actual death or diagnosis of serious illness to begin to grieve; even the threat of loss can invoke the grief response. Think of how you feel when your loved one is extremely late arriving home, when you hear rumors that your company is downsizing, or when your doctor tells you to go for more tests. The beginning of a grief reaction will vary for each person, but often the process begins well in advance of the actual loss event.

☐ Origin and Function of the Human Grief Response

It is a curious paradox of the human condition that perhaps the most painful experience a person will suffer in life is also, at its primitive roots, the most necessary for survival—not only for the individual but for the continuation of the species as well. An *exquisite witness* must understand the origin and function of attachment theory as the basis for understanding the human grief response in order to provide effective care for grieving people.

In the following section, we will review the biological and psychosocial basis of the human grief response—from the neurological separation distress signal to the role of attachment in survival. We will also cover the formation of attachment styles that influence relationships and ultimately the nature of how we grieve a loss.

Experimental Research and Human Attachment

"The non-verbal music of grief comes out through the body."

P.D. MacLean (Personal Communication, October 12, 2001)

Separation alert signal. In the 1950s, National Institute of Mental Health neurologist Paul MacLean introduced the concept of a limbic system in the mammalian brain that governs emotional reactions, fight–flight response, and sexual behaviors (MacLean, 1952, 1955a, 1955b; MacLean & Pribam, 1953). MacLean (1973) later wrote about the limbic system's role in three functions: (a) the separation distress call, (b) maternal nursing behavior, and (c) play or social affiliation. Each of these processes is designed to protect and enable the survival of the individual to reproductive age. Of special interest is the separation or isolation alert signal that MacLean (1985) characterizes as probably the "earliest and most basic mammalian vocalization" (p. 405).

A young mammal senses the distance between it and its mother by changes in the intensity of smell, a drop in temperature, the loss of tactile contact, and/or critical visual distance from the mother. Acting like a security system, the limbic part of the brain sends an automatic message, resulting in a *distress cry*. When the mother receives this signal, her own brain connections trigger her protective reaction to restore physical attachment to the baby, and she leads it to safety and comfort.

Survival basis of attachment

A baby may reach out, grasp, seek its mother's nipple, utter continued sounds of distress, and engage in searching actions in order to restore the physical proximity. These behaviors are what Bowlby (1969) calls *attachment behaviors*. The agitation generally subsides when reunion is accomplished. Animal babies whose genes do not provide a well-developed separation alert system may be eaten, die of exposure, or starve to death. MacLean theorizes that of the earliest little mammals on the dark forest floor, only those who had this alerting system survived (personal communication, May 6, 2003). Professor Karl Pribram of Georgetown University reinforces the idea that the neurological process that drives the offspring to maintain attachment for survival is the basic level of the human grief response (personal communication, July 16, 2003).

I have composed the tale below to further illustrate the work of Paul MacLean (1973) on the primitive survival basis of attachment; the foundation for understanding the normalcy of the human grief response.

On the Dark Forest Floor

Many, many years ago there lived on the dark forest floor a tiny little baby mammal named Dino. He looked a lot like his great-great-grandfather—the one they called "lizard face." Dino had a longer snout than his cousin Tina, who was also was very young. Dino had claw-like feet and could run faster than Tina, but he was unable to make a sound with his throat. One day, Dino wandered away from his mother. He heard a commotion and turned to see a big, hungry lizard coming toward him. He began shaking his long snout from side to side; but his mother, in the dark forest-floor world, could not see this visual signal for help. Tina was nearby and heard the noise of the hungry lizard, too. She immediately squealed out her vocal distress signal. Her mother came running and led her quickly to the safety of an underground burrow . . .

Tina tells this story to her grandchildren, who all were born with the ability to emit vocal distress call signals that bring their mothers whenever they are too far from her body. Dino was never seen again; and all the other baby mammals that looked like great-great-grandfather "lizard face" also disappeared.

As the little mammals, Dino and Tina, in the story above demonstrated, the development of the human grief response is a matter of survival.

Psychobiological attunement in attachment

Experimental psychologist Tiffany Field (1985) has further contributed to the understanding of learned behaviors associated with attachment and separation by identifying the psychobiological attunement process in the mutual feedback loop of actions and reactions between mother and baby. As mother and baby learn a series of signals and cues by which they modify their behavior, their bond develops beyond their initial instinctive behaviors. These cues take the form of crying, clinging, hearing and repeating sounds, feeling the comfort of being held and caressed, and seeking and greeting actions. "Each partner provides meaningful stimulation for the other and has a modulating influence on the other's arousal level" (p. 415). For example, a mother's smile and cooing may stimulate sounds or facial reactions from the baby, and this causes the mother to pick the baby up and cuddle it. While babies initially focus on bonding with their mother, they eventually include their father, siblings, and later, as the individual matures, peers, life partners, other family, and friends.

The nature of bond formation will influence future adult pair bonding as the individual matures. It is the pattern of individual attachment style that affects the character of the relationship, and this has a direct bearing on features of grieving when the attachment bond is severed.

We have much to learn about the complex nature of attachment and maternal care behaviors. The role of organic brain function in the underlying attachment behavior has been given increasing attention in the laboratories of experimental psychologists investigating the role of brain chemicals in stimulating receptors for separation distress (Insel, 2000). Clearly, an understanding of how and why we attach to others is essential to understanding how and why we grieve.

Attachment Theory and the Human Grief Response

Attachment theory is based on findings from ethology (the study of behavior in different species), evolutionary biology (the study of the transmission of instinctive behaviors from parent to offspring), and psychological studies of both animal and human behavior. The human grief response is a complex set of feelings, thoughts, and behaviors following the loss or threat of loss of an attachment bond. In addition to brain researchers, several writers have contributed to our understanding of human attachment behavior. We will begin with the work of British psychiatrist John Bowlby, considered by many as the "father of attachment theory."

Bowlby (1969/1980, 1973, 1979, 1980) has written extensively on how and why human beings attach to each other, and what happens when we are faced with separation or even the threat of separation and loss. His work, often in collaboration with Mary Ainsworth (1991), focuses not only on the nature of early attachment bonding between the very young and their maternal caregivers but also on adult attachment throughout the life cycle.

According to Bowlby, young mammals maintain a close physical tie to the mother in order to survive predation, starvation, and other physical harm that would prevent the baby from reaching reproductive age. Attachment behaviors are therefore a mechanism for individual survival and continuation of the species. This drive to survive is carried forward from birth to death (Bowlby, 1969), manifesting itself later in life as adult pair bonding.

When an individual is unable to restore the contact with a person or other significant lost object, the result is protest, agitation, and separation distress—the behaviors we identify as a grief reaction. A very young child who has been separated from its mother will cry, scream, look in the direction she was last seen, stand up in the crib, shake the crib framing, and possibly flail and throw things. In healthy, secure attachment bonds, this agitated distress will abate when mother returns. But what if the mother or caregiver never returns, has died, or has left? In these cases, the period of agitated hyperdistress will often continue and initiate the beginning of mourning.

The ability of a mother or other caregiver to identify and seek out the baby when he or she is in distress or threatened with danger is part of a reciprocal system of relationship and protection (MacLean, 1975). This system of action and interaction between offspring and maternal or other primary caregiver is an essential part of the development of attachment bonds. The manner of early attachment formation begins a pattern of relationship style that ultimately plays a role in how an individual grieves.

> *Care providers* should obtain background information regarding the grieving person's relational history in order to fully appreciate the nature of current grief. Taking a careful history of how the individual has made and broken affectional bonds can do this.

Utilizing direct observational studies of children, Bowlby (1969/1980, 1979) and Ainswsorth (1970, 1971) identified typical separation behaviors of very young children and their mothers at the time of separation and upon reunion. These observations form the basis for modern studies of adult attachment patterns (Fraley, 2002; Fraley & Shaver, 2000; Hazan & Shaver, 1990; Simpson & Rholes, 1998; Wayment & Vierthaler, 2002). Studies investigating adult attachment styles strongly suggest that the way an individual makes and breaks social bonds in childhood is carried forward into later relationships throughout life (Fraley, 2002). These three prototypes of attachment are described below.

The style of attachment has a strong influence on the way an individual grieves the loss of an affectional bond—whether as a result of death, life-limiting illness or injury, divorce, or separation. Attachment styles are developed in childhood, and adults, who are faced with loss of a bond partner, demonstrate similar separation distress behaviors as those described for children.

Attachment Styles

Three Attachment Bond Styles

- Secure attachment
- Anxious–ambivalent
- Avoidant–ambivalent

Secure Attachment Bonding

When a baby in distress has been responded to promptly by the mother (or other primary caregiver) and receives a rich set of caring behaviors—holding, caressing, singing, talking, feeding, cleaning—a *secure* bond will be formed. Such a child can eventually create a stable inner image of the attachment figure, is able to tolerate periods of separation, and is confident enough to explore the environment.

Anxious–Ambivalent Attachment Bonding

When the response to a child's distress signals is consistently delayed or absent, and the nature of maternal interaction is also limited, the child is unsure of the availability of the mother and how much she will actually provide protective caring. Infants with *anxious–ambivalent* bonds make unsuccessful and unrewarded attempts to connect with the mother or other caregiver (Hazan & Shaver, 1990; Parkes & Weiss, 1984). As adults, such individuals generally have a pattern of relational anxiety, may be insecure about the other's commitment ("She loves me; she loves me not!"), and are possessive and controlling.

Adults with anxious–ambivalent attachment patterns are typically at high risk for chronic grief complications when a bond is broken because of death or separation (Hazan & Shaver, 1990; Parkes & Weiss, 1984). Typically, they may fear abandonment and hold on to the attachment figure through clingy, possessive, and controlling behavior (Feeney, 1998). They also possess an underlying fear that their bond partner cannot be counted on for safety and support in times of distress. Furthermore, they are likely to become stuck in grief due to their inability to alter their inner representation of the lost attachment figure. They typically have great difficulty letting go of the deceased loved one as a living bond mate. This can result in chronic grief complication, which is discussed in chapter 9.

I have found that when one member of a couple who has lost a child has an anxious–ambivalent attachment style, there is often conflict because the anxious person perceives the other as not being available. Individuals with an anxious–ambivalent attachment style may resent the lack of attention to his or her grieving needs—listening, holding, close proximity—and develop painful relationship conflicts.

Care providers may find it necessary to help these couples decrease their emotional distancing and enhance their communication as well as build the level of support skills of both parents. For example, couples who learn active listening techniques and schedule time for conversations often discover that the ambivalent partner becomes less anxious over time.

Avoidant-Ambivalent Attachment Bonding

This type of bonding results when infants make no attempt to secure the mother figure's attention or social interaction because they have learned that such an expectation will be unmet. Subsequently, they develop an internal style of coping with distress. These children typically seek emotional distance and independence and resist help from others during and following a crisis.

The adult with an *avoidant-ambivalent* attachment style will typically seek safe emotional distance and flee from intimacy. Such people have learned to consciously or unconsciously suppress or deactivate the attachment system in a time of distress (Fraley, Davis, & Shaver, 1998).

In either of the nonsecure attachment types (anxious–ambivalent or avoidant-ambivalent), grieving people are not to be condemned for being "too demanding or too distant." They are simply engaging in those attachment behaviors that have been shaped by their early life experiences.

Care providers need to obtain a thorough relationship history in order to understand how best to support bereaved individuals with a history of insecure attachments. The care provider can invite the grieving person to relate the story of his or her relationships. This can yield some insight into how this individual will grieve. A clingy, anxious person may be more likely to suffer prolonged and debilitating grief. A bereaved avoidant, distancing individual may be more likely to suffer physical complaints.

☐ The Three Conditions of Grief

Broken or Altered Bond

We grieve when a bond has been broken or unalterably changed (as in Alzheimer's disease). Death or permanent separation from an attachment figure brings on the grief response as we have described in the above section on attachment theory.

Threat to Bond

We also grieve when there is a threat to the attachment bond. A relationship that is at risk, a loved one with a terminal illness, a workplace undergoing massive reorganization, a recently detected breast lump, a child late coming home from a party—all these can bring on a grief response as intense as it would be if the loss had already occurred.

Unestablished Bond

Finally, we grieve for that which never has and never will happen—the relationship you never established with an alcoholic father or mother, the child you were never able to conceive, the promotion you never obtained, or the partner you were never able to court. These ongoing grief issues may become linked with more current, acute losses, intensifying the grief reaction.

The care provider must gather information about the multiple sources of grief impinging on the grieving person. What old and other current losses may be adding to the person's grief reaction? What "Cowbells" are ringing for the grieving person? This can be accomplished by taking a comprehensive loss history that is discussed in chapter 8.

☐ The Components of Grief: Psychological, Physical, Social, Spiritual

Grief is expressed in feelings, thoughts, and behaviors. These manifest themselves within four aspects of an individual's life: the psychological, physical, social, and spiritual components of grief.

The Four Components of Grief at a Glance

The Psychological Component
Emotional Aspects of Grief—feelings of grief

    a. Sadness
    b. Anger
    c. Fear
    d. Guilt
    e. Shame

Cognitive Disturbances of Grief

The Physical Component

Health Factors
Physical Symptoms

The Social Component

Family and Other Relationships
Society and Attitudes Towards Grief

The Spiritual Component

Faith Resources and Life Philosophy

The Psychological Component of Grief

The psychological component of grief is divided into two parts:

Emotional (feelings)
Cognitive (thought process)

The role of the *exquisite witness* care provider is to be fully present and to accept and normalize all feelings and thoughts that the grieving person wishes to express. As discussed earlier in the section on attachment, the human grief response is a normal response to loss or the threat of loss. Normal grief is not an illness to be cured but (for most persons) an expected pattern of behaviors that are necessary for healing to take place.

In some cases, grief may become complicated and even have associated psychiatric disorders. Such grief may be overly prolonged and intense, filled with debilitating anxiety, depression, or physical symptoms. (See chapter 9 for further details on complications of grief.)

Emotional Aspects of Grief

Sadness.   Sadness and grief are terms which many people use interchangeably. The pain of grief is usually associated with crying, sobbing, sighing, blowing the nose, wringing hands, shaking the head, and verbal expressions of pain and hurt. You can expect anything from soft sobbing to vigorous wailing. I've heard clients say things such as, "This is going to kill me!", "I will never get over this!", "I don't want to live without her.", "It hurts so much.", "When will this awful pain stop?", "I feel so empty inside.", and "I'm afraid I will never stop crying." We recommend that care providers never shove a tissue at a crying person. This may send the message that we want the crying to stop. Instead, I suggest placing easily accessible boxes of tissues around the room so that grieving people can reach for one when they need to. Grieving people will often say that they have very little opportunity to express their sadness because others in their lives "do not want to hear or see them cry." Sad, hurting, and aching hearts may need to weep and sob. As one client once told me as she cried copiously, never once reaching for a tissue, "I want to feel the wetness on my face and know that I am really grieving."

Sadness often comes and goes in waves. People will feel good one day and awful the next. There is no straight line on the graph of grief feelings, and not all people will express sadness in the same way. I have met some bereaved persons who show little or no outward expressions of grief. Some individuals who have had a nondeath loss believe they are not entitled to cry and mourn. Although the losses connected to the work-place—mergers, downsizing, and reengineered work roles—can feel very much like a death loss, those affected may withhold their grief feelings because of pressure from management or because they don't feel entitled to have a grief reaction (Jeffreys, 1995).

There are also individuals who show none of the usual and customary emotional reactions to a loss due to death (Bonanno et al., 2002; Wortman & Silver, 1989). Such persons are described in the literature as *resilient* "people who [after a loss] have positive emotional experiences and show only minor and transient disruptions in their ability to function" (Bonnano, 2004, p. 20).

While there is continuing research to determine the reason for what is believed to be nonpathological absence of the symptoms of grief, the people I have worked with in clinical practice, hospitals, and workplace settings who suffer a loss continue to demonstrate the natural and expected expression of sadness and other feelings of grief. Where these reactions were absent or minimal, there have been adequate explanations for such absence. These include but are not limited to restrictions on expression of feelings learned in childhood, fear of loss of control, resistance to acknowledging the painful reality of loss, and intervening practical responsibilities to others which place the person's grieving on "hold."

There are also mourners who do not grieve because the nature of the relationship with the person who died was abusive, controlling, or sufficiently negative to leave them feeling liberated. For such persons, the loss generates positive feelings which are contrary to the feelings and thoughts friends and family may have been expecting. Absence of grief reactions have in the past led to the diagnosis of complicated grief and the person had to deal with others wanting to know why they showed no sadness but rather a sense of freedom and an enthusiastic view of their new future (Elison & McGonicle, 2003). Many persons caring for a very ill loved one for months and years feel very relieved when the ill one dies. Care providers must help to normalize these feelings and assist with any guilt that may follow the feeling of relief and freedom from burden.

Anger.   Take a rattle away from a baby and the baby cries—a quavering vibrato, which is usually accompanied by a reddening face. This is the cry of anger, a natural reaction to loss. Missed out on a good parking space when another driver slipped in ahead of you? Anger! Lose your car keys or a contract bid? Anger is not unusual in any of these cases. But when life, a relationship, or a job is at stake, anger can take on frightening proportions.

A grieving person's anger can be intimidating. He or she may scream out, bang fists, slam doors, and/or have hostile outbursts. The care provider needs to view this as part of the grief response, and be available to the person despite the expression of rage. Anger may be directed to anyone connected with the death, diagnosis, layoff, or other loss situation; or to God or a belief system. Anger may even be directed toward the care provider who then becomes a part of the safe space for the grieving person. An *exquisite witness* will understand that this is part of the grieving process for this individual and will provide a "space" for release of such anger. However, this does not mean that physical violence against the care provider (or others) is to be tolerated. (See "Externalization of Grief Feelings" in chapter 8.)

Anger also has a quiet side. It may go underground and cause internal emotional and physical damage. A client may sit in your office gripping the armrests with white knuckles and deny feeling angry or claim that his anger will "go away on its own." But anger doesn't simply disappear; it has to be acknowledged, accepted, and released safely.

Fear.   Many grieving people will express specific fears and general anxiety as part of their grief reaction: "I don't believe I can make it on my own.", "I'm afraid I will be alone for the rest of my life.", "Maybe I (or a loved one) will get sick and die too.", "I'm afraid I will go crazy!", and "I don't know why I am frightened but I just am." Underlying all of these statements are fears about one's physical and emotional survival.

One woman who lost her baby told me, "I'm afraid my husband won't come home alive from work." She also feared that she would never get pregnant again. Children who lose a parent usually express fear for the health of their surviving parent. Children who lose a brother or sister may fear that they will die of the disease that killed their sibling.

Guilt.   "Guilt is a normal and expectable aspect of the grief experience" (Rando, 1984, p. 31). Much of the guilt we see in grieving people is related to the "imperfection of human relationships" (Raphael, 1983, p. 45). Guilt is often most pronounced in bereaved parents and survivors of suicide.

Guilt usually comes from two sources: the nature of the death and its preventability, and from relationship issues (Archer, 1999). Some grieving people may have a clear and valid reason for their guilt—they were responsible for another's death or severe injury through neglect or error in judgment. In other cases, the guilt comes from "shouldisms," that is, from what they believe they *should* have done or not done in the relationship while the deceased was still alive: "I didn't visit her enough.", "Why did I not hear his call for help?", "I should have called 911 sooner.", "I should have insisted on a third opinion." or "I should have visited her more often and taken a greater role in her care."

Sometimes, the guilt has no rational or tangible source: "I just feel guilty because I am still alive and he or she is not." Other clients focused on self-reproach as a way of creating some meaning in a situation that has no precedent or suitable explanation. Bereaved parents often express profound guilt at not having protected their child. Though there usually is no basis in reality for such feelings, parents may go to great lengths to find cause for self-blame. Here is a personal reflection:

> As have many other parents who have lost a child to a protracted illness, we agonized many, many times over what we might have done differently. We wished we had let him stay home from school more often, helped him and his siblings to better understand his medical condition, and made more time for our two other children.

In cases where the death may have been prevented, or where the grieving person was somehow responsible, guilt is a reasonable reaction and must be approached differently than guilt that is obviously not rooted in reality (see chapter 8 for helping with guilt issues).

A special type of guilt arises when the relationship being mourned was characterized by ambivalence, conflict, or distance. The imperfection of human relationships forms another source from which guilt is fed. The mourner may ruminate, replaying the times he or she was angry or unkind to the deceased or very ill person. A woman I saw professionally had frequently quarreled with her adolescent son about his hair and dress; after he was killed in a car crash, she nearly suffocated in self-reproach for not resolving her relationship with him when she had the opportunity.

Sibling Guilt.   Similarly, surviving siblings often feel plagued by guilt if they were jealous of or angry with a sister or brother who was ill and later died. They may also suffer from *survivor guilt*, the guilt of having survived while others died. Bereaved parents may also suffer survivor guilt. Many employees who survived layoffs carry a sense of guilt as well (Jeffreys, 1995). Another type of guilt arises among caregivers or family members who devoted themselves totally to the care of another and now feel relief when the death finally occurs.

According to Worden, "Most often the guilt is irrational and will mitigate through reality testing" (2002, p. 13). However, grieving people who have continuing distress and dysfunction due to complications arising from guilt must be given special attention to facilitate healing. (Chapter 8 provides suggestions for helping with guilt issues.)

Shame.   Shame is related to guilt. People who feel shame are often concerned about their social status. When ashamed, people say things like, "I can't admit to anyone that my husband died of a drug overdose.", "I do not want the funeral service or the obituary to reveal that our son died of AIDS.", "It's so hard to be with our friends since Jack killed himself.", or "I just know the whole neighborhood is talking about my being laid off."

Certain types of loss are more prone to producing shame as a part of a grieving person's emotional reaction—death by suicide or drug overdose; criminal behavior such as driving while intoxicated; losses due to failure at school, layoff, bankruptcy, divorce, or legal misconduct; and stigmatizing illnesses and conditions such as AIDS or schizophrenia. When persons or families feel ashamed or disgraced, they may isolate themselves from their customary social support systems. They should be directed to support groups composed of others who have similar situations.

Summary of Emotional Aspects.   The degree to which grieving people feel comfortable expressing the emotions of grief is related to the emotional climate of the family of origin and their culture. Some ethnic traditions inhibit the expression of anger, sadness, and/or anxiety at a time of crisis. About one-third to one-half of the audiences I address indicate that they did not feel free to be emotionally expressive as children. Typically, I have found that people who were inhibited from expressing themselves as children will have more trouble expressing their grief as adults. They may know that giving in to their feelings would be helpful, but they can't shake the messages they heard when they were young—*Don't cry! Act like a big boy or girl.* Sadly, such grieving people may want desperately to cry out—but cannot.

Care providers working with people who are blocked in this way need to assess the extent to which the individual is blocked and the basis or reasons for the emotional withholding. Therapy can focus on facilitating insight and the opportunity for the release of feelings. Methods for assisting with the release of feelings (externalization) are presented in chapter 8.

Cognitive Disturbances of Grief

People who are grieving may find that their thought processes are also affected. The unreality of their new situation violates their assumptions about the world. Loved ones are gone or are terminally ill, careers have been aborted, and lifestyles and dreams have vanished—but the individual's inner picture of the old pre-loss world does not match the painful new external post-loss world reality, and a discrepancy exists. This is really hard to do for most people and can fatigue and disorient the mind.

Some common cognitive disturbances to this inconsistency include the following:

- *Responding sluggishly* to questions—a long lag between question and answers
- *Difficulty concentrating*—easily distracted from tasks; lack of focus
- *Memory loss*—unable to locate things, recall appointments
- *Loss of interest* in usual activities—work, sports, games, collecting, social clubs, hobbies
- *Loss of pleasure*—avoids sex, entertainment, food, and social events
- *General numbness*—shutdown of reactions to social stimuli, no pain, and no joy
- *Intrusive thoughts* about the loss—constant barrage of thoughts, images associated with loss
- *Confusion and disorientation*—difficulty with time sequences, location
- *A sense of futility* about life—"What's the use?" and "Why bother?"—apathetic attitude
- *A sense of helplessness*—"Can't do anything to help myself"—sense of impotence
- *Uncertainty about identity*—"Who am I now?" and "How do I present myself to others now?"
- *So-called "crazy" thoughts*—hearing or seeing the lost loved one; feeling like they can communicate with them
- *Mental fatigue*—too tired to figure things out, mind just won't work

Many of the above symptoms, especially those relating to confusion and inability to concentrate, naturally dissipate over time. However, questions associated with personal and social identity may persist and require continued support. As grievers confront the question of meaning and identity in the post-loss world, they may ask, "Who am I now?", "What do I do now?", "Why did this happen?", "If I have been a good person, why am I being punished this way?", or "Where was God?". For some, absorbing the traumatic loss event into a larger worldview, such as a religious or philosophical belief system, can help make sense of a tragedy. Others may be driven to review police or medical records. Those coping with workplace change and trauma may initiate grievance actions to obtain answers to the questions of "why?" and "how?".

Some people simply need to tell and retell their stories over and over again. Frequently, time with the care provider is the only time when they can do this. It is through this making sense of the loss that people come to grips with the cognitive aspects of grief (Frankl, 1977).

> *Care providers* should be aware that these cognitive changes are frequently associated with depressed mood, and there is a tendency to diagnose a grieving person as depressed. Providers need to determine whether the level of depression requires special treatment or a referral to a mental health professional. When in doubt, make the referral. Further discussion of grief and clinical depression is provided in chapter 9.

The Physical Component of Grief

Health Factors

Nerves, muscle, bones, hormones, viscera, senses, the immune system, the heart, and circulation—all of these parts of our physical being are affected by the trauma of loss or threatened loss. According to Klerman and Clayton (1984), bereaved children and adults are "at greater risk for a variety of adverse health consequences" (p. 15). In addition, grieving people have been shown to be at increased risk for mortality, aggravation of existing medical conditions—especially cardiovascular problems—and such health-threatening behaviors as substance abuse, smoking, and poor nutrition (Osterweis, Solomon, & Green, 1984; Parkes & Weiss, 1993). Further, continued grieving is stressful, and chronic stress lowers the ability of the immune system to protect the body from infection. Vulnerability to colds is not unusual among grieving people.

Physical Symptoms

Grieving people complain of various combinations of the following physical complaints. These symptoms are not unlike those experienced by depressed persons.

Common Physical Complaints of Grieving People

- *Lack of energy*—physical fatigue, too tired to do daily activities
- *Stomach aches*—cramps, spasms, burning
- *Chest pain and tightness*—dull ache or throbbing twinges
- *Shortness of breath*—awareness of breathing, can't catch their breath
- *Dryness or lump in throat*—continued need to drink, throat muscle spasms
- *Multiple pains* and other muscle aches
- *Dizziness*—head spinning, difficulty with balance
- *A perception of empty space within the body*—a "hole" or sense of something missing
- *Frequent colds*—lowered immune function and colds, coughs, fevers
- *Nausea*—feeling like they could vomit or simply a low-level queasiness
- *Sleep and appetite disturbance*—unable to fall asleep, waking during the night, overeating, lack of appetite
- *Body change*—loss of weight/weight gain
- *Sexual dysfunction*—lack of desire, inability to engage in sexual behavior

Care providers can help by advising good eating and sleeping habits, physical relaxation, physical exercise, and specially designated "time outs" from active grieving. At the same time, care providers need to take clients' continuing physical symptoms seriously and refer those with lingering problems to their physician. This not only treats the grieving person with utmost respect but also enlists the medical practitioner as part of the grief support team. For example, grievers who develop clinical depression need to be evaluated to determine if antidepressant medication is indicated. Those exhibiting features of post-trauma stress should likewise be assessed for possible medical treatment.

The Social Component of Grief

Family and Other Relationships

Grief changes the individual's face to the world. Social roles, family relationships, and identity are all modified by significant loss. Some individuals shrink from social contact while others overextend themselves socially.

Here is a personal recollection regarding the effect on my life of the death of my mother.

> I was 16 and the only kid in my group of teenage friends whose mother had died. Every time one of the guys said, "My mother says . . . " I would feel a stab in my heart and become silent and withdrawn.
>
> The death of my mother from cardiac arrest following surgery was a major change-producing event in my life. I was 16 and my sister was 10. My mother was 36 and her death put into motion a number of life-altering changes, as premature deaths must do.
>
> The remarriage of my father during the early stages of our grief introduced a new person into the family system and limited our ability to talk comfortably about our loss. We moved out of state, away from friends and family, and what support may have been available was then cut off. The grief for my mother was buried deep within, and the priorities of college, military service, as well as later becoming a husband and father, filled my time and attention, further burying my grief for my mother.
>
> Five years after our son Steven's death in 1975, I attended a "Life, Death, and Transition" workshop given by Elisabeth Kubler-Ross. As I began to work on my pain over his death, I found myself weeping for mother. It took two workshops, as well as personal grief therapy, to get back to Steven and obtain some relief from the stored, unfinished grief material from my mother's death. I say "some" relief because my own awareness of grief and my clinical work with grieving people have shown me over and over that we never expunge grief completely from our hearts. Rather, we learn to manage and live "side by side" with grief as a part of who we are.

The death of my mother severely shifted the course of my life, and this is true to some extent, of all loss in life. We are pushed, pulled, buffeted, seek, and find places of satisfaction and even joy. Yet, pain of loss can also serve to highlight the times of blessings and peace.

Society and Attitudes Toward Grief

In a similar way, people react in special ways to a person whom they know has suffered a loss. Some individuals in the griever's social network avoid them—remember the "Safeway Samba" reported by a bereaved father? Others are overly solicitous, seeking out mourners and offering "should" advice.

Regrettably, some well-intentioned people say very hurtful and inappropriate things to grieving people. A couple who lost their first baby to SIDS was told, "Maybe you will be more careful with your future children!" A mother whose son was shot and killed was asked after 6 weeks, "When are you going to stop crying?" A woman who suffered a miscarriage was told, "It was just a fetus, why are you so upset?" I spend a good deal of time helping clients to cope with the avoiders, the advisors, and the hurters.

Grieving people are also hurt by lack of attention to their loss. One newly widowed woman was bewildered when no one at the family Thanksgiving dinner mentioned her recently deceased husband. Families frequently do not know what to do about "poor cousin Sue" who is now a widow, has three young children, and is sad and tired all the time.

Many fathers mourning children are hurt by the assumption of others that they need less sympathetic support than their wives. They hear comments such as, "This must be so terrible for your wife." Or, "How is your wife doing since the baby died?"—as if their loss and pain were unimportant.

> *Care providers* can help by normalizing much of the social discomfort a grieving person experiences and by identifying external support systems. The provider can also bring family members of the bereaved together to educate them about how to be supportive to their relatives in the post-loss world. Further, the care provider can assist the grieving person by suggesting ways to respond to unwanted advice and hurtful words.

The Spiritual Component of Grief

Faith Resources and Life Philosophy

The human grief response is typically bound up with spiritual considerations. Many people suffering loss will turn to their belief system for help with death-related rituals, prayer support, comfort, and for advice on placing the loss within a greater spiritual context.

Families and friends are usually drawn together to participate in funerals, burials, and memorials.

It is a time when many reach back to their traditions for connection with some sense of comfort and understanding. Others may reject any notion of God or a Higher Power because they see their tragedy as incompatible with such a concept. Many ultimately reconnect with their faith systems, and some never do. There are also people who may have no particular faith system and seek comfort and answers in a nontheological, humanistic, or other secular philosophies of life.

> *Care providers* can help by determining the grieving person's desire for religious or other spiritual support and assisting in locating clergy or other spiritual advisors in the community.

☐ Past Loss Survey

One of the best ways to learn about grief is to use our own loss material as part of the subject matter. This is an opportunity to look for our own Cowbells. Let yourself become your own consultant to that part of you that may still be holding unfinished loss material. Understanding our own loss material—"heart" dimension—provides personal data that can be related to the theoretical material on the grief process that will follow. Please complete the exercise below to help you identify some of your unfinished grief material or your Cowbells. (This can be done on a separate sheet.)

Exercise 3: Past Loss Survey

1. List two important losses you have experienced. In addition to death, illness, and separation, consider other losses (pets, a home, dreams, and jobs as well). Choose one from childhood if possible.
2. Locate the degree to which you still have feelings and thoughts concerning the two losses and mark the spot on the line between (1) and (10) to indicate to what degree each is still having a continued effect on your daily life. Please also list one or two feelings (if any) that still come up about this loss.

LOSS

1: _____

No *Current* Effect   Major *Current* Effect
(1)   (5)   (10)
Feeling raised:

LOSS

2: _____

No *Current* Effect   Major *Current* Effect
(1)   (5)   (10)
Feeling raised:

3. Briefly describe the ways in which your own loss experiences have helped and/or hindered your own personal or professional growth. Please be specific. (For example, does any particular loss make it uncomfortable for you to work with others who have experienced the same type of loss? Does your own loss experience give you a sense of comfort with a particular type of loss?)

_____

You can use this survey for purposes of stimulating thinking about your own Cowbells. The exercise is a technique to start the process of uncovering unresolved grief material that may be interfering with your comfort in working with certain loss situations. It is not a clinical diagnosing instrument but rather a thought-provoking exercise.

You can do this survey repeatedly and get new material each time. The material that comes up can be placed in a journal and added to the Cowbells that you are gathering for self-discovery purposes. I have used it in training programs for care providers and also with grieving people who are seeking to identify the extent that old loss material is affecting current grief. If feelings have been stirred up by this exercise, this is "gold" for you. Do some journaling and/or talk to a trusted friend before continuing.

☐ Grief Process Theories: From Bowlby to Neimeyer

Understanding the nature of normal grief and how it heals is the foundation of the *exquisite witness's* "head" or knowledge dimension. This understanding enables the person who is helping grieving people to have a sense of the range of reactions to expect from grievers. Additionally, the value of being aware of the several models that are presented below provides a variety of possibilities for explaining the many variations of the human grief response, and implications for various supportive and clinical interventions.

The literature on loss, grief, and the healing of grief contains the work of several important contributors who have studied and written about this human phenomenon from several perspectives. The following summary will highlight the main features of each writer's contribution to the understanding of grief and healing. This will be followed by a synthesis of seven conceptual points on the path to healing.

> *Note*: While various writers have used different formats and emphasized one aspect of healing grief over another, the purpose for all of the explanations is to arrive at an understanding of how grieving people can be helped to heal. I have divided the theoretical material into two groups of writers: those who use a stage or phase design (Bowlby through Rando), and those who do not (Stroebe through Neimeyer).

Several writers have conceptualized the process of grief as a series of phases or stages. For those explanations organized in stages, be advised that the boundaries between such stages are fluid, that following a proposed sequence may or may not happen, and that some grieving people may skip some or all of the phases.

John Bowlby

John Bowlby (1969/1980, 1973, 1980) outlined a four-phase process of what happens when a human being is separated from an attachment bond figure, such as mother, lover, sibling, friend, and pets. He includes symbolic losses (such as future dreams) as well as loss of youth, health, function, roles, and home.

> **Phase I—*Numbing*.** An initial period of shutdown, denial, and unreality lasting for a few days to several weeks. Grieving people may

appear to be doing "very well" during this time because they do not grieve outwardly.

Phase II—*Yearning and searching*. A time during which the grieving person attempts to recover the person or other loss object. This is "attachment behavior." Mourners experience agitation and distress as they seek contact by calling out the name of the deceased loved one, wearing items of clothing that belonged to the deceased, and ruminating about that which was lost.

Phase III—*Disorganization and despair*. A sad time during which hopes for reunion fade and the mourner acknowledges, "She or he's never coming back." Despair, fatigue, loss of motivation, and apathy are common. One bereaved father called this "the bleeding stage of grief."

Phase IV—*Reorganization*. A new definition of self is established as grieving persons create new patterns of thinking, feeling, and acting. "Who am I now?", "How do I fit in with others now?", "What new ways do I have to adopt?".

Elisabeth Kubler-Ross

Elisabeth Kubler-Ross (1969) suggests five stages of loss as an outgrowth of her work with over 200 dying cancer patients and their families. These stages are still perhaps the most familiar to the lay public and should be referred to as descriptions of observed behaviors rather than required steps for healing grief.

Stage I—*Shock and denial.* "No! It can't be!" "There must be some mix up with the x-rays." "Let's get another blood test." These expressions of shock and denial are common immediately after a loss or the threat of loss.

Stage II—*Anger.* Rage, resentment, bitterness, irritability, hostility, and violence are all expressions of the anger that grieving people may feel and express. Anger may also take the form of passivity, stubborn refusal to eat or comply with medical advice, or even to speak with family or medical staff.

Stage III—*Bargaining*. "If I start praying again, or pray more, maybe I will get well." "Maybe if I come in earlier and stay later, I will survive the next layoff." These are examples of bargaining through which a person seeks an extension of time or at least freedom from pain and discomfort.

Stage IV—*Depression*. Many individuals withdraw to prepare for the final act of dying. During this stage, patients may literally turn their back to visitors and staff in an attempt to conserve energy. They may spend time thinking about their lives, the meaning of life and death, and/or religious or other spiritual truths.

Stage V—*Acceptance*. This is perhaps the most misunderstood of these five stages. It refers to the fact that some terminally ill or bereaved persons may *intellectually* accept the unavoidable reality while at the same time remaining depressed, angry, and frightened.

Parkes and Weiss

The three tasks outlined by Parkes and Weiss (1983) are based on data collected from the Harvard Bereavement Studies completed in 1973.

Task I—*Intellectual recognition and explanation of loss*. Mourners need to understand their loss, to have it make sense.

Task II—*Emotional acceptance of the loss*. In this phase the bereaved can recall the deceased without a resurgence of pain. To accomplish this, the bereaved must repeatedly confront memories and express feelings of pain.

Task III—*Assumption of a new identity*. This transition to a new way of thinking of oneself—as a widow, as an orphan, as unemployed—is often a turbulent time of painful reality testing.

These tasks provide for some of the basic requirements for healing: emotional release and the creation of a new identity in the post-loss world.

William Worden—Four Tasks of Mourning

William Worden (2002) has made a major contribution with his conceptualization of four task-based categories of behavioral goals that must be addressed in order for healing to take place.

Task I—*To accept the reality of the loss*. A grieving person must realize intellectually that the loss has occurred before progress toward healing can take place. The primary objective at this time is to ultimately integrate the reality that the loss is irreversible, and to neither deny nor minimize it. Examples of minimizing a loss include a teenage boy who told me, "My mom was sick for so long that I didn't get to spend much time with her anyway, so I don't miss her that much now," or an executive who reacts to being laid off by saying, "I knew it was time to move on anyway."

Task II—*To work through the pain of grief.* Pain in this context refers not only to emotional pain but also to the physical and behavioral pain associated with loss. Worden (2002) (as do Bowlby and Parkes) emphasizes the importance of experiencing this pain in order for grieving people to heal. Further, when this task is not sufficiently addressed because of avoidance or suppression of memories or images of the deceased, healing will be impeded, and the result may be emotional complications of grief or physical problems. Worden is clear that "not everyone experiences the same intensity of pain or feels it in the same way . . . " (2002, p. 30). However, those who do need to express their feelings should have the opportunity to do so in a safe and healthy way.

Task III—*To adjust to new environment after loss.* Worden divides this set of tasks into three subsets: (a) *external adjustments*—adapting to such everyday functioning as cooking, shopping, and working; (b) *internal adjustments*—developing a new identity in a changed world; (c) *spiritual adjustments*—necessary changes in beliefs, values, and assumptions about the world.

Task IV—*To emotionally relocate the deceased or other changed condition and move on with life.* "Moving on with life," in this case, means being able to hold on to the inner picture of the person or other loss object and function in a changed world. The bond with the deceased or other loss is altered yet continues in the post-loss world.

In chapter 8, we will use Worden's four tasks to describe how care providers can offer support and clinical interventions.

Therese Rando—Phases and Processes of Mourning

Therese Rando (1984, 1993) divides the responses of grieving people into three broad time periods or phases:

Avoidance: a time of denial, disorganization, and confusion
Confrontation: a time of intense grief
Accommodation: a time of diminished grief and re-entry into the world as a changed individual

Rando describes six processes of mourning that are grouped into each of her three phases. She advises that these processes need to be addressed for healing to take place. When some interference prevents a process from occurring, a person is at risk for complicated mourning (Rando, 1993).

Rando's Six Processes of Mourning

Avoidance

1. Recognizing the loss—acknowledging and understanding the loss.

Confrontation

2. Reacting to the separation—experiencing pain and feelings of loss and secondary losses.
3. Recollecting and re-experiencing the deceased in the relationship—reviewing and grieving.
4. Relinquishing the old attachments—both to deceased and to pre-loss assumptions about the world.

Accommodation

5. Readjusting to move adaptively into the new world without forgetting the old attachments—revision of world assumptions, creating a new relationship with deceased, a new identity, and new ways to function in the post-loss world.
6. Reinvesting energy formerly absorbed by the living bond into other relationships or activities, causes, or hopes.

The following writers describe the human grief process in a non-stage-based format.

Margaret Stroebe—Dual Process Model of Grief

Margaret Stroebe's (1999) dual process model was developed as an alternative to stage-based models of human grief. In this view, the grief response is explained as having two different focuses:

Loss-oriented focus—behaviors that express feelings of grief. These may include expressing a range of emotional reactions such as feelings of grief, as well as reviewing and reminiscing, yearning, and missing the lost loved one or prior condition.

Restoration-oriented focus—behaviors that reorganize the self in the new, post-loss world. These include learning new skills, constructing a new identity, or relocating the inner image of the loved one.

Feelings in this area of focus can range from pride of accomplishment to fear of the unknown.

Stroebe also describes an *oscillation* phenomenon—the grieving person moves between engaging in the *loss-oriented focus* and *restoration-oriented focus* in the post-loss world. In this system, the care provider enables emotional release as well as confronting the new meanings in the post-loss world.

Dennis Klass—Continuing Bonds After the Loss

Dennis Klass (1988, 1996) initially explains the healing of bereaved parents as the development of a new inner representation of the deceased child and an adjustment to a new social world.

> *New inner representation.* Parents must ultimately revise the inner image of the child and find equilibrium with the new world reality. It is then possible to form a bond with this new image of the child, a bond that continues throughout the life of the parent. In a similar way, the continuing of bonds with other deceased loved ones facilitates healing in the post-loss world. This concept of continuing bonds has been extended to bereaved people of all ages.
>
> *Reestablishment of social equilibrium.* In both the inner and outer worlds, parents must evolve an authenticated picture of who the lost loved one now is and who the bereaved parent now is to the outer world. The Compassionate Friends support groups for bereaved parents and other grief support groups provide a social network where the "bereaved parent," "grieving child," or "widow" identity is normalized and accepted by others. In a similar way, groups for "cancer patients," "unemployed," and "family survivors of homicide" provide such acceptance and understanding.

Thomas Attig—Relearning the World

Thomas Attig's work (1996, 2001) regarding the importance of the grieving person's need to relearn the world emphasizes the importance of the care provider helping the grieving person to "make sense" of the post-loss world, to reinvent self in a world missing who or what used to be. Attig also endorses continuing bonds as necessary for healing grief.

Robert Neimeyer—Meaning Reconstruction in the Post-Loss World

Robert Neimeyer (1998, 2001) emphasizes the need for many grieving people to restructure the meaning of their lives in order to reclaim them. He views each of us as developing a "self-narrative," defined as "an overarching cognitive-affective-behavioral structure that organizes the 'micronarratives' of everyday life into a 'macronarrative' that consolidates our self-understanding, establishes our characteristic range of emotions and goals, and guides our performance on the stage of the social world" (Neimeyer, 2004, pp. 53–54). Seen in this way, the basic meanings that constitute our life stories are not simply thoughts or cognitions, but are instead passionate assumptions that provide the existential, spiritual, social, and personal grounding for our unique life stories, for our sense of identity (Neimeyer, 2002).

When trauma or loss occurs, these meanings and assumptions are challenged and often profoundly disrupted, and have to be adjusted to help us find orientation in the new reality of the post-loss world in a way that secures the validation of significant others in our family, community, and culture. In emphasizing this quest to reaffirm or reconstruct a world of meaning that has been challenged by loss, Neimeyer would help the mourner seek answers to such questions as, "What do my loved one's life and death mean to me? Who am I now? What can I no longer take for granted in this changed world? What do I need to learn and who do I need to become in order to integrate this loss and move forward with my life?" In some respects, Neimeyer's theory recalls the work of Victor Frankl (1977), who urged those who suffered devastating losses to seek meaning in them in order for healing to take place.

Summary of Grief Process Theories

The above review of important explanations of the human grief response and how grief may proceed over time is a necessary part of the care provider's understanding of the predictable aspects of grief behavior—the "head dimension" of the *exquisite witness*. Understanding the origin and function of the human grief response demystifies the process and imparts to the care provider a sense of the normalcy of grief and its importance in the healing through loss of grieving people. Appendix A contains lists of suggested readings that the reader may wish to consult for further study.

☐ **The Path to Healing**

The seven basic concepts below are drawn from this chapter and can provide a summary of the material for understanding grief and formulating a plan for helping grieving people.

1. *Attachment is an instinctive behavior* occurring from infancy throughout adulthood, which has as its purpose the protection and survival of the individual. Early individual patterns of attachment affect the nature of relationships throughout life as well as issues associated with mourning. The goal of attachment behavior is survival.

2. *Grief reactions are a normal part* of the human behavioral repertoire and will occur whenever attachment bonds are broken or threatened. Grieving people must be helped to see the normalcy of their grief responses. Under certain conditions, grief can become complicated and pathological.

3. *The human grief reaction* manifests in four aspects of an individual's living: psychological, physical, social, and spiritual. The thoughts, feelings, and behaviors that compose the grief response may include shock, avoidance, physical and emotional pain, confusion, and other cognitive disturbances, withdrawal and other social disturbances, and spiritual questioning or seeking.

4. *The expression of emotional pain*—anger, fear, sadness, guilt, shame—surface in many grieving people as they confront the reality of their loss or threat of loss.

5. *The reconstruction of a grieving person's life story*, identities, and social meanings in the post-loss world is a critical part of the healing process.

6. As a grieving person *relearns the world* after a loss, the inner representation of the lost loved one or lost condition changes. This enables the grieving person to maintain a connection or *continuing bond* to that which was lost in a way that matches the new reality.

7. We can discern several *predictable patterns* in the way that people show their grief over time. However, the *exquisite witness* care provider needs to learn and respect the individual differences of grieving people that derive from personal styles of coping as well as from the person's family, culture, and society. *Predicting the nature of any individual's grief is at best an estimate of what to expect.*

☐ Conclusion

Whether you are a family doctor, a hospice volunteer making a home visit, an oncology nurse, a faith-based bereavement worker, school counselor, clergy, friend or family caregiver, or a professional mental health provider, understanding the nature of the human grief response and its complexities over time will give you the comfort of knowing what to expect when working with grieving people.

There are many instances where the volunteer or professional care provider will just simply listen with heart and soul to provide a safe space for the grieving person to tell his or her story. The ability of a family to listen to a dying or bereaved person is an intrinsic part of the social support for grieving people. As providers, we must help families learn to listen to each other.

Loss and grief typically occur within the context of family. The *exquisite witness* care provider must learn about current family relationships and dynamics in order to provide optimal care. These issues will be explored in chapter 3.

Loss and Death in the Family

☐ Introduction

Family

Think family whenever you are working with a person who is faced with a loss or the threat of loss. Family is the basic social unit for the individual, and grief will play itself out among the members of that unit. Family members will typically be the most affected by a loss event, and their reactions will become part of the emotional climate of the grieving person.

Family Change

Any significant change in a family creates a shift in its balance and a need for the realignment of relationships and responsibilities, and the reallocation of resources, including time, energy, and money. Death, divorce, separation, birth or adoption, chronic or terminal illness, disability, natural disaster, job loss, relocation, and the blending of families are all change events that require the reestablishment of balance. Even though some of these changes bring joy, they are always accompanied by a loss of the *world that was*, and this can generate grief responses. We will discuss the family as it is affected by such changes so that the care provider will have an understanding of how to help families who are coping with death, illness, and other significant loss.

In this chapter, we will look at the family as a system with its own needs and unique forms of grief reactions. Among the factors we will consider are the stage of the family in terms of life-cycle events and the role of unfinished grief that moves down through the generations to mix with new grief. We will also consider the needed realignments and shifts in the organization of the family as grief unfolds. These changes in family organization sometimes cause additional and ongoing grief for its members. Family tasks that must be addressed in order for healing to take place will also be reviewed. The special nature of the grief of children, parents, and older adults will be discussed in chapters 4, 5, and 6.

Family Defined

I define family as intentional as well as biological units. Therefore, groups of single people, gay couples, religious communities, and long-term neighbors who have developed a highly connected social network can all be considered families. In addition, long-standing workplace colleagues or those who bond through the intensity of their task—that is, fire, police, and military—can serve an extended and supportive family role. It is important for a care provider to learn who makes up the grieving person's support system so that they can play a role during the grief process.

☐ Death/Loss and Change in the Family: Primary and Secondary Factors

"The pain of death touches all survivors' relationships with others, some of whom may never have even known the person who died."

(Walsh & McGoldrick, 1990, p. 3)

Rippling Effects of Primary Loss

When a family is affected by a primary loss such as death, divorce, disaster, or job loss, there is a painful transition from the world that was. The hopes, dreams, and predictions that could be counted on in the pre-loss world are shattered, and grieving people find themselves thrust into an alien world. Family members are propelled into a new life stripped of their old assumptions, identifications, and meanings. Their pre-loss world is simply gone.

Family members must also cope with the sudden awareness of the end of or threat to existing plans for the future. Attending college, buying a new car or home, changing jobs, looking forward to familiar activities and routines—all these are either thwarted or put in jeopardy. When a beloved grandmother dies, a family may lose the sense of comfort they enjoyed which was associated with spending the holidays together at her house. Even expected and positive changes such as the children going off to college or taking new jobs bring an end to those great Sunday morning breakfasts together.

Secondary Losses for Family Members

The secondary losses that result from the primary loss—death, illness, disability, and layoff—also create changes in the life activities of the family and a trail of loss and grief in their wake. When there is a death or other traumatic loss in a family, it is natural for each family member to evaluate the effect of the loss or threat of loss on his or her life. The following examples illustrate secondary losses that flash into the minds of the surviving loved ones:

- A newly widowed mother and her children have a session with a counselor to figure out how to reorganize their lives. The pre-teen daughter announces with anger and some anxiety, "How will I get to camp without Dad's paycheck to count on anymore!" Her older brother says nothing, but he's thinking about the bill for his next semester's college tuition that arrived a week after his father's funeral.
- A young man, recently a father, is about to be promoted to a much more responsible position at work when his wife is killed in an auto crash. He finds himself grieving not only for his wife but also for the likelihood that his single-parent responsibilities will end his chances for a promotion at work.
- A mother of two pre-teens is bedridden with severe cardiac dysfunction. At night in their room, the girls cry together over the after-school club activities they will no longer be able to attend now that the household responsibilities fall on their shoulders.
- At a Compassionate Friends meeting, an elderly woman points out that the death of her 50-year-old daughter means not only the loss of her only child but the loss of the person she counted on to care for her as she aged.

When the primary wage earner has been laid off, the family must not only deal with the anxiety about the loss of financial support and/or health insurance but also the unhappiness of the person now out of work. Family members may also fear that others may view them differently as a result of the job loss. When a parent becomes seriously ill or disabled, children lose not only the attention of that parent but also find the caregiving parent much less available. Children and adolescents may feel painfully different from their peers. Many new widows and divorced women find themselves in a downward economic spiral that forces them to move into less expensive housing, curtail their children's activities, and to severely reduce their food and clothing budgets.

Separation and divorce bring many other changes besides the end of a marriage. Often children have to balance their time between two homes, cope with conflicts which continue beyond the physical separation of parents, worry about how they "look" to others, care for lonely parents, and adapt to new routines. The aftershocks of traumatic loss in the family continue to trigger grief reactions through the family's future generations (Bowen, 1991). The absence of one parent from the life of the children, from the grandchildren, and from special life transition events can have lingering effects on the family system through the years. Additionally, the lack of homelife stability and the associated limitations on financial resources continues to yield ongoing losses.

As a care provider, you will need to gather sufficient background information regarding the rippling effects of the secondary losses that flow from a primary loss event such as death, job loss, relocation, financial hardship, separation, and divorce in the family. Some people talk about their concerns over these secondary losses easily. Others have a harder time. Many feel guilty.

As a care provider, one of your most helpful functions is to assure family members that thinking "What do I lose?" is a normal reaction and part of the grieving process. When people understand the nature of "secondary loss" and accept that their responses are natural, they often feel more willing to share their grief experience with each other.

If family members are reluctant to talk about their concerns over what they have lost, care providers can initiate the discussion by making a general statement about how most people automatically inventory what will be different as a result of their loss.

Care providers can also give examples of how other grieving people have thought about losses, and can even compile a master list of "What do I lose?" items as a teaching device.

☐ Factors Influencing the Family Grief Reaction

The family's grief reaction—their thoughts, feelings, and behaviors—will be influenced by the factors listed below. The care provider will need to be aware of these influences on grieving behavior and consider them when deciding how to help a particular family.

Factors Influencing Family Grief

- Stages of the family life cycle development
- Family values and belief systems
- The role of the dying or deceased person in the family
- The nature of the death
- The age of the person dying, deceased, or bereaved
- The nature of the attachments to family members
- The nature of the family's functioning
- Disenfranchised grief
- Additional factors affecting the nature of grief

Stages of the Family Life Cycle Development

A newly married couple with young children will have different needs than an elderly couple with grandchildren. At each stage in the life of a family, different goals are affected by the loss. For example, the death of a young father leaves a woman alone as a single parent with different issues than an older widow with grown children.

Family Values and Belief Systems

Family values flow from social and cultural heritages and unique family traditions that develop over time. Attitudes toward life and death, dealing with death-related rituals, and patterns of communication about grief vary and require great respect and sensitivity from the care provider.

The Role of the Dying or Deceased Person in the Family

Each role—wage earner, elder, patriarch, matriarch, problem-solver, entertainer, social convener, mechanic, financial advisor, turkey carver, pie baker—has its own set of expectations that are lost along with the person. Care providers may need to locate additional resources for a family to fill the holes that have been left by the loss.

The Nature of the Death

Grief varies with the circumstances under which the loss occurred. Some loss events can complicate the grief reactions; sudden, violent, and unexpected deaths, for example. Family members who have witnessed violent deaths are more likely to develop problematic grieving such as post-traumatic reactions. Lengthy illnesses can drain a family of energy, time, and motivation to engage in other aspects of life. Further discussion of types of death are as follows.

Sudden Deaths

Sudden deaths do not allow for any preparation time for the family. There is no opportunity to have developed internal images (fantasies) of the future without the loved one. There is no chance to say good-bye, and survivors may feel guilty that they are still alive.

Lingering Deaths

Lingering deaths do provide time to prepare, to begin the grieving process, to experience many changes and anticipate the changes to come. The family system is altered gradually. Painful medical procedures may be part of the experience, and resentment at the disruption of life caused by caregiving may occur. This anger and resentment may also be followed by guilt. Siblings may be jealous of the attention their sick brother or sister receives—this is normal. Opportunities for saying good-bye and having a dignified and spiritually affirming death are possible.

With the lingering death of a homebound terminally ill person, more than the body is lost. The after-death removal of the hospital bed, medicines, oxygen, and other medical support apparatus leaves a gaping physical hole; the departure of outside nursing help creates a sense of emptiness. Caregivers may also be physically and emotionally exhausted from the prolonged dying of a loved one. Families, therefore, need to expect a reaction at the end of their caregiving, and the provider can help to normalize this reality for them.

Suicide

Suicide reportedly claims the life of over 30,646 (National Vital Statistics Report, 2004) each year in the United States. Families who have experienced the death of a loved one who has taken his or her life typically have a very difficult and complex grief journey. Parents bereaved by suicide have, in my experience, an enormous level of intense grief and may require long periods of provider support. Emotions range from rage to pain, guilt, shame, and fear. The unfinished business of the loved one who has completed suicide is left in the lap of his or her family. Families sometimes are reluctant to talk about the death as a suicide and even omit this fact from obituaries. Guilt is a prominently expressed feeling in a suicide death and must be listened to and not belittled but not supported. Later in the grief process, guilt can be gently reality tested. Should guilt or rage become a fixed part of the grieving person's sense of self, referral to a mental health provider may be required. Support groups for family survivors of suicide are available. (See appendix B for listing.)

Homicide

Death by homicide presents its own sense of horror for family members. They are tortured by images of their loved one being terrified, in agonizing pain, and helpless. They may have rage at the perpetrators and have no way to express it directly. Legal procedures may keep the wounds open for a protracted period of time. This may also be the case for drunk driving and other vehicular deaths. There are a great number of homicides that go unsolved and often unprosecuted. Surviving loved ones of such deaths are at high risk for endless grief. There are special support groups for the family survivors of homicide and for victims of drunk- driving deaths. (See appendix B.)

The Age of the Person Dying, Deceased, or Bereaved

Grief reactions are typically influenced by the age of the person who has died. Normally, the death of an older aged adult is a considered an expected death while the death of a child has been labeled "unthinkable" by Rosen (1990, p. 61). However, the loss of an older adult can be just as painful. I've been with teenagers who sobbed as they recounted the loss of beloved grandparents and even great-grandparents. Here is an example from a family I know.

> I listened to the deeply sad words expressed by a bereaved great-granddaughter in a family discussion at her grandmother's home after the funeral of her great-grandpa. The teenage girl talked about her many visits to great-grandpa in the nursing home, how he loved to tell her of his early days in this country. She enjoyed this time and now sobbed as she expressed grief at missing his smile when she came into his room and also pushing him in his wheelchair around the floors and grounds.

Certain deaths—that of a child, the loss of a spouse on the threshold of retirement, or of a parent just before one's wedding—provide a sense of "untimeliness" that adds an additional thread of pain to the grief reaction. "Why now?" we ask ourselves.

I've also heard women at Compassionate Friends meetings who have lost grown children question the intensity of the grief reaction of women who suffered miscarriage or neonatal deaths. They felt that the younger the child, the weaker the attachment bond, and therefore the more attenuated the grief should be. However, each type of loss has its own misery. Parents of deceased grown children mourn the people they knew and loved; parents of infants mourn the loss of the opportunity to be parents and the loss of the child they would know.

We cannot pre-judge the effect of age or timeliness on the nature or intensity of grief.

Care providers can help a family and their friends to understand that there is no one right way to grieve. All grief is valid regardless of who, when, and how the loss occurred. Various examples of normal grief reactions can be mentioned, and it can also be a time to teach some of the basics of the how and why we humans grieve.

The Nature of the Attachments to Family Members

The intensity of the attachment to the person who died, the degree of dependency, and the quantity of unfinished business with that person all affect how we grieve.

If the surviving member of a couple was very dependent upon the other, or derived his or her self-image from the lost loved one, grief may be intense, prolonged, and interfere with daily functioning. Survivors of ambivalent or abusive relationships often have to deal with unfinished business before they can focus specifically on the loss.

The care provider can offer an opportunity to discuss these issues or arrange for a referral to a mental health professional. Problematic relationships lead to complicated grief reactions such as chronic grief, distorted grief, or clinical depression.

The Nature of the Family's Functioning

The degree to which the family members communicate with each other and with people outside of the family can have an impact on grief. The existence of social connections to various parts of the community—faith community, social clubs and recreational groupings, workplace friends, and neighbors—can yield rich levels of support. Some families choose to remain more secluded from their social surroundings or do not know how to express their needs and receive support. Family therapists have found that many Western culture families who have a more open style of communicating both within and outside of the family are generally more open to support and heal more quickly than families that have relatively "closed" patterns of communication (Walsh and McGoldrick, 1991).

Families with pre-existing conflicts among their members may reflect this in their grief during and beyond the mourning rituals, and add additional stress to an already stressful situation. They may lack connection, fail to support each other, and even continue hostilities. The Melbourne Family Grief Study comparing families coping with death from cancer which were rated as *adaptive* (high cohesive, expressive) or *maladaptive* (low cohesive, low expressive) found that there is "a close link between family functioning and the psychosocial outcome of bereavement" (Kissane et al., 1996, p. 665). Low-communicating families had the highest intensity of grief, and maladaptive families had the highest levels of depression and overall psychological distress (Kissane et al.). I have seen some families remain at odds and erupt in angry turmoil during discussions of inheritance and distribution of the deceased person's belongings.

Other families are able to effect a temporary truce during the early period of mourning, and have even been able to use the period of bereavement as an opportunity to begin the healing of old wounds.

> *Care providers* should be aware that while many families can benefit from external support, individuals, families, and cultures vary in the function and value placed on sharing their feelings. This is true for communication within or outside of the family boundaries. The care provider can get a sense of the family's style of communication during informal discussions and by observing how the family interacts. Additionally, being with the family at home, in the hospital cafeteria, in the visitor's lounge, and in the hospital room can also yield important information on how family members communicate.

Disenfranchised Grief

The grief of certain groups—children, the mentally ill, the intellectually retarded, elderly, gay partners, ex-spouses, clandestine lovers, and legal offenders—is frequently invalidated (Doka, 1989). Medical and pastoral care providers, schoolteachers, classmates, and work colleagues also may be overlooked as grievers. Not only can certain grievers be disenfranchised but also certain types of loss are open to invalidation. Grief for abortion, miscarriage, giving a baby up for adoption, pet death, and death of a friend are examples of disenfranchised losses. The grief of the disenfranchised has sorrow that may be hidden and/or unrecognized by the people in their lives. Such people grieve alone . . . painfully alone.
    Some individuals disenfranchise themselves. Here is a personal story.

> I participated in a local funeral for a husband, wife, and their daughter who were killed in a small plane crash. The community was devastated, and several close friends of the family gathered in a small room prior to the ceremony. I attempted to comfort a man I know who was especially distraught. He looked up and said, "Oh, I'm OK. I'm just a friend."

Nondeath Losses

Zinner (2002) points to the need to take a broader view of loss and to legitimize the grief reactions to nondeath loss events. She cites a number of examples of disenfranchised nondeath losses gleaned from grief research: aging and dementia; childhood trauma; community disasters; chronic illness or disabilities; hearing, speech, vision, and other impairments; injuries; mental retardation; alcohol and drug abuse in the home; marital dysfunction; loss of romantic relationship; immigration; pet loss; and relocation.

Often, nondeath losses are not considered valid reasons for grieving. Families whose primary wage earner is laid off experience grief and mourn the loss of the sense of financial security they had before the loss. Children who overhear their anxious parents discussing financial concerns may carry the burden of uncertainty with them to school, playground, and the neighborhood. Teachers, guidance counselors, and other school staff must be sensitive to such loss events and the continued effect they may have on students.

Zinner (2002) describes how some people may determine the validity of a loss using the "Hallmark test"—"If Hallmark™ Cards has a card for it, then the loss is legitimate." If not, we tend to believe that people don't have a valid cause to mourn (p. 391). Where does the ex-wife sit at the funeral? How does the partner of a man who dies of AIDS participate in the funeral that has been planned by the partner's parents? Adults may not want to listen to a young person grieve after a cat dies.

Infertility

Couples who have tried repeatedly to have a baby and have been unsuccessful represent another group of hidden grievers who receive little social support. This is partly because infertility is not usually a topic of discussion. However, even when it is known that they are "trying" but have not gotten pregnant, family and friends are reluctant to call or somehow offer some support. The grief over what is not happening ripples outward to the couple's parents, grandparents, siblings, and close friends. It is very sad and frustrating for couples who are so very anxious to begin a family.

> *Care providers* may have to help the couple avoid displacing anger on each other and teach them how to keep lines of communication open. The provider may need to help the family take the initiative to reach out to those grieving people who are disenfranchised and offer support by including them in rituals and reminiscences. When this is not possible, the provider may want to contact the grieving person directly and offer support.

Adoption

While adoption can be a wonderful and positive experience, it may sometimes present difficulties and represent another potential area of loss and disenfranchised grief. Some problematic areas are: (a) the grief of the birth mother who lives with the loss of the child she gave up, (b) grief for those adoptive parents who continue to wonder what their own biological children and grandchildren would have looked like, and (c) the adopted child's grief at some point when he or she learns of the adoption and the loss of the birth parents.

> *The care provider's* role is always to enfranchise, to empower the grievers to sigh, cry, and express their rage and their fears. Frequently, other hidden losses impact on current grief and may be unrecognized as a factor in the intensity of their grief reaction. Providers can educate families about the ramifications of the added grief from these "undercover" losses to further their awareness of the sources of grief and help them to cope with their current loss.

Additional Factors Affecting the Nature of Grief

Education level, economic realities, spiritual resources, cultural expectations, and available community resources will have an effect on how family members grieve. For example, people who are expected back on the job after a 3-day "bereavement leave" are not likely to have had time to grieve. A family whose financial resources have been drained caring for a terminally ill family member will have additional anxieties to cope with on top of their grief. Some families are isolated because they have had to relocate so many times and have no local family or long established friendships to count on for support. In other cases, family mourning behaviors will be affected by the traditions of their faith and cultural heritage. Some families may not be part of a religious group, and the care provider will have to help them seek available social support in the community. (See appendix B for a list of support groups found in many communities.)

☐ Family Life Cycle Stages and Objectives

Family Life Cycle Stages

As families develop, they pass through various transition periods during which certain tasks have to be accomplished for the health and well-being of its members. During some periods, there is a natural moving away of family members—from home to school, to jobs, to marriage, to retirement. The life cycle stages presented in Table 3.1 provide a road map of the natural tasks that families typically address at each stage. When a traumatic loss or threat of loss occurs, the objectives may be severely compromised. In some cases, traumatic loss or threat of loss has the effect of drawing people back into the nuclear family against the flow of natural development. This disruption of the work in each stage creates yet another series of losses for family members (McGoldrick & Walsh, 1991a; Rosen, 1990).

The care provider needs to understand how the disruptions to a family's natural developmental inclinations at each stage add additional stress to grieving. Realizing what is at risk for family members at each stage of the life cycle when there is a death, separation, or other loss will give the care provider a fuller understanding of the grief reactions of family members.

The material in Table 3.1 has been drawn partially from concepts gathered from the work of McGoldrick and Walsh (1991a) and Rosen (1990), as well as from my family therapy practice.

Effects of Traumatic Loss in Each of the Stages

The effects of traumatic loss in each of the stages of family development depend on whether family members are moving toward or away from the family unit in a given stage. A death, a frightening medical diagnosis, disability, or other traumatic loss event has the potential for thwarting the natural push outward of younger family members and creates a strong force pulling them back into the original family unit.

A college age child, for example, may decide to attend a local school and live at home to help out in the face of an impending death or serious illness of a family member. An engaged couple may postpone their marriage. A young adult may turn down a good job opportunity in another city. This "push-pull" effect, described by Rosen (1990, p. 51), is at work in every stage but is more prominent during adolescence (Stage 4) or young adulthood. In Stage 5, family members who should be experiencing greater independence may resent being pulled back in at a time of crisis. Young adults, who have invested great energy in launching a career

TABLE 3.1. The Family Life Cycle Stages

Developmental Stage	Objectives Being Addressed
1. Young adult moving between families	Become independent of family of origin and new parents; establish adult role in family college or job; seek and obtain a mate.
2. Newly joined couple	Form new nuclear dyad; realign and reconstruct new attachments to family of origin.
3. Family with young children	Learn parent roles; integrate children into couplehood; further develop connections to family of origin.
4. Family with adolescents	Adapt to children who are beginning the move away from family; redirect energy back into couple.
5. Empty nested	Adapt to new freedom as a couple and reconstruct the relationship; continued adaptation to children as adults, and to grandparent role; manage health issues for self and own parents.
6. Later life	Adapt to retirement; coping with physical decline and multiple losses of advanced age; facing death of spouse and own mortality.

or a serious relationship, may be heavily conflicted when a parent becomes terminally ill or dies and leaves a surviving parent in need of assistance and care.

The anguish of a young person caught in such a conflict can result in resentment, guilt, and anxiety regarding the balancing of the push-pull equation as well as fear of sliding back into a dependent relationship with the parent. This may lead to chronic anger toward the parent.

People who are newly coupled (Stage 2) or creating a family (Stage 3) feel a strong pull into their young family unit, and they are establishing new boundaries with family of origin members. ("Mom, please don't come over next week, we want to spend more time with just the three of us.") In Stage 5, couples also pull inward as they reestablish themselves as a two-person household once again. ("Sorry, dear, we can't babysit; we're off on a trip for the weekend.") A death or other traumatic loss in these stages can impede the formation of newly independent family units. ("I need Mom here all the time since I miscarried.")

The widowed or divorced mid-life man or woman (Stage 5) may find that they are isolated in their grief. Children are grown with families of their own; peers may avoid them as they represent "our worst fears!" "Single again" men and women frequently have referred to themselves as the "fifth wheel" at gatherings of family and friends. At a time when the couple should be enjoying their couple commitment, death or illness undermines the pull toward each other and may create a dependency on children or other relatives for managing grief and creating a new life.

There is always the issue of how much time can be comfortably spent with married children or a brother or sister's family. Conjugally bereaved mid-life individuals must create a whole new sense of identity in order to make sense of the new world in which they find themselves.

> *Care providers* may need to help such individuals establish ground rules for visiting family, and find resources to assist in developing plans for personal growth and development as well as financial independence. When desired, support groups for widows and widowers can do much to help them re-enter the social world with their new identity.

Older adults (Stage 6) have multiple loss issues to deal with when a spouse dies or when one becomes ill and perhaps has to be placed in a nursing home. The hopes for retirement leisure, increased freedom from work, and the pursuit of nonwork activities may be dashed when traumatic loss occurs. Added to this is the disenfranchisement of elder grief that we will take a closer look at in chapter 6.

☐ Unfinished Grief and Emotional Inheritance

Current grief is typically fueled, in part, from the leftover energy of old grief. This stored loss material is called "unfinished business" and can add to the intensity of the grief response. The unfinished business may come from the individual's own personal history (Cowbells), or it may have originated as unresolved issues in earlier generations (Bowen, 1991). Care providers must have an appreciation of how such loss material has infiltrated the current grief response. Often, grieving people talk about older losses as they tell the story of a current loss. The care provider needs to attend to this material. Unfinished business from an older traumatic loss becomes an important part of the grieving person's story and part of the healing process.

The Unfinished Business Model

The Unfinished Business Model (Jeffreys, 1995) presents the three sources of unfinished material that are stored (Fig. 3.1). Such old grief material

Unfinished Business Model

Threat of Loss   Breaking of Bonds

Developmental Loss

FIGURE 3.1. Unfinished Business Model (Source: Jeffreys, 1995)

may or may not be obvious to the grieving person or to the care provider. Compiling a thorough loss history using this model will help the clinical care provider and grieving person gain the best perspective so that the unfinished material can be addressed. (This will be discussed in greater detail in chapter 8.)

Aspects of this model are outlined below.

Developmental Loss

We naturally store loss material that is created by the normal and expected changes that occur throughout human development—moving from diaper to potty, from being at home with mom to going to school, from being a couple to welcoming home a new baby, or moving from work to retirement. Each time we make a transition to the next stage of development, we lose what went before—all that is comfortable and familiar—and this can create a grief reaction.

The Threat of Loss

We store up loss material when we live under a constant threat of loss. The threat of loss can arise from having to cope with chronic financial insecurity, physical and emotional abuse, a life-threatening illness, a history of traumatic losses, or an unsafe environment.

The Breaking of Bonds

We also store up loss material when bonds we have made are broken or severely altered—when people die or leave, pets die, a beloved Teddy

Bear is lost, we move to a new city, friends reject us, we are dropped from a team, we lose a job, or a loved one develops Alzheimer's disease.

In summary, grief reactions that are not given the opportunity of expression and acknowledgment are stored as unfinished grief material. Grieving people are vulnerable to the reappearance of this material each time a new loss occurs. These are their Cowbells ringing.

Care providers can help to identify unfinished loss material by taking a loss history. This will alert the grieving person as well as the provider of old loss material that may need attention. This can also be addressed by having the person talk about the most difficult times of life or by having the individual compose an autobiography that includes a time line indicating losses and their effects.

☐ Family Loss Genogram

Material in this section was drawn from Bowen (1991), McGoldrick (1991a), McGoldrick and Gerson (1985), Rosen (1990). The work of Murray Bowen provides us an understanding of the effects of past family deaths on current loss. He refers to unfinished business and tension left over from deaths in earlier generations as an *emotional shockwave* that moves down through the years and mingles with reactions to new deaths and traumatic loss. Some of the energy feeding such a shockwave is the result of lack of knowledge as to the cause of a death, secrets or suspicious circumstances around a death, lack of sufficient medical information regarding an old illness or death, relationship secrets, tensions, and breakups in earlier generations.

Again, to fulfill the "heart" dimension (personal grief awareness), the provider must look first to him or herself. The family loss genogram exercise below is included to provide you with an activity that can further inform you of death-associated tensions coming from your own family system. Understanding how this is revealed in your own family loss genogram can be of assistance in working with individuals and families who need to understand the role of unfinished business on current grief.

I will very briefly summarize three generations of my own family in terms of health issues and age at death as a guide to this exercise.

As I look back over the ages at death and the nature of serious illnesses of my parents and grandparents, and their siblings as well, a history of cardiovascular disease, cancer, and stroke are obvious. Our family has had its share of death due to illness, and I am aware that the fear of loss

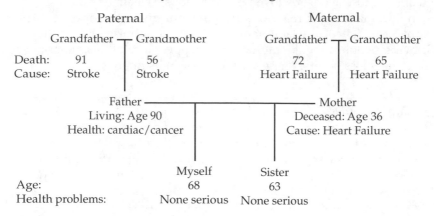

My Personal Genogram

	Paternal			Maternal	
	Grandfather — Grandmother			Grandfather — Grandmother	
Death:	91	56		72	65
Cause:	Stroke	Stroke		Heart Failure	Heart Failure

Father ——————————— Mother
Living: Age 90   Deceased: Age 36
Health: cardiac/cancer   Cause: Heart Failure

	Myself	Sister
Age:	68	63
Health problems:	None serious	None serious

of a parent was very much in evidence in both of my parents. My first awareness of fear of loss of a loved one due to death from illness occurred when my mother's mother had been diagnosed with diabetes and was hospitalized for amputation of a gangrenous leg. I saw the fear in my mother's face as she prayed for the survival of my grandmother. I was 5 years old.

The death of my father's mother at age 56 from a stroke threw me into the worse case scenario we had feared when my other grandmother had her amputation. Now the reality of a loved one's potential loss was firmly in place. Four years later my mother, who had suffered from heart disease, died and the horror of my fears came true. All of this loss became a backdrop for the unthinkable: the death of my 8-year-old son.

When care providers work with an individual or with the family, information gathered from an exercise such as the loss genogram can yield history that bears directly on the nature of current grief. With this in mind, please complete the exercise below.

Exercise 4: Family Loss Genogram

On a separate sheet of paper, compile the following information for three or four generations of your family following the directions and model below. Use squares to designate males and circles for females, putting males on the left and females on the right. Indicate miscarriages or abortions.

1. Starting with your grandparents' generation, list the **names** of living relatives and **ages** (or **age** at death and **cause** of death) of grandparents and current state of **health**.
2. Do the **same** for your parents and their siblings.
3. Do the **same** for you and your own siblings.
4. Do the **same** for your children.

Brief Family Loss Genogram

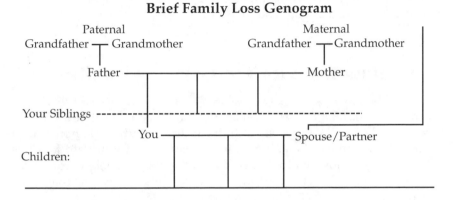

Answer the following questions about the information you have recorded:

1. What was the earliest death in your family that you can recall?

2. Which deaths do you know the least about? Do you know why this is?

3. How many deaths did you list in this exercise? Is this a surprise?

4. To what extent were you included or excluded from rituals and conversations about death?

5. What patterns of "cause of death" do you notice?

6. How does the above material influence the way you respond to death?

In addition to insights you may have gathered by completing the genogram and answering the six questions above, what images and feelings are you aware of? If you have been journaling or are willing to begin a journal, write down your images and feelings and keep a record of emotional reactions as you read this book.

☐ Healing Tasks for the Grieving Family

Worden's (2002) *Four Tasks of Mourning* have been adapted by family therapists (Rosen, 1990; Walsh and McGoldrick, 1991) to demonstrate a set of action-oriented behaviors and outcomes that will help families adapt to the post-loss world. I have drawn the material below from these sources as well as from my own practice of family therapy. The role of the care provider is to help the family address these tasks.

Task I: Sharing Acknowledgment of Death or Other Traumatic Loss

Denial vs. Acceptance of Reality

It is important that the family ultimately recognize that the loss is final and irreversible. Denial may be useful to permit the acceptance of reality in small doses; however, the goal of this task is to have family members share their sense of the loss. Funerals, memorials, prayer services, wakes, sitting Shiva, viewings, and other rituals can help achieve this.

Closed vs. Open Intrafamily Communication

The more easily and openly a family communicates, the more they can engage in necessary sharing. Planning memorials and traditional rituals as well as other joint family events can help move people toward a more open discussion of the reality of a loss event. (Note: The degree to which a family communicates may vary greatly by virtue of cultural traditions, which may support or restrict open communication either within or outside of the family.)

Inactivity vs. Activity

While it is important for individuals to have private time to mourn their loss, healing is often eased when family members undertake a joint activity. Planning religious services, receiving visitors, sending appreciation cards, creating the obituary, and notifying others in their social network about the illness or death are all useful actions. Again, family and cultural traditions will play an important role in determining how this is accomplished.

Closed vs. Open Communication Beyond the Family

Connecting with extended family, friends, faith community members, support services, and work colleagues can provide families with the opportunities to deliver the painful news and receive support.

Task II: Sharing the Pain and Grief

Storytelling

Much of the sharing of pain and grief will take place as the family engages in storytelling with each other and with extended family, friends, and others in the social network (Nadeau, 2001). Grieving people typically need to tell and retell the history, describe characteristics of the loved one, relate medical information, the circumstances of the death or other loss, and consider what they will miss and how different life will be.

Conspiracy of Silence

In some families, however, there may be a conspiracy of silence, an unstated agreement that "We don't talk about it." Other families simply say, "We are all fine, thank you." The reluctance to share their needs with others may limit the family's support from outside sources. This may be a function of cultural or family customs.

> It is not *the care provider's* role to confront resistance to open communication head-on, but rather to offer the family opportunities to share feelings or express emotions indirectly by delivering eulogies, telling stories, speculating on the future, using drawings, and creating personalized memory albums.

Expressions of Emotions

Sharing expressions of disappointment, helplessness, relief, guilt, anger, anxiety, panic, or the need for quiet withdrawal are all possible responses to loss; and useful for others in the family to hear and acknowledge. The expression of these emotions can vary widely among family members (Rosen, 1990, p. 90). Couples can show great astonishment at the level of pain felt by the other spouse. The family rule may be one of "keep your pain to yourself." Lack of awareness of how others in a family are feeling can give the false impression that "No one else is as upset as I am." or "You don't really care so much about our child's death."

Guilt and anger are particularly difficult feelings to express to others in the family, but it can be an extraordinary relief for a family member to find out that he or she is not alone in having those feelings. Caution must be taken with those ethnic groups whose customs restrict open communication.

> *Care providers* can help alleviate guilt, anger, and shame in the aftermath of a loss by enabling family members to discuss their feelings with one or two others and even doing some journal writing or letter writing to the deceased loved one.

Task III: Reorganizing the Family System

Realignments and Reallocations

The realignment of relationships and the reallocation of roles may begin as the family prepares for a funeral and other death-related activities. Who chooses the pallbearers? Should we have an open casket? Such decisions may need to be made as a very ill person fades from active participation in family life: "Who will make Thanksgiving dinner this year since Mom can't?" Everyday household responsibilities may be shifted. Who takes out the trash, pays the bills, and services the car? How do couples reestablish their relationship after the death of a child? What responsibilities are shifted to the middle child when the oldest has died? How well do siblings bond with each other when the parents are focused on a dying child?

Care providers must be prepared to raise questions in a family meeting about the future of the family—routines, finances, reorganizing responsibilities at some point when the family decision maker has died. All eyes may turn to the surviving spouse for answers to such questions. If the family is unable or reluctant to discuss their needs for the future, the provider can assist by having a meeting expressly for planning limited to the immediate future. This should concentrate on discussing how family members will take on new responsibilities.

Evaluation of Ambiguous Limits and Rules

Uncertainty may follow immediately after a death, life-threatening diagnosis, separation, loss of job, or disabling accident. Sustaining a loss can usher in a period of confusion in family life, and members may need to be guided into a process of setting limits for children and establishment of interim schedules and responsibilities for such activities as homework, household cleaning tasks, shopping, and meals.

Care providers can help guide families to consider when and how to reestablish rules and delegate roles as needed. This can be approached as a problem-solving/brainstorming session with the provider facilitating the creation of a proposed list of changes in family limits and rules. This may also be a time when outside support from extended family and friends can be sought.

Adopting New Family Organization Structures

The opportunity to abandon old patterns and adopt new, more functional structures in the family is available to grieving families, especially if the deceased was the dominant family member. Whenever there is a significant change, there is the opportunity to review old traditions and seek new ways to have recreation, family meals, create and implement a budget, and relate to others outside of the nuclear family.

The care provider can introduce the idea that new traditions can be established in the wake of loss. A note of caution: This idea should not be brought up before the family has had the opportunity to spend time mourning their loss. Some families may need weeks or even some months to be ready to create new traditions and routines for living. Approaching holidays typically prompts a family to consider other traditions and routines. Here again, a brainstorming session with all ideas accepted and listed for consideration can be helpful.

Starting a Subsequent Pregnancy

The question of choosing when to start a new pregnancy at some point after a miscarriage or neonatal loss, and whether to have another child after a pregnancy loss or the death of a child is a very sensitive and highly individual issue. Many couples have been advised to wait a year or more so that they can complete the grief for the loss, but this is not a uniform need. I have seen young couples, for example, who have sustained a traumatic loss but were able to direct their attention and emotional resources to the joys and anticipation of a new baby much sooner than a year.

In these circumstances, *care providers* need to be particularly sensitive to the couple's emotional needs during the first several months of the new baby's life. This period can be filled with extreme anxiety and can complicate the grieving process. If complications in the grieving process arise—chronic acute grief reactions, extreme anxiety issues, clinical depression—the care provider needs to suggest a consultation with a professional mental health provider. There is no single formula for healing; much of how the couple reacts to a new baby after previous pregnancy loss or the death of a child depends on the coping resources and social support the couple receives from family and friends.

Other Replacement Concerns

Other replacement concerns typically occur after the loss of a spouse or life partner. Social conventions and resistance from the family may influence when a grieving person should decide to resume his or her social life. Pressure from immediate family members may be for the widow/er to find a new companion or to keep him or her unattached as long as possible. I have seen some individuals enter the social scene as soon as they are able and others who resist this indefinitely. For many, there is the awkwardness felt by existing family members and their resistance to accepting a new person into their lives. Children may resent Dad or Mom's new friend. In-laws may be hurt by the daughter-in-law or son-in law having a new relationship. This may be especially difficult for grandparents who perceive a new spouse as replacing their deceased adult child; they may also fear being left out of their grandchildren's lives.

The care provider can work with bereaved individuals on specific areas such as relationship concerns, improving self-confidence, entering the current dating scene, and strategies for integrating a new partner into the family system. Support groups also can be helpful as others can share how they approached difficult or awkward situations.

Other Traumatic Losses

In the case of other traumatic loss—layoff, financial crisis, divorce, destruction of home by fire, or other disasters—families may be as devastated as if an actual death has occurred. The prospect of living with a severely reduced income, parents living apart, and the loss of a home and all personal belongings has secondary effects beyond the initial loss event. Children are especially vocal and blunt about their concerns for survival. "Where will we live?" "How will we pay for food?" "How will I get to school?" "When can I see my friends?"

Too often such nondeath losses are not viewed as legitimate causes for grief reactions. The survival concerns, the many secondary losses, and the traumatic experience are truly justifiable reasons for mourning.

The losses and changes not only require reorganization to get the family restabilized but also provide windows of opportunity to create new patterns for the family to live by.

The care provider can help by arranging for resources to meet the immediate needs of the family and helping to reassure children—and adults as well—that they will not starve and will have shelter. Providers can help the family review and reorganize to meet the new realities. They can also direct the family to resources which can help them secure part-time jobs, develop careful budgeting, and provide for consistent childcare, fair custody arrangements, or temporary new shelter.

Providers are not expected to do all of this on their own. Faith-based organizations can be called upon. Local government and community service agencies have provisions for emergency assistance and can offer longer term support. (See appendix B for a list of support organizations.)

Task IV: Creating New Directions, Relationships, and Goals

Moving on in the Face of Loss

This is usually accomplished slowly over time. People realize that they can continue to honor the memory of a loved one while making changes in their present-day lives. For instance, a surviving spouse can renovate her home as she and her late husband had planned, but may allow herself to make certain changes that she alone wanted. A child who felt pressure to attend his deceased father's alma mater may decide to attend the college he or she really wants to go to.

Creating New Traditions

Sometimes, overidealization of the deceased or past traditions and routines may prevent people from initiating new ideas that more adequately meet the needs of the family as it is now. Many family members will keep certain traditions and routines because Dad or Grandma always did it that way. Some of these family customs may serve to keep the members attached to the deceased loved one while others can be replaced by new and more satisfying ways of doing things.

Care providers can help families achieve a balance between memory and idealization of the way they were. In this way, family members can stay connected to the past or the loved one while feeling free to explore new options and experience new possibilities. Providers can help family members to give themselves permission to explore such new options for living. Brainstorming sessions with the family can be held to review existing routines and schedules and list new ideas for these basic requirements, as well as for recreation, finances, and addressing holidays.

☐ Factors Interfering with Healing

There are a number of specific issues arising from certain losses that may prevent family members from expressing grief emotions and thinking about how to reorganize their lives and create new meanings in the post-loss world. Below are a group of reasons that make it difficult to move ahead in the healing process.

Factors Interfering with Healing

1. Loss event is too painful to express grief.
2. Early childhood messages inhibit expression of feelings.
3. Relationship was problematic, engendering anxiety, anger, and/or guilt.
4. Old loss material overwhelms the current loss, creating an overload.
5. The mourner feels disenfranchised.
6. The mourner has a pre-existing psychopathology.
7. There is a lack of social support.
8. Lack of tangible evidence of death—no body recovered.

The Loss Event Is Too Painful to Express Grief

Often a loss is too painful to talk about and denial is needed in order to survive each day. Denial serves a useful function and enables the grieving person to take in the awful reality in doses. Sometimes denial can limit the freedom to communicate with other family members and friends. The dread of "bringing it up" can keep mourners from communicating and create distance that may become problematic. The internalized pain of grief can also become somaticized and show up as physical health problems. Not everyone needs to express pain and talk it through with others. However, for those who have a need to express themselves and fear to do so, some assistance must be provided to help them slowly start the process of externalizing their emotional pain.

Early Childhood Messages Inhibit Expression of Feelings

In many families it was not acceptable to show anger, express fears, or cry. These early childhood messages often linger in the inner core of our self-concepts and direct us to restrain our expression of sadness, anger, or fear at the very times when it would be helpful to do so. People who find themselves unable to express feelings may need to learn or relearn that they are entitled to express their pain and talk to others about their grief.

Relationship Was Problematic, Engendering Anxiety, Anger, and/or Guilt

The level of guilt, anger, and pain that may still be present as unfinished business can interfere with the grieving person's expression of these upsetting feelings.

Old Loss Material Overwhelms the Current Loss, Creating an Overload

Accumulated loss material ("Cowbells") may overload the capacity of the grieving person to let much out. The old grief combines with current loss material and it can feel too unsafe to open up at all.

The Mourner Feels Disenfranchised

When the grieving person feels unentitled to grieve or gets the impression that others around them do not see why they are so upset, it can shut them down. An ex-wife, a coworker, a neighbor, or a lover can all be given the message that your grief doesn't count.

The Mourner Has a Pre-Existing Psychopathology

Various emotional disorders make an individual highly vulnerable, and they may withdraw from active mourning. Some may be on medications that impede the expression of feelings. For example, people who have a history of depression and are extremely fragile may seek to protect themselves by avoiding active grieving. In some cases, antidepressant medications may keep the mourner's mood at a consistent level and hold off active expression of grief.

There Is a Lack of Social Support

When the safety net of emotional and practical support is absent, the grieving person may be too preoccupied with practical matters of self and family care to take the time to express his or her grief. They may also feel isolated and unsafe for allowing strong emotions to surface.

Lack of Tangible Evidence of Death—No Body Recovered

When there is no tangible evidence of death—missing in action, sea and air disasters, or explosions—there is no recovered body. Some simply remain unconvinced that their loved one will never return. Others cannot engage in the traditional funeral and other death-related rituals that allow for the grieving person to grasp the reality of the loss. During the aftermath of the disaster at the World Trade Center, a massive search continued for months to find any identifiable body parts so the families could have some tangible evidence of their losses.

Creative alternative rituals such as imagery funerals, or saying goodbye exercises, can be of some help to mourners who lack a body and any tangible evidence of the death.

The care provider, when taking a formal history or informally gathering background information about a family, must be aware of all of these grief-complicating factors. If anyone in the family is having particular difficulty with the grieving process, the provider should try to determine if any of the above issues are the cause. Where the provider is not trained to address the issue of traumatic or pathologic grief, a referral should be made to a mental health professional.

☐ Conclusion

In this chapter, we have considered loss in the context of the family system. We must consider the grieving person's family and family history in order to truly understand the realities in which they live out their mourning. The family's communication style, their cultural influences, the life-cycle stage of the family, and the nature of the intrafamily relationships all affect human grief responses.

Within the family system, there are members who require some special consideration as grieving people: grieving children, parents, and older adults. Chapters 4, 5, and 6, respectively, give special attention to these three groups of grieving people.

4
CHAPTER

The Grief of Children and Adolescents—Loss of a Parent

☐ Introduction—The Grief of Children

"The loss of a parent to death and its consequences in the home and in the family change the very core of the child's existence" (Worden, 1996,

p. 9). Children are also influenced by the nature of the grief expressed by the adults in their lives.

Here is a clinical observation of the delicate interplay between the parent and child grief reaction:

> Two little girls sat in my office. I had already talked to Dad (who was now sitting in the waiting room). The younger child, age 6, had an eager look, made eye contact, and waited to hear what I was going to say. The older girl, age 10, looked down at the floor, appeared sad and reluctant to have any conversation. Their mother had died 3 months earlier, and Dad was concerned about what he believed was his older daughter's lack of mourning. Many parents express such concern and bring their children into counseling or therapy with the hope that I can somehow "prime the grieving pump."
>
> In response to my questions about how things had been for them since their mom had died, the younger girl told me that she missed her mommy and that her Daddy had to hold her when she cried. Her older sister was less willing to share information but did let me know that she was also sad. When I asked her if she ever cried like her sister, she said she did. She said her crying was restricted to her bedroom at night. I expressed interest in these remarks and told her that her dad was concerned because he never saw her crying. When I asked what kept her from crying when her dad was nearby, she said, "I never cry in front of my dad; it upsets him too much."

Too often, adults expect children to grieve in some specific way. According to an African proverb, "It takes a village to raise a child." It also takes a village to *heal* a child! Grieving children need a supportive network of adults and, at times, need adults who have expertise in working with bereaved children and who also understand the life experiences that mediate the nature of their grief.

Children have rich internal lives, and their grief can be both similar and vastly different from that of adults. We form attachments in order to survive. When an individual loses the person whom he or she depended on for survival, the grieving person may react with panic, dread, bewilderment, despair, and/or rage. Even the *threat* of loss of our primary attachment figure (usually mother) can result in the grief reactions. Children, no matter what their age, have an inborn drive to survive, and their grief response to loss is part of this drive. To help children who have lost loved ones, the adults in their lives need to be aware that:

    a. children do grieve,
    b. their grief needs to be acknowledged, and
    c. the nature of children's grief varies widely with age and maturity.

All of these issues will be addressed in this chapter. (Loss of a sibling is discussed in detail in chapter 5.)

☐ General Considerations for the Grief of Children

Before we examine the differences in each of the developmental stages of children and how to provide help to grieving children and adolescents, we will review several general considerations regarding their needs. These are briefly listed and are further elaborated upon below.

The Needs of Grieving Children at a Glance

Children need:

1. To be allowed to grieve as a child.
2. To be heard.
3. To be part of the family's grieving process and participate in family grieving rituals.
4. To be appropriately included in the information loop.
5. To have usual schedules, routines, and limits maintained.
6. To be hugged, held, and shown love by a parent or other caring adult and reassured regarding safety and other survival concerns.
7. To be reassured that their feelings are okay and have opportunities to express them.
8. To be reassured that they are not the cause of the death or illness.
9. To have accepted time-offs from grieving.
10. To be able to ask questions and have them answered truthfully.
11. To be prepared for questions and comments from neighbors and others in the community.
12. To not be singled out for special consideration by teachers and other adults.

1. Children Need to Be Allowed to Grieve as Children

Children are often overlooked as credible mourners, and their grieving may be very unlike that of adults. Too often, their grief is evaluated on the basis of an adult's expectations for seeing and hearing adult mourning. Adults frequently expect children to grieve as they do, but children may appear not to be grieving according to this expectation. Children grieve in idiosyncratic ways: Some may not appear sad or distressed at all; others withdraw; still others may cry, sob, and talk about missing the parent or sibling and then go back to playing as if nothing has happened to change their lives. This shifting back and forth should not be misconstrued to mean that they are not deeply affected. Some children appear to put off their grieving for several months. This may alarm the parent and sometimes results in a request for counseling. Some children may regress to younger age behavior and wet the bed, become clingy, or act out by hitting other children or by refusing to do schoolwork.

 Doka (2002) states, "When a loss occurs, [societal] grieving rules [tell us] not only how one is to behave but also how one is to feel and think" (p. 6).

Below are some basic guidelines for differentiating the grieving of children and adults.

> Children do not usually grieve continuously; they take breaks. They grieve in small portions and may actually delay much of their grief for weeks or even months.
> Adults grieve fairly constantly and are usually not delayed.
> Children's grief behaviors may be mixed with play activity.
> Adults typically separate grief from play.
> Children's understanding of death is limited to their cognitive development.
> Adults are aware of the irreversibility of death.
> Children (prepuberty) may have difficulty retaining the image of a deceased person.
> Adults have a more fully developed memory of the deceased.
> Children are dependent upon adults for support; they may not be able to articulate their needs.
> Adults can seek help and are usually able to meet their needs independently. Both need their grief to be heard and acknowledged.
> Both children and adults need the support of caring people.
> Both need to know it is normal and acceptable to mourn and express feelings.
> Both may express similar feelings of sadness, anger, fear, guilt, and shame in their mourning.

2. Children Need to Be Heard

It is not unusual for children to be excluded from participation in family rituals for burial and grieving.

Too often, children are not fully appreciated as grievers in the family system, yet they are very much affected by the grief of others.

The story of how I learned of my grandmother's death points out how easy it is to disenfranchise children's grief.

> When I was barely 12 years old, my father's uncle and his son's pounding on the front door awakened us. I ran to the door and let them in. Uncle ordered me to get my father right away. I woke Dad and Mom up, and Dad went out to see what was happening. Suddenly my father began to cry. I asked Dad's uncle what was wrong and he said, "Figure it out!" This was the only answer I received. My dad was sobbing; my mother was pale and holding him. I was terrified, but not at what had happened. Seeing my father cry for the first time in my life alarmed me.
>
> The sudden death of my grandmother from a stroke sent a stunning wave of horrible reality through my senses. Her funeral was my first. It was the first time I saw a dead body and attended a burial. I was mostly frightened, however, by seeing all of the important adults in my life crying, bent in pain and sorrow. People hovered around my grandfather, my dad, and his sister and brothers. No one seemed to be concerned about how my sister or I were feeling. I assumed that no one was supposed to.

Care providers may need to offer opportunities to talk or to simply be with children as they play. Providers can also coach parents or other family members on how to provide special alone time to "talk about the deceased." Children can be helped to express their grief by drawing, playing games and role-playing fantasies, or reading some of the many children's books about loss and grief.

3. Children Need to Be Part of the Family's Grieving Process and Participate in Family Grieving Rituals

Children should be able to observe the surviving parent crying and realize that the parent can still function as a mom or dad. They may interpret a lack of evidence of mourning as, "We must hide our grief." Parents and other adults can let the children know that we are sad because our loved one has died and it's okay to cry and feel very upset.

Even though younger children may not grasp the permanence of death, it helps to have them participate in funerals, burials, and memorial services—if they are willing to go and the adults can prepare them, answer their questions, and offer reassurance. The funeral, the grave, and the cemetery not only provide visible evidence that death has occurred but also reassure children that "we are not alone in our mourning" and "that this has happened to others as well." For older children, these rituals "constitute proof and confirmation of the fact that the deceased has passed away from our world and will remain only in our memory" (Smilansky, 1987, p. 111).

Generally, young children will use only the information they need and block out or not register the rest, as the following example illustrates:

> When my aunt died, we asked my 4-year-old grandson Zack if he wanted to see her at the family viewing. He agreed. Picking him up, I showed him the body in the casket, explaining that she was no longer living. Together we touched her forehead and felt the coldness. I asked if he had any questions. "What happens to her now?" he asked. I told him that the top would be closed and then after the funeral service we would take her to a cemetery where she would be buried in the ground. "Okay," he said. "Can I go and play now?"
>
> At the cemetery, Zack played with the pile of soil next to the grave and watched with interest as the casket was lowered and covered with shovels of earth. Zack participated in this ritual and played with the mound of earth. Back at my aunt's house, Zack asked me, "Papa, what was in that box anyway?" I explained that our aunt's body, the one we saw in the funeral home, was in the box. "Oh yeah, that's the one we buried." Despite his question, I felt as if he benefited from being with us and participating in the family ritual.

4. Children Need to Be Appropriately Included in the Information Loop

"Parents and children need to know the facts about a loss. This information lessens fear and creates a foundation from which to grieve" (Goldman, 1996, p. 69). It is vital that children not be overlooked as part of the family's grief process and that they not be patronized or dismissed with clichés. Being kept out of the information loop is a frequent complaint I hear from adults who experienced a childhood death of a parent or a sibling.

5. Children Need to Have Usual Schedules, Routines, and Limits Maintained

Children need structure in times of crisis; therefore, bedtimes, curfews, mealtimes, and other familiar limits need to remain in place. These provide a sense of security, assuring children that there is a sense of control and that the family system will survive. When children are missing the needed structure, they may act out behaviorally until an adult provides the structure and limits they need.

6. Children Need to Be Hugged, Held, and Shown Love by a Parent or Other Caring Adult and Reassured Regarding Safety and Other Survival Concerns

Caregiving adults should give physical connection and loving reassurance. This lets children know that, even though a terrible thing has happened, they are loved and will be taken care of. Children are very aware of and worry about how the family will survive financially. They must be given a sense that they are safe and that the family will continue to provide for their needs.

7. Children Need to Be Reassured That Their Feelings Are Okay and Have Opportunities to Express Them

It is important that the feelings of grief—sadness, anger, fear, guilt—are reacted to as normal and acceptable by the adults in their lives. Nongrieving times must be free of disapproval. Visitors to the family may judge the children or teens critically because they are playing games, watching TV, or even singing. Grieving children should be protected from those who want to interfere with how they grieve. An understanding adult needs to explain that children are not being disrespectful or unfeeling, but rather that they "need to escape from the terrible reality from time to time." Often they incorporate their feelings about their loss into their play. It is also helpful for adults to facilitate the release of such grief feelings.

Care providers and family members can encourage children to express their feelings of grief by supplying them with paper and crayons, puppets, a tape recorder, and other means of emotional expression through play. Care providers can help neighbors, friends, and relatives understand that it is not unusual for children to play and even laugh while adults are grieving in the next room.

8. Children Need to Be Reassured That They Are Not the Cause of the Death or Illness

Young children may engage in fantasies about why a loss or other tragedy has occurred. The fantasy may include the idea that they were bad or possibly had a bad thought about the loved one. Some children carry these thoughts for years and are troubled by them into adulthood. Keeping the lines of communication open and asking children what questions or concerns they may have can encourage them to express these concerns. Play activities can also reveal these concerns. For example, while engaging in doll or puppet play with the child, the adult can set up a story similar to the loss situation and work in statements that show the child in the story is not at fault for the death or illness of the parent.

9. Children Need to Have Accepted Time-Outs from Grieving

Adults need to accept the fact that children often grieve intermittently. This may be because they can only allow themselves to feel the pain in small portions, or because of a short attention span, or because they do not have the mental maturity to engage in prolonged episodes of painful grieving. For all of these reasons, they need time out from grieving.

10. Children Need to Be Able to Ask Questions and Have Them Answered Truthfully

Children struggle as adults do with "Why, why did this happen?" They may have basic questions such as "When will Nanna come back?"; "Where is he or she now?"; "Why do we bury dead people?"; or "Will I ever see Papa again?" Answers may be strongly influenced by cultural beliefs and customs. Questions are a way that children attempt to make sense of a situation at their own level of cognitive development. Answers should be brief and as specific as appropriate. Excessive and detailed information will not be useful and could be confusing to the child. Lying to a child is not only disrespectful but may haunt the parent at a later time when the child learns the truth. It's okay for a parent or other family adult to say, "I don't know the answer, but I will find out for you." Coming back to an earlier question asked by the child can also be an opportunity to have a conversation about other areas of concern—over the child's guilt fantasies, anxiety regarding survival of the family, or other unspoken needs of the child.

Care providers can help the child's grief by educating the family about his or her needs and grieving patterns. Teaching the parent and/or other family members about what to expect and how to help the child express his or her feelings can achieve a lot in creating an environment of understanding and comfort for grieving children.

---

11. Children Need to Be Prepared for Questions and Comments from Neighbors and Others in the Community

Children need help to know how and when to respond to other children and adults who ask them questions about their deceased parent or sibling. It will be helpful for them to have some preparation for this. Though they may not bring up and discuss such conversations with people outside of the family, the comments and questions of others outside of the family can be upsetting to them.

Care providers can help prepare children for these questions by role-playing with them and helping them to find words to use to respond to the questions of others. Family members can also benefit from such activities. For example, the provider can coach the child to say, "I really don't want to talk about my dad's illness now." "You will have to ask my mom that question."

12. Children Need to Not Be Singled Out for Special Consideration by Teachers and Other Adults

As a rule, children seek conformity with peers and are uncomfortable being identified as "the kid whose brother was killed" or who has a dying or incapacitated parent, grandparent, or sibling at home. They may be reluctant to have friends over because of the need for quiet, or because the home has a depressive quality to it—some houses of mourning may be "off-limits" to playful children. Children may also be reluctant to invite friends over fearing that these friends may witness their parents in tears. All of these issues need to be discussed with children to help them cope with awkward situations as comfortably as possible.

Summary of Grief of Children

As the child matures, fuller awareness of the reality of a loss may bring a painful realization of the changes in his or her life. Grieving becomes more adult-like. Further, older children and adolescents may have unfinished business as a result of earlier losses or traumas that may be triggered by the current death or other circumstance of loss. Regardless of age, children need lots of hugs and kisses, reassurance that they are not to blame for the death or that they are not bad because they have survived the loss. It's natural for them to want to talk about their feelings. Adults should provide for this, and children should also be aware that it is okay *not* to grieve.

☐ Developmental Stages and Children's Grief: Helping Grieving Children

Helping Grieving Children

The material in this section is drawn from the work of Bowlby, 1980; Rando, 1984; Raphael, 1983; and Worden, 1996, as well as from my own clinical experience.

The child's reaction to the death of a parent has two components: an emotional response and an intellectual processing of the reality of the loss. Younger children are able to respond emotionally before they are old enough to really grasp the implications of what has happened. The emotional feelings arise from the separation from a parent or other primary loved one. This reaction is usually referred to as *separation anxiety* and is related to the fear that comes from loss of proximity to the person who has ensured their survival. This response is reflexive and takes the initial form of crying out when the distance between child and mother reaches a point of alarm for the child.

This reflexive response is reminiscent of Paul MacLean's (1973) *isolation distress call* discussed in chapter 2. It is a response to a loss or a signal for the threat of loss (e.g., mother is putting her coat on, wearing her "going out" perfume, walking toward the door) and does not entail intellectual processing. Behavioral responses to actual or to threatened separation include crying, reaching, screaming, moving toward mommy, and looking and searching in the direction she has gone. These behaviors will vary according to the child's age and developmental stage. They represent the *attachment behaviors* Bowlby (1980) described as part of the "protest" phase of the grief process.

As children mature and are better able to comprehend the world around them, their understanding of the meaning and consequences of separation or threatened separation deepens. Thus, their emotional reactions to separation will be further intensified by the realization that mommy or daddy is never coming back and that a new chapter of their lives is beginning. The realization of the finality of the loss and the multiple changes that occur increasingly become part of the grief process as they get older.

Here are three brief stories about children that illustrate their reflexive survival reactions:

- Jake was almost 4 when he and his older brother Zack were listening to me read them some bedtime stories. I began to tell the story of Jack and the Beanstalk with increasing drama. Jake was really engrossed when I got to the part where "Jack had quietly taken the magical singing harp from the table while the giant slumbered and snored. As Jack began to creep out of the window, the harp screamed out to the giant who awoke and reached out to grab Jack." At that point, acting as the giant, I thrust my hand toward Jake who screamed out in terror, "I NOT JACK, I NOT JACK!"

- A colleague was running a workshop in Northern Ireland for bereaved children who were given an opportunity to release pain and anger by beating on pillows and letting it "all come out." One 5-year-old was so angry at the circumstances of his life that he cursed and said he wanted to get rid of all of the grown-ups in his life—"except for you!"—and he pointed to my friend. When they completed the session and went to lunch, the boy was asked why he said, "Except you!" He answered matter-of-factly, "Well, somebody has to feed me."

- I was seeing a family who had very recently lost their dad. During the course of the session, the 10-year-old daughter emphatically stated, "Well, what are we going to do now? We won't have Dad's paycheck to count on every week!"

As these three children contemplated the consequences of loss, the survival-oriented reactions ran the gamut from a reflexive "I not Jack!" response to the more studied "Well, what are we going to do now?" Each reaction to loss or predicted loss is governed by the ability of the child to reason and evaluate circumstances. In the first story, Jake's knee-jerk screaming out "I not Jack!" was remarkable self-preservation behavior. In the next story, the young boy was clear on the importance of where he believed his next meal was coming from. The young girl in the last story voiced a concern for the whole family. Children typically cut to the bottom line of survival. This is why it is so important that they be given early reassurances that they will be secure and cared for.

The brief outline below summarizes how children grieve at various ages—along with some recommendations for helping them. While some grief reactions are particular to a certain age range, there is a great deal of overlap. Each child or teenager must be viewed according to his or her own personality, family situation and history, cultural influences and religious affiliation, and developmental stage, which result in unique grieving needs. We serve children best when we take our lead from them and learn about their grief from them.

Helping Children Under 2 Years

This child responds to the emotional reactions of the surviving parent or caregiving adult. The very young child is unable to understand the irreversibility of death and reacts to the separation and changes in energy of the surviving caregiver, that is, how much attention the adult is able to pay to the child. If the emotional climate of the family has shifted to agitated or depressed, the child will mirror this change. In the case of death of a mother or other primary caregiving adult, older infants may protest and search for the mother, alter their sleep and feeding schedules, and generally be fussier. (A substitute caring adult can be a source of comfort and continuity of attachment comfort.)

Helping Children Ages 2 to 5

The mourning behaviors of children in this age category are intermittent. They lack the capacity to view the loss as irreversible or understand feelings of distress. Regressive behaviors such as bedwetting, acting out, becoming clingy, reverting to baby talk, or insisting on sleeping with the parent may appear. The surviving parent may not be available due to his or her own grief. (Here again, another caring adult can provide some level of structure, comfort, and continuity.)

These children may have difficulty understanding the reality of the loss until they are able to master the concept of death's finality. They may believe that the parent is still going to come back to them and take care of their needs again. Each sound of a car driving up, a door opening, the dog barking may bring the expectation that mommy or daddy is going to walk through the door. Children may need to be told repeatedly and tenderly that their mommy or daddy is not there. They can be given a sense of security in spite of the loss with continuous and loving care from the surviving parent or a surrogate caregiving adult. Keeping as much as possible to established schedules and routines would enable them to feel safe and content.

Showing children under 5 photos of the deceased parent can also help them to create an inner image of the mom or dad who is no longer here with them. They will need to hear that the surviving parent and/or grandma, aunt, or adult friend are all okay and are going to be here to take care of them. The message, given at whatever level of understanding the child has is "Things are different now and you will still be safe and taken care of."

Helping Children Ages 5 to 8

Children of these ages are better able to grasp the consequences of death due to their increasing cognitive maturity. They may, however, use denial to avoid the reality they can now grasp. Grieving may be more internal than outward. They may repeat questions in an attempt to integrate the implications of the death. Some regression may take place: bedwetting, thumb or pacifier sucking, seeking to sleep in bed with the parent or other adult. It's best to provide a patient and caring response to questions and accept the regression as normal and temporary.

Children often engage in fantasies or "magical thinking" associated with their belief that they somehow caused the death by bad or angry thoughts about the parent. They should be encouraged to discuss these fantasies and be reassured that they were not to blame for the death or illness.

These children may also need a clear repetition concerning the "facts of death" appropriate to their understanding. There should be no fiction told about "daddy being away on a long trip" or "working very hard at the office and can't come home yet." Questions should be answered accurately and as completely as he or she truly needs without overwhelming the child. When there is love and care from the surviving parent and/or other caring surrogates, the child can move forward in his or her development, secure in being well taken care of, loved, and cherished in spite of the absence of the deceased parent. In time, the concepts of finality and irreversibility will be integrated into the sense of self and new meanings of the world without the missing parent.

Normalizing Feelings.   Children ages 5 to 8 will have a more developed sense of the finality of death and may have upsetting emotional reactions to this awareness. They should be helped to view the emotions as normal and acceptable ways that people feel when a loved one has died. Many times children will ask why mom or dad died. Answers should be given calmly. Explain to the child that a part of the body stopped working because of the accident or illness, and that ended the person's ability to stay alive. If there are life experiences the child has had—loss of a pet that was handled in a positive way (not a goldfish flushed away) or another family member's death—this can be used to help explain what happened to the parent and "how people were sad and upset when that happened, too."

Some children may want to believe that the parent will not stay dead and will come back to be with them again. A gentle reaction to such a normal and understandable statement would be to say, "I know you would like that to happen and so would I, but that is not what will happen because when people die they don't come back, but it's all right to want that to happen."

Modeling Mourning Behaviors.   Adults can be helpful to children ages 5 to 8 by modeling mourning behaviors—crying, sighing, expressing words of sadness, and using facial tissues. Tissue boxes can be left around to remind the child that this is what people do when someone has died—"We are sad, we cry, and we blow our nose." Children need to feel that they have permission to let the feelings of grief out and may do some of their externalization of grief through play with dolls and other human figures. For all age groups, art materials, dolls, puppets, a chalkboard, and clay, and/or a sand table should be made easily accessible. Children can be invited to use them.

Helping with Anger.   When a 5- to 8-year-old expresses anger, it should be viewed as okay to have and to communicate with but not in a way that is harmful to another or to him or herself. Children may need to have some time with an adult who can help them explore nonhurtful ways to vent anger.

Helping with Memories.   Reviewing and reminiscing with the 5- to 8-year-old for purposes of gathering feelings while building recall of the deceased parent is an activity children can participate in with the surviving parent and siblings. Creating a memory book or album with photos and memorabilia, and writing notes or adding stickers on each page can provide an ongoing activity that several family members can do together.

Helping with Current Family Conditions.   Telling a story using dolls and props can be another way for children to work out their understanding and feelings about the death of the parent and the secondary losses that have already occurred. A child may say, "The daddy [doll] is very sad and doesn't have time to play with the children." "The children are at the dinner table, and they hate the food their grandma is cooking." "Their daddy doesn't know how to tuck the children in at night." Statements like these can become part of a discussion of how it is now in their home since their mommy died. Encourage the children to talk about what is different now. They can be encouraged to teach Daddy how to do a "proper tuck in" and how to suggest that Grandma cook some other kinds of food. Other feelings can emerge during play or while informal conversations are taking place. Children can be guided into talking about this new world they are in and to making suggestions to the adults in their lives on how to make things better for them.

Locating the Dead Parent.   Artwork depicting where the 5- to 8-year-old child believes the parent is now may help those children who need a specific image of where the deceased parent has gone. This can be a comforting idea for many children. If needed, it can lead to an exploration of their ideas about "heaven."

Helping to Deal with Guilt.   Guilt and regrets should be given some attention so that children do not feed into larger, more complex issues of self-blame and despair. Asking the parent in a letter to forgive any misdeeds may be a way some children can let go of continuing guilt thoughts. Open discussions with other children may give some comfort with regard to the normalcy of guilt feelings. Hospice, schools, religious, and other community organizations usually run bereavement groups for children and may be enlisted to assist the child.

Care providers can assist 5- to 8-year-olds with methods for externalizing anger, such as encouraging the free expression of feelings with drawing materials using crayons, finger paints, or chalk; clay or other molding material; or hitting a pillow or a punching bag. Writing and reading a letter out loud to whoever is supposed to hear the anger is another way to release feelings. Young children can use storytelling as an adult writes down or tapes the material. Most important is making clear that anger is an acceptable feeling to have and express but not in a way that will harm the child or someone else.

Helping Children Ages 9 to 12

Children in this age group have the intellectual capacity to understand the finality of death and generally use less denial. This age, frequently referred to as "preteens," may exhibit behaviors which are similar to the 5 to 8 age group ("magical thinking" about the cause of the death, seeking parental attention, fears associated with survival) and may also imitate some of those we typically see in adolescence (distancing, investing emotional energy in friends, seeking autonomy). It is a time when peers take on an increasing importance and the need to be like the other kids is a priority. Some of their needs may feel "babyish" to them, and they may therefore be reluctant to express feelings or ask for help. This holding back of feelings also helps them to maintain a sense of control. Preteens are often very aware of the family's vulnerability when the primary income-producing parent has died or is seriously ill.

For the preteen, talking with other bereaved children will help them feel less isolated and different. They do not want to be singled out as the kid whose mother or father died. School personnel should be advised to avoid drawing attention to bereaved children with special privileges and relaxed requirements.

The grief process will be helped along if children in this age group are included in family decision-making (e.g., preparing and participating in the funeral service, reallocating household chores and responsibilities) and in creating family memorial projects that can help them remember their loved one. They also appreciate it when they are given the opportunity to mourn. Children this age need to feel free to have their grief unfold on its own course. Sometimes this includes long periods of not grieving.

Helping Them Feel Normal.   Adults in the life of the child from ages 9 to 12 must help them to feel "normal" not only in terms of their fears, sadness, and bewilderment about the tragic changes in their lives but also to assure them that they still belong to a world where they fit in. Participation in school, religious affiliations, athletic groups, and other community activities such as music lessons, dance, and martial arts are places where they can feel some of that old "I'm okay-ness." These activities should be continued and supported by the parent and other adults involved in the family. Children in this age group grasp the finality of death and may seek solace by escaping to peers.

In addition to separation anxiety and pain, the feelings of grief may be associated with their greater understanding of the consequences of the death. They may feel a need to withhold feelings as a way to defend against the pain of their grief. They may deny that they are upset as a way of preventing a sense of regressing to younger age behavior. They may be frightened with regard to the well-being of their surviving parent and withhold grief and anger in order to protect the parent from more burdens. They may take on the responsibilities for younger siblings as a way of coping and also as a way of reducing dad or mom's stress.

Helping with Aggressive Behavior.   Children of this age group who typically have more freedom to come and go may also find themselves acting out and getting into fights or trouble in class, in afterschool programs, school yards, in the neighborhood, and at shopping areas. Releasing anger in this way can be an effective way to hold off the terrifying pain about what has happened and the fear of what the future will be like. "Does Mom have to get a job now?" "Is Dad going to start dating?" "How will we make it financially?" "Will we be able to buy food?" These questions may not be vocalized but should be given an opportunity to become part of a family discussion of "how are we going to manage and organize to meet our needs." If the parent is unable to do this, some other caregiving adult may be able to discuss with the child fears he or she may be having about how they will manage to survive now.

Care providers can help preteen children gather their thoughts and feelings by keeping a journal or diary of what has been happening; doing "past, present, and hopes for the future" drawings; writing letters of good-bye; listing all the things that are missed and what we still have as a family; and sharing some of this material in family meetings. Some children get very creative and do documentary productions with audio and/or videotape. Others may be interested in producing theater in the form of brief skits to demonstrate the world before their parent's death, the world afterward, and the possible future world.

Helping Adolescents Ages 12 to 18

Adolescents often feel conflicted by their drive toward autonomy clashing with their desire to be with family in times of crisis. Feeling drawn back into the family can activate bitterness and/or depression and withdrawal. They may seek to minimize the effect of the loss and bury their grief, or they may use anger to control an aching desire for the lost parent. Secondary losses that have to be faced relate to autonomy, future planning, and involvement with peers. If, in the course of normal adolescent rebellion, an adolescent had fought with the parent who died, he or she may also experience a residue of guilt. Additionally, adolescents may have a recurrence of grief when they acquire a more mature understanding of the consequences of their loss. Young people in this age group can benefit from bereavement support groups and the opportunity to release anger, sadness, and guilt.

As stated above, the adolescent is already coping with much emotional turbulence and disruption of the status quo as the transition to adulthood looms closer and closer. The drive for autonomy and natural pull away from family may have been disruptive and led to multiple clashes with his or her parents and left unfinished business. The death of a parent pulls the teenager back into the family and occurs at a time when there may already be an existing web of conflicts in the family system.

The risk of an aggravated grief reaction is high for the bereaved adolescent. It's not cool for boys to cry. Thus, grieving may need to be kept private from adults, and the natural expression of sadness may have no easy outlet. While there is often overlap between genders, boys generally are more likely to show anger and hide tears; girls are more likely to seek comfort and express their pain more openly. Young people in this age group can benefit from bereavement support groups for teenagers that can provide the opportunity to release anger, sadness, and guilt.

Remember, the pulling back into the family system may also raise feelings of resentment and guilt for having this resentment. Anger may also be the easier emotion to express publicly for a young person who wants to maintain the "sense of maturity" recently acquired.

The effect of the parent's death on the adolescent's plans, freedom, and purchasing power is no small issue. The loss and its consequences may form a depressing outlook of what should have been a high energy and enjoyable period of high school years. The demands to be available to help with family needs, academic and extracurricular requirements, the drive for peer acceptance, an emerging sexual awareness, and social activities all create a mix of pressure, already at a high pitch before the death of a parent or other loved one.

A care provider or some other trusted adult who can hear the guilt, fears, anger, and frustrations can normalize them and provide assurance and a calming presence for the bereaved teenager. The grief of the adolescent is one that needs much support from family, other adults, and peers. The teen needs a sense of "I'm okay and I can manage this tough time." The care provider can play an important role for a grieving household by imparting some basic adolescent psychology to the parent and other involved adult family members. There are a number of excellent books available for children of various ages to read or have read to them. Additionally, there are also books that are useful to parents and other family members as well as for care providers to use when helping to facilitate the grief of children. (See appendix A under suggested reading for helping children and adolescents in grief.)

The surviving parent, who is aware of some of these dynamics thundering within the adolescent child, hopefully will choose to respond less with anger and more with understanding and respect. It will be helpful for the adolescent to understand the many emotions that are triggered by the loss of a parent, sibling, or close friend and the possibility of some mental confusion as well. Understanding that physical aches and pains, sleep, and appetite pattern changes are also a natural part of the grief response can also help to alleviate some of the unspoken fears that the adolescent may have been holding on to.

At each stage of development, the way grief plays out will be influenced by a variety of life conditions and past experiences, which all affect the meanings the child will place on a death and its consequences.

☐ Other Mediating Influences on the Nature of Children's Grief

These mediating influences affect the intensity and the duration of the child or adolescent's grief reaction.

The Nature and Circumstances of the Death

Who died?—father or mother? How was the child informed of the death? Was the death expected? Was the death the result of a long or brief illness? Was it sudden? Was it a violent death? Was the child present at the death? Did the child receive care and support after he or she learned of the death?

The death of mother or other primary attachment figure will typically result in a more intense grief response. As a child matures, the nature of the evolving relationship will play a large role in grief behavior. A child may feel more prepared for the death of a seriously ill parent if he or she was old enough to comprehend the possibility and was kept informed. Sudden and violent deaths—especially those in which the child was present, may result in post-traumatic reactions (nightmares, high anxiety, phobias, extreme startle reactions, hyper-vigilance, engaging in re-enactment of the traumatic event) and may require special care from a mental health professional.

The Nature and Circumstances Surrounding the Death-Associated Rituals

Did the child see the body? Was the child at the funeral or memorial service? Did the child participate in the service or attend the burial or cremation? How was the child prepared for these experiences?

Seeing the grave and the other graves in the cemetery confirms not only that the death has occurred but has occurred in other families as well. "The irreversibility of death as well as its universality gradually penetrates the consciousness" (Smilansky, 1987, p. 112). In my own experience, increasing numbers of children attend funerals. One long-term study found that "95% of the bereaved children attended the funeral" (Worden, 1996, p. 23). Unless a child is vehemently opposed to attending the funeral and/or burial, every encouragement should be offered. Children should be prepared in advance for what the funeral service and burial will be like. Arrangements can be made in advance for them to leave early should they become unable to tolerate the experience. Children should never be made to feel bad or guilty if they do not attend the funeral or if they have to leave early.

Participating in the preparations and the actual service can help the child acknowledge the death, honor the memory, and begin a different relationship with the deceased parent, as well as feel included in the ritual event. Some children have helped to choose burial clothing, select flowers, music, and food to be served, and have written and read the eulogy. Decisions about what role he or she will play must involve the child. Again, children who wish to participate need to be prepared as to what will happen and what they will do. This can help them determine what they may want do to in the funeral, burial, and other rituals.

The Nature of the Family Relationships Prior to the Death

"The child's responses to death and loss must be viewed in the family context," writes Raphael (1983, p. 114). What are the patterns of relationships in the family? How did people typically respond to each other and to crisis in the past? Were they open, intimate, and willing to share or cold and withdrawn from each other? What, specifically, was the nature of the relationship between the parents? What were the family's attitudes toward death? How much did the family concern itself with "what the neighbors think?" How much were they invested in the "status quo" and aversive to change? What is the loss history and medical status of the surviving parent? What is the loss history and medical status of the child or children? How chaotic and unstable has life been in this family? Are they financially solvent or are they marginally surviving? Is this family connected to the community and/or an extended family? Are they isolated and without community support? What cultural, ethnic, or religious traditions are relevant to the family's grieving process?

The patterns of communication between family members, attitudes toward expressing feelings openly, level of support and caring in the parents' relationship, and connection to outside resources will directly affect the way a child grieves and feels permission to express his or her grief. If supportive community and extended family members are available to help, children often do well.

If there is a history of conflict between the parents, if the home was disorganized, chaotic, nonexpressive, and insecure, children will be more likely to experience intense grief and also be at increased risk for social and psychological problems (Kissane et al., 1996).

The Nature of the Family Conditions After the Death

Is there a surviving parent? Is the surviving parent the mother or the father? What is the emotional condition of that parent? How intense is his or her grief reaction? What is the nature of the relationship of the child and that parent? Is the child going to reside with the surviving parent? How will the surviving parent balance work requirements with time for the child or children? To what extent are other family and friends involved in providing continuity of support and care for the child or children?

The emotional state of the parent who must care for the child will play an important role in how much the child feels able to express his or her grief feelings. As discussed earlier, children will protect the surviving parent from their own pain and stifle their crying. They do so out of love and concern for the parent, as well as out of their need to survive. If the surviving parent is overwhelmed with his or her own grief and/or the responsibilities for maintaining a home and making a living for the family, the parent may not have much time left over to devote to sharing their feelings of grief. In cases like this, children may be literally on their own to cope with a multitude of feelings about the death of the other parent. Depending on the age and level of independence of the child, the surviving parent may need to seek support for the child from extended family, friends, the faith community, or from social service agencies.

The physical health of the surviving parent and other children are also of concern. Grief is very stressful and drains the body's capacity to withstand colds, flu, and other infections. Grieving families need proper nutrition and medical attention. The organized help of supportive people can provide food and other care for extended periods of time. I've seen friends, extended family, and members of a family's faith community step in to provide this kind of care for weeks and even months.

All of us have assumptions about the world and so do children. The loss of a parent, sibling, or other important loved one shatters the assumptions and expectations held by the child. The hope for a cure, the wish for return of a parent, the expectation that all will be well and secure may evaporate with a death or other tragic loss. Children must be given a sense of safety and security in the post-loss world and an opportunity to restore the assumptions of survival and continuity (Goldman, 2002).

The Role of the School in the Life of a Grieving Child

To what extent has the school staff been informed of the parent's death? How are they preparing the classmates for the return of the bereaved child? How well do the teachers and other school personnel understand the grief of children? Do they know what age-appropriate grief behavior to expect? How does the school maintain communication with the surviving parent or surrogate caregiving adult? How will the school accommodate the needs of grieving children who do not want to be given special consideration or do not want to be seen as different from the other students?

When necessary, a mental health professional should be made available to the staff to orient them to the needs of grieving children and the nature of their grief. Each subsequent teacher that the child encounters should be informed of the child's loss; this can spare the child being asked awkward or hurtful questions. Some form of communication with the home should be established so that the child's educational progress is maintained.

The Role of Peers in the Grieving Process of the Child

Does the child have a friend or friends with whom he or she can maintain contact with during this difficult time? If parental death was due to a lingering illness, were peers in contact during the period of illness? To what extent does the grieving child feel stigmatized by having had a parent die? Have the grieving children been able to express their pain and even cry with friends? Do friends bring up the dead parent and are they comforting to the bereaved child or children? Does the bereaved child "hide" or avoid the fact that he or she has lost a parent? Is the child ashamed because the parent died by suicide or homicide, or because of drugs or alcohol? Were friends at the funeral or memorial service? To what extent have friends been to the home since the death?

It is not easy to be a bereaved member of a peer group. Some of the friends may say things that are disturbing or describe an experience with their parents that can cause the grieving child to withdraw. It's also common for the child to feel envious or even angry with those who have two parents and an intact family.

☐ What to Expect from Grieving Children

Much of the outward signs of children's grief and adult grief are similar. Below are some of the ways that children express normal grieving:

- *Physical pain and health problems:* Headaches, stomach and intestinal disturbances, more than usual colds and fatigue, sleep disturbance (too little or too much), and appetite changes have been reported by parents of bereaved children;
- *Regression to younger age behaviors:* This may include bedwetting, soiling, thumb or pacifier sucking, "baby" talk, clinging and seeking to sleep in parent's bed, not wanting the parent to leave, "playing" sick in order to stay home, and seeking attention more than usual;
- *Mood shifts:* Irritability, emotional ups and downs, episodes of anger, periods of despair and withdrawal, feelings of being anxious, fears for safety and well-being—fighting at home, school, or neighborhood—being disrespectful and blaming the surviving parent for death of the other parent;
- *Poor school performance:* Drop in grades, misbehaving at school, and/or does not do homework;
- *Apathetic and a lowered self-esteem:* Helpless sense of the future, and feelings of guilt and regret;
- *Socially withdrawn* or overly socially active.

☐ Clinical Concerns

There are danger signals that children and adolescents display that indicate a need for more than good support for normal grieving. These signals and, in some cases, high-risk conditions indicate that there may be complications in the child's grieving process and a mental health professional should be consulted. (See chapter 9 for a discussion of complicated grieving.)

Danger Signals for Clinical Concerns

1. The complete and continued absence of any reference to the loss or evidence of sadness, crying, or questions about the absence of the parent.
2. Threats or actions of self-harm; suicidal ideas, plans, or attempts.
3. Physical abuse of animals or other children.
4. The child is continually clingy beyond appropriateness; panicky and/or fearful of being without an adult present.
5. Extreme change in appetite, weight, and sleeping patterns.
6. The child states he or she has not been told the truth about the death.
7. The child had a conflicted, ambivalent relationship with the deceased parent.

8. The child is extremely withdrawn and refuses to make any social contacts.
9. Use of drugs or alcohol.
10. Extreme and sudden change in behavior: failing in school, personality shifts to very low energy or very high energy, aggressive actions, extreme and prolonged regression to earlier age behavior (bedwetting, soiling self, thumb sucking, returning to crib, baby talking), and/or a display of delinquent behavior.
11. Continued physical complaints: headaches, stomach pains, muscle spasms, and tightness in chest.

> *The care provider* should alert the parent, other family members, and/or caregiving surrogates about these signs. Concerns must not be pushed aside. Referrals to appropriate professional resources should be provided for the families if needed.

□ Conclusion

This chapter has provided a brief overview of the nature of the grief of children and adolescents who have suffered the death of a parent. Children live in an adult world and often are expected to mourn like adults do. They have often been ignored as grieving people.

When either of these occurs, it is not only disrespectful to children but also reduces the chances for a healthy and healing grieving process. The adults in a child's life must have availed themselves of the information about how children grieve, what to expect from bereaved children, and how to help them do what is necessary to adjust to a world without their mom or dad. When the usual, normal process of grief goes off course, it is important that children and adolescents receive the special attention required to help them continue on a path to healing.

Chapter 5 will discuss the grief that parents, siblings, and others have when a child has died.

5

CHAPTER

The Grief of Parents:
An Upside-Down World

☐ Introduction

From a biological perspective, the parent is the physical agent whose function is to send the genes received from earlier generations into the future. This biological imperative intertwines the parent and child in a

117

very special relationship, the essence of which is reflected in the way our culture and society defines the role of parents as well as the expectations placed upon them regarding the protection of their offspring. When a child dies, the generational continuity is cut off. Added to the biological attachment for survival, psychological, cultural, and social factors impact on the attachment and create a uniqueness that is the parent-child bond. Each becomes attuned to the other's needs and expectations over time to form a reciprocal system of actions and reactions (Field, 1985).

Parents frequently experience massive guilt when a child dies. Many explain their loss as a failure in fulfilling their own job description. Archer (1999) discusses the connection between family closeness and the level of involvement in ensuring the survival of the young. The closer the family member (i.e., parents and siblings), the more intimate the involvement in the care of the young. It follows then that we should expect that the more intimate the childcare role, the greater the intensity of grief if that child happens to die. While this is understandable, parents and siblings aren't the only ones who mourn the loss of a child—grandparents, aunts, uncles, cousins, and friends grieve as well. These close family members and friends should also be accorded the highest validity as grievers. It is fair to say, however, that the parental grief response is the most complex. For in most families, parents are heavily invested in "providing and doing for children [via the] roles of provider, problem-solver, protector, and adviser" (Rando, 1984, p. 120). The losses that are grieved are much more than the death of the child—they are all the things that you won't share for the rest of your life.

> "When you lose a child, you don't heal."
>
> **Carroll O'Connor**

This comment of the late Carroll O'Connor (best known for his roles in the popular television programs "All in the Family" and "In the Heat of the Night") at a televised press conference after his son's death, calls to mind a phone conversation my wife had years after our son Steven's death:

> My wife had received a phone call from an old friend. During the conversation, the woman said, "I don't know how you survived the loss of your son. I would have died." My wife answered, "I did. The person I was is gone."

My wife's remarks to her friend and the statement by Mr. O'Connor reflect a sad truth. The title of "bereaved parent" reflects the parent's new and permanent identity, and healing typically becomes a lifelong process.

About 10 years after Steven's death, my wife and I saw a man we had not seen for some time. He shocked us by bluntly asking, "Have you two gotten over the death of that son of yours yet?" "No," I answered, "and we probably will grieve for life." Many grieving people hear remarks like these, which only reveal the sad lack of understanding and, at times, a lack of tolerance for those who are bereft.

☐ The Grieving Parent: A Look Inward

"O my son Absolam, my son, my son Absolam! would I had died for thee, O Absolam, my son, my son!"

David upon learning that his son had been slain.
II Samuel: 19 (King James Version)

Who is the grieving parent? What is his or her life like now? What do they think and how do they feel? How do they cope with the upside down world they now find themselves in?

In the selection below, a mother relates a fear many bereaved parents have.

"How Many Kids Do You Have?"

A bereaved mother sat in my office and shared her sense of dread about an upcoming school meeting for parents of new pupils. Her daughter was starting a new school, and she ached with pain at the thought of that terrible question she knew she would hear from the other mothers: "How many kids do you have?" She wept as she heard herself say those words that brought back with ripping pain her memories of the little boy who was struck and killed the year before while playing outside.

This woman's experience isn't unusual. Other grieving parents have expressed horror at the thought of being with people whom they didn't know well and were unaware of their tragedy. Excessive talking by others about their alive and well children may be hurtful to bereaved parents who frequently report that such conversations feel like a knife in the heart. This alone makes many parents feel like withdrawing from social contact.

The "Upside-Down World"

Not only is the world of the bereaved parent lonely, but it's also truly upside down. Parents are not supposed to outlive their children. The bereaved parent is forced through a crack in the universe into a world where expectations are turned inside out. The death of a child before the death of the parent goes against the grain. Here is an ancient folk tale:

> After waiting in vain for years, an emperor was overjoyed at the birth of an heir for his throne. He and the empress invited royalty from far and wide to attend a great celebration. The royal poet was commissioned to create a special poem for the occasion. On the day of celebration, the newborn son lay in a royal cradle between his parents. After all of the guests had eaten, the emperor called for the royal poet to deliver his poem. This is what the poet said: "Grandfather dies; Father dies; Son dies." The emperor was enraged at the poet for connecting death with his newborn child and called for the poet to be executed on the spot. But the poet interrupted. "Sire," he said, "is this not the best course for history? Each generation should die in sequence, the younger outliving the older."

The devastation of having your child die before you do is reflected by me in the following journal entry written 22 years after our son Steven's death.

Kaddish—A Memorial Prayer November 23, 1997

> It seems so stupid to say Kaddish for a little boy.
> Kaddish is a prayer of respect for the dead—for a dead parent usually,
> Or an uncle or an aunt or a grandparent
> Or maybe even for an older brother or sister.
>
> But for an 8-year-old boy?
> Who now has been dead for 22 years . . .
> It just doesn't fit.
>
> I am sitting in front of a
> Roaring fire in our living room.
> When he died, we kept a fire burning
> During the several days before
> His funeral, and for
> Many, many days after
> He was buried.

Tending a fire gives me an
Activity, a distraction for the moment.
The hissing flames cry out
The pain that is still in me
Twenty-two years later.

I'm not sure why
I am so sad and listless
This year.
Last year I almost didn't remember it was November 23rd again.
I find myself irritable

And very sad at odd times throughout the day.
This year I just want to sit and tend to the fire,
And not say Kaddish
Or light a memorial candle.

It feels stupid to say
Kaddish for a little boy.
He should be saying it
For me!

©1997, J. Shep Jeffreys

Once at a regional Compassionate Friends (bereaved parents support) meeting, some of the parents argued as to which is worse: losing a baby or losing an older child. I asked them, "When is the best time for a child to die?" They answered, "After me!"

Parental Guilt

The lament of grieving parents I have worked with over many years echoes the *Kaddish* verse above. They find themselves in a disoriented, new, and achingly strange world, unable to make sense of their loss. The guilt of bereaved parents flows heavily from the wound of loss. The guilt is composed of:

1. Regrets—about the quality of parenting
2. Misgivings—about medical treatment and other decisions involving the child
3. Unresolved past conflicts with the child—about anything
4. Practically every aspect of the relationship and childcare that may be examined and used for parental self-blame

Some view their grief as a possible punishment for misdeeds, either an omission or commission, in the parental role. I hear them tormenting themselves with such questions as:

- "Why did I (or didn't I) let him go out that night?"
- "I should have checked who was driving the car."
- "Why didn't I look in on the baby sooner?"
- "We should have gotten another medical opinion!"
- "I should have known she was so desperate."
- "We had a terrible fight the night of the accident."
- "I should have visited her more often in the hospital, been nicer, told her I loved her."

This is just a small sample of the kind of painful self-evaluation that parents engage in when they feel guilty for "failing to keep their child alive," failing to fulfill their "job description." For most of the parents that I have worked with, the issue of guilt has been raised as a disturbing and demoralizing feature of grieving.

Guilt comes in a variety of forms and is a powerful influence on both physical and mental health (Johnson, 1987). Guilt may arise out of a parent feeling implicated in the death. For example, parents whose child died in the car they were driving or whose child died from drowning due to lack of supervision may relive the terror of the child's death over and over again. Still other parents feel guilty because they are not grieving enough, not experiencing enough pain or even are having moments of laughter and contentment. (See chapter 8.)

Survivor's Guilt

Many parents feel guilty because they are alive and the child is not—regardless of any possible connection to the cause of death. This is called survivor's guilt; siblings and grandparents can be affected similarly. It is also not unusual for some women in a family to feel a type of survivor's guilt because they have a healthy newborn and their sister or other close relative has suffered a recent miscarriage or is unable to conceive.

Secondary Losses

"Parents who depended heavily on a child for need-fulfillment can also experience complicated responses" (Solsberry, 1984, p. 82). The child may have filled the gap left by a physically or psychologically absent spouse. Some parents have stated that they lost not only their child but their best friend as well. One man indicated he lost his fishing partner, a mother lost her confidant, and another lost her business partner.

Children also provide a sense of status or self-esteem that has meant so much to the parent's self picture. Mothers have said things like, "Once I gave birth to her, I really felt like I was finally important." For some people, having a child depend on them gives them a real sense of purpose in life, one that provides a great responsibility and a continuing job to perform. Having a child and developing a relationship with that child can also provide the parent the opportunity to give to another the love and care that he or she was deprived of as a child. The death of that child ends the opportunity of need-fulfillment and creates significant additional loss.

Much of the guilt parents experience will melt away over time. When this doesn't happen, it may be that the grief has become complicated, yielding chronic despair, guilt, anger, and physical complaints that can linger for years. Continued guilt can give rise to complications in the grief process, resulting in depression, low self-esteem, alcohol and drug use, self-sabotaging behaviors, and overextension into work and other activities. (See chapter 9 for details on complicated grief.)

Care providers should anticipate the expression of parental guilt and listen to it, never agree with it, and confront it only when the parent is ready to work on this. Often, listening to the guilt of parents helps them to unburden the pain and feel some relief. At an appropriate point in counseling, reviewing medical information, police reports, and eyewitness accounts of the accident can help to relieve the guilt burden. These are reality-testing activities. Seeking forgiveness can also alleviate the intensity of remorse. (See chapter 8 on forgiveness as a healing tool.)

Parental Anger

Grief can also give way to extreme bitterness. Bereaved parents feel that their core identities have been ripped out and a "chasm exists between the person that I was and the person that I am" (Rothman, 1997, p. 11). The world, the entire universe, stops making sense for the bereaved parent. The search for meaning is typically fruitless, at least at first. Their anchors in reality have vanished with the conclusive realization that their beloved child—an extension of their being, their stake in the future—is no more and will never be again. This terrible finality may give rise to bitterness. I have found that the outward rage and bitterness is a way that some parents cope with depressed or hostile feelings toward themselves. In other situations, the rage is directed at people who are seen as having had some role in causing the death of the child—the driver of the car, a neglectful babysitter, a health care provider, or a spouse. Anger is sometimes directed at the dead child or at God. Parents who feel betrayed by their faith may reject any support from their religious community. Parents may even direct their anger toward surviving children, distancing themselves as a way of self-protection from additional losses; and in some cases protecting their children from parental sorrow.

Regardless of the source of the bereaved person's anger, it is an expected component of grief. The care provider must provide a safe place for it to be expressed. It is not unusual for angry, bereaved people to lash out with rage and trigger aching feelings of grief that were lying just beneath the surface.

Care providers may find that anger may even be directed at them. In these cases, the provider needs to internally reframe the situation and view the outburst as a part of the needed release with a safe person. The provider can also reflect this feeling back to the grieving person by saying, "Who else would you like to hear those feelings?" This helps to put the anger in a more productive context. Providers who are not experienced in working with highly explosive individuals must exercise caution with persons who are prone to violent and explosive rage. When in doubt, get a consultation and consider referring the individual to a colleague specializing in rage issues. Techniques for helping the parent understand and discharge stored anger are discussed in chapter 8 under Externalizing the Feelings of Emotional Pain.

Coping with Other People

Sometimes a grieving parent will find it necessary to educate friends and family as to what is and isn't helpful in order to create a useful social support system. We have found that the bereaved parents' loved ones generally welcome such guidance. However, grieving people need to be aware that there are people in their lives from whom they will never get the support they would have expected or desire. It is usually a shock for a bereaved parent to realize that his or her own parents or siblings cannot be supportive to them and instead may distance themselves. Other people may be at a complete loss for words and not know what to say, or else may say hurtful and destructive things, such as, "You will just have to move on.", "When are you going to stop crying and get a life?", and "I really don't care to be with you when you are so down all the time." It's best for grieving people to avoid such individuals.

The care provider can help grieving people find tactful ways to respond to uninvited advice, judgmental statements, and other non-helpful comments from people who may be available support if they had some direction. I have found that a clear and firm message without any sarcastic overtones works well. Some examples include:

"You can help me most by just listening to me for a while."
"Advice is not what I need right now."
"I really don't want to talk right now; I hope you understand."
"That comment was not only unhelpful, it hurt me."
"Can you just sit with me while I cry for a little while?"

Parental Fear

In addition to the hurt, pain, and anger expressed by grieving parents, there is a special type of fear and anxiety that surrounds their hearts—the fear of losing other children or any close person. We attach to survive; and when the critical parent-to-child (or sibling-to-sibling) bond has been broken, the individual may become sensitive to the reality that it could happen again. Sometimes this causes bereaved parents to overprotect surviving children, spouse, other relatives and close friends, and this in itself may become a serious energy drain, causing problems in other relationships. Sometimes the anxiety-related overprotection of grieving parents spreads to their own health concerns and that of their loved ones.

New Me in a New World

As bereaved parents search to define their new identity, they need to restore both their inner sense of the dead child and their ability to create a new social equilibrium—that is, to answer the question, "Who am I in the outer world?" (Klass, 1988; 2001). The inner representation of the lost child—whether it was a fetus, an infant, older child, or adult child—must be converted to the image of a child who exists within but is now no longer physically available as an external reality. ("I know I have the picture of my child in my mind, but I don't expect him or her to come to the table for dinner.") The same is true for the dreams, hopes, and wishes they had for the future with this child—they too are gone.

The parents must also create a new internal picture of who they are in the outside world. Parental grief at varying levels of intensity may continue to be a part of their awareness. Holidays, as well as birthdays, graduations, weddings, and births, will all serve as powerful reminders of loss as we confront who is not there, whose life story will never unfold, whose own marriage and family never happened. How do we act on Mother's Day or Father's Day, or at the graduation of the children our deceased child once went to school with?

Bereaved parents often point out how differently they feel from other parents wherever they encounter them—on the playground, at school events, during family occasions, or at any other social activity. Their loss and grief accompany them everywhere they go. Others may be aware of their loss but seldom bring it up. This often causes bereaved parents to feel as if they were wearing masks—they look fine to the outside world and feel like an impostor inside. One grieving mother shared how rejected she felt by family and friends in the months and years following her son's death because of their lack of sensitivity.

Painful Reminders

Seasonal reminders of loss are part of a bereaved parent's reality. Here is a personal journal entry regarding one seasonal occurrence that never fails to take me back to a painful time.

Halloween Is Still Painful October 24, 1995.

Ah, yes. It's pumpkin time again. Driving down the highway, I see them, in all their shapes and sizes dotting the roadsides. The sight snaps me back to the time of unrelenting terror when there was "no way out of this prison of pain." Halloween—twenty years ago. Steven just didn't have the energy to go trick-or-treating, and I so wanted him to; just as he did when he was well and not dying. He refused to let me carry him piggyback. He couldn't even put on his costume. Ghosts and goblins came to the door all evening. They didn't know.

There may be many, many reminders each week. Some you notice and others slip past the corner of your eye. Newly bereaved parents may suddenly find a sock in the laundry that catches them unaware and causes them to wince, sob, or even scream. Robert Neimeyer (1998) states that grieving parents must ultimately "redefine [the inner] connection to the deceased while maintaining our relationship with the living" (p. 98). Over time, the parent reorganizes the inner picture of the lost child from one who is available in a real, physical sense, to images of the deceased child that is available only in memory. As a way of continuing the bond with the deceased child, many parents continue to relate to the inner image of the child, reminisce with others about the child, and think about how things would have been had the child lived.

Continual acknowledgment of the child can be a part of family events—holiday rituals, visiting the grave, and religious ceremonies. Many parents want to hear their child's name spoken and may continue birthday celebrations. Adapting to a world without the physical child is aided by developing a capacity to bring the image and memory of the child into the post-loss reality. The parent can feel as if he or she is still connected to the child as life goes on—not necessarily without pain but with the knowledge that the memory of the child remains available. This is very normal and a part of the continuing bond, which is vital to the healing process.

Linking Objects and Continuing Bonds

One of the most common ways that parents maintain the continuity of a relationship with their deceased child is by linking objects, locations, or events associated with the child. Parents find that this process can connect them to the child or specific memories of the child, reduce their anxiety, and be a source of comfort (Klass, 1999). Many diverse items have served as linking objects: toys, games, clothes, jewelry, photos, music, dried flowers, stuffed animals, dolls, a hospital identification bracelet, a strand of hair, hand or footprints, coins, stones, a sonogram of the fetus, a blanket, stamps, cards or a coin collection, school artwork and homework papers, a pet, a plant, a garden plot, an infant car seat, and even a fragment of bone recovered from an accident scene. Linking these objects with the child not only validates the existence of the continued connection to the dead child but also affirms that he or she *did* live for a time.

Frequently, parents will attend school sporting events, graduations, and other community functions that their children would have participated in. Visiting the site of the accident and marking it with flowers, a stone, cards, artwork, and religious symbols, and attending veteran's parades and other memorials further serve to maintain contact with the dead child.

As the grief journey proceeds, many linking objects and activities weaken in their strength as the need for them diminishes. Linking items may be placed in a box and kept nearby in a closet or night table drawer. Some items may be displayed while others may be distributed to relatives, friends, and community organizations associated with childcare or hospital pediatric waiting rooms.

Here is my linking object story:

> Steven wore a baseball cap when chemotherapy caused his hair to fall out. After he died, I placed his cap under my pillow. Each night I could reach under my pillow and make contact with the hat and feel some connection to Steven. It was always a good feeling. It remained under my pillow for a year and has been in the drawer next to my bed since. I seldom look at it now, but I know it is there.

The continuing spiritual bonds and linking objects provide a support for grieving parents as they gradually reconfigure their identities and the new ways of being in the world without their child. The bonds are thus not severed but rather remolded in a way that allows them to create a new relationship with the dead child in a new world. For many, this provides a sense of comfort and restores a sense of equilibrium, but not for all.

Reunion Fantasies

I have heard many parents state that they simply do not wish to be in a world without their child. Parents may express a desire to join their child; and while any self-destructive remarks must be taken seriously, the reunion fantasy usually exists on its own, without any plan for implementation. Parents need to know that it is safe for them to express such thoughts to the helping person. (See chapter 8 for suicide assessment procedures.)

The Bereaved Parent Lives in Two Worlds

A bereaved parent often says, "It's not right!" "It doesn't compute!" —and these bizarre, unreal, and not-right feelings spread to other parts of the grieving parent's life. This means that the ripples of this horror not only flow inward, affecting one's sense of self, but also outward—to the couple's relationship, the deceased child's siblings, as well as to extended family and friends. The waves of grief also flow out to school friends and teachers, health care providers, neighbors, workplace peers, the faith community, the people from whom the family buys food and services, mail delivery people, and anyone else who has regular contact with the family. All are affected and nothing will ever be the same again in any of the social systems connected to the family that has lost a child.

Bereaved parents operate in two spheres. In one world, parents grieve, connect with the internal image of the dead child, reminisce, engage in rituals, and attend to the legal and business affairs dealing with the child (insurance claims, tax accounting, estate law, and in some cases, courts and attorneys). The other world in which the parent lives in is the daily and weekly business of living, working, planning for the future, caring for other children and family matters, functioning, or not functioning in these pursuits. Which world predominates? It varies. Families may focus on the inner image of the lost loved one and grief-related activities, or on accommodating to the new post-loss world (Rubin, 1996; Rubin and Malkinson, 2001; Stroebe and Schut, 2001).

This came to me very clearly when I visited Steven's grave just before the anniversary of his death.

Visiting the Grave Site November 21, 2003

Leaving Steven's grave is like drawing away from grief.
Walking towards the car is facing away from one reality
And looking in the direction of the world without him.
Driving out of the cemetery and turning onto the street
Is reentering life as usual, life with traffic, people, stores.
A few minutes earlier I stood looking down at my son's grave.
I prayed, I told him how much I still loved him, missed him.
I sang a song he sang before he died and I also sang
"Morning Has Broken,"
The song we sang at his funeral 28 years ago.
Then I walked a few steps to the left and
Prayed at the duplex gravesite of my father-in-law and
mother-in-law.
I sat for a while on an adjacent marble slab.
The sun was warm. It was peaceful, quiet and filling there.
Then I looked back at Steven's grave marker, got up and
Walked towards the car.
Leaving Steven's grave is like drawing away from grief,
Walking between two worlds.
I belong to both.

© **J. Shep Jeffreys, 2003**

Care providers may need to refer grieving parents to other sources of community support, such as Compassionate Friends, Bereaved Parents of the USA, religious or spiritual groups, or health care professionals. Many parents or other family members who have embraced their faith have found solace in spiritual activities. (See appendix B for a list of support organizations.)

☐ Parents Whose Child Was Murdered, Completed Suicide, or Died from Other Violent Causes

There are clearly differences in the needs of parents who are coping with a murder, a suicide, a drunken driver, or a disaster that claimed the life of their child. The suddenness, the unexpected change in their lives forever, wreaks an abrupt concussive blow to mental and emotional balance. Their assumptions about the world are violently torn away, and grounded reality is gone. Their sense of safety, predictability, and personal identity is shattered in a moment. A family sits at the Thanksgiving dinner table filled with happy expectations as they await one more of their family to join them. After a period of time elapses, the phone rings. It's the hospital chaplain calling from the emergency room. Their loved one was killed on the way to their home. Life changed in seconds. The cold reality flows over and through them. (See chapter 9 for traumatic death of a child and grief complications.)

Parents of Murdered Children

Homicide and suicide loss, "as compared with other types of bereavement, renders a significantly pathological appearance" (Rando, 1993, p. 537). Parents of murdered children feel that this form of child loss sets them apart from other bereaved parents. The unnatural elements surrounding homicide—intentional violence, possible violation or mutilation, and the imagery of the suffering of the child can yield a high level of parental anxiety, recurring horrible images, and the increased risk for post-traumatic stress.

Parents of murdered children may have lingering involvement with the legal system as the killer is sought, taken into custody, tried, and sentenced. Trials and sentencing may require long periods of courtroom presence. The media may also create continued or sporadic revisiting of the horror for the families. The process may take months or years and impede healing their grief. In some cases, the killer is either not caught, not prosecuted, or receives a sentence less than the parents felt was just. This leaves the family with unfinished business regarding justice not being done. Help in coping with this incompleteness must be given. One mother commented on how helpful it was for friends simply to allow her to "rant and rave" and not interject any advice. These parents will need extended support during this time.

Care providers can help by educating parents as to the typical emotional and cognitive reactions they may expect. It is not always easy for a parent to find friends who can be present, listen, and also be comfortable with strong grief reactions. Most local prosecutor's offices have a victim support program in operation. Support groups typically provide a climate of understanding, acceptance, and caring for bereaved parents whose children have been murdered. (See appendix B for community resources.)

Suicide Completion

Suicide completion by a child leaves the parents with guilt, rage, intense hurt, and frequently many unanswered questions. In addition to working with parents individually or as a couple, there are special groups that are available for them. (See appendix B.) I have used externalization of feelings with very angry people and found that once they were able to release their pain and anger, they could connect with their child through rituals and forgiveness exercises. The reader is referred to the Externalization, Rituals, and Forgiveness activities in chapter 8. When there are unfinished issues between parent and child, these must be addressed in professional counseling sessions. Parents who have lost a child to suicide are at risk for complications of grief. (See chapter 9.)

☐ Impact of a Child's Death on a Couple's Relationship

"When our baby was born, a mommy was also born," said a very sad woman who was sitting in my office one day. Her husband, who sat apart from her, without touching or looking at her, just looked down. My initial impression was that he was grieving the loss of his child. When he later spoke, I realized that he was not only grieving the loss of his child but also the loss of his wife who no longer seemed involved in their relationship. As his wife related her lament—a lament he'd heard many, many times in the several months since the sudden death of their infant—he slowly shook his head.

Just as the birth of a child has a major impact on the life of a couple, the death of a child has the potential to bring cataclysmic waves of change. Some couples simply lack the skills to make contact in the aftermath of such a tragic event in their lives. The hopes, dreams, and expectations for life's journey in the company of their child as a vital member of their family system were ripped out from under them. Whether the death was sudden or the result of illness, the empty space in the home and in their hearts frequently causes them to retreat into their private worlds of grief. Separately they struggle to emotionally keep their heads above water. Many report a sense of drowning. Suffering from a serious loss of control and uncertainty as to how to approach their partner, they hurt too much to do anything. "Where do we go from here?" couples frequently ask me.

> *Care providers* must help couples set some outcome goals for counseling, and to begin a sense of direction and structure that is usually a comforting first step. Even some brief homework assignment to spend an agreed upon interval of time together can start the process of reconnecting.

Subsequent Pregnancies

In my experience, many couples who have suffered the loss of a fetus, a stillbirth, an infant, or even an older child, are often anxious to have another child fairly soon after the loss. They may seek guidance from a mental health or medical care provider to determine how long they should wait. There is no clear-cut answer, but we can offer them a way to evaluate their readiness so that they can make the most intelligent choice for themselves.

There are several important issues that must be resolved in order to make some recommendations. First, what is the medical status of the woman and what does her physician advise regarding her health needs? Second—and admittedly this may be difficult to ascertain—to what extent have they mourned the child who has died? According to Rando, "The couple must have achieved some resolution of the loss of the deceased child" (1984, p. 140). How can we find this out? One way I have used is to determine to what extent each parent has addressed Worden's four tasks of mourning as described in chapter 2. This requires some time to assess, but most parents who seek guidance for this issue understand the importance of making this determination and are eager to help however they can. As Rubin and Malkinson (2000) state, "The need to maintain an ongoing attachment to the unique child who died, and to allow for the formation of a distinct attachment to the unique child who is to enter the family, are important benefits of experiencing the grief and loss process" (p. 232).

Care providers can help a couple with their own assessment of readiness to have another child by teaching them some basic understanding of grief and the healing process. Worden's four tasks, Rando's six processes, or Neimeyer's meaning reconstruction are examples of explanations that can be the basis for this learning. (See chapter 2.) The couple can then become participants in their own evaluation because they have some basis for understanding what they have and have not yet done regarding those methods for understanding grief process over time.

The High Divorce Rate Myth

Bereaved couples do not have a high divorce rate.

Many couples that have lost a child do feel like strangers in their own relationships, but the high divorce rate story simply isn't true! Oliver (1999) reports "most empirical studies have found that a substantial minority of couples experience marital difficulties after the death of a child." Additionally, a major study of bereaved parents reports that "Overall, 72% of parents who were married at the time of their child's death are still married to the same person" (The Compassionate Friends, 1999, p. 11). Of the remaining 28% of marriages, 16% ended due to the death of a spouse, leaving only 12% truly ending in divorce. Of those couples whose marriages ended in divorce, only one out of four reported that the death of the child contributed to their breakup.

In addition, an extensive review by Schwab (1998) of studies designed to measure the degree of marital discord and divorce following a child's serious illness and/or a child's death from many different causes found that only a "relatively small percentage of bereaved parents do divorce in the aftermath of a child's death but many parents reported [either] no change [in marital status] or [definite] positive effects of [the] child's death on their marriage" (pp. 460–463). Some parents described their relationship as being closer because of their mutual grief. It is important that care providers educate grieving parents and their families regarding the erroneous *our marriage is doomed* myth.

However, in spite of the low rate of divorce after a child dies, many grieving parents do experience some marital strain and have to make some readjustments in their marriages. People who lose a child naturally turn first to their spouse (or even an ex-spouse) for support and at times to place blame. The trauma of child loss can escalate an anxious attachment that creates increased need for emotional support (Oliver, 1999). The parent who does not need high levels of emotional support may feel overloaded and withdraw just when the other has the greatest need for talking, physical contact, and reassurance. The person who feels as if they are not receiving the care and comfort expected may detach and withdraw from contact. This then can lead to further hurt, distancing, lack of communication, and deterioration in the couple's functioning; counseling is indicated when this happens.

Care providers should expect some disruption of marital communication and assist couples with understanding why their post-loss relationship feels strained and how normal this is. Providers should also give couples opportunities to reconnect, using techniques for building mutual support. Communication enhancement activities such as structured, scheduled periods of contact and sharing how each is feeling and what each needs can be a focus of couple's counseling. Keeping a diary of feelings to share at the agreed-upon communication sessions may also relieve some of the need to express thoughts and feelings frequently to the other spouse. Friends and other family can become part of an inner circle of support. Self-help support groups can also play a role in meeting the need for a place to safely express the feelings and thoughts of a grieving father or mother. (See appendix B.)

Inhibited Grief Expression

In addition to the issues discussed above, we will now discuss other specific reasons why couples inhibit their grief expression after their child has died.

Grief Varies in Timing and in Intensity

When couples feel out of sync in terms of their grieving styles and rhythms, breakdowns in communication occur. Let's return to the couple described at the beginning of this section. The bereaved father admitted that he was "tired of hearing his wife's grieving all of the time." They both complained that there never seemed to be "time to talk" because each seemed to be in a very different phase of the grief cycle. He had spent the day in a nonchild environment with few painful reminders, and he was ready to relax. His wife, however, had spent the day at home trying to avoid the baby's room filled with never-used furniture and accessories, hearing the sounds of little children playing outside, glimpsing television shows interrupted by baby food and diaper commercials, and images of late-model vans loaded with happy, healthy children. She couldn't escape from her shattered dreams. The depth of his wife's grief made the husband feel helpless and unable to come to her aid. When they left my office, I suggested that he not use his computer as an escape and that he and his wife engage in conversation.

Men and Women Often Grieve Differently

A summary of studies by Rosenblatt (2000b) on bereaved parents' styles of grieving indicates that men and woman differ in the length, intensity, and degree of public openness of their grief. It was reported that mothers typically grieved longer and were more openly expressive than men. Couples interviewed by Rosenblatt frequently cited the communication problems resulting from these gender differences as causing stress in their marriages. How does this play out at home? A woman who thinks nothing of giving vent to her feelings may have a husband who does not know how to be with his sobbing, despairing, and sometimes bitter wife.

So many husbands say they "don't know how to make it better for her"—and too often this "problem-solver" role is what men believe they are supposed to do. They often feel helpless because they don't have the magic words that will make their wives feel better. The masculine ways of managing grief can easily be misinterpreted by the wife as, "he has no feelings about this tragedy; he just doesn't care about me and goes on as if nothing has happened." This can result in increased withdrawal, isolation, and bitterness.

On the other hand, women don't want solutions or magic words; wives report that they feel abandoned by their husbands when they fail to listen to them. "He wants to advise me or solve my problem, but all I want is for him to listen to me, even for 15 minutes!" Some grieving people need to be heard, frequently over and over again. Others grow impatient and are eager to "move on." Most of the lack of conversation and resistance to expressing grief is a natural and human desire to avoid pain.

While many women may need to confront their grief directly, many men elect to take a more indirect route. I've met men who work out their feelings of anguish by exercising, doing home improvement projects, and by throwing themselves into their work. This isn't a problem unless grief begins to take partners down such different paths that they don't spend any time grieving together. A wife may also withhold her expressions of grief so as not to upset her husband and seek comfort in a relative or friend. This also contributes to an increase in their interpersonal detachment. Communication is the life energy of a relationship—when it goes, the relationship goes.

The care provider must encourage the couple to be conscious of any distancing and help them to find ways to connect. Ground rules for communication can be developed as a way of guiding couples toward connecting and speaking. Couples can agree, for example, to let each other know how they are feeling, no matter how sad they are, even if it may cause the other to start to cry.

To hold back reduces mutual grieving. Couples can enhance understanding and closeness when they share some part of their grief.

At some point my wife and I became aware that there were gaps in our sense of each other's grief:

> After Steven died, my wife and I realized that we were sometimes unaware of each other's grieving. We discovered that both of us were holding back so as not to "bring the other down." We made a pact not to hide our expressions of pain in order to protect the other. Many times her sadness made me cry, just as my tears broke her heart. However, we agreed to make our grief part of our experience as a couple. While we each still had private grieving times, we also grieved together.

Some of the differences in grieving may result from the fact that each parent has a unique relationship with the child. The nature of this relationship affects how each parent grieves. The primary caregiving parent will face a different set of secondary losses after the death of a child than the parent who has been significantly less involved due to work, travel, withdrawal, separation, or other causes of disconnection. It is also true that those parents who considered their children as companions, confidants, or business partners will feel additional losses and may grieve more intensely as a result.

Sometimes, in spite of the best of intentions, each partner is so emotionally drained from coping with personal grief that there is no energy left over to support each other (Bernstein and Gavin, 1996). This is especially true when there are other children to care for, and if one or both parents have demanding jobs outside the home.

Care providers can help by assisting couples to understand the reasons for their isolation and the factors preventing them from communicating about grief. Further, couples should be helped to develop some simple, brief check-in procedures that will begin the process of reestablishing some workable mutual support. For example, some agrees upon a time to make contact by phone once or twice a day and once in the evening—just to say, "Hi, how are you doing? I'm feeling . . . " or "What's been on your mind the past half-hour?"

Old Childhood Messages Influence the Rate and Depth of Sharing Feelings

A couple's communication patterns are based on each person's life experience and develop before they are born. Individuals who grow up thinking that they may not express feelings of sadness, anger, or fear may have trouble expressing these feelings as adults. If such a person marries someone for whom emotional expression comes easily, they could have conflicted styles for communicating inner feelings. Such conflicts can be exacerbated when grieving for a child.

A care provider must help couples like this build bridges to each other during the grieving process. Providers must continually remind couples to be respectful and tolerant of the different styles of grieving, explaining that each individual has a different pain and grief threshold that can be tolerated at any given moment. Some need to give vent to grief; others need to limit or avoid these expressions. Care providers can also help couples realize that even though they may grieve in different ways, they still have opportunities to grieve together. They can create family rituals, visit the gravesite, review and arrange photos. They can also hold family discussions, include their children, and talk about their grief. This can be an opportunity to learn how grief reactions are different for each person.

Some Parents Find It Too Painful to Express Grief Directly to Their Partners

Some grieving parents cannot grieve in front of each other because "It hurts too much!" or "I just can't let him or her see me like this" or "I feel judged when I cry with my spouse present." For many, it is simply not wanting to hear themselves cry and feel the devastation again. In such cases, the sound of the other parent's own sobbing can add further to the anguish and is avoided by distancing, distracting, and any avoidance behavior available.

Care providers can help couples begin to gradually share their grief using letter writing (either handwritten or e-mailed to each other), sharing written diaries, and listening to audiotapes the other has prepared in private. Providers can also suggest specific homework assignments, such as asking that one partner tell the other how he or she is feeling, what is missed most, and what each thinks the other person is going through.

Couples That Have Lost a Child Frequently Raise the Issue of Sex

For some men, sex may serve as a comforting and releasing activity, whereas women report that grief is inconsistent with lovemaking and that their pain makes this impossible for them. As a result, men often react with frustration, anger, and a sense of abandonment, while women end up feeling "How can you not know how I feel?"

> *Care providers* can help couples communicate about what each wants sexually and how they can achieve their goals. It's helpful to determine what issues regarding sex predated the loss of the child (i.e., "What is different about their sex life now?").

In the case of pregnancy loss or death of an infant, some couples are eager to resume having sexual relations as soon as permissible to hasten a new pregnancy. As indicated earlier in this chapter, help the couple to assess to what extent their grief for the dead baby will interfere with their focus on a new pregnancy and infant. There is no rigid determination system. I have seen couples who wanted to become pregnant as soon as possible, but were still so absorbed with the loss of the recent pregnancy or with the death of a week-old infant that they delayed pregnancy for almost 6 months. Others felt clear of the need to mourn and started a pregnancy within 2 months. For many couples, the return to an active and mutually happy sex life symbolizes their return to a somewhat normal life.

> *Care providers* must help each member of the couple understand that each individual grieves differently. Each must appreciate and respect this reality, as well as the need to grieve privately. Couples need help keeping lines of communication open, contacting community support resources as well as attending to the needs of other children in the family. (We will explore this further in the section on sibling grief below.)

☐ Sibling Grief

Each year approximately 1.8 million American children, from birth through 18 years of age become bereaved siblings (Hogan and DeSantis, 1996).

A friend of mine in his early '60s told me that he had borne a painful guilt from the time he was about 9 years old regarding the death of his younger brother. He and his brother had gotten into a fight, and he kicked his brother in the stomach. Some months later his brother fell ill and died of an intestinal disorder. My friend remained convinced that he was the cause of his brother's death and kept this secret for decades. It became part of his deep memory, surfacing mostly upon hearing of the death of a child. During psychotherapy, the unfinished material about his brother surfaced. He felt much relieved, only to discover upon subsequent investigation of his brother's medical records, that he was not at all responsible for his brother's death. He also told me somewhat ruefully, how different his life would have been had he been able to talk to his parents about his fears, and had them reassure him that he did not kill his brother.

The effect of terminally ill siblings and the death of that sibling on brothers or sisters is too often neglected. This is unfortunate as the grief reaction of surviving siblings is a critical part of the emotional climate of the bereaved family. As mentioned in the previous chapter, children grieve differently from adults and have varying understandings of death, depending on their age and stage of cognitive development. Adults need to help children deal with their own feelings of loss in ways that fit their level of understanding.

Many Varying Influences Impact on the Nature and Extent of Sibling Grief

Information Flow

It's hard to keep secrets in a family. Children read signals and often ask difficult and evocative questions—"Is he going to die?" "Does she know how sick she is?" Other children may not ask questions because they fear upsetting their parents and also may not want to really know the truth. When siblings are kept out of the information loop, however, they may fill in the gaps with troubling fantasies. They may worry that they will take ill and die. They may fear that their parents will be killed in a car crash on a trip to the drugstore to fill a prescription. It is absolutely vital to consider the sibling's need to know what is happening with an ill child or what has happened to a child who has died. Children need to be encouraged to ask questions and to have these questions answered. The health and healing of the family depend on it.

Lack of information may not only make children feel afraid and guilty but can also create a chasm between the sibling and parents. Many changes in the family are set in motion when a child's brother or sister dies. Rosenblatt (2000a), Fanos (1996), and Repole (1996) have shown that the death of a sibling can yield long-term effects on the mental health of an individual, especially when the experience has been a traumatic one and there has been no opportunity to express the feelings and thoughts of grief. Children have a right to know the facts regarding the illness or death of a brother or sister. They must also be dealt with honestly and in a way that is appropriate to their age. On the other hand, "just as one can err by trying to shield children from grief so one can err in the other direction and overwhelm them with grief" (Scherago, 1987, p. 3). Parents must be careful not to give children more information than they can use or that is inappropriate for them to have. Troubling details regarding sudden, violent, and mutilating deaths, those regarding agonizing pain of a degenerative illness, or any other potentially traumatizing details may need to be omitted from the information provided to young children.

Availability of Parents

Children heal most effectively from the death of a sibling when their parents remain in their lives, caring for them, playing with them, doing homework with them, and going out together. As indicated earlier, this may be difficult to achieve, particularly if the parents are consumed with their own fears for the life of a seriously ill child or are so devastated by grief over a child's death that they are left with no emotional and physical energy to spare for their other children. Faced with demands from work and household responsibilities, it can be tempting to put the needs of the children off for another day. However, surviving children can see this as rejection, and it can lead to resentment that can linger for years.

> *Care providers* should alert parents to the need for continuous communication with their children about how they feel and what they need from them. Family meetings for the purpose of sharing feelings and concerns and answering questions can keep the other children in the parent's awareness and provide needed attention. Family projects, such as memory albums, and planning recreation and other activities, can help siblings to feel included. When parents cannot possibly be emotionally present to their well or surviving children, providers will need to arrange for surrogate adults to be available.

The Nature of the Parents' Grief

Parental grief will have a direct effect on the reaction of siblings. Parents who don't cry or seem not to be distressed out of a desire to "protect" their surviving children can give children an unrealistic picture of grief. When parents grieve openly, children learn that it is OK to feel and express grief. When parental grief is shared, children get the message that this is a natural and acceptable human behavior. Some families may have conflicts over how much and how deeply children should be grieving the loss of a brother or sister. At these times more than ever, open communication can be an essential part of a family's grieving and healing.

> *The care provider* must be sensitive to the differences in cultural and ethnic communication patterns. What is an acceptable level of sharing in one culture may not be in others. Providers can seek this information from a family member or other person who knows this family's traditions.

Parental Understanding of Children's Grief

Chapter 4 gives a detailed discussion of the variations in the grief of children and common misinterpretations regarding how it differs from adult grief. I have counseled families in which the parents were worried that a grieving sibling was not grieving enough—they feared that this reflected a lack of love for the deceased sibling or that this would affect their emotional health adversely. In many of these cases, I discovered that parents usually were not aware of the differences between adult and child grief. Also, I frequently learned from the child while the parents were in the waiting room that he or she was grieving but doing so privately—so as not to upset their parents.

> *Care providers* can help in these situations by making sure that parents understand how grief varies from child to child, and the type of grieving behavior that might occur during each age. (See chapter 4 for details on developmental stages of children's grief.)

Nature of the Illness or Death

The nature of the illness or circumstances of the death of a child's brother or sister will influence their grief. In some cases—prolonged lingering illnesses or sudden, violent deaths—complicated grief reactions can occur. Risk factors for complicated grief are discussed in chapter 9.

Death due to a lingering illness characterized by numerous relapses and remissions, hospitalizations, painful treatments, debilitating medications, and drastic changes in the sick child's physical appearance can traumatize the surviving siblings. Some parents send their well children to stay with relatives or friends in an attempt to spare them from the harrowing details or to free up parents so they can spend more time at the hospital with the sick child. This can provide relief for parents but may severely diminish the sibling's awareness of the seriousness and limit their participation in the grief process. Where siblings have closely experienced long-term illness leading to the death of a brother or sister, they will need to talk about their fears, anger, guilt, anticipatory grieving, and any other issues that they feel.

Sudden, violent, or avoidable deaths send shock waves through the family, creating the potential for complicated grief reactions in surviving siblings. Their anxiety and diminished sense of security may result in post-traumatic reactions, and they may become fearful, hyperactive, sleepless, and/or easily startled.

Fear, Shame, and Guilt

Siblings may experience shame or embarrassment simply because their families are so different from those in which all of the children are alive and healthy. Preteens and teens are particularly sensitive about feeling different. In addition, the resentment that naturally builds up as parents and visitors are absorbed with the ill brother or sister usually leads to feelings of guilt after the death has occurred. Siblings typically regret their angry thoughts and feelings and how they acted when their brother or sister was alive. This guilt can become part of unresolved grief that may surface years later. Further, many siblings express feelings of being medically vulnerable and fear that they too will either contract their sibling's illness or meet a similar sudden death.

> *Care providers* must facilitate the flow of appropriate information to children and opportunities for them to ask questions and receive answers they can understand. Such information may in fact help them begin their grieving process. They must also be reassured that they will be cared for and that they are still important to their parents. This can be verbally expressed or demonstrated by such parental behaviors as engaging in rituals, spending quality alone time, reading to them, playing board games, engaging in family art projects, going on outings, and having unstructured "hangout" time.

Care providers can help families to open up the lines of communication between parents and siblings—both during a child's illness and after a death has occurred. Because younger children have their own timetable and ways of grieving, the family should come together from time to time in such family projects as sorting through the deceased child's possessions; creating a memory/photo album; rearranging and redecorating the room, closet, or play area; creating a memory collage or family mural; writing letters to the dead child on his or her birthday (or other special days); and planting trees, flowers, or shrubs together in honor of his or her memory.

Children should be given the opportunity to talk about what it was like during the illness, or upon hearing the news of the accident, and how they are now feeling about the death of their sibling. This can provide the surviving children the possibility of hearing each other as well as sharing whatever they are able to. Referral to children/adolescent bereavement groups can also offer a grieving child the opportunity to learn that other families experience tragedies too and other kids have the same guilt and regrets. (See appendix B for resources.)

Replacement Expectations

Although there is always some reshuffling of family roles after a death, "parents may inappropriately place expectations on children that repress the children's own identities in an attempt to keep the deceased child alive" (Rando, 1984, p. 125). Some parents who lose a child may consciously or unwittingly communicate to surviving children that they are expected to take on a part or the entire role of their dead sibling. Such parents may deify the dead child, enshrine his or her room, and focus on the dead child to the exclusion of the surviving siblings. The reactions of these children can range from resentment to mild or serious psychological disturbances.

A single mother spent over a year as caregiver and emotional support for her seriously ill young adult son. Her son greatly appreciated her efforts but her daughter resented her mother's attention to the brother. After the son's death, the mother remained absorbed in grief, which caused her daughter's resentment to deepen. Deprived of her mother's attention even after her brother's death, she withdrew, and eventually the two became estranged.

Siblings Speak

Children who lose a brother or sister can benefit from the opportunity to express their concerns, resentments, and fears regarding the tragic changes and the waves of unhappiness and turmoil sweeping through their lives. It is important that they have the opportunity for conversations at various points during a sibling's illness or during bereavement. The need for information and expressing feelings will differ from child to child. In some cases, the lack of upsetting information is welcomed and, in others, it is resented. I have, however, found that in later life, many adults are very glad to be able to get completion on some old leftover Cowbells material related to a childhood sibling loss.

Birth order will affect the self-pictured role of children in a home where a child is very seriously ill and after death has occurred. Typically, the oldest child will serve as a stand-in parent for the younger children and will be more likely to identify more closely with the parents' pain. Oldest children typically express concern for the well-being of the parents and seek more information than younger children. Below are the memories of Steven's sister and brother 13 and 28 years after their brother's death.

As my wife and I look back over the years of Steven's illness and death, we are aware of how much we did not know and how much we wish we would have done with and for our two other loved ones. It became painfully clear much later that they had their own grief reactions and continued to experience these effects long after Steven's death.

> **At 13 years after death of brother: sister, age 28**. I had a major issue with not being included in the realities of Steven's illness. I was aware of Mom and Dad getting more and more withdrawn from things. I remember how much he (my brother) hated going to the hospital and his screams of, "I don't want to go!" I felt incredible responsibility for both of my brothers, especially when we heard Steven screaming in pain. I felt reluctant to discuss my brother's illness with friends and felt great pain for my parents as well as a need to be strong for them and for my other brother. I was angry at receiving no information about when periods of remission began and ended. I felt cut off, and this scared me.
>
> I was angry that this was happening: "Why him?" "Why this family?" I remember waiting, always waiting in the hospital waiting room. I still feel angry that I was not told that my brother was going to die. I felt him distancing himself from me as he got sicker and sicker. He was in his own world of doctors and pain, and pushed us away. I feel cheated out of not having a brother who would be 20

now. I miss the friendship we would have had, and have dreams about him and feel his presence. I have painful memories when I see friends of his now. I wish we could have explored more alternative healing methods.

I found that I was able to keep up my usual activities. My mom made a great effort to keep things normal around the house. My parents were there for the big things and supportive adult friends were there. I feel that other subsequent deaths have been easier for me. Now, as a brand new mother, I am aware of how horrible it must have been for them, and I have fears about losing my own son.

At 13 years after death of brother: brother, age 25. My brother's illness became a way of life. I was jealous of his presents in spite of Mom's explanations. I still felt competitive with him in games. I worried when he was in pain and moaning when I was babysitting for him. I never pictured that he could be "dead." I just wanted him to get well; so we could play as we did before he got sick. I was frightened by his thinness and seeing his heart beat through his chest. I was not aware of the true life-threatening nature of his illness. I remember the music played at his funeral and always feel close to him when I hear it. When you have a younger brother, you always have a playmate. I am angry that I have lost the "older brother" role. I feel cheated out of the experience of having him in my life. I had the "protector" role. I wanted to keep his room intact. I lost the availability of my parents when they took trips to the hospital.

I have guilt over fighting when we shared a room, when I tore up a club certificate in anger when he was well. I feel that I have more crying to do and want to visit his grave and fill in some memory gaps. I now feel different from others as a result of his illness and death. I feel that I know what life is really about and that I grew up faster. I feel guilty when asked about siblings and I answer "a sister." I find myself castastrophizing whenever I have physical symptoms.

At 28 years after brother's death: sister, age 43. I think of him now whenever I see a kid with a baseball cap whose hair is cut short. I wonder how he would look if he were still alive today. What kind of uncle would he be? I feel cheated out of his kids. It gets harder to picture being with him and to remember the original experience. I wonder how much of my memories of him are "memories of memories?" I worry about my own health because I would never want my parents to go through that again.

We did not talk about it enough. I had a sense that it was bad, but did not know he was dying until the last few months of his life. I thought what we were doing medically was going to make him better. Even on the night he died, I didn't believe he was going to die. I remember the ride home after he died. There were no pangs of pain from him when we hit bumps in the road. We all slept in the same bed that night.

I felt very responsible for my other brother and had to stay strong in order to not be another burden for my parents. We were absorbed with the death of my brother and still trying to maintain some kind of normal life. My teenage friends were crucial to my support. They listened to me and didn't judge me. I have had fears about my children as each of them reached the age my brother died. They have grown up hearing and knowing about their uncle. This has given them an awareness of death and life because of our talking about him and other loved ones who have died.

I am aware that I overreact to my children's illnesses for fear of losing them.

At 28 years after death of brother: brother, age 40. I look at people who have brothers. A brother is a lifelong friend you can do things with. I have flashbacks when I play with my son, of being back with my brother. It's a neat feeling like unlocking a mystery as sudden memories surface—collecting cards, playing games. When my kids got a hamster, it took me back to my brother's gerbil and secretly buying him a new one when our cat Felix got the first one. Sad memories when I pass an area where my brother and my father and I took an overnight trip to an amusement park. He was weak and felt ill. I could see his heart beating. It rained all night. I still have a weird feeling whenever I see that amusement park. I still feel regrets over ripping up that certificate for a club we made up after a fight we had. He cried and we were mad at each other.

Sometimes my son's crying reminds me of my brother's crying. I remember my brother said, "I'm dying." Now, I take extra time with patients to see where they are with the issue of dying. My wife and I wonder what it would be like if he had lived. How would he be in our lives?

The care provider must help parents balance their grief focus by providing attention to their surviving children so that they can apportion time for both mourning and parenting. Parents may need to be educated regarding the risk for possible problems the surviving children may develop. These may take the form of unresolved anger, feelings of guilt, sense of abandonment, and/or distancing from parents. When the parents are too emotionally bereft to function effectively, other supportive adults will have to be found and brought into the family system.

☐ Impact of a Child's Death on Grandparents, Extended Family, and Friends

Grandparents

Grandparents are exposed to double pain when a grandchild dies. They feel grief because of their own child's loss while at the same time they have to cope with their own grief. Much of what we have said about couples and their need to respect different styles of grieving also pertains to grandparents, other relatives, and friends (Rando, 1986). Grandparents have a stake in the future that is cut off when a grandchild dies. In some cases, it is the end of a family's lineage. It is important that the grief of grandparents be taken into consideration and they not become disenfranchised grievers, for they have many special needs.

Grandparents may be seen as the stable entity within the family and are looked to for courage and guidance. This may make it difficult for them to do their own grieving. Unfortunately, they may also be left out of the information and decision-making loop and thus not have an opportunity to express their grief. Not only is there a lack of support groups specifically for grandparents, but also few materials have been written that address this population (Galinsky, 2003). Sadly, "there remains a deficiency of specific information to assist grandparents to survive an event they never believed they would live to experience" (Reed, 2003, p. 1). Grandparents often become surrogates for children whose parents are unavailable due to the intensity of their own grief reactions.

Extended Family

Family social systems reach beyond parents and grandparents and include aunts and uncles, cousins, and close family friends. As such, their grief expressions are a vital part of the healing process. If such people are not allowed to express their feelings, unspoken tension within the family can create an emotional shock wave that will affect the family for years to come.

Often, family conflicts do arise—over the definition of what constitutes appropriate grieving, the role religion should play in bereavement rituals, and attempts to assign blame for the child's death. Grandparents' opinions may differ from their children and in-laws, giving rise to other conflicts as well. For example, in one situation, the child's parents had decided on a closed-casket funeral service, but the grandfather insisted that it be open. Some issues are continuations and variations of conflicts that have troubled the family for years.

> *Care providers* can encourage family meetings that can include grandparents, and all participants can be invited to express their grief and their needs. All family members can also be helped to support each other as best they can by regularly communicating, listening, and being nonjudgmental.

Close Friends

Close friends may easily be overlooked in the mourning process. Since they don't share a blood tie, they may not feel entitled to participate; they may stay on the periphery and frequently remain outside of the family grieving process.

The Admission Ticket to Grieving Is Love

I was at the memorial service for a mother, father, and daughter who had lived in my community and died in a plane crash. When I joined the sole surviving daughter and several friends who were preparing for the funeral service, I noticed a man I knew was weeping, and I asked if there was anything I could do to help. He said, "No thanks, I'm okay—I'm just a friend."

This man had disenfranchised himself as an entitled griever—yet this family friend was an invaluable emotional and practical support to the bereaved young woman and very much entitled to be part of the grief process. Not all friends react in such helpful and heartfelt ways. Many of the parents I have worked with complained that some family and friends distanced themselves in the aftermath of the death of a child for various reasons. Some people feel the family's pain is too great. Some fear, superstitiously, that death may be "catching." They may come to the funeral or memorial service and make an initial visit to the home, but beyond this, they avoid the family.

Parents often say that the best support came from neighbors and friends who were not that close. According to the Compassionate Friends study (1999), many parents indicated that the most helpful support came not only from family and friends but also from coworkers. In addition, many bereaved parents turn to their faith communities and community groups for ongoing support. During the period of time immediately following a child's death, families often state that they feel surrounded by care and love, but as the weeks go by, support seems to melt away. One mother said to me just a month after her child died, "Where did everybody go?"

> *Care providers* can help bereaved couples by helping them identify their needs for support and by obtaining the support they ask for. Cultural backgrounds may play a role in who will be involved. Some cultures keep a tight boundary around the family unit. Pre-existing family conflicts must also be taken into consideration in determining who can play supportive roles.
>
> Find out who will make the parents feel most comfortable. Many times grieving parents ask for people who ultimately are not helpful and may even be hurtful. Care providers can help sort out those friends and family members who can help from those who can't. This is an important distinction says Paul Rosenblatt (2000b).

> *Care providers* can also help parents judge with whom they can share information and who needs to be kept more at arm's length. In addition, providers can help mourning parents discover creative and healing ways to include family and close friends in various rituals surrounding the death.
>
> Finally, *care providers* can help devise networks composed of friends and family to greet visitors who come during the mourning period, to answer the phone and doorbell, and to tend to household needs. Keeping the lines of communication open and providing for the needs of all family members beyond the first month is very important. The care provider may have to create the initial structure for this to happen by contacting family, the faith community, and other available support systems.

☐ What Grieving Parents Ask from Care Providers

Bereaved parents are valuable sources of information about their various needs. Here are some of the comments I have gathered from grieving parents:

- It's very hard for the average person to understand what we are going through.
- Everyone, especially my family, has a different plan to help me, but the support I want is to have someone just listen.

- I don't want anyone to tell me that I should or shouldn't feel the way that I am feeling. It makes me feel discounted or dismissed. I don't want a judgment—just a listener.
- Members of the clergy should ask the family to inform them about personal traits of the child if he/she didn't know them or let a family member speak. Clergy should not make general comments that indicate that they didn't know the child.
- I am still a mom even though I lost my only child. I would have liked someone to listen. Don't ignore me. I am not invisible.
- I still miss him after 10 years—I wish others could acknowledge my pain about this.
- I am being avoided by friends whom I have known all my life. I wish they were here for me.
- I really would have liked to have the support of my family regardless of the geographic distance. I need the recognition of my daughter by friends and family.
- Other people give sympathy, not support. Sympathy is not what is needed. Moral support is needed very much at this time.

Many bereaved parents feel misunderstood by those who they feel should know better—family, medical and mental health providers, and clergy. The comment I hear most frequently from grieving parents is that they don't want sympathy or advice; they do want another human soul to listen to them. Many parents want to talk about their child. They want to hear their child's name said at family events. Bereaved parents do not want to be treated as if they are not there.

Care providers can help by facilitating a flow of information to all who are connected with grieving people about what they need and what they don't need. A goal of the *exquisite witness* care provider is to disseminate information throughout the family's community as to how to be with grieving parents and siblings. This can be done informally at home or during hospital visits, or in connection with funerals, wakes, sitting Shiva, and other death-related rituals. A care provider can also call several family members and/or friends, school personnel, or workplace associates to provide information about the needs of a family.

Providers can also give more formal presentations at bereavement classes, PTA, religious communities, and at workplace or community group events.

☐ **Summary of Clinical Considerations**

Because bereaved parents grieve in unique ways, I will summarize this chapter by including the bereaved parent's version of the seven principles of grief that appeared in chapter 1.

Seven critical points to remember when working with bereaved parents include:

1. *You cannot fix or eradicate grief.* Parents have embarked on a painful journey, and the care provider will support and accompany them. As *exquisite witnesses*, we serve as exquisite listeners. Many grieving people, especially parents, will ask the provider, "Why?" "Why did this happen to us, to our child, to our family?" *Why* is not a frivolous or obstinate utterance. It usually is asked with no real expectation that an answer, satisfactory or otherwise, will be forthcoming. Yet, you may be tempted to answer, to give a response—perhaps a philosophical or spiritual statement in lieu of a medical explanation. I welcome the question and find it to be an opportunity to reach into the heart of the grief. "Oh yes," I often say. "The question of 'why' is so much on all of our minds. I wish there was an easy answer. Even though I cannot give you an answer, I can listen to what is in your heart." By listening, I learn that bereaved parents have many thoughts connected to the question of *why* this happened. In this way, asking "why" is like opening a door.

   Some parents are asking for answers; they want their pain fixed or cured like a cold or headache. They may be pleading for relief from the despair that threatens to engulf them. As care providers, you can normalize these reactions so that parents feel less different, less "crazy." Assure them that these feelings are not unusual and that most parents say similar things. If medical symptoms persist, however, refer the individual to the family physician.

2. *Everyone's grief is different.* In any situation where there are multiple grievers, there are variations in the nature of the response to the loss. As previously discussed, men and women tend to grieve differently, and this can lead to conflict in the relationship. Men are characteristically described as wanting to act, to restore equilibrium, obtain answers, gather resources, and provide for the safety and well-being of the family members. Women are described as needing to express their feelings. They want to reduce their pain by seeking solace in relationships. Though this stereotype is often quite true and exploited in the

entertainment media, there are, naturally, many exceptions. Essentially, we all grieve differently, and this can lead to misunderstanding.

> *The care provider's* goal is to educate grieving people about the variations in grief styles and to help each person respect individual differences. The provider also needs to arrange family meetings as conflicts arise and facilitate or secure a counseling professional to enable resolution of the disagreements.

3. *Every loss has multiple ramifications.* The loss of a child, at any age, means more than the loss of the body and being. It is also the loss of what was expected, looked forward to, and dreamed of. It is also the loss of that part of self that has or would have interacted with that child. For many, understanding this multiplicity of loss can help to explain the intensity of their despair. When people know what is happening to them and what to expect, they may feel comforted, and this restores some degree of normalcy to their lives and the lives of their surviving children.

4. *There is no set timetable for the grief journey.* Personal grief does not unfold on a schedule or according to a calendar. We all have our own timetables and roadmaps; often, healing isn't linear. It may be two steps forward, one step back. Think of standing in ocean surf. At times, a wave knocks you down; at other times, it barely touches your feet. You can be flooded with cold water and still remain standing upright.

   Once again, care providers need to remind family members about how unique each grief journey is, and how important it is to respect individual differences. When others urge mourners to "get over it," care providers need to help grieving parents give themselves permission to take as long as they need to heal.

5. *We extend the boundaries of what constitutes "normal" grief behavior for bereaved parents.* "Do you think I am going crazy?" Bereaved parents often ask care providers this question. When we ask what prompted this question, we learn that the parent dreams of the child night after night, talks to a photo of their child, keeps the child's baby seat in the car and converses with the child, believes they saw or heard the child calling out, feels the presence of the child, or thinks that the child is guiding their decisions. These experiences are not unusual; they often give the parent a sense of connection to the child. They may occur soon after the child has died or occasionally appear over time. In most cases, they are not evidence of being "crazy" but rather a desire to have a continuing connection to the child. Bereaved parents often

report other "normal crazy" experiences, including hearing their child's voice, seeing the child in a distant group of people, or having intense dreams about the child. These are normal, typical, and natural continuing connections to the child.

6. *Life changes bring about many losses, and this results in compound grief.* The loss of a child sets in motion a ripple effect in the lives of parents, siblings, other family and friends, classmates, workplace colleagues, members of the faith community, and the neighborhood. Some of the changes are swift and obvious, while others are more subtle and creep in over time. The empty crib or car seat, the crashing silence in the house, the absence of hearing the child's name spoken, the unoccupied seat at the table, the cessation of treatment and trips to the hospital, the restaurant reservation for three instead of four, the lack of an answer when you call out the child's name, and the nightmare question: "How many children do you have?" These are all reminders of the depth and breadth of one's loss.

7. *As an exquisite witness, the care provider must be available to meet the needs of the grieving parents in an authentic way.* To be available means more than setting aside sufficient time for a consultation. It means being aware of our own Cowbells and processing our own unfinished loss material so that we are more available to enter the bereaved individual's space—a space that may be filled with pain, anger, fear, guilt, and shame. Processing our own Cowbells facilitates our being emotionally and mentally present to the grieving parents. Further, the provider must be sufficiently aware of the nature and range of parental grief so as to know what to expect from particular bereaved parents, and have a repertoire of appropriate skills to apply. Availability to grieving parents is therefore affected by the "head," "heart," and "hands" dimensions of being an *exquisite witness* care provider.

☐ Self-Help Support Groups

An important way a care provider can help grieving families is by referring them to appropriate community resources. Parents, siblings, and grandparents need a safe place to share with other people who are grieving the loss of a child. This gives the griever a sense of belonging, of identification—"I don't feel like such a weird person when I am in here."

Self-help support groups for bereaved parents can be found in communities throughout the United States, Canada, and overseas. Among such resources are the Compassionate Friends programs and the local chapters of Bereaved Parents of the USA, Inc., as well as a variety of programs for bereaved children and their families that are operated by hospice, religious organizations, community social service organizations, and private care providers. The bereaved parent groups often have subgroups to accommodate the variety of circumstances surrounding the death of a child and for those with special needs, such as parents who have suffered miscarriage, SIDS, suicide, homicide, or other forms of child loss. (See appendix B and consult telephone directories for local phone numbers and more information.)

In the safe haven of a self-help group, parents typically discuss their grief, their children, and how they cope—with birthdays, death anniversaries, holidays, and life in general. Compassionate Friends groups develop rituals, such as candle-lighting memorials to help members survive difficult times (like the holidays), and birthday cake and photos when their child's birthday falls in the month of the meeting. Members share feelings, pictures, and memories, providing parents with the opportunity to deepen their bond with their deceased child in a very accepting environment.

Not all bereaved parents benefit from group meetings. For some parents—or, as is often the case, for one of the parents—this type of support experience is not for them. Some feel overwhelmed by the level of pain in the group. In this case, they can be encouraged to return in a few months when they may be more open to the group sharing experience. Such parents must be respected for their choices and given the option of seeing an individual support person—a counselor or spiritual advisor.

I have been both a member of and a speaker at our local and regional Compassionate Friends support groups. I have found a sense of honesty among the bereaved parents I have met and a willingness to help each other that is comforting. It diminishes the sense of isolation so many of us experience. (For information about other support programs such as Mothers Against Drunk Driving and support for homicide, suicide, and neonatal deaths, see appendix B.)

Care providers should familiarize themselves with the various programs by attending some meetings. Visiting groups will give the provider insight into the appropriateness of the group and its helpfulness to a particular set of parents. The care provider will be better able to explain to parents what they can expect should they desire to attend. It is also useful for the care provider to get acquainted with the contact persons for the various support programs and to receive the organizational newsletters.

☐ Hope for the Grieving Parent

For many grieving parents, hope is sometimes there, up ahead, around the next bend, but not quite within their grasp. In the early stages of grief, parents can seem lost in helpless despair and apathy. To tell them "hang in there," and that "it gets better over time" rings hollow. What can you say to comfort people whose light of life has gone out?

In the most despairing times, I might simply offer parents something to read with a spiritual message, a beautiful piece of music to listen to, or some lovely artwork to contemplate. Even books designed for children that are about nature and the cycle of life can comfort grieving adults. Books can soothe the younger inner self when there is pain. I've listed some of these books in appendix A.

I include this poem of hope that I wrote the day after I'd been to a bereaved parents' meeting, as I walked around a nearby lake on a snowy, wintry morning in March.

A Robin in the Snow—March 11, 1999

I move into the day,
Once more.
The sky is blue and
The bright sun stretches down
To touch the fringes of brilliant
Snow around the lakepath.
And the air is frigid,
Almost painful, as I
Breathe it into me.
Signs of winter's retreat
Surround my walk,
And I hear the aching words of
Parents in grief—
"Oh how I hate spring!"
What a contrast
What a paradox.
Who doesn't feel some excitement stirring
From the prospect of warmth,
And green growth's return?
For grieving parents renewal of life is soured, and
Inner pain screams out against
The coming rebirth of earth.
And then, I see nearby
In the cold whiteness . . .
A robin in the snow.

© J. Shep Jeffreys, 1999

We may not be able to change reality, but we can help to move some of the pain aside and start the process of turning the upside-down world right-side up.

Chapter 6 will address the realities of bereaved older adults and consider the needs of family caregivers.

CHAPTER

Older Adult Grief

☐ Introduction—Realities of Aging

> An 88-year-old woman came to see me because her only child, her 55-year-old daughter, had died. There were no grandchildren. She had been a widow for many years and had no family left. Though she was in good health, she wanted very much to die. "Why hasn't God taken me?" was the question constantly on her mind. She had expected her daughter to be part of her final years; now, she had no one.

This woman's story is the story for many older aged grieving people. The deaths of close relatives and friends leave many elders wondering why they are still here. Even though the loss of an older adult's spouse is considered by society to be an expected or "normative" death, the survivor typically enters a world that is strange, lonely, and sometimes unfriendly.

Death becomes a much greater part of life's experience for aging people than it is for those in childhood and young adulthood (Marshall, 1996). This issue needs serious attention because the population of people over age 65 has been increasing for decades—and the post–World War II "baby boomers" are joining the ranks of seniorhood at a very rapid pace.

Many older adults have been learning the "language of loss" over time. In fact, we are all introduced to changes in our bodies very gradually during the initial phase of mid-life. We become aware of the need for various aids that make it possible for us to be able to read, chew, or manage chronic back pain. Perhaps we have had to cut down on certain foods to curb weight gain or keep cholesterol, blood sugar, or blood pressure readings in the normal range. These gentle reminders of the deterioration of our bodies gather momentum as we age and little by little scoop away energy, our ability to heal quickly, as well as our overall physical functioning. Of course, it is important to distinguish the symptoms of treatable disease from normal changes that accompany the aging process.

However, not all older people are frail, confused people. The range in physical and cognitive limitation is wide, and many senior citizens lead active and healthy lives. The purpose of this chapter is to assist care providers in understanding the needs of the older members of our communities who experience the death of a loved one or a close friend. Additionally, we want to alert the care provider to the special circumstances that in-home caregivers (frequently a spouse) who may be caring for a very ill and/or disabled husband or wife may face.

Defining Old Age

There are a number of terms used to define that part of our population that is considered *old*. The terms frequently used are the following: *elderly, old, older adults, senior citizens*, and *young-old* as well as *old-old*. The actual age range ascribed to a particular term for older adults is continually shifting as "middle age" thrusts up into what has been known as "old age." This is affected by increasing life spans and the popular drive to eat healthy, keep fit, and stay active. Terms that refer to adults past middle age are frequently used interchangeably. Age and stage of life are less defined by a number and increasingly defined by a person's state of mental and physical health and degree of social activity.

In addition, older adults can bring a richness of life experiences to the challenges they face in later life. The insights gained are well used for both themselves and for others. The term *elders* has a connotation of wisdom, of having negotiated and survived transitions and problems of earlier years. This wisdom is also available to provide confidence and guidance to younger individuals. I recall one older man's comforting wisdom in the story below.

> Many years ago when our nation was coping with the threat of atomic bombs and so many people were openly frightened about the world coming to an end, an older neighbor man said to a group of us, "There has always been a world, and there will always be a world." Months later, while filled with frightening news of the gathering cold war tensions, I was very comforted by that statement and was certain that he had some special wisdom.

Physical Health Factors

As older adults enter the later years, certain health conditions and physical limitations affect their quality of life. Some of these are biological—a function of wear and tear. Some limitations are related to sudden events such as a fall; others result from a disease process that might have begun earlier in life or are the result of multiple chronic conditions. Many of these disease processes and conditions can and should be treated.

Examples of health factors that may influence the grief of an older adult are as follows:

- Physical changes in the form of cumulative deterioration of basic body systems: cardiac, neurological, digestive, endocrine, muscular-skeletal, and immune;
- Decreased ability to heal and restore the body after injury, illness, or surgery;
- Increased vulnerability to chronic infectious disease;
- Changes in physical appearance due to loss of muscle tone, wrinkling, and loosening of facial skin and other visible skin changes; decrease in range of joint flexibility and spinal curvature due to arthritic processes;
- Decrease in muscular strength and physical endurance;
- Loss of balance;
- Loss of bowel and/or bladder control;
- Diminution of the senses—smell, taste, touch, hearing, and vision;
- Dental changes and resulting problems in nutrition;
- Side effects or interactions of multiple prescription and over-the-counter medications;
- Undiagnosed depression or other mood-altering conditions.

Care providers must also be cognizant of alcohol use for self-medication and its potential negative effects due to interaction with current medication. Counseling for alcohol abuse may be required.

Cognitive Factors

At the same time that the physical body is undergoing transition, changes in cognitive ability can also occur. This can affect the performance of familiar tasks and make people feel inadequate. They may find themselves confused trying to drive to the home of an old friend or trying to fill out a health insurance form. There can be short-term memory loss, slowed-down reaction time, decreased alertness, and/or decreased ability to select appropriate words. Some cognitive change is reversible and can be caused by such factors as minor as inadequate hydration, drug interaction, or a urinary tract infection. For other people, small strokes or the beginning of a disease process such as Alzheimer's disease may be the underlying condition for memory loss or other cognitive change. The care provider should not assume that the reduction of cognitive ability is either permanent or a normal sign of aging unless the older adult's primary physician has verified the diagnosis.

Transition in Life Roles

New words enter our vocabulary as we approach our later years, reflecting the emerging choices we make about our future. These are all continuing issues that confront people of advanced years. The ability of individuals to plan for their future is reflected in words such as "retirement," "advanced directives," "long-term care insurance," and "burial planning." Other events bring up challenges not easily predicted ahead of time and require other words: "Hospice" and "caregiving" are two examples. Whether these events lend themselves to pre-planning or coping, they express experiences common to us as we age. The point is that transitions and losses in later years can occur against a backdrop of recurring and cumulative physical and cognitive limitations. The older the person, the better chance there is that these limitations can impact coping abilities. From this perspective, it's easy to see how bereavement in later life can be more intense.

☐ Factors Affecting the Grief of Older Adults

When providing services to the bereaved senior, the care provider must take into consideration certain social and living conditions that can impact on their grief reaction.

Isolation

Limited social contact is a reality for some older adults regardless of where they live. Even those living in settings with many people around, such as assisted living and nursing homes, can be very lonely. Seniors living independently may be isolated because of lack of transportation; mobility limitations; or loss of family, friends, and neighbors. Distance or unsatisfying family relationships make older adults feel terribly lonely because their children and grandchildren live at great distances from them, or live close enough but don't come to visit often.

Some older senior citizens may experience isolation because so many of their friends may have already died, leaving them no one with whom to reminisce. At the same time, many older people have less opportunity to meet new people and make new friendships. Finally, loss of the role created by work or volunteer involvement can result in social isolation when not replaced.

Care providers should facilitate older adults being active in the community. They need opportunities to connect with others and have the benefit of social interaction. Intergenerational work opportunities can also be sought for increasing a sense of contribution to the community. Information about social activities and work or volunteer possibilities can be found in local senior centers and/or regional offices on aging. Providers should also be aware of programs offered by religious organizations and other community human service agencies.

Disenfranchisement

Older adults are frequently not credited as having the same level of grief and fears about death as younger people do. I have heard younger members of a family take the view that the elder is "used to people dying" because he or she has lived for such a long time. This lack of validation can result in the withholding of grief expression. This in turn can lead to physical, mental, and emotional problems and conditions.

> *Care providers* can assure seniors and their families and friends that age doesn't diminish the grief response and that our elders are entitled to all of their feelings as well as the opportunity to share them. Efforts must be made to include all seniors in death-associated rituals.

Social Devaluation

We reject the use of the term *elderly* because it frequently conjures up stereotypical images of people who are frail, unproductive, sexless, and unimportant. Older adults may be rejected because they are viewed as old, unattractive, and cognitively impaired and require medical care and are possibly depressed and/or grieving. They typically no longer work; they might need the radio or TV volume turned very high, and may have difficulty with mobility. They may like to talk about the "old days," and the "way we used to do things when I was growing up." Their values may conflict with the younger generation. They just may not fit in to the current youth scene. Middle-aged people may already feel out of touch with the younger fads and styles.

While our society seems willing to provide health care, medication, and assisted-living facilities for older adults, we may also be missing the true value of people of advanced years—people who have stories to tell and wisdom to share. In many cultures, older adults are highly respected, valued, and revered.

> *Care providers* need to educate families, and especially adult children, about the unique needs of older people who are grieving so that they are not shunted aside. Elders can supply a wealth of family history. Families can create opportunities for their elders to share their memories while involving grandchildren in creating journals, family history albums, and taping interviews on audio or video.

Multiple Losses

A bereaved elder experiences death within a web of other losses. These losses may include the health problems listed above as well as the loss of the following:

Fiscal independence. Loss of income and purchasing power can shift people into a different state of control over their lives.

Work role and status. Occupational roles have contributed to self-identity for so many years; with retirement and loss of the work-place role, there is potentially loss of status, productive activity, income, a sense of self-worth, social connection, and identity.

Community roles. Giving up the workplace can frequently affect community roles on various organizational boards and committees as well. Declining health and lack of transportation may be other reasons the older adult forgoes community roles. Moving out of the home of many years ends the "neighbor role" and requires emotional energy to establish connections in the new residential setting.

Mobility. Inability to drive or walk will increase isolation unless public transport or organizational provisions for carpools, busses, and/or vans can be arranged. Family and friends may also become involved in providing transportation.

Death or distance of life-long friends, siblings, and other family members. When such members of the older adult's social world die or move away to live with their children, isolation is increased. One important part of healing grief is the ability to reminisce. With age-mates diminishing, the options for reminiscing also become limited.

Care providers need to be aware of the multiple loss concept whenever an older adult sustains a loss.

Providers can help grieving elders by arranging for family contact and bereavement-related rituals and activities—religious service attendance, visits by clergy, activities with grandchildren, and social activities with peers. Additionally, there must be an effort made to help the older adult find and develop new meaningful roles in the community. This can be effected as part of an organized group effort such as neighborhood improvement or holiday commemorations, or by joining a community organization's volunteer program in hospitals or schools. Even planning for and helping to set up for meetings, lunches, and trips can give the individual a sense of making a contribution to others.

☐ Losses of the Older Adult

Death of Spouse

Individuals married for many years create a closed system in which they have each become each other's primary attachment figure. This is "a system of roles, traditions, and mutual experiences, which are in turn reflected in an identity shared by the couple" (Moss, Moss, & Hansson, 2001, p. 246). The loss of one partner may literally leave the other without an anchor in reality. Widowers find themselves anxious at the prospect of having to fulfill the homemaker role their wives held. Widows are now responsible for unfamiliar or physically demanding tasks that the spouse may have handled prior to the loss.

One study found that anxiety in older men who had lost their spouses was the dominant aspect of their grief reaction—more so than loneliness or depression. This is explained as *separation anxiety*—loss of their primary attachment figure and difficulty adjusting to living alone (Byrne & Raphael, 1997). We have seen many men who were so dependent on their wives that they had very limited relationships with friends outside of the marital dyad. The shock of the death of the long-term "bond-mate" and subsequent anxiety response pattern is reminiscent of *isolation distress behavior* of MacLean (1973) and the *agitated protest behavior* of Bowlby (1980). (See chapter 2 for attachment theory.)

Older women typically have women friends and may not suffer as great a level of isolation distress as a result. We have observed that women who go to the senior centers and participate in other community activities arrive with one or more female companions. Men are more likely to arrive alone.

Yet, both widowed men and women say things like: "What will I do without her/him?", "How can I go on?", "I'm so used to being with him/her that I can't get a grasp on who I am or what I'm supposed to do now."

Others may withdraw into the silence of despair and become clinically depressed or ill. In families where the adult children and other relatives are geographically distant, the bereaved elder may be without social support in several weeks or even days after the funeral as their children return to their own lives. Unless other social support resources are in place, the individual can be isolated and may be very lonely. This is especially true for same-sex older couples. When a life partner dies, the surviving person may lack the social support traditional couples have. Care providers must also be sensitive to the variations in death-associated rituals and communication patterns due to the growing cultural diversity of our population.

Care providers (or a family member), at an appropriate time, can introduce the widow(er) to the idea of participating in the many structured senior-citizen activity programs in the community such as exercise classes, current-event discussion groups, and lecture and lunch programs. Many older seniors can benefit from being coached on finding resources—who or where to call for information on what is available from groups such as the area agency on aging, religious organizations, town recreation departments, and the American Association of Retired Persons (AARP). The goal is to neutralize the isolation and provide social interaction to reduce the level of anxiety and loneliness.

Care providers should be aware that the trauma of losing a mate might aggravate other existing loss conditions as well as trigger old loss material (Cowbells). Individuals may need referrals to support groups that provide support and encourage productive physical as well as mental activity.

Some older people resist participating in structured support groups. When they do, however, they usually enjoy the meetings. Care providers and family members need to acknowledge that not every elder will be physically healthy enough or psychologically inclined to make the effort to participate in a support program. For some who have never been "joiners," the inclination to attend simply is not there.

Many older adults find great solace in their religious affiliations. According to Weaver and Koening (1996), "the religious community is central to the lives of most older Americans" (p. 496). It is estimated that 80% of older persons are members of a religious community. The services and observance of rituals provide an ongoing set of meaningful activities; the spiritual comfort they find in such affiliations can help them develop a sense of meaning in their new lives.

Death of an Adult Child

When an older person loses an adult child, being able to carry a positive picture of the child in the mind's eye may be a comfort—even though this may cause tears. Photos and memorabilia, talking about the deceased, and acknowledging the child in memorials and other family events can bring the lost loved one into the present.

Adult children also represent potential caregivers to the aging parent and such deaths increase fears about not having care needs met in the future. This is a normal reaction and one that we hear from older bereaved parents in self-help support group sessions.

Care providers can facilitate the family's awareness of the need to help bereaved seniors achieve balance in their lives so that they can attend to their spouse, living children, grandchildren, as well as engage in memorializing their deceased child. When possible, other members of the family should be included in rituals and activities of remembrance. Grandchildren should be especially included in these activities as they are reminders of the future and can help the bereaved older individual focus on the blessings that are now part of their new life.

Death of an Adult Sibling

"Perhaps the most frequent death of a close family member in later years is the death of a sibling" (Moss et al., 2001, p. 245). However, many older adult siblings are disenfranchised as grievers. They are often not included in the inner circle of mourners along with the sibling's spouse and children. There are no grieving elder sibling support groups. Typically, the only support most bereaved older siblings may find is from their surviving brothers and sisters when they take the time to review the past and reminisce together.

Care providers can make every effort to have families they are working with include older adult bereaved siblings in memorial services and remembrance rituals.

Death of a Grandchild

In a study reviewing the differences between the grief of parents and the grief of grandparents, Ponzetti (1992) found that "grandparents' concerns focused on their children" (p. 69). Grandmothers are generally more involved with the bereaved parents than grandfathers. Grandparents' grief was found to be threefold: They grieve for the loss of life their deceased grandchild has suffered, for their own child's grief, and for their own loss of the grandchild. (The grief of grandparents has been discussed in greater detail as part of the death of a child in chapter 5.)

Older Adults and Suicide

Research indicates that "older adults who attempt suicide die from the attempt more often than any other age group" (Miller, Segal, and

Coolidge, 2001, p. 358). This reality indicates how deeply emotionally and physically exhausted surviving spouses can become. Older people tend to choose lethal weapons to end their lives—hanging themselves and discharging firearms are the most common (Miller et al., 2001). They are less prone than younger persons to inform others of their suicidal thoughts or plans, or to seek out crisis hot lines and mental health services.

Many suicides, however, are believed to be a result of undiagnosed and/or untreated depression. Since the primary care physician most likely has frequent contact with the older adult, more effort should be made to increase the awareness of these providers with regard to screening senior citizens for symptoms of clinical depression (P. Madachy, Administrator, Howard County, Maryland, Office of Aging, personal communication, December 19, 2003).

Care providers must assess bereaved older people for suicide risk because suicide rates increase with age and are highest among Americans aged 65 years and older. Also, suicide rates among older individuals are highest for those who are divorced or widowed (CDC, 2004). Post-assessment follow-up contact by care providers is critical with elders at risk. (See chapter 8 for assessment procedures for suicide risk.)

☐ Helping the Bereaved Older Adult

There are several ways of helping the older bereaved individual. As we will discuss in chapter 8, these interventions can be supportive, clinical or combined interventions.

Supportive, Clinical, or Combined Interventions

Supportive helping. Supportive helping is generally preventative in nature and may take the form of making a friendly home visit, facilitating attendance at a senior center activity, doing the shopping, helping to prepare food, or helping to plan for future needs.

Clinical helping. Clinical help may take the form of bereavement counseling, prescribing medication, or making an assessment of cognitive and/or emotional functioning. (See Chapter 8.)

A combination of these interventions. A combination of supportive and clinical interventions may occur when individuals are engaged in a self-help support group, attend a grief and loss workshop, or participate in a discussion group on a grief-related topic.

We will concentrate on the *combination* of supportive and clinical interventions in this chapter. (For more detailed supportive and clinical techniques and interventions when grieving becomes problematic, refer to chapter 8.)

No bereaved person should automatically be referred for grief counseling or other clinical treatment simply because he or she has sustained a loss. Grief is not a disease (Raphael, Minkov, and Dobson, 2001). There are many people who can provide a first line of care and support for the bereaved as they grieve and work on the four tasks for healing. (See chapters 2 and 8.) In addition to family and friends in the community, clergy or other spiritual advisors should be in contact with the bereaved if the family welcomes such contact.

Support Groups

When the time is appropriate, an older bereaved person can be made aware of various community resources available. There is no single best time to introduce the idea of attending a support group. However, sometime during the first or second month of bereavement, the concept should be suggested. The family member or care provider can introduce the group as "people who share the same or similar losses and are able to get and give help to each other."

Many support groups are self-help groups. This means that other similarly bereaved persons make up the groups and serve as facilitators. Professional facilitators lead other support groups. Some bereavement support groups are specific to the nature of the loss (spouse, child, suicide, homicide) while others are mixed. Some widow-to-widow groups are organized by age, which is preferable since similarly aged people generally have similar needs and concerns. There are a growing number of services provided by local offices of aging and other organizations available in many communities. Family and their support persons should avail themselves of these resources.

Here are some resources for locating support groups (see appendix B for additional details):

- Local hospice
- Area agencies on aging
- Senior centers
- Churches, synagogues, mosques, and other faith communities

- Religious-affiliated social service organizations
- Funeral homes
- AARP
- Red Cross
- Alzheimer's Association
- National Caregivers Association

For child deaths or deaths due to drunk driving, suicide, or homicide, contact:

- The Compassionate Friends
- Bereaved Parents of the USA
- Mothers Against Drunk Driving
- Homicide victim support programs run by local district attorneys' offices
- Parents of Murdered Children
- SEASONS suicide support

Care providers may also find that older individuals can benefit from some coaching on how to seek information—for example, referring to local directories, accessing information from the library, or using the Internet. Many seniors appreciate it when they can find what they need themselves; it facilitates independence.

Study Findings: Older Adults and Self-Help Support Groups

Lund and Caserta (1992) have conducted longitudinal studies on how self-help bereavement groups help older seniors. Some of the groups that were studied ended after 8 weeks; others continued beyond 8 weeks on a monthly basis for 1 year. Their findings are listed here:

1. Participants derived help from helping others (the act of giving assistance to another person yields a sense of self-value and a useful activity).
2. The opportunity to share successes and disappointments provides valuable reciprocal emotional and social support.
3. Participants stated that entering a group within the first 4 months of bereavement was most beneficial since this was usually a very difficult time.
4. Being able to express thoughts and externalize feelings with others as well as keeping busy was very beneficial.

5. The best results were attained by participants who were actively involved in each group session.
6. Participants in the longer-term groups had greater benefits from the group experience than those in the shorter-term groups. The idea of attending a group and sitting and talking with strangers can be very daunting to a bereaved person.

Care providers and family members may need to raise the subject more than once. We use a "three-time rule"—we offer to arrange transportation and attend with the bereaved elder three times a few weeks apart. If after 2 or 3 months the senior has not expressed any interest in attending such a group, but seems to be in need of one, then we repeat the three-time offer. If self-help groups don't seem tenable, other activities may be feasible.

Workshops, Lectures, and Other Programs

These activities may be sponsored by all of the community organizations listed above, as well as recreational and/or educational programs—trips, classes, exercise programs, lunch programs, speakers, and movies. Senior centers represent a growing resource in local communities and may be sponsored by an office of aging, a community center, or religious-affiliated organization. Sometimes, the older bereaved person who attends these activities decides to seek professional help as the program material makes the elder aware of personal needs in specific aspects of physical and mental health.

Bereaved senior citizens may be sad and lonely but should never have to be isolated.

☐ Family Caregivers

When we discuss the older grieving person, we must discuss the *primary home caregiver*. This is usually a spouse, or sometimes an adult child or sibling of a seriously and/or terminally ill man or woman. It is estimated that about 80% of caregiving for the elderly is provided by a family member (Beery et al., 1997). Spouses caring for a terminally ill wife or husband living at home make up the majority of home caregivers. Many of these individuals, while not professionally trained, have typically received some form of care instructions from a home care nurse or other professional providers.

Health Risks for Family Caregivers

The family caregiver may grieve the loss of a once healthy loved one to terminal illness prior to the actual death. They may mourn not only in terms of anticipatory grief for the ultimate death of their spouse but also for all that they have given up in order to assume the caregiving role. Many show signs of pre-loss grief complications such as depression and anxiety (Beery et al., 1997). (See chapter 9 for complications of grief.)

Family caregivers frequently resist the term *caregiver* to describe their roles. They portray themselves rather as a wife, or husband, a sister or brother, a son or daughter. They often do not allow themselves adequate validation for the critical but often overwhelming tasks associated with providing constant care for a loved one. In spite of this, many describe their role as rewarding. Providers must recognize that they are at high risk for depression, resentment, physical fatigue, and illness. Some family caregivers have been known to treat their depression with tranquilizers and alcohol in an attempt to cope with the demands and stress of their responsibilities.

Loss of Future

One caregiving spouse lamented that she had lost the future she and her husband had planned for. The dream of having quality time as they grew older together was shattered. Some realize this gradually, others feel it as if they were hit by a devastating wall of reality. The buildup of resentment and frustration can cause the caregiver to have periodic explosions that can seem "out of proportion" to an outside observer. A visitor may be surprised to hear the anger that pours out, but may not be able to understand the path of problematic events that led up to the emotional release.

Loss of Freedom

For many, the realization of severe limitations on their own lives creeps in subtly and gradually as they find themselves increasingly unable to attend family and other events outside of their homes: a graduation or wedding, an outing with friends, a walk with a grandchild, or necessary shopping. Still others continually postpone their own health care appointments. For many, recognition of a shrinking social world comes abruptly after a hospitalization for stroke, heart attack, acute illness, or a traumatic injury.

For many aging adults, there is mutual caregiving that forms part of their couplehood. The balance can shift rather quickly when one falls or has an acute medical crisis, leaving them impaired. Many report a sense of growing "imprisonment" in the home and cite the reluctance of the loved one to have anyone else provide care while they have some time to themselves away from the home. They often say that they are not always aware of the grief, the resentment, or the guilt that is building within.

Caregiver Grief

Family caregivers (spouses, children, siblings, or close friends) are grieving people who have already lost the healthy, functional, and available aspects of the relationship with the care recipient. They also have lost the potential for engaging in activities that are outside of the caregiving responsibilities—they have lost the freedom to choose how to spend their time. Much energy is also consumed in medical, legal, insurance, and financial responsibilities of the caregiving role. Grief reaction is also triggered by anticipation of the actual loss of the loved one to death, dementia, or coma.

Care providers can play an important role in mitigating the risk of burn out to family caregivers by facilitating their awareness of the threat to their own physical and emotional health. The incidence of depression among family caregivers is not so much a result of involvement with the loved one's activities of daily living, but because of the caregiver's inability to engage in activities that are personally fulfilling and recreational. They need to be convinced to have periods of respite and cope with the objections of their loved one and arrange for other family members to participate in some of the home health care responsibilities. Engaging professional home health staff or hospice care will give the family caregiver an opportunity to take advantage of much needed downtime. Even a short break can reduce the potential for depression and enable family caregivers to regain their equilibrium.

The provider should also normalize the many reactions that family caregivers have: resentment, guilt, grief, anxiety, fatigue, depression, disorganization, and the feeling of being overwhelmed as well as feelings of being crazy. The goal is to help caregivers understand the humanness of their feelings and the need to take some action, not only to preserve their physical and emotional health but also to enable the provision of the best care for their loved ones. Providers can also refer family caregivers to the various community support groups that are becoming more and more available so that they can share their reactions, hear how others are coping, and know that they are not alone in this difficult role.

Support for Family Caregivers

Support services of various types have been growing in local communities. Some family caregivers have been able to avail themselves of support groups especially designed for their loved one's particular illness or condition. These may include support for family members caring for a loved one with cancer, Alzheimer's disease, dementia, Parkinson's, chronic illness, or memory loss, as well as workshops on how to balance caregiving and a career.

In all communities the area agency on aging provides education and selected direct services (such as respite) to family caregivers, funded by the National Family Caregivers Support Program (Administrator, Howard County, Maryland Office of Aging, Madachy, P., personal communication, April 30, 2004).

One local office of aging holds a day of workshops and lectures devoted to the needs of family caregivers. Some community agencies provide a training service for family caregivers by nurses who go into the home and teach basic nursing skills. There are respite programs where the caregiver can take time off and have a competent person provide the caregiving temporarily. These services charge a range of fees. There are many publications produced by regional agencies for aging adults that give suggestions for the caregiver's personal health and emotional care—including stress reduction and ways to balance the caregiving with meeting his or her own needs.

The issue for many home caregivers is their resistance to letting go of the role for some rest and recreation. The reason usually given is that they feel the care for their loved one will suffer if they are not the one providing it. In some instances, the loved one being cared for will resist having a substitute caregiver and block his or her caregiver from taking time off. Many local communities have day programs where ambulatory individuals can spend a day participating in activities and socializing with peers. This gives the family caregiver an opportunity to catch up on personal time and recharge their energy.

To summarize: Too many caregivers are not aware of the risks that "no time off" places on their own physical and emotional health, as well as the effects on the quality of care they can continue to render. Further, they may have no way of knowing what is available in their own community in the way of home caregiver support services.

Care providers should remember that family caregivers are knowingly or unknowingly coping with an ongoing bereavement for the loss of their loved one as he or she once was. While they may reject the idea of leaving him or her in the hands of another caregiver, the provider should make them aware of the benefits of respite and of the availability of a range of such support services in their local community. Providers are referred to regional agencies for aging adult care for available support services for family caregivers. (See appendix B for additional resources.)

When the Family Caregiver's Loved One Dies

Many family caregivers face a great emptiness when their loved one dies. The grief they feel is not only for the person who is now gone but also for the empty space and unfilled time left as a result of his or her death. There are various bereavement groups the caregiver can attend. In time, many people who served as family caregivers find themselves volunteering in a nursing home, hospice, or hospital where they can help others in need as they continue on their own grief journey. An experienced family caregiver can also be a great help to other caregivers. In this way, the illness and death of the loved one can ultimately become a gift to others.

☐ Conclusion

We have reviewed the realities of the various losses the older bereaved adult must cope with as he or she mourns a current death or serves as a caregiver to a loved one. Older persons must not only be able to grieve their losses but also reclaim life in a world that may appear to be less friendly than it once was.

Care providers should help the grieving older adult to obtain the support he or she needs in order to address Worden's four tasks for healing, to reach out for social support, to maintain their physical and emotional health, and to connect with spiritual resources where desired.

Providers must also reach out to family caregivers who are truly disenfranchised grievers. They need help both during the caregiving role and beyond to address their grief and to find new meaning in their post-loss life.

In chapter 7, we will look at the issues faced by families and their loved ones who are dying, terminally and/or chronically ill, or have a life-limiting disability. For the family and the dying loved one—the "end of life" experience can be both tragically devastating and a fulfilling spiritual experience.

CHAPTER **7**

Chronic Illness/Disability, Terminality, and Dying

"Illness is a family affair."

Richard M. Cohen (2004, p. xiv)

☐ Introduction

And now, the story of grief continues with the world, invisible to so many of us, of people who are coping with ongoing loss due to serious illness, chronic physical limitations, and those coping with the threat of the ultimate loss—death.

You never know whether the person walking by you has a loved one at home lying in a bed of pain or if the woman sitting at the next table in the coffee shop has just come from visiting a dear one who no longer recognizes her. You may not know that the man buying tickets at the theme park is waiting for a child with braces who is being helped out of the car in the handicapped parking space or that the family in the pew behind you is praying for a loved one who is in a coma and not expected to live much longer.

While attention is drawn to people who have a loved one actively dying or who have recently lost someone, chronic, life-limiting conditions become less attended to by friends and neighbors after a while. For some, *chronic* can indicate "we have become accustomed to the situation at the house down the street, and don't think about it much anymore." For the family members providing continuing care for the chronically ill, there is no such thing as forgetting about it; they cannot "turn their eyes away." They become part of a less visible world of grievers who must cope daily with both multiple, accumulating, and anticipated losses.

The Many Faces of Grief

As we have mentioned earlier, the human grief response is not reserved for death or separation only. In addition to the grief of the bereaved, care providers must also be aware of the grief experienced by those individuals who are seriously ill, those living with permanent physical or intellectual challenges, and those with a lingering terminal illness, as well as the grief of their family members. The climate of grief surrounding such families is often less understood than that of those who are bereaved. Consequently, these families may be less supported than those who have already lost a loved one. The difference comes from the fact that the ill, disabled, and dying persons are still here—breathing, eating, and requiring some level of care, love, and attention. Some are at home, yet many more are in hospitals, hospices, or nursing homes. Teno et al. (2004) found in a study of "last place of care" that about 70% of dying people are in a hospital or a nursing home. Of the remaining 30% who die at home, 36% have no nursing services, 12% have home nursing, while slightly more than 50% receive home hospice services.

The Dying

Tending to the dying requires a different consciousness than tending to the memory of the no-longer living. The expectations families have for health care services may be significantly inconsistent with the actual quality of the care delivered. According to the Teno et al. (2004) study, family perceptions of the quality of end-of-life care differed according to the location of the dying person. Families whose loved one died at home with hospice services reported the greatest overall satisfaction with care. However, about a fourth of all families reported that there was inadequate pain management, and roughly another fourth complained of insufficient help with breathing problems. Additionally, "many people dying in institutions have unmet needs for symptom amelioration, physician communication, emotional support, and being treated with respect" (Teno et al., p. 88).

When we convert the concerns of dying patients and their families into care provider goals, we arrive at five recommendations for providers. (See box below.)

Care providers working with dying persons must (a) be respectful of the patient, (b) provide physical comfort and emotional support, (c) engage the patient and family in decision-making, (d) include family members in the information loop and give them emotional support, and (e) coordinate the person's care regardless of the care setting.

Wherever the ill or chronically disabled person is in residence, the continuing grief of family members will be affected by medical reports, mood and symptoms of the ill person, reactions of the family as well as interactions with medical and other care providers. The more effectively care is coordinated, the greater the potential for patient and family well-being.

Regardless of where the ill loved one is—at home, in a hospital room, a nursing home, rehabilitation center, or other residential setting—all care providers will need to communicate with other staff who are concerned with the case: nurses, physicians, aides, pastoral care, mental health staff, and volunteers. For optimal care, it is vital that all care providers involved in the care of a family's loved one have a cooperative team approach and respect for the various contributions each team member makes.

☐ Definitions and Statistical Realities

Definitions

Palliative Care

Palliative care has as its primary aim the provision of comfort and enhancement of quality of life for people with advanced life-threatening disease, and assistance for their families. It means that the primary medical treatment goals have changed—medical teams are no longer seeking a cure. Instead, the intent is to provide a broad range of support, comfort, and freedom from the pain and debilitating side effects of medicines and procedures. Palliative care is described as "patient centered"—that is, the focus is on sick or disabled people rather than on disease or medical technology (Institute of Medicine, 1997). The goal is to "address the physical, psychological, social, and spiritual needs of patients with advanced disease and their families" (Addington-Hall, 2002). Palliative care can be provided at home, in hospitals, hospices, nursing homes, and other residential settings.

The six skill areas of palliative care are (a) communication, (b) decision-making, (c) management of complications, (d) symptom control, (e) psychosocial care of patient and family, and (f) care of the dying (Institute of Medicine, 2001). These care goals require full communication with the patient and family about the illness and prognosis as well as involving them in decision-making regarding care options. There is management of the treatment side effects to further the goal of comfort and control of such symptoms as pain, weakness, nausea, constipation, and depression (National Cancer Institute, 2003).

Hospice

Hospice is a program that offers palliative care from a multidisciplinary staff. These services are provided at home, in dedicated hospital rooms, or in freestanding hospice facilities for people who are terminally ill—typically in the U.S. with 6 months or less to live.

According to Dame Cicely Saunders (2002), well known for her role in the establishment of the hospice movement in Great Britain, hospice care provides a program of care that affirms a quality of life free from pain, supports the dignity of individuals, helps people to deal with emotional distress, and seeks new ways to understand the quality of life as one is dying. Hospice further supports the completion of important end-of-life-arrangements and includes the family and friends as an important part of the care.

Dying Person

The dying person is a person with a life-threatening illness who may be at any point along the living–dying interval (i.e., the time period from diagnosis to death). Many U.S. hospice programs, however, will not accept persons who have longer than a 6-month life expectancy.

Life-Threatening Illness

This is an illness that may be chronic by virtue of its lingering nature and usually results in an individual's death. Examples are the following: cancer, acquired immunodeficiency virus (AIDS), amytrophic lateral sclerosis (ALS), multiple sclerosis, cystic fibrosis, emphysema, end-stage renal disease, advanced cardiac illness, Parkinson's, Huntington's, and Alzheimer's disease.

Chronic Illness

While this category overlaps with life-threatening disease conditions, the people who are chronically disabled from illness, injury, or developmental disorders are not necessarily faced with immediate threats to their mortality. Their conditions are *life-limiting,* often requiring long-term care. In these situations, there is a significant impact on the quality of life for the individual as well as for his or her family. Examples include the following: traumatic brain injury; mental retardation; permanent paralysis; diabetes; hepatitis; dementia; cognitive, intellectual, and developmental disabilities; and certain psychiatric disorders.

Shortly after our son Steven died, I had an interaction with a friend who has a developmentally disabled daughter. She told me that she suffered a "death-like" loss when she learned that her child would have profound life limitations. People with a loved one who was born with or develops a severely life-limiting disability often report feeling the "death of their dream of how it should have been."

Family

I use *family* in both the conventional sense, referring to people who are related by birth or marriage, and also for people who live together and spend much of their lives in close proximity because of social and occupational needs. Examples may include life partners; very closely connected friendship; groups; work teams who are dependent on each other, such as fire, police, rescue, and military groups; and closely knit faith communities.

Statistical Realities

Table 7.1 lists the leading causes of death for the year 2002 in the United States. Many of these deaths come after varying periods of chronic illness, requiring care for months and in some cases years. Table 7.2 provides estimates of selected newly diagnosed life-threatening conditions.

There are an estimated 50 million family caregivers in the United States (U.S. Department of Health and Human Services, 1998), and 50 million are grieving for ill and disabled loved ones.

To restate the significance of the 1,716,033 deaths reported in Table 7.1, many of the deaths represent months and years of families coping with lingering, life-threatening illness. For instance, it is estimated that 9 million persons in the United States have a history of cancer and that in 2002 about 1.3 million people were diagnosed with cancer (National Institutes of Health, 2002). The 58,785 Alzheimer's deaths for 2002 no doubt took place after years of agonizing progressive loss and family caregiving. The American Brain Injury Association reports that 1.5 million people in the United States sustain a traumatic brain injury (TBI) annually and that an estimated 5.3 million people currently live with disabilities resulting from TBI (Centers for Disease Control, 2001).

Table 7.2 presents several of the debilitating medical conditions that have an impact on people and their families. We must, however, also add to this list such additional conditions as developmental, cognitive, and emotional impairments and disorders. The sheer volume of terminally and chronically ill who require care points to the growing need for family caregivers and professional care providers and volunteers to work with ill, disabled, and dying persons and help them with their continuing grief reactions.

TABLE 7.1. Leading Causes of Death, 2002, United States

Diseases of the heart	695,754
Cancer	558,847
Stroke	163,010
Chronic lower respiratory	125,500
Diabetes	73,119
Alzheimer's	58,785
Diseases of the kidneys	41,018
	1,716,033

Source: National Vital Statistics Center, The Centers for Disease Control and Prevention (2004), p. 4.

TABLE 7.2. Annual Estimates of Newly Diagnosed Cases of Selected Life-Threatening Conditions

Traumatic brain injury	1,500,000[1]
Breast cancer	175,000[2]
HIV/AIDS	43,681[3]
Spinal cord injury	11,000[4]
Multiple sclerosis	10,400[5]

[1]CDC. (2001) "TBI in the US: A Report to Congress"
[2]American Cancer Society. (1999) "Cancer facts and figures: Selected cancers."
[3]CDC. (2001) "HIV/AIDS Surveillance report, US HIV and AIDS cases reported through Dec. 1999."
[4]CDC. (2001) "Safe USA—What you should know about SCI."
[5]Multiple Sclerosis Society. (2001) "MS, the disease."

☐ The Relationship Between the Sick, Dying, or Grieving Person and the Care Provider

While the care provider can be identified as a professional or volunteer with a specific helping role, and the sick, dying, or grieving person as the recipient of this help, the formal distinction between the two can melt away as two human beings merge in this relationship. The *exquisite witness* care provider connects with the person in need at a level of human being to human being—beyond titles, beyond medical treatment procedures. In this way, the helping person can provide a level of presence that provides a safe place for the person being served to explore feelings and thoughts regarding his or her life and death.

A friend with whom Isadora Duncan went to stay after her two young children drowned demonstrates the essence of this relationship. Her friend encouraged her to repeat all their little sayings and ways. The friend never told her to stop her grieving, but grieved with her, and for the first time since their death, Isadora felt she was not alone (Duncan, 1927).

The relationship between the care provider and the grieving person is complex. A sacred trust is developed between two human beings. The trusting nature of the relationship is not based on a care provider's professional degree, but rather on the capacity to be present to the person receiving care. I heard a story about a 4-year-old boy who visited his next-door neighbor whose wife had just died. He walked over to the man and climbed up into his lap. When he returned to his mother she asked him what he said to the man. The boy replied that he didn't say anything.

He just "helped him cry." Many grieving people yearn for a helping person who will simply help them cry and feel the feelings of grief without any judgments, time limits, and admonitions to move on with life.

Following is a personal reflection of my work with a man with AIDS that illustrates the relationship between the care provider and a terminally ill person.

> I looked into the eyes of the dying man and I thought to myself, "I wonder if he's thinking what I'm thinking. I wonder if he's thinking that in an hour I will leave this hospital and go home, and he will still be here. I wonder if he's thinking, as we talk about his depression and his sense of helplessness and doom, that he is very, very ill, and I am well. I wonder if he's thinking——that he is dying, and I am not?"
>
> What do I see when I look and listen to him? Often, I see more than sadness, more than isolation. I see much more. I see a masked rage at the losses that have occurred and continue to occur as the virus ravages his body, disfigures him with cancerous lesions, wastes his muscles and flesh, drains his energy, and prematurely ends forever the social and professional life he so much enjoyed. I see his anger for so many men already dead of AIDS, which intrudes itself as a dreaded interruption of life, a loss of control, and as the messenger carrying the horror of a death sentence. There is more than a man with AIDS lying there in that bed. There is a past that continues to play a role in who he is. There is a present that bears down hard on his physical and mental self. And there is a future that is uncertain at best. And here am I, a man still able to plan a future and in this way different from him, and committed to his care.

Working with the Dying

For many care providers, working with dying people is profoundly satisfying and uplifting spiritually. Others are affected in ways that make them view their work as futile and depressing. Sometimes this happens because many of the people do not get well and the effects of their illnesses can be devastating to some care providers. Sick people and their loved ones may be very sad. Further, a care provider's own Cowbells (personal loss material) may become overwhelming. Their own unfinished material around grief and loss prevents them from being sufficiently available to those who need care. As a result, care providers may feel burned-out, develop physical or emotional problems, and provide less than optimal care for their clients. In most cases when such individuals take the time to identify and discuss their own unfinished business (Cowbells) with a trusted friend or colleague, most are better able to be available to seriously ill, dying, and bereaved people. Some care providers, however, are unable to get past a sense of futility and depression. They may say, "I only want to work with people who are going to get well." In such cases a change of work setting is a good idea. Care providers are needed in all types of health care settings; and those who need to move on to other venues deserve our support to do so.

What does "dying" mean? What do you say to a dying person or to the spouse, or child, or sibling, or parent, or best friend of a dying person? How do you offer comfort without crushing hope or raising it unrealistically? What do you ask? What can you do to help?

When I enter the room of a dying person, I feel as if I am entering a sacred place. It may be dark or brightly lit; the television may be blaring or it may be very quiet; it may be hot and have an unpleasant odor. It is not unusual for a seriously ill or dying person to confide in me about concerns that they feel they cannot discuss with their families. Often, they want to protect other family members from pain. I may not speak very much; I hope to listen intently.

Being with a person who is at the very end of life can be an awesome experience. Family members need to be encouraged to use the final hours or moments to the fullest. I make every effort, within the scope of family and cultural traditions, to facilitate conversation, physical contact, saying good-bye/facilitate forgiveness in whatever way the family members are willing or able to do so. This may also be a time for religious or spiritual practices. The final moments with a dying loved one remain as a "memory photo" throughout a lifetime.

Visiting the Dying

Before I make a visit, I seek the following information in order to learn as much as possible in advance:

- The nature of the illness or condition that the individual is coping with;
- The history of this person's medical condition;
- Who the primary family or other caregivers are;
- The family history and current functioning;
- The amount of medical information already shared with the person and with the family;

- The cultural background and religious belief system of the ill person and family;
- The extent of outside support systems for this person and the family.

> *Care providers* should view the patient's room at home, in the hospital, or nursing facility, as the province of the dying person and his or her family. Permission should always be requested before entering, and providers should make an effort to match their volume of speaking to that of the patient and family members. Suggestions should be offered rather than stated as commands or requirements. Effective listening skills will enable providers to learn what medical information the family knows, the way that people are relating to each other, and how they are interacting with their dying loved one. Care provider Cowbells must be attended to so that negative energy is not brought into the setting.

☐ Five Rights That Preserve Patient Dignity

It is the responsibility of the care provider to facilitate preserving the dignity of the person with a life-threatening illness. Five rights or ways to preserve the dignity of dying people are listed below and described in the following text.

1. The right to know as much of the truth as can be handled.
2. The right to be free of pain and have hope for some quality of life.
3. The right to participate in decision-making at one or more levels of care.
4. The right to talk about death when ready.
5. The right to externalize emotional feelings and complete unfinished business.

The Right to Know as Much of the Truth as Can Be Handled

Patients and their families have a right to know about their condition. Such information gives them a sense of control and a framework for thinking about the future. Care providers can arrange for members of the medical or nursing staff to deliver health-associated information to a seriously ill or dying person and his or her family. Before arranging for this, it is important to check with the individual and/or family to determine what has already been conveyed and to get a sense of whether additional information is desired or if any material needs to be clarified.

It's essential that patients learn only as much as they really want to know. I once worked with a woman who seemed very eager to more fully understand her prognosis. Yet after the doctor spoke with her, she became distressed and regretted her decision. I realized that I should have spent more time discussing with her what she believed was already happening to her body and how much additional information she truly was seeking. One way to prevent overloading a person with information is to give it in small increments and stop as soon as verbal or nonverbal cues indicate a negative reaction.

The Right to Be Free of Pain and Have Hope for Some Quality of Life

Strange as it may seem, hope can always be part of a dying person's worldview. When I work with clients, I always explain that hope is on a continuum. We begin by hoping we stay healthy. If a terrible diagnosis is received, we hope there was a mistake. When we know the diagnosis is accurate, we hope for a cure. When a cure is not possible, we hope for long remissions and a quality of life that is pain free; one where we retain control and personal dignity. When the end of life comes, we can hope for a peaceful, pain-free death with our loved ones close by. Finally, we can hope that our loved ones will heal after we're gone.

The Right to Participate in Decision-Making at One or More Levels of Care

The antidote for depressing and anxiety-producing helplessness that many dying people experience is for the individual to participate in as many choices as possible. This is an extension of the already existing right that patients have in making decisions about their health care, even the right to refuse treatment and life-support measures. Even though seriously ill or dying people cannot take as active a role in making health-related decisions, they can still maintain some control over their lives. They can decide to raise or lower the bed, how to rearrange their pillows, when to have a bath or be moved, whether the TV should be on or off, what food to eat, whom to see during visiting hours, and what music to listen to.

The Right to Talk About Death When Ready

Many dying people complain that they never have an opportunity to discuss dying. However, many families do talk about dying—away from the loved one. I've frequently had family members whisper to me, "The doctor said it won't be more than a day or two, but we really haven't talked to Mom about this, and no one wants to be the one to upset her." There is often an unwritten agreement that the family won't bring it up and the dying person won't ask. The care provider can offer an opportunity to talk about this final phase of a person's life with the individual and encourage family members to do so as well when appropriate.

The Right to Externalize Emotional Feelings and Complete Unfinished Business

Dying people who want to externalize their feelings of grief, rage, and fear should be provided opportunities to do so. In this situation, the care provider becomes an exceptional listener, allowing the dying person the chance to express all feelings. Care providers need to be prepared to stay with the person for as long as needed at a particular session. During this process, the dying person may bring up unfinished material about other relationships.

It is also easy for a very ill person who is in pain and emotional distress to keep his or her feelings locked up inside. The ill person may believe that such feelings are inappropriate or too unpleasant to talk about. He or she may be reluctant to share these feelings with family members in order to protect them from pain. Families may be uncomfortable with the true feelings of their dying loved one, and this may inhibit honest expression by both the family and the loved one. The release of stored feelings can aid in emotional healing before death by allowing the dying person to focus his or her energy on saying good-bye and letting go. In chapter 8 we further discuss externalization of emotional pain and the care provider skills required to facilitate this activity.

Care providers can ask the person what he or she is thinking about or ask, "Have you ever had any thoughts about what may happen when your body just wants to stop working?" "Do you have some thoughts about what is happening in your body at this point?" The dying person may be very relieved to finally be able to talk about the forbidden topic. At other times the dying person may not want to talk about death with the family in order to protect them from pain. In these cases, the care provider can offer the patient the opportunity to have a discussion about dying. Even a short talk can be useful. However, sometimes the dying person does not want to talk about it. This must be respected with no pressure. It's important to avoid saying things like, "I'll come back later to see if you've changed your mind." Say instead, "We can talk about whatever you wish, whenever you wish."

☐ What to Expect from the Dying Person

The Dying Person

The dying person is a grieving person, and the grief begins very early in the process, perhaps as early as the first awareness of troubling and persistent symptoms. Dying people are unique in some important respects from other people in their lives and are different from each other as well.

I've found that some dying people:

Can be so drained by their disease that they do not have much energy left over for thinking about dying, death, and the consequences for all concerned.

Are likely to be sick at heart knowing that they will be leaving loved ones, their life activities, and their hopes and dreams for the future. At the same time, they are filled with uncertainty, wondering what's ahead as the reality of their death permeates their conscious awareness.

May appear to have adapted to the idea of life ending for them and the awareness of their loved ones' grief.

May be able to place the ending of their lives into the broader context of their religious beliefs and their belief in God; in a secular, universal philosophy of life; or the concept of life-after-death as depicted in the media and literature.

Can be frantic, panicked, depressed, and very frightened at what will happen to them during the active dying process—"Will I be gasping for air?" "Will I be in excruciating pain?"—and fear of what it will be like after death—"Blackness?" "Oblivion?" "Heaven?" "Some other dimension of existence?" "Reincarnation?" "Be with deceased loved ones?"

May be comatose much of the time and uncommunicative, or wax and wane between alertness and sleep due to a morphine drip or to the effects of such medical conditions as renal or congestive heart failure, encephalopathy, or septicemia.

Can be withdrawn, fatigued, drained, depressed, and in this state cannot be expected to interact very much with their family caregivers and visitors.

All these varied reactions have an effect on family members, friends, and others who are close to the dying person. They are all grieving people, coping with losses due to the illness as well as loss that anticipates the death of the loved one.

The Final Hours

Sometimes family members will not know what to do in the final hours and minutes of their dying loved one's life. They may sit in the room, nearby or at a distance, looking at their loved one—or trying not to look. Some may congregate outside the room—waiting. They say things like, "He isn't really here anymore," or "She isn't really Mom anymore." Still others may climb right into bed and embrace the dying man or woman. They may hold the person's hand, caress her face or wipe it with a damp cloth, or touch her arm, neck, or shoulders. They may talk to their dying loved one, saying, "I love you." They may express gratitude and find a way to say "good-bye." Some ask for or give forgiveness if this has not already been done.

Care providers should be aware that not everyone is able to have such a close physical and final connection. Providers should educate or even coach family members who are hesitant about staying close by to remain in the room, to talk to the dying loved one, to touch his or her feet and/or hands, and to say whatever they need to say by way of good-bye. Once they see and hear the last breath and know that life is over, they can acknowledge that death has come. They may want to hear the physician pronounce the loved one dead. They can even touch their loved one or wash his or her hands and feet. Sometimes, people who were unable to be in the room to witness the death wish to come in afterward to say good-bye either silently or out loud or through some form of physical contact. People typically find this closeness at the time of death to be not nearly as scary as they imagined it would be. Rather, they experience it as an opportunity to make a final emotional and spiritual connection. They may experience it as a sacred time. Remember though that cultural traditions differ, especially with regard to physical contact at the time of death and afterward. The care provider needs to learn what the family's traditions require at this time.

For many, healing begins during the moments of close contact at the time of death and immediately after death. Even though a patient is comatose or has been pronounced dead, it is useful for the loved ones to say their good-byes. Prayers offered later, at funerals or memorial services, at graveside or at home, are also an important part of the healing process for mourners. For those loved ones who are comfortable with a belief that a spiritual connection has been made, some healing and the beginning of a new form of bond with the deceased has begun (Bowlby, 1980).

Here is an account of a family's experience with end-of-life bonding.

> A young physician on weekend duty was called in to see an elderly woman who was dying on an inpatient medical unit. He was surprised to find only one visitor standing outside of the woman's room. When he inquired as to the whereabouts of the rest of the family, he was informed that a number of others, including the woman's adult children and her grandchildren, had been sent home so Grandma "could die in peace." He immediately had the lone relative phone all of the family who had been sent away and had them all return. He invited them into the room, had them circle the bed, make physical contact with the dying woman, and say their loving good-byes to her. Later as they departed, they tearfully thanked the doctor for enabling this never-to-be-forgotten gift. This was their "memory photo."

The physician in the story is Steven's brother, Dr. Ronald Jeffreys.

☐ Factors Impacting the Dying Person and Family

There are 12 important factors described below that directly impact the family of a terminally ill loved one.

The Heartbreak of Remission and Relapse

People undergoing treatment for cancer and other illnesses must have frequent tests to determine the growth of the tumor or the progress of their disease. Their hopes rise and are dashed depending on the outcome of these tests. Life begins to feel like a perpetual roller coaster, continually up and down. As the time for the next blood test, spinal tap, or x-ray gets closer, the whole family can become very tense as thoughts dwell on the possible outcome. Sometimes they breathe a long sigh of relief, and at other times they gasp in horror at the diminishing odds for survival. There can be long intervals of remission where the family begins to emerge from a type of darkness and have some real hope. The ill loved one may appear to look healthier and act like his or her old self again. Life at home starts to regain a less dread-filled atmosphere. This can continue for a long enough period to be considered a cure. The family and medical staff may then be lulled into an expectation that "It's going to be OK!" Then, a follow-up lab report pulls the rug out from under them, and the care provider will need to be in close support to help the family deal with their renewed grief.

A study of fathers who had children with life-threatening illnesses (Davies et al., 2004) describes the raising and diminishing of their hope for their children's survival. Fathers portrayed this experience as "living in the dragon's shadow." Even when remission occurred or treatment was concluded, the shadow of the underlying illness (the dragon) haunted their thoughts. I recall the never-ending and recurring fear that would arise during Steven's periods of remission. There would always be another blood test or spinal tap waiting up ahead to confirm that he was still in remission. We were never really at peace.

Grief Reactions

In addition to grief over the loss of remission, grief occurs for losses already incurred during the course of the illness, as well as for the anticipated future loss of the loved one. The family is bereaved well before the terminally ill person actually dies. Grieving occurs as a result of what has already been lost in terms of the loved one's limitations, discomfort, and distress. Elisabeth Kubler-Ross has often referred to this as the thousand deaths that occur before the actual death. This is seen dramatically with people who have ALS (Lou Gehrig's disease) where functions are disappearing, seemingly inch-by-inch, week by week. Each upsetting change may bring on additional grief from the person with ALS and his or her family members.

Changes in Social Life

Loss of work and other social roles shrink the world of a dying person. The dying person has to let go of an increasing number of attachments. These include the connections to people in the workplace, in the neighborhood, and in community activities, and to family members who may live a distance away or even others who choose to avoid the situation as much as possible. As a person's illness progresses, the dying individual and his or her loved ones may recede more and more from social contact as do the expectations of others for their participation in social events significantly diminishes.

Financial Pressures

Loss of income and the costs of treatment and care may drain financial resources and intensify stress among family members. Even good medical insurance may not cover all charges. Financial statements from various specialists, laboratories, and other health care services show up in the mail monthly to remind the family what is *not* being covered by insurance. Loss of family income due to caregiver responsibilities creates further anxiety for the loved ones.

Physical Pain, Impairment, Disfigurement, and Fatigue

Relentless pain and physical limitations create depression as do the upsetting changes in appearance. The "face" of illness is very apparent to the sick person as well as to the others in his or her life. When my cousin was in the later stages of AIDS, he would tell me that when he looked in the mirror he now saw "Auschwitz." During the course of a long-term debilitating illness, the loss of strength, control over hands and fingers, bladder, and bowel all add to the multiple losses accumulating and adding to the individual's and the family's grief.

Emotional Distress

Many people experience depression, demoralization, and anxiety that wear away at the dying person's and loved one's abilities to have hope and the strength to cope, and to maintain the medication and other care procedures. This additional stress and tension deprives the ill person of the stamina to deal with the distress of the illness and contributes to hopelessness.

Existing Family Dysfunction

Pre-existing and newly developed conflicts take their toll on the dying person and the family members. This may interfere with care and further demoralize the terminally ill loved one. Some families observe a truce during the interval between life and death. Others are simply unable to do so. It is very important that wherever the loved one is—at home or in a hospice, nursing, or rehabilitation facility—the care provider be aware of such energy-draining issues and help the family with resolving conflicts and focusing on gathering resources to cope with the health care needs of their ill loved one. When conflict resolution is not possible, it will be necessary to keep the energy of negative interactions far away from the loved one.

The Reactions of Others to Progressive Decline

Dying people are often jolted to the reality of their illness by watching the faces of those who come to visit them. Often these faces register the decline in the patient's health since the last visit and remind the patient of the inevitability of approaching death. Some dying people want everything to be above board; they want honesty and openness with everyone. Others are glad not to have any negative reactions shown to them.

Degree of Information and Uncertainty

Most people I have worked with report that knowing their diagnosis and its implications reduces their anxiety and allows them the structure and direction to make plans for treatment and care. Lack of knowledge can make people feel uncertain, despairing, and fearful. There are some who appear to be content with little information, however, and say they are leaving it all in the hands of their doctors. In some cultures, medical information is given to a designated family member other than the ill person. The family determines when, what, and how much information is shared with the ill loved one.

Dependency

Many dying people are terrified that they will have to depend on others for their basic needs. This kind of dependency is another assault on their self-image. In *Tuesdays With Morrie* (Albom, 1997), Morrie Schwartz, a man with ALS (Lou Gehrig's disease), says that he is horrified by the thought of another person having to wipe his backside. However, when the time arrived that Morrie actually needed this kind of care, he was able to appreciate and accept it. There are activities of daily living that a seriously ill person or one who is physically limited due to illness or injury has to surrender to another person. For some, this is initially a very difficult loss of personal dignity. Care providers must be sensitive to this shift in status in dependence. For people who have been very independent, this may be a very painful loss.

Painful Procedures and Medication Side Effects

Much of the physical and emotional distress of cancer patients and others who are receiving chemotherapy comes from the side effects of the medications: hair loss, nausea, vomiting, weakness, itching, and vulnerability to infection. Medical procedures can be uncomfortable at best and very painful at worst. For some, chemotherapy must be discontinued because of the seriousness of the side effects. Other progressive illnesses have their own distressing medication side effects and procedures—spinal taps, mylograms, and painful injections—which add to the total suffering of patient and family.

Difficult Decisions and Upsetting Dilemmas

Having to make decisions regarding treatment and care can create painful and upsetting dilemmas for dying patients and their families. Each treatment has its negative effects. With increased choices, there is the potential for increased anxiety. Medicine frequently offers a patient and family several options, and each has its good and not so good aspects. Side effects and potential risks have to be considered. Fathers in the Davies et al. (2004) study commented that they often had to make what seemed like split-second decisions about a medical treatment.

Having to make medical choices that have major consequences on the outcome of a loved one's survival as well as his or her level of discomfort can place a family in an agonizing position and add greatly to the already existing high stress level.

Care providers can help the family get all of the information they need to make the best choice at any given time. Providers need to help families think through their issues involved with the above factors and know when to call in other resources, such as members of the clergy, medical, and mental health professionals.

☐ The Needs of the Patient's Family

The family and friends of a very sick and dying loved one may feel as though they are trapped in a nightmare. The situation can be frightening, draining, painful, unrelenting, and seemingly endless. In reality, there is an end—the death of the very ill person. The conscious acknowledgment of this usually invokes a guilt reaction in the family member or friend.

People may feel anger and resentment over the restrictions in their lives, the cost of care, the time they spend visiting and tending to other details, and the emotional ups and downs that ravage their emotional stability. Family members may feel that their lives and future plans are suspended and that they will remain that way as long as their loved one lives and requires the care that they are providing.

In sum, the dying person's family has a set of needs and all care providers can play a role in meeting these needs. Below is an abbreviated list of care provider actions for meeting family needs. Each of the items is expanded further. Care providers can play a significant role in meeting the family's needs by:

Normalizing the family's feelings;
Providing for the needs of all members;
Helping to balance denial and acceptance;
Facilitating accurate, clear, and open communication;
Continuing to relate to the dying person as a member of the family;
Balancing the person's increasing dependency with autonomy;
Helping with grief, anticipatory grief, and guilt;
Helping family members say good-bye;
Assisting with the event of dying and after-death rituals.

Normalizing the Family's Feelings

Many grieving people question whether some of their feelings are disloyal or inappropriate. They are often angry at the dying person and at the intrusion of the illness into their lives. Secretly, they may wish that it "were all over," and then experience intense feelings of guilt and shame. People need to know that all of these feelings are simply part of the process. One of the benefits of participating in support groups for family of persons with life-threatening conditions is the opportunity for hearing that other family caregivers also feel angry, resentful, depressed, and/or guilty.

Care providers will let families know, preferably in advance, how usual the above reactions are. Family members are typically very relieved to know that they are not bad or disloyal to their loved one if they feel resentful, irritated, or guilty. Where local support groups for family members of patients with Alzheimer's, cancer, Crohn's disease/colitis, and lung disease are available, these should be offered so that the family anguish may be reduced.

Providing for the Needs of All Members

Some family and extended family members get overlooked during the course of a loved one's illness. Children, elders, in-laws, classmates, colleagues, and neighbors are among those who may be disenfranchised during the living—dying interval and after death as well. Care providers should alert the family in advance to the needs of these important but frequently less noticed members of the dying person's social network. Effort should be made to include them at appropriate times—information updates, organizing support services, rituals, organized visiting, and healing prayer circles. Family friends can shop or do other basic chores, keep a fresh supply of flowers in the room, read aloud to the ill person, pray with him or her, relay neighborhood or workplace gossip, or just sit quietly with him or her.

Care providers can include the disenfranchised by giving them information and involving them in some aspects of the caregiving. Children should have an opportunity to spend time with the dying person even if he or she is comatose. They can make cards or other artwork and bring it to the bedside and be given an opportunity to ask questions or share feelings afterward.

Providers can also arrange informational services for the larger community of the dying person. If a child is dying, for instance, the care provider can arrange for a counselor or nurse to visit the child's classroom to relay information about the sick child and answer questions. Similarly, a care provider can arrange for an employee assistance counselor or human resource staff person to speak to the colleagues of an ill person in the workplace. Note: Always check to see if the family approves of such activities.

Helping to Balance Denial and Acceptance

Throughout the living–dying interval and after the death of the loved one, family members will use various levels of denial to cope with grief. At the beginning of the process, the care provider may need to help family members balance their desire to avoid the reality of the terminal illness with their need to accept it. Families can be helped to acknowledge the true nature of the medical condition if they are encouraged to obtain accurate medical information, share their feelings with each other (if this behavior is appropriate for this family's traditions), and organize caregiving activities such as gathering medical, financial, spiritual, and logistical resources.

The care provider's interventions regarding denial depends on the nature and effects of the denial. Providers need to understand that some denial is healthy and that each case is unique and should be evaluated individually. For example, a dying woman who was making plans for her funeral decided to purchase a new car. Her family supported this because it gave her a sense of control and made her feel happy. In this case, the care provider did not intervene to prevent the car's purchase. However, in another case, a care provider did intervene when a couple decided to put all of their savings into buying an expensive new home even though the husband had terminal AIDS. This decision, rooted in denial, was a potential financial disaster for the wife. When the couple reevaluated and discussed the home buying with their accountant, they dropped the plans prior to settlement.

Facilitating Accurate, Clear, and Open Communication

Each family has its own unique way of understanding and communicating medical information. Many families use the language of medical technology as fluently as their doctors and are familiar with treatment options and the statistical realities of survival. Other families—because of education, language barriers, family communication styles, or by choice—appear to know little about the medical options and treatment plans. Often, one family member serves as the communication bridge between the dying person and the rest of the family, and sometimes to the various care providers on the health team as well. The person in this role may need to be present when medical or nursing providers are supplying medical information. If appropriate, he or she can plan to meet or use a telephone conference call with the other members of the family to share information.

Children should also be included in family-wide discussions when appropriate, or at least be given the information arising from such discussions. They are often asked by neighbors about the health of an ill family member and need to be able to respond comfortably or to feel comfortable saying that they can't respond. I have found it useful to talk to children separately so that they can express feelings and raise questions away from family adults.

The care provider must determine how much information the family really requires, what's preventing the information that they want from getting through, and who and how best to communicate the information so it will be understood. A good way to initiate a conversation about this is to ask a general question regarding what the family already knows about the patient's medical condition and proceed from there.

Providers working with the family should obtain parental permission before speaking with children. Children should be given an opportunity to express their concerns and their needs. The conversation should be confidential unless health and/or safety issues arise.

Continuing to Relate to the Dying Person as a Member of the Family

My wife was visiting her mother in a nursing home when the physician stopped in. He checked my mother-in-law's vital signs and started to relate his findings to my wife. "Talk to me!" my mother-in-law told him in a powerful voice she hadn't used since her condition began to deteriorate.

It's so easy for care providers or family members to forget to honor the dignity of an ill and/or dying person. Some simply talk to each other about the dying person as if he or she were not in the room. You can easily imagine how irrelevant the dying person must feel. While there are some cultures that view medical decisions as the family's responsibility and not the patient's, care providers should make every effort to encourage continued involvement of the dying person as much as possible where this is not in conflict with family or cultural traditions. Always ask if you are not sure.

> *Care providers* can also help families sustain their relationship with the dying person. Many times, families withdraw prematurely—they stop visiting comatose Grandpa on sunny days, and then stop visiting altogether. In these cases the family needs to be reminded not to abandon the dying person. It's not always satisfying to spend time with people who are drifting in and out of a coma or who have dementia, but it is important for family to be there in case the fog does lift—if only for a few moments—and provide the dying loved one with the opportunity to talk to the family and say whatever still needs to be said.

Another form of discounting the ill person is to treat him or her like an infant. I heard a health care worker say to an older ill gentleman, "Are we going to be a good boy and make all gone our dinner today?" The old man spit the food out, cursed, and said, "The only thing I want all gone today is you! Just who do you think you are talking to, a 1-year-old?" Infantilizing very sick persons denies them their dignity. Even when they are not as verbally emphatic as this man or perhaps not even saying anything, they are likely thinking in the same way. I have had such reactions to being patronized quietly confided to me later. One older dying woman kept firing her home health aides as a way to let everyone know she was still lucid and in charge of her care.

> *Care providers* can remind families to accord dying loved ones the respect they are due. Even patients who have regressed mentally and/or emotionally need to be treated with respect.

Balancing the Person's Increasing Dependency with Autonomy

As mentioned earlier, one way to preserve the dignity of a very ill and dying person is to continue to keep him or her involved in making decisions about health care and treatment options. Care providers need to find ways to maintain a person's autonomy as much as possible. For example, if a patient were no longer able to go to the toilet, the next step would be to use a bedside commode rather than go right to a bedpan. In this way, the person still feels some control over care.

Care providers can help the family caregiver identify intermediary steps in terms of bathing, eating, and other functions of daily life. The goal is to preserve the individual's dignity and provide opportunities for the person to continue to make choices as long as possible.

Helping with Grief, Anticipatory Grief, and Guilt

A family who has a dying loved one is already grieving. As the disease progresses, they have had to cope with multiple losses as the loved one's condition worsens and his or her appearance changes before their eyes. In addition to the deterioration of the body and diminished functioning of the loved one, there are losses due to changes in the family system. Things the family can no longer do and/or things that they now must do alter the normal family patterns. Family members are learning to let go. At the same time, the family is also envisioning what's to come: the death, the funeral, and life without their loved one. This is anticipatory mourning. The care provider can help a family move through this process by encouraging them to talk about their thoughts and feelings.

Care providers can help family members to understand the grief reactions that occur long before a loved one has died. Explaining and normalizing the grief response may ease any guilt and remorse that may arise when a family member engages in fantasies of the loved one's death. Care providers should help family members understand that they may be grieving over what has already been lost as well as for the anticipation of what is yet to be lost. They should be assured that such feelings are completely normal and are a part of the grief reaction.

Helping Family Members Say Good-Bye

Saying good-bye may occur at every step of the journey from terminal diagnosis to the moment of death. I find it useful to ask family members what they feel they need to say in order to say good-bye. Good-byes can be said silently or out loud and at any point in the process. People will usually have a sense of what they want to say even if the person has slipped into a coma. If they need assistance, the care provider can suggest some general ideas of what to say and then let people fill in their own details.

Assisting with the Event of Dying and After-Death Rituals

We come into the world with a single breath, and we leave after a single breath. As life has begun, so it is finished. Most medical personnel at a hospital or hospice describe to families what may occur during the moments of death. Knowing this in advance is very useful and allows the family members to stay in physical and verbal contact with the dying loved one as he or she slips away. Saying final words and touching the person, as life is suddenly no more, can give them an experience of the sacredness.

Care providers need to be prepared for a variety of emotional reactions on the part of the survivors; some become agitated, some cry and sob, some withdraw into silence. Unless requested or if it is obvious that a loved one is in extreme distress and agitation, there is no need for the care provider to be other than an observing *exquisite witness* at this very important time.

The question of provider funeral attendance often comes up. While there is no detailed set of criteria regarding this determination, in general, I am in favor of funeral attendance. However, this will be influenced by time constraints on the provider and the wishes of the family. Some loved ones look upon the providers as part of their own family and even request that they attend their funeral. Attendance enables the provider to say his or her own good-byes and lets the family know of the provider's continued support and concern for them and their loss. Conversely, the presence of the provider may serve to remind the family of what they see as the failure of medical science, the hospital, and/or the provider to keep their now deceased loved one alive.

☐ Adapting to Life After a Terminal Illness Diagnosis

While every family adapts to the diagnosis and progression of a terminal illness in its own way, there is a pattern of behavior that often emerges. The care provider can assist the family members as they journey through the three phases of this process.

Phase 1: The Beginning

The process of grief for the terminally ill individual and family members can begin at any point from the first occurrence of troubling symptoms to the diagnosis of a fatal illness. When the patient receives a prognosis and treatment plan, some families rapidly "circle the wagons" to strengthen their connection and keep the terrible news inside the family. Others actively seek all of the resources they can connect with—other family, neighbors, clergy, community services, the Internet, library, and others who have experienced the same or similar diagnosis. There are some families that are so stunned or without a sense of what to do that they take little action beyond that required by the medical system.

The initial grief responses may include fear, anger, denial, panic, and disorganization. Some family members may withdraw or seek some form of distraction. Those who have a strong faith belief system may embrace prayer and seek the prayers of others. Reactions may vary from absolute panic to very controlled emotions. Denial of the reality of the illness or its ultimate consequences is to be expected, at least from some of the family members. Denial softens the horror of a terrible diagnosis. For many, such a diagnosis is considered a death sentence and a grief reaction is immediate. For others, taking action may include information-seeking, calling in resources, and organizing care. There is no single right way to do this.

Phase 2: Living with a Loved One with a Fatal Illness

The family begins to organize the caregiving responsibilities. They become familiar with medications, medical procedures, various therapies—respiratory, physical, radiation—and establish routines. They confront the daily challenges of caring for the loved one both physically and emotionally, and such care takes a definite toll. The relentless cycle of "good days/bad days" and the heartbreak of remission and relapse drain energy and hope. Some family members (frequently children and elders) may be left out of the caregiving process. If so, they need to be attended to. During this time, it's not unusual for existing family conflicts to go underground or become aggravated by the stress and anxiety involved in coping with a dying loved one. Failure to express the inner stresses and tensions can impact on caregiving and the quality of life of the loved one and other family members. Families need to secure outside support to help in the daily or weekly routines. The involvement of hospice provides good support and relief for the family caregivers.

Phase III: Ending Phase

Much of the denial concerning the terminal nature of the illness has melted away by this time. Now, it is *"when"* rather than *"if "* he or she dies. Underground conflicts may burst into the open as the temporary "truce" has been shattered. The family may circle the wagons even closer. Sometimes a "bunker" mentality emerges as the end approaches. Family members may need to discuss issues of abandonment that they are experiencing as well as begin to make plans for the actual death.

Care providers should be aware of the above general description of how a family adapts to life with a loved one who has a terminal illness. Each family will present many variations on the themes included in the three phases above. Normalizing reactions can help family members to know that they are responding as many people do in this circumstance. Families should be informed of how they can use the time in the latter phase of the journey to complete unfinished business, engage in forgiveness where appropriate, and say good-bye.

☐ Signs and Symptoms of Approaching Death

Health care providers are in the best position to guide the family with regard to what to expect from a dying person. It is important preparation for family caregivers and other persons close to the family who may be present at the time of active dying. While every individual dies in his or her own way, we have included below some general information regarding what may be observed and experienced as a loved one dies. Clinical medical material in the following sections have been drawn from information provided by Dr. Ronald Jeffreys, Internal Medicine, Franklin Square Hospital, Baltimore, Maryland (personal communication, September 12, 2003).

The Process of Dying

To help the family be prepared as death approaches, the following signs and symptoms are included and should be reviewed with the family by a health care provider.

Prior to the Final Dying Period

The following symptoms occur roughly 3 weeks before death (typically due to inability to clear toxins in the body): diminished eating and drinking, restlessness, withdrawal, confusion, agitation, increased periods of sleep, persistence of wounds and infections, and swelling of bodily extremities. Nurses frequently report dying persons' accounts of seeing deceased persons and their repeatedly saying that they are dying. It is also usual for many dying people to seek completion of unfinished business and make financial arrangements.

Final Phase of Dying

This phase includes the following signs and conditions that occur about 3 days prior to death: periods of lethargy alternating with extreme agitation, inability to swallow fluids or ingest food, urinary and/or bowel incontinence, decreased urine output, swelling and puffiness, and a drop in blood pressure. Hands and feet become cold and turn blue. Dying people may slip into a coma or become very hard to arouse and are reluctant to speak even if not comatose. Change in breathing patterns include breathing through open mouth, very shallow breathing, and lengthening in the intervals between breaths with periods of no breathing extending from 5 to 30 seconds and up to a full minute. This is called *Cheyne–Stokes breathing*. As fluid builds up in the lungs, crackling sounds are heard in the chest. Dying people often repeat that they "are dying." They may also complain of being very cold and maintain a rigid body position. Toward the end, however, they may experience a sudden resurgence of energy and appetite, as if miraculously returned to life for one or more days of well-being. This typically is followed by rapid deterioration and death.

The Signs at Death

Although family members may be prepared for the process leading up to death, they may not be equipped for the actual moment of death. Care providers can be helpful by ensuring that all family members of a dying person know the signs that indicate that death has occurred. These include no breathing, no heartbeat, release of bowel and bladder functioning, and no response to sensory stimuli. The eyes of dead people remain slightly open and enlarged pupils fix on one spot; there is no blinking. The jaw is relaxed and mouth slightly open. When they believe that death has occurred, family members should notify the appropriate medical or nursing provider.

Spiritual and Emotional Changes

In addition to the physical signs of approaching death, spiritual and emotional changes are taking place. Some dying people seem to let go of their agitation and become calm and accepting of the inevitable. They may take on a sense of wisdom about the meaning of life and seek to pass this on to loved ones.

People who have never been much for prayer and worship may embrace this as a final connection to the mystery of life, death, and transition. One couple, in which the wife was dying and who came from different religious backgrounds, were fascinated by the "life after death" literature and united in the exploration of available articles and videos concerning the reports by people who had "near-death experiences." Other dying patients may withdraw and seem to be relating to people who are unseen by family members, and still others may become gracious, seeking to say good-bye to as many of their family, friends, and colleagues as possible before they die. The two different dynamics are closely interrelated and interdependent. Both the physical and the spiritual-emotional changes are normal and natural.

Care providers and family members can help the dying person by enhancing physical comfort, supporting the release of emotions, meeting his or her spiritual and religious needs, encouraging letting go of attachments, and moving toward the transition. Any such provider activity must be appropriate to family traditions.

Providers need to know the family's wishes. What happens after death is determined largely by the family's traditions. Some family members may stay to wash or touch the body, say good-bye, or simply be present at their final time together before the formal death rituals begin. Some families wish to spend extended time with the body of the deceased. In these cases, care providers can attempt to arrange for the body to be moved to another location in the hospital, nursing home, or hospice so the family can have the uninterrupted time they desire. It is also a time for the family to begin the process of letting go of the body.

Providers should also find out if a post-mortem is to take place so that they can prepare the family for this. Decisions regarding donation of organs may or may not have already been made. Families should discuss this possibility in advance. This may also be the time for contacting the funeral director, clergy, family, and friends who may be needed for support and handling of some of the details of arrangements. Care providers need to give the family the opportunity to let go at their own pace and do as much of the planning and preparation of after-death rituals as they desire. Care providers should make an effort to coordinate care for the family after the death has occurred. Continued teamwork and communication are in the best interest of the deceased patient, the family, and the care providers. Those providers who connect with the family during and after the funeral give both the family and themselves a gift of care and closure.

☐ Bedside Guide at the Time of Death: Saying Good-Bye

Many family members have their first experience with dying when a loved one dies. Often, in a hospital room, nursing home, or at home, a family will not know what to do as the final breaths are taken. Care providers may be present and can assist the loved ones in having a healing experience or can educate the family in the event that the provider is unable to be present. The following guide for people who may be at the bedside of someone who is dying has been adapted from material prepared by Patricia Wudel, Director of Joseph's House Hospice, Washington, D.C., and her staff.

1. Take several breaths and turn off the TV. You are on holy ground. Quietly pull a chair close to the head of the bed. It is natural to feel anxious or afraid. Be patient with yourself. Take the hand of the dying person and give thanks for the opportunity to be connected as he or she travels the last mile of this life.
2. Assume that even in the last moments of life the dying person is able to hear. If you are a family member or have been especially close to the person who is dying, this is the time to say your good-byes. Where appropriate, let the person know that he or she is loved and/or will be missed, but that you will be all right and that you want him or her to be in peace. If your tears come, that is OK. If no tears come, that is OK, too. *There is no one right way to be or one right thing to say.*
3. Respect the dying person as a full human being as long as he or she is alive. Use the person's name when talking. If you need to talk about the dying person to someone, step outside of the room and close the door. If you forget, be gentle with yourself but keep practicing deep respect.
4. If the dying person is a person of religious faith and you feel comfortable talking about this faith, do so. You may want to read from the

Bible or other spiritual books, or any passages that may have special meaning. You may be inspired to sing hymns, lullabies, or songs of comfort that communicate love and care.

5. Keep distraction to a minimum. If others in the room appear overcome with grief, comfort them, or step outside of the room with them for a few minutes so you can gently care for them.

6. The moment of death is different for each person. As you watch, keep your heart soft and open. Take a moment to sit quietly in the room to honor the passing and sense the world with his or her living, physical presence no longer in it. Allow your feelings to come out—tears, sighs, sobs. Have mercy on yourself. You have just shared an awesome moment with someone dear to you.

Care providers must be aware of the fact that not every death experience may be filled with awe and spiritual significance. In some cases, the end comes as family watch the end of breathing or the critical changes in vital sign monitors. Some report an unreal feeling as the loved one breathes in and then out and the next breath never comes. Some deaths are very upsetting to witness. The loved one may be struggling for breath or calling out to be saved from death before they lapse into a final irreversible coma. Every opportunity must be taken to allow as peaceful a death as possible, and providers must be sensitive to the effects of upsetting deaths on some family members.

☐ Chronic Illness/Disability and the Family

As stated earlier in this chapter, long-term life-threatening and chronic non-life-threatening illnesses are overlapping conditions that, in many cases, carry a high mortality rate. (See Tables 7.1 and 7.2.) Some chronic, life-limiting illnesses or injuries that do not have a mortality risk may linger for many years but can enable vulnerability for other medical problems. These conditions include chronic bed sores, infections, depression, demoralization, and other emotional disorders. For conditions that require long-term care, the individual may be significantly impaired either physically, mentally, or both and live for many years. My own grandfather, who suffered paralysis from stroke, died at the age of 91, unable to walk and partially paralyzed for many years. He lived with my aunt and her family who provided long-term home care for him.

Effects of Life-Threatening Illness

The existence of a life-threatening illness in the family shifts the focus of attention and energy to the affected loved one and alters the psychosocial climate. Family members will need to adapt to new ways to view their family unit and the way they relate to the outside world.

Below is an account of our family on vacation when Steven was ill but still well enough to travel to Disney World. It demonstrates how the picture of a family shifts, especially when out in the world away from the privacy of home and neighborhood.

> During the 3 years from the time of our son Steven's diagnosis of cancer until his death at age 8, we were a family living with a chronic, life-threatening illness. He actually had about 11 months of remission—his hair grew back, he returned to school, and he even rejoined his soccer team. When the crushing news of his relapse came just before spring break, we decided, with his physician's approval, that the five of us would take a trip to Disney World. It was during this trip to Florida that we truly saw how different we were from other families. Steven was weak and not able to do very much in the way of rides or waiting in line. My wife and I were uncomfortably aware of other people looking at us. We overheard some young children ask their parents, "Mommy, why is that boy in a wheelchair?" Even when people didn't say anything about Steven, we detected subtle reactions to the fact that our family was "different."
>
> The oral chemotherapy medications made Steven sick some of the time, and we had to cut outings short so that he could get back to the hotel and rest. I worried that Steven's siblings resented this. We worked hard to make sure that our other two children were having a good time. Yet we were always aware of Steven's schedule and of our overriding need to care for him. We were also very aware of the other families there—carefree, active, and happy, whose only worries appeared to be which ride to go on, which exhibit to enter, and where to have lunch. In our minds, we stood out as very different from them. Later, we began to notice other family groups who were different—a mother in a wheelchair, a child in braces up on her father's shoulders, a teenager with a portable oxygen tank and nasal tube, and several families with Down's syndrome children. As I mentally reviewed these other families, I felt an unspoken connection to them—a sense of community with family groups who were different.

This personal experience underscores many of the challenges faced by families coping with a family member with a chronic illness. It includes the frustration of family members with the many new restrictions on their lives, especially the limitations on socializing at home or away from home. Children and adolescents may be reluctant to have friends over because a handicapped parent or a bald sibling may be intimidating or embarrassing. Family members may suffer from chronic sorrow with few periods of well-being. There may be little joy in some families while others find ways to have some fun or quality of life between periods of great pain. Family life is different. Life itself is different.

To further illustrate the adaptations that families must make in the face of chronically impaired members, a case of chronic disability due to injury in one family and how they have reorganized their life to care for their daughter is presented below.

> I visited Sue (not her real name) in her nursing home; she is 35 years old, a victim of traumatic brain injury suffered as a result of a motor vehicle accident. She has been a resident of the nursing home for 14 years. She was in nursing school prior to her injury.
>
> Sue was in a reclining wheelchair, and her hair was neatly pulled back with a pink ribbon. She looked well nourished and well cared for. Sue is fed with a gastric tube, has no control over her environment, and is totally dependent. Her color was good, and she moved her head from time to time and had her eyes open. She is unable to speak or make obvious communication gestures. Her head is always kept elevated to prevent aspiration of fluids. While we were together, her mother maintained constant physical contact with her.
>
> Sue gave no noticeable reactions to my talking to her although she did move her head and appeared to be looking around. Her parents indicate that Sue reacts with a smile when she recognizes her aide's voice. They also point out that she will turn away when a motor vehicle accident is shown on the television and will move her body closer to her mother when her mother gets into bed with her. These reactions give her parents a feeling of connection to her, and their faces are happy when they tell me this.
>
> Sue's parents visit her twice daily, and she comes home on holidays because they want her to be present with the family. They feel that she is getting good care at this facility and have special praise for her aide.

I asked both parents what they believe constitutes good provider care, and in addition to their responses, which are summarized below, they recommended that people who are training to work with the chronically physically impaired would benefit from spending time in a wheelchair with their hands bound in order to get a sense of the loss of control and the experience of total dependency.

The parents suggested that good care providers have the following characteristics:

1. Good skills in physical care—feeding, bathing, moving, and dressing.
2. Compassion and empathy.
3. Ability to treat the care recipient with respect by

    a. Telling the person they are caring for what they are going to do: "I'm going to bathe you now; feed you now; turn the TV off so you can get some sleep."
    b. Talking to the person; telling him or her what is going on around them.
    c. Never assuming that people who cannot express their needs have no feelings.

4. Ability to provide auditory stimulation that is especially significant to the patient—music, singing, cheerful talking.
5. Ability to provide touch, massage, and physical contact with loved ones.
6. Ability to provide opportunities for some level of control over their environment whenever possible: "Do you want the TV on now? Your lunch now? Bed adjusted up or down? Vanilla or chocolate ice cream?"
7. Ability to share stories from the care provider's own life that can be appreciated by family members.

Four million people in the United States suffer from traumatic brain injury. One and one-half million people are diagnosed with traumatic brain injury annually (Brain Injury Association, 2003). Some people who have suffered traumatic injury to the brain are left in a state of complete dependence while, for others, recovery enables the reclaiming of life. In one case, a man who suffered a brain injury as a child related that the most important message he has for care providers, family, and friends as well as to persons with brain injury impairments is to learn to understand the cognitive and behavioral deficiencies, accept them, and adapt life to the new reality.

When asked what advice he would give to people adapting to life after they have had a brain injury, he had the following suggestions:

1. If you need help, don't be afraid to ask.
2. Keep communication lines open to family and friends.
3. Don't let problems accumulate unresolved.

4. Ask family and friends for feedback on your behavior so that you can make corrections.

Consequences of Chronic Illness and Conditions on the Family

Families who have a loved one with chronic illness or other disabling physical or mental conditions may be affected in one or more of the following significant ways.

1. They are always aware that they are different from other families.
2. They live with ongoing concerns for the health and well-being of the ill or handicapped loved one and always need to balance these concerns with the needs for other members of the family.
3. They experience various levels of resentment and anger at the limits and restrictions imposed by the situation and the consequent guilt and shame that frequently follow.
4. They despair at the "no end in sight" nature of the chronic condition, and at the uncertainty of life with a chronically ill or disabled person in the family.
5. They undergo grief reactions regarding their past losses and anticipated losses.
6. They feel angry at other relatives, friends, and neighbors who are happy and seemingly unaware of the continued impact of chronic illness on "our family."
7. They feel tired of caregiving and are emotionally drained.
8. They may express the desire to withdraw into themselves and spend increasing time away from the family.
9. They are proud of their ability to reframe the way the family thinks of itself. They may now consider themselves a family unit composed of independent, caring members who can adapt to one of life's most challenging situations: coping with chronic illness and exceptional conditions.

Family Caregivers

Family caregivers are family, friends, and neighbors who serve those they love in the face of terminal and chronic illness, disability, and dying (McLeod, 2002). "They may bathe, feed, dress, shop for, listen to, and transport frail parents, spouses, children, friends, relatives, neighbors, and even strangers" (McLeod, 1999, p. 3). Family caregivers require special attention; they are subject to their own grief reactions, including depression, burnout, physical breakdown, and substance abuse, and may have difficulties with work and nonwork relationships. When a man or woman is caring for a chronically ill life partner of many years, the losses are many and continuous. The loss of the "way we were" is an ever-present reality as the loved one's physical and mental condition deteriorates and the caregiver strives to provide the care that will keep him or her at home. Parents caring for a chronically ill or disabled child must cope with the "way we never will be."

The strong desire to care for the loved one can lead to a form of stress called *compassion fatigue*. This is the decreasing ability to continue care at the level that the caregiver feels he or she must provide (McLeod, 1999). "Competing demands on time and energy . . . fears for the future . . . [lead to] distress such as loneliness, exhaustion, anxiety, and sadness" (p. 103). In addition to the direct care services that must be addressed, there are medical, financial, and legal issues as well. When caregiver guilt, depression, and resentment are added, there exists the potential for ending family caregiving at home for that loved one.

There are growing support services for family caregivers and an increasing range of care placements for the loved one when home care is no longer possible. Many regional agencies for aging have caregiver support groups. Local family and children service agencies offer training programs specifically for family caregivers, and a new specialty in *geriatric care management* (McLeod, 2002) has emerged to assist the family in managing care for their loved one. (See appendix B for resources from the National Alliance for Caregiving, the Family Caregiver Alliance, the National Association of Geriatric Care Managers, and other various support organizations devoted to people with specific diseases and disabilities.)

Care providers need to let families coping with chronic illness know that they are not alone and that their frustrations and other reactions are normal. They can direct families to specific support groups that include other families coping with similar illnesses or disabilities. Care providers can help family caregivers assess their level of burnout and when they need to seek respite services to assist with the loved one receiving care. Family caregivers must maintain their own physical and emotional health so that they can continue to be available to their loved one.

☐ Medical Dilemmas, Patient Rights, and Bioethical Considerations

With the growing capacity of medical science to extend the life of terminally ill and critically injured persons and with the rising consciousness of the rights of patients and families to participate in medical decisions, the potential for conflict over decision-making has increased. Conflicts may be between the patient/family and the health care staff, and also among family members themselves, including the patient. We will focus on the bioethical considerations associated with medical and general care decisions and patient autonomy. Patient autonomy dilemmas can arise in hospitals, hospices, long-term care facilities, and in the home. Care providers may find themselves faced with conflicts arising from differences of opinions among family members regarding a loved one's treatment and end-of-life care decisions. Providers may find families need help with difficult decisions associated with using or terminating life support.

Family Dilemmas

Dilemmas can occur when a shift from curative treatment to palliative and/or hospice care is being considered. Patients and family may feel that shifting to palliative care means that their medical providers are giving up on them. Family members may disagree with each other regarding the cessation of active, aggressive treatment in favor of comfort care. A sick and weak person may be overlooked in the decision-making process.

Here is an illustration of an extreme family conflict in response to initiating palliative care.

> An older widow with advanced metastatic cancer was being cared for by her daughter who lives nearby. The daughter has two brothers, both of whom live out of town and have been minimally involved in their mother's care. The oncologist, the mother, and her caregiving daughter agreed that it was time to shift to palliative care, and a referral to hospice was made. When the two out-of-state brothers learned of this, they immediately came to town and attempted to take over their mother's care. Sidelining the caregiving sister and their mother, they attempted to convince the mother that she "would be well again," and they had her admitted to another hospital against medical advice and the wishes of their sister who felt anguished over this decision. Within a day, the new hospital staff affirmed the original decision for a hospice referral. The two brothers reluctantly agreed and home hospice care was arranged for. The mother lived for 2 more weeks, the broth-

ers departed, and the caregiving sister was left emotionally distraught and estranged from her brothers.

Several elements of this story are common. First, it is not unusual for out-of-town family members to show up late in the course of an illness and attempt to impose their wishes for the dying loved one to "hang in there and we'll get you well." This is upsetting for the person who has been the continuing caregiver. It may raise doubts or cause guilt and/or anger at last minute attempts to reinstate aggressive treatment. It is also very human for adult children who have been out of the daily care picture to seek intense involvement as a way of holding on to their parent. These efforts exemplify John Bowlby's "protest phase" (Bowlby, 1980) and a struggle with reality that is characteristic of early grief.

In the above case, the mother was moved to another hospital before her sons accepted her terminal reality. Their decision to overrule their sister and the physician was also a function of old, unfinished sibling issues as well as the fact that they were in a different part of the grief process than their sister. The mother, confused, and extremely weak because of her illness, was unable to participate in medical care decisions. She typically had left these medical decisions to her physicians and her daughter. Second, the flaring up of old family struggles—in this case, a long history of sibling conflict—erupted and continued after the mother's death. Resentment of siblings usually does not begin at the time of a health crisis but rather has its roots in past relationship issues. In many families with a similar pattern of internal conflicts, the discord continues after the parent has died when inheritance and property disposition issues are considered.

Care providers can help a family examine options based on medical information and consider the consequences for each option available. However, a clear resolution of all dilemmas may not be possible. Medical staff and other resources may need to be called in to resolve conflicting positions. Hospitals and other health care facilities have established ethics boards to advise those with difficult decisions to make. In some cases, the institution's legal department may need to be consulted.

Treatment Choice Dilemmas

Patients and their families must make decisions about treatment options. These decisions may be in conflict with medical staff recommendations. When the judgment of medical staff and patients and/or their families come into conflict, the results can be very unpleasant for all concerned.

Disagreements can occur with regard to the selection of a treatment, the continuation or discontinuation of aggressive treatment, the extent of patient pain and discomfort, the continuation or the termination of life support, and other end-of-life medical care. Examples of medical treatment dilemmas that confront a patient and family include the decision to move a person to the intensive care unit (ICU), whether or not to provide breathing with a respirator, the decision to resuscitate, whether or not to feed with a gastric tube, and decisions regarding fighting infections or not. Patients and family must be given a clear picture of what the implications of ICU medical realities are. Patients may be unable to communicate, may have their ribs cracked during aggressive resuscitation procedures, or may have their hands tied down to prevent their interfering with vital lines and tubes. Sometimes there is disagreement among the family with regard to the use of heroic lifesaving methods.

Medical care providers should discuss a clear and understandable plan with the patient and family before a move is made to intensive care. This will reduce any mistaken expectations on the part of the family about what should be done to help a person survive. It will also help to clarify what procedures they do not want done. Sometimes staff will feel that certain heroic measures are futile and may view the request by the family as denial or false hopes. Yet the decision rests with the family. I encourage as full a discussion of this staff concern as possible and recommend that consideration be given to the needs of the family and their loved one to "have at least one resuscitation and/ or give the patient 72 hours of all opportunities to survive."

Another area where there is concern over the best decisions for care is shifting from aggressive, curative treatment to palliative care and/or a hospice program. Care providers must give families clear and understandable information and allow them full participation in what can be a traumatic and guilt-producing decision. Control of pain and comfort for their loved one must also be assured, and such concerns responded to promptly.

One of the ways to reduce the extent of confusion at a point where decisions must be made in a very short amount of time is to have an up-to-date advanced directive in the patient's chart.

Advanced Directives

Advanced directives are documents signed by an individual and witnessed. They generally detail two specific areas of concern regarding medical treatment decisions in the event that a patient becomes too disabled to act on his or her own behalf. First, a *health agent* or proxy is identified who will make such decisions; a backup person may also be appointed in the event that the first listed is not able to perform this role. Second, the *lifesaving and/or life-preserving procedures* that may be used in the event of a medical crisis are laid out. Examples are the following: Do not resuscitate (DNR)—no actions taken to restart the heart; do not intubate (DNI)—no actions taken to provide artificial breathing; no feeding tubes—in the event that swallowing is not possible; no dialysis—in the event of kidney failure; no antibiotics—in the event of infection; no blood transfusions—in the event of loss of blood. Some advanced directives stipulate that life-preserving measures will be used only for a period of 72 hours and terminated at the end of that interval if no improvement is determined. There are many different forms of these documents, and most states require that all patients entering a hospital have a signed copy in their medical records.

The purpose of advanced directives is "to define a level of intolerable indignity at which death becomes, for them, preferable to continued existence" (Cantor, 1998, p. 630).

Advanced directives are most helpful when family members have discussed them early on. Family members who have never discussed what each would want done (or not done) are at a disadvantage when a medical crisis occurs and an unconscious loved one cannot articulate their desires. Even in the best of circumstances, problems arise. Some ill patients clearly stipulate their wishes to avoid life-prolonging measures, yet, at the moment of decision, families may be unwilling to enforce do not resuscitate (DNR) or do not intubate (DNI) orders. It's as if they suddenly realize, "Sure, Dad wanted it this way, but if we order DNR, DNI, or refuse dialysis, blood transfusions, antibiotics, fluids, and feeding tubes, we'll be killing him!" In short, advanced directives are only as good as the designated health agent and the physician who are responsible for carrying them out.

In a study of cognitively normal seniors over 65 by Gjerdingen, Neff, Wang, and Chaloner (1999), most respondents did not desire life-sustaining procedures such as CPR, ventilatory support, or artificial nutrition if they were to develop any level of dementia. Further, most said they would not want to be hospitalized or given antibiotics if they were no longer able to recognize their loved ones or care for themselves. As dementia is a condition common to many deteriorating illnesses, it is important that families have a conversation about desired life-prolonging measures while loved ones are capable of making decisions for themselves. The decisions should be included in an advanced directive, including specifics regarding point of discontinuing life support.

Other problems can arise. Sometimes the advanced directive document is vague and too general. If, for example, the siblings and the spouse of a comatose patient don't agree on the level of DNR, it's possible that one resuscitation can be tried and then the DNR goes into effect. This may or may not be what the patient wanted, but it resolves the family conflict.

Treating for illness other than the primary disease also involves a shaky judgment call. Should an antibiotic be administered if a dying person spikes a fever? Should the person be placed on a ventilator and run the risk of developing pneumonia from the aspiration of fluids? Should a feeding tube or a line for fluids be used? There are many areas of decision-making that are not provided for in the standard advanced directive document. The family should be in communication with the physician regarding these concerns.

In addition, *the patient may change his or her mind.* I have seen this frequently in an inpatient medical unit. A patient who is frightened may suddenly terminate the original "do nots." People do change their minds and the care provider must be aware of this to avoid problems of over or underserving a patient's needs and requests. Here is an example of end-of- life ambiguities.

A woman, age 89, has been transferred to a hospital from a nursing home. She is incoherent, very sleepy, and unresponsive. Her advance directives only indicate that her four children will serve as her health agents if she is unable to make decisions for herself. Two daughters and a son meet with their mother's attending physician to review her medical history and assess her present condition. The doctor, seeking direction in terms of taking heroic, life-saving measures, asks the children which life-saving procedures and treatments they want placed in their mother's medical chart. The children decided that she would receive resuscitation and antibiotics for any disease whose course could be reversed. At one point the mother becomes alert just long enough to refuse any artificial breathing procedures. She continues to survive for another week—sleeping, breathing on her own, and receiving fluids and small amounts of food orally. One day, she opens her eyes and says, "Where am I and what is happening?"

The woman spent the next 6 months at home with health aides and wished she had died and never returned home. She was very angry with her children for enabling her to live. She couldn't walk, hated having "strangers" in her home, and fired and rehired her home aides every other day. After a brief period of being clouded, noncommunicative, and completely bedridden, the family met and

decided to add DNR, no feeding, and no antibiotics to the life support orders. However, a week after the family met, she died peace-
fully in her sleep.

The care provider must be aware of the potential difficulties that
arise from the inability of a typical document to cover all of the possible
medical scenarios. This is why it is so important for the family to have
prior conversations with their loved one and with the physician as well
about the multiple provisions of an advanced directive document.

Further problems with advanced directives have been cited by Cantor
(1998). These include the low percentage of patients completing the document, and the use of terms that are not sufficiently specific (i.e., terminal
condition, significant recovery, and personal dignity). Studies reported
by Cantor found that 598 of 688 advanced directive documents were
uninformative and lacked descriptive elements that spelled out which
life-sustaining measures will be withdrawn or not initiated as well as
how this would be determined.

To help families decide what to do, Cantor offers an advanced medical
directive model (Cantor, 1998, pp. 648–652), which contains five categories of concern. (See appendix C.) His model seeks to enable a person to
"identify crucial personal values or considerations to be used in end-of-
life decisions." The profile provides the individual with a list of conditions and a rating for level of intolerability at which they do not desire to
be kept alive. It guides determination of the levels at which feeding and
hydration will be provided or discontinued. Additionally, each of the five
conditions includes a description of circumstances under which the person wishes to be kept alive.

The five conditions for ranking the level of "intolerable indignity"
from "intolerable" to "unimportant" are

- Pain and suffering,
- Mental incapacity,
- Physical immobility,
- Physical helplessness,
- Interests of loved ones.

This model includes a place to designate primary and secondary
health care representatives, other family members to be consulted, living
arrangements desired or rejected, and medical interventions accepted or
rejected. There are places for signature of patient, health care representatives, and witnesses as well as provisions for periodic review. While this

model will not necessarily overcome all of the difficult decision-making issues that occur at the end of life, it does overcome many of the weaknesses of earlier developed, overly general, and vague documents.

An advanced directive is a continuing process that takes place from the first signs of a change in the status of a patient and moves along a continuum of adaptation to patient circumstances and needs until death. Decisions regarding changes in health care provisions are always based upon the experiences a patient has during a particular hospital admission or phase of the living–dying interval.

> *Care providers* must familiarize themselves with the nature of such available documents and determine whether the dying person has completed an advanced directive, whether the family is aware of its existence, and if the document is up-to-date and still viable. Many advanced directives now include the provision to terminate all life-support measures if the patient doesn't improve after 72 hours. Where appropriate to family traditions, an open discussion of these matters is desirable. The communication process is most important and the advanced directive should never supplant this needed interaction (Goodman, 1998).

In his discussion of the responsibility for end-of-life communication, Goodman (1998) states "the overarching goal of advanced directives is to inform caregivers, family members, and others about preferences for end-of-life care" (p. 722). Goodman urges medical providers to initiate a discussion of options, values, concerns, and decisions and not leave it to the patient to bring up or turn it over to other staff. His conclusion is that there is resistance to doing this due to the lack of sufficient training in medical education in the area of death, dying, and communication skills (Goodman, 1998).

Medical treatment decision-making in the provision of end-of-life care extends beyond the concrete consideration of advanced directive documents to the role that cultural diversity plays in influencing choices. As indicated in chapter 1, not all cultures view the decision-making process in the same way as many middle-class, Western families do. As Koenig (1997) points out, bioethics in America stresses the Western values of patient autonomy. She indicates that discussions regarding the continuation or cessation of aggressive treatment with a patient and family may require a translator who is sensitive to the ethnic and cultural mores of that family.

In some cultural traditions, family members do not share the extent of the disease and the fatal nature of the diagnosis with their loved one. Either family members make the decisions for the loved one or the decisions are left up to the medical staff, with the assumption that all will be done to prolong the life of the patient. In these cases, medical information is not easily conveyed because of language and communication barriers.

Care providers working with such families must facilitate the sharing of diagnosis, prognosis, and treatment options within best ethical practices as well as in accordance with the patient's cultural traditions and culture. Advanced directives, in concert with family traditions, may need to be written in both English and in the patient's native language.

☐ Conclusion

We have discussed the nature of the dying process, the needs of the dying patient and family, ways to say good-bye, and how to support people through this difficult aspect of living with a serious, chronic illness. Bioethical issues were also considered. The dying person is a bereaved person as are his or her loved ones. The losses that occur daily (and sometimes even more rapidly) cause the family to rewrite the narrative of their lives constantly. Terminal and chronic life-limiting illnesses and disabilities have an extraordinary effect on the family as members see themselves as different from other families and in some cases restricted in their lifestyle options.

Care providers can help families with a dying loved one by understanding the family issues and dynamics, being sure that the needs of all family members are being considered, and helping all to maintain the dignity of the ill person. Enabling opportunities for open communication in areas of conflict and concern can help families with chronic, life-limiting situations.

In chapter 8 we will focus on the "hands" dimension of the *exquisite witness* care provider by furnishing a review of both general supportive and specific clinical interventions for helping grieving people.

Helping Grieving People:
A Continuum of Care for Healing

"Bereavement is choiceless, but grieving is not."

(Thomas Attig, 1996, p. 32)

☐ Introduction

Thus far we have focused on the "heart" and "head" dimensions of the *exquisite witness* grief care provider. We have had several personal awareness exercises and have reviewed social, cultural, and psychological aspects of grief, the effect of grief on family systems, unique grief and ethical issues associated with chronically ill, disabled, and dying people. This chapter will concentrate on the "hands" dimension, that is, on general guidelines and the specific skills or interventions the *exquisite witness* care provider can supply. The interventions fall into three categories: (a) supportive behaviors, (b) the four tasks of mourning, and (c) clinical tools. These overlapping categories of helping actions form a *continuum of care for grieving people.*

☐ General Guidelines for All Care Providers

How can we, as unique human beings possessing our own background culture and skills, help grieving people? Let's first look at some general suggestions for providing care that can be used whether you are feeding a dying person ice chips, listening to a widow's pain, or helping a bereaved father express his rage. Explanations for each of the guidelines follow:

- Offer yourself.
- Be respectful.
- Become comfortable with silence.
- Be a skilled listener.
- Normalize practically everything.
- Avoid judgment.
- Take action! (don't do "nothing!")
- Don't do everything by yourself.
- Keep your promises.
- Teach the "side by side" or the intermittent approach to grieving.
- Be sensitive to cultural, ethnic, and family traditions.
- "Bracket" your "Cowbells" when they surface.
- Be aware of and respond to your own compassion fatigue.

Offer Yourself

Remember that you want to make a caring connection with the person who is grieving. The amount of time that you spend with him or her is less important than the quality of time. Don't appear rushed; avoid looking at your watch. Be fully present—look at the person and listen attentively. Let the grieving person know that he or she has been heard. Know that there will be times, however, when there will be no conversation and you will simply be present in the silence. Be sure that you have allowed appropriate time for the interaction. Keep aware of your own personal Cowbells that may have already been triggered by the person or the loss situation.

If appropriate, offer to perform a simple task, like picking up some dry cleaning, buying some groceries, or changing television stations. Even the smallest offer to help will be appreciated. This is a golden opportunity to connect with the grieving person. A little caring goes a long way.

Be Respectful

Let an ill person know that despite the circumstances, he or she is still a unique and valuable human being. Don't talk down to an ill person even if the behavior you observe has become childlike. If another person is in the room, look at and talk directly to the ill person when the conversation refers to him or her.

Become Comfortable with Silence

Quiet time together can be golden. There is no need to fill up every moment with conversation. You can light a candle, set some flowers in a vase, listen to some music, or simply sit relaxed and wait for the person to speak.

Be a Skilled Listener

To be truly effective as a listener, you will need to focus and give the grieving individual your complete attention. True listening connects the care provider to the grieving person in a way that can bring a sense of acceptance and healing into the process. Make eye contact, maintain an attentive posture, and match the volume and speed of your voice to theirs. Refrain from asking too many questions and let them steer the conversation. Nod and affirm, saying words of encouragement. Provide a sounding board by reflecting back to them the meanings and feelings you hear them saying. Grieving people will then be more willing to share their stories and express their feelings to you. People in grief and distress from illness want to be heard. They may need to tell their story over and over again, and sometimes the care provider may be the only one who is still willing to listen.

Normalize Practically Everything

Grieving people feel a wide range of emotions: confusion, helplessness, hopelessness, a sense of dread, and a feeling of being stuck in a nightmare without an end. They worry that they are going crazy. Often, they lose their appetite for food, sex, and/or entertainment. These reactions are all normal, and care providers need to normalize them. Normalizing is never done in a patronizing or belittling way. Instead, assure people that what they are feeling is an unfortunate but usual part of the grief process and that the need to talk about it is normal as well. Say things like, "It's okay to feel this way," "Of course you're angry," "I would feel this way too," and "It's good to let those tears out." Grieving people need to be able to express themselves without worrying that they are burdening the care provider.

Avoid Judgment

Try to keep the "why" or "shoulds" out of the conversation. If your loved one (or the person receiving care) says, "It's hopeless," don't respond by saying, "You shouldn't feel that way." Also, don't allow your facial expressions, body language, or gestures to give away your thoughts. For instance, be careful of the telltale "raised eyebrow" which signals judgment. Instead, acknowledge the person's expressions of helplessness and continue to listen. Counselors may wish to introduce gracefully a "let's count our blessings" conversation when the time is appropriate to do so. Keep in mind that we are entitled to every feeling we have; don't judge the person if he or she says something that strikes you as strange or provocative.

Take Action! (Don't Do "Nothing!")

Help people who are bereaved to become active. They can write obituaries, plan the funeral, create other mourning rituals, block out schedules, send out acknowledgment cards, fill a vase with flowers on Mother's Day, invite special friends over to reminisce, make a donation in honor of the deceased, get into an exercise routine, and/or take a class. People grieving due to a serious or life-threatening diagnosis can research the latest developments concerning their illness, make a list of all the medical specialists who are conducting studies or research on their disease or condition, and locate local support groups related to their illness or loss situation.

Doing "something" gives us a sense of control and purpose; it's a perfect antidote for feelings of helpless despair. (Keep in mind, though, that there are times when grieving people welcome inactivity as a respite from being overextended.) In the case of perinatal loss, nurses in hospital obstetric units have increasingly "provided opportunities [for parents to] name, see, and embrace their deceased babies" (Leon, 1992, p. 7). Having an extended period of time to sing, hold, dress, and grieve before leaving the child, provides a physical being to let go of and an opportunity to say good-bye. Parents frequently will take a blanket, identification bracelet, or other article as a comforting, connecting link to the deceased infant.

Don't Do Everything by Yourself

Don't turn it into a one-person show. Widen your circle of support. Identify social, spiritual, and health care resources. Locate family, friends, clergy, neighbors, colleagues, other care providers, and community services that can become part of the "team." Clergy and congregational members can be invaluable sources of support for the grieving–healing process. If, during this process, an individual experiences physical symptoms as a result of grief, a referral to the primary care physician is advisable. *Don't try to fix everything*—some issues may not require fixing while others can be put on hold. For example, it is not necessary to respond immediately to condolence cards. When the grieving person's energy and inclination are there, writing such cards can be a useful action. If the person is exhausted, the care provider can help to legitimize putting off this task until the individual is physically and mentally ready to do so.

Keep Your Promises

If you make a commitment—to visit, run errands, prepare a meal, or even make phone calls—do everything possible to keep that promise. This builds trust. People who are confined to bed usually look forward to visits from family and friends. When the anticipated visit does not materialize, the confined or ill person may experience sadness, depression, or a sense of being forgotten or of not mattering.

Teach the "Side by Side" or the Intermittent Approach to Grieving

Very few bereaved people maintain grieving behaviors on a continuous basis. I encourage "time-outs" from grieving and prescribe activities such as taking a walk outdoors, working out at a health club, taking time out for a hobby, watching a funny video or television show, scrubbing the kitchen floor, and even retail therapy at a nearby shopping mall to temporarily distract the grieving person. Sometimes people need permission *not to grieve*—to do or think about something else. Most grieving people can learn to take brief time-outs and then return to their grieving. I have found that bereaved people who state that their grief is a measure of loyalty to their deceased loved one can gradually allow themselves brief time-out periods. These can become gradually longer intervals, allowing increasing time periods for adjusting to the realities of the post-loss world.

Be Sensitive to Cultural, Ethnic, and Family Traditions

An individual's background influences the way grief is expressed, how one plans for end-of-life rituals, and how one makes decisions. It also affects expectations for the care provider's role. Care providers need to learn how each family interprets its own cultural, religious, and ethnic traditions—sometimes all it takes is asking someone in the family. Don't be surprised to learn that a particular family does not follow the presumed pattern for their cultural group. The more information obtained, the better equipped the care provider will be to intervene appropriately to avoid making unproductive interventions that impede rapport with the family.

"Bracket" Your Own "Cowbells" When They Surface

Ask not for whom the Cowbells toll, they toll for thee—and for me. Everyone grieves at some point in his or her life, and it is not unusual for our own Cowbells suddenly to surface—often when you least expect them. You may be in the middle of a conversation with a bereaved or a dying person and suddenly feel the urge to cry. This may be an empathic reaction to the other person's situation, or it may be your own Cowbells ringing. At moments like this, the care provider should remember that he or she has the capacity to put personal feelings to the side, to "bracket" them. We do this by consciously assuring ourselves that we will address our own issues as soon as we are finished talking to the person we are working with. The next step is vital—we must talk to a colleague, friend, or someone to whom we can express our bracketed feelings. If we don't discuss and acknowledge our unfinished loss material and express feelings, we may hear Cowbells ring the next time we're working with someone who is grieving, and our Cowbells may drown them out.

Students frequently ask if it is okay to cry when they are with a grieving person. This is very individual and should be based on the provider's comfort with sharing his or her feelings at a time of sadness. I have, at times, shed a tear when I was saddened by what was being said, and simply told the person that I was "very moved" by what they were telling me. A care provider should not overly emote to the point of making the other person uncomfortable. The bracketing of strong emotions should be used in those situations.

Be Aware of and Respond to Your Own Compassion Fatigue

When providers reach a point where they find their own Cowbells coming up frequently, they may have reached a point of compassion fatigue or burnout. Accept that you have your own issues to deal with; that you may feel resentful or angry with a loved one, client, or with the situation; and that you may begin to wonder who is going to give *you* some loving care. This is normal—but it is also a signal that you need a break and some outside social and/or spiritual support or personal counseling.

☐ Interventions for Helping Grieving People

Interventions are the actions taken by persons who are assisting grieving people. They can range from sitting silently with an ill or bereaved person, listening and responding to them, offering specific suggestions, making referrals to various specialists, or engaging in clinical actions taken by professionally trained care providers. These interventions are grouped below according to the role of the care provider; they are supportive behaviors for family caregivers, the four tasks of mourning, and clinical tools.

General Supportive Interventions for Family Caregivers

These caregiving functions, sometimes referred to as the "chicken soup component of care," can be initiated by a person who desires to help an individual in grief. Activities may include taking care of everyday needs (shopping, cooking, cleaning house, running errands), listening, adjusting the television, reading out loud, and arranging for family and community resources. Family members, friends, and/or neighbors typically perform these care functions in addition to performing certain nursing activities as instructed by a physician, nurse, or other health professional.

These areas include administering medications, providing a massage, and also assisting with bathing.

Family Caregivers Are Grieving People Caring for Loved Ones

Based on census data, over 50 million people (over a fourth of the adult population) serve as family caregivers for a loved one (National Family Caregivers Association, 2002), providing about 80% of all home health services, estimated at a value of $257 billion annually (Arno, 2000; Arno, Levine & Memmott (1999)).

Family caregivers include family members, friends, and neighbors who provide care to someone who is ill, incapacitated, in need of help, and/or may be dying. Family caregivers, whether serving as the primary (full-time) or as a secondary (part-time) caregiver, may also be in grief themselves. As they care for loved ones who are ill and/or dying, they are subject to their own feelings of grief and loss, are coping with physical and mental fatigue, and often feel overwhelmed. Sometimes they may feel taken for granted. In short, they must address several issues in addition to grief. These issues include the following: depression, living a life outside the norm, relinquishing their own dreams, and perhaps being faced with the overwhelming responsibilities for the financial, legal, medical communication, and hospitality functions. They, perhaps more than most, experience the "thousand deaths that occur before the actual death" (Kubler-Ross, November 20, 1981, personal communication).

Family caregivers also assist the ill with toilet and other activities for daily living. They answer phones; greet visitors; cook; clean; shop; handle finances, insurance, and other business matters; interface with medical and other care providers; and worry, love, and grieve for what was and what will be lost. They are nurse, counselor, and at times spiritual advisor. Their most critical role is not that of a "fixer" but rather one who will be there for the long term and will honor the individual and his or her illness and needs. To most effectively engage the loved one, the family caregivers may wish to enhance their communication skills. Effective listening techniques can ease the flow of conversation and assist in understanding the expression of needs. Questions using the word "why" should be used sparingly as this can be taken as judgment on the part of the loved one. Reflecting feelings ("It sounds like you are upset, or angry, or sad"), rather than "Why are you so angry?" can show care and respect as opposed to criticism.

Caregivers must also be careful to talk and treat their loved one with respect and dignity. Talking in a patronizing way can be hurtful and reinforce behavior that is unnecessarily dependent and childlike. When the loved ones are talking about their feelings, stay focused on their agenda and, hold back your own material for a while. Cultivate the art of just being there, in silence with no obligation to keep a conversation going.

Affirm the ill loved one and give yourself permission to be okay with their tears, anger, fears, guilt, or shame. These are all normal grief reactions, particularly when the medical condition is one that causes physical deterioration. For many caregivers, the role can become a spiritual practice in which a level of honesty with the loved one reaches deeply into his or her own awareness of life and its meanings. The ever-present changes due to illness also confront normal denial of the reality of loss of function and death leading to the possibility for the deepest levels of honesty in communication. When the end of life does come, the caregiver can know that he or she has had not only a difficult, draining, and grief-filled experience but also a spiritual journey that will forever change his or her own meaning of life in the post-loss world.

To be available as a family caregiver in the healthiest way for both the loved one and for oneself, there are self-care interventions or guidelines that must be part of the process. These guidelines will help to maintain the caregiver's own physical health and psychological equilibrium.

Guidelines for Maintaining Caregiver Physical and Emotional Health

- Avoid making decisions that can be made by the person being cared for; whenever possible, offer him or her choices. This not only reduces decision-making stress, but also keeps the ill person involved in the process.
- Avoid doing things for the ill person that he or she can do without help. The individual being cared for may be able to do some self-care—feeding self, use of bathroom, and adjusting the TV—on his or her own.
- Take care of yourself: Eat regularly, exercise, rest, and get enough sleep. Caregivers' routines should include self-care activities daily.
- Take care of your own spiritual needs; attend religious services or have them at your home if possible; attend a workshop on a topic of interest; take a nature walk.
- Make sure the home is safe: Check any hazards regarding electrical appliances; security of medications, poisons, and household chemicals; and make sure bathing areas are safe from slippery surfaces.
- Have emergency phone numbers and important resources (legal, insurance, medical, financial, home repair) readily available.
- Encourage the drafting of a "living will" or advanced directives. If the ill person isn't willing to do this, talk about what specific life-saving or life-preserving measures he or she wants. Seek assistance

from a nurse or another person who has experience with these issues.

- Anticipate future needs so that you will not be caught by surprise when health care or household needs change; learn about hospice or available home health care services.

- Don't do it all alone. Connect with social support systems, including other family, friends, clergy, and community services. Let people know specifically what you need done—shopping, repairs, transportation, housecleaning, a prescription picked-up, other errands run, and visits with the loved one—so you can have a "time out."

- Don't let your loved one's illness or disability overshadow your entire life. Honor and value yourself by finding ways to pay attention to yourself. Become your own advocate as well as that of your loved one.

Guidelines for Visitors

Family caregivers play an important role in educating and managing visitor behavior. Many people who come to visit an ill or dying person are unsure of how to act; sometimes they irritate rather than soothe. To make visits more helpful, visitors should be apprised of all of the "interventions for helping grieving people" listed above, and of the following specific guidelines for visitors:

- As a visitor, you are making a commitment.
- Look at the person you are visiting.
- Talk directly to the individual.
- Make physical contact.
- Bring something as a connecting activity.
- Don't persist in probing for medical information or express concerns for the person's condition.
- Bring news of the outside world.
- Use humor when appropriate.
- Keep advice out of the conversation unless asked for.
- Be aware of your own feelings and respect them.

As a Visitor, You Are Making a Commitment.   Whether this is an ongoing activity or a one-time visit, it is a time devoted to supporting the person you are visiting. The agenda belongs to the ill person being visited. If you are too conscious of "doing a good deed," the person you are visiting will resent rather than welcome your presence.

Look at the Person You Are Visiting.   If you avoid eye contact, the person may conclude, "I must be too terrible to look at" or "I'm worse off than I thought." In addition to feeling insecure about one's physical appearance, the ill person may feel embarrassed. Stay focused on the person you are visiting and refrain from allowing every sound outside to pull your gaze away from him or her. This does not imply staring so intensely that the other is made to feel uncomfortable. Look away from time to time and then look back.

Talk Directly to the Individual.   Talking to another person in the room about the person whom you are visiting is discounting and hurtful. Additionally, using the "Royal We" ("How are *we* today? Would *we* like our meds now? Are *we* ready for lunch?") is hurtful. Just converse normally.

Make Physical Contact.   Approach the person, whether he or she is in bed or in a chair—and it's always best to *ask* if it's okay—hold a hand, wipe a forehead, or massage a foot. Offer to bring a drink or food, rearrange pillows, take a walk, or take a wheelchair stroll.

Bring Something as a Connecting Activity.   Anything that interests you or that you know interests the other person can be used as a good ice breaker: a novel, magazine article, prayer book or book of psalms, scriptures, cards, checkers, chess, or other games to play. You can also pray or reminisce together.

Don't Persist in Probing for Medical Information or Express Concerns for the Person's Condition.   Allow the person you are visiting to talk about his or her medical status or not. Share your concerns with and get additional medical information from the family caregiver.

Bring News of the Outside World.   Talking about the neighborhood, larger community, or workplace gives the person a sense of ongoing connection with the outside world.

Use Humor When Appropriate.   Some people will appreciate hearing new jokes; others will want to read humorous books or watch funny videos or DVDs together.

Keep Advice Out of the Conversation Unless Asked For.   If you want to make a suggestion, speak to the family caregiver. Such advice is not always met with enthusiasm; be prepared for this.

Be Aware of Your Own Feelings and Respect Them.   Visiting a very ill, disabled, or dying person can be a profoundly sad and possibly a scary experience. If you begin to feel overwhelmed by these feelings, it's time to say good-bye and make a promise to return. If possible, give a specific time when you will come back.

The Four Tasks of Mourning

There are care provider interventions listed below that require professional skills training. These are noted with an asterisk (*).

Worden's (2002) "four tasks of mourning" will be used as a structure for organizing care provider interventions that help the grieving person address each task for healing grief. Additional material on the four tasks of mourning appears in chapter 2. Trained volunteers, and professional health and pastoral care providers, as well as educators, workplace human resource, and employee assistance personnel, funeral directors, school counselors, and police/fire/rescue workers can address the four tasks. As previously mentioned, some care provider actions require no special training and others should only be engaged in by professional providers.

While there is some overlap between the areas of intervention, the extent to which care providers use the suggestions listed under each of the four tasks of mourning or in the clinical tools section below will depend on the background and training of the care provider.

Some of the care provider behaviors will be used in more than one of the tasks. Providers of different specialty areas may address each of the four tasks from their own point of reference (i.e., spiritual, medical, nursing, counseling, hospice, school, or workplace). The suggested activities represent a generalized response in each area, and the provider is expected to adapt these interventions to the unique needs of the grieving person(s).

Task I: Accepting the Reality of the Loss

As we discussed in chapter 1, people absorb the reality of their loss and its consequences at different rates. When grieving people are ready to confront their "loss as reality," providers must be particularly sensitive to their continuing need to strike some balance between facing the loss and avoiding the loss event. Also, be prepared for the *head/heart split*: Some people intellectually recall loss events with little or no accompanying physical or emotional reactions because the "head" knows the terrible truth but the "heart" has still not registered it. Thus, the grieving person may act as though the loss had not occurred. The activities that follow are designed to reconnect the grieving person with the reality of the loss and facilitate intellectual acceptance of its irreversibility.

Listening—The First Provider Action

Exquisite witnesses will listen first and provide ample opportunity for the grieving person to tell the story of the loss. This is the beginning of a long process of registering the awful truth of a death, a diagnosis, a paralysis, or a layoff. If the grieving person doesn't want to talk, suggest that he or she write thoughts down in a journal, speak them into a tape recorder, or write a eulogy and bring them to the next counseling session to share with the care provider.

Facilitating Insights Regarding a Terminal Illness Diagnosis*

When this task is to be addressed by a terminally ill individual, the care provider can review, clarify, or summarize a patient's current medical information by asking some of the following questions: "What is your understanding of your current medical condition?" "What specifically has the doctor or nurse told you?" "What do you believe your body is telling you?" "Who was with you when the doctor told you the diagnosis?" "What is the effect of this information on you?" "What do you believe the next steps are?"

Dealing with a Death*

To help with re-introducing the reality of the death or other loss condition, some of the following questions can be used: "How did you find out about the death?" "Where were you when you found out?" "What happened then?" "Who did you speak to next?" "Who made the funeral arrangements?" "Was there a viewing?" "How was that for you?" "Were you there when (he or she) died?" "Can you describe what happened?" "What was that like for you?" "Who else was in the room?" "Were you able to say good-bye?" "What did he or she look like?"

Recalling Rituals

Returning to the death-associated rituals can also help to reintroduce the reality of loss. "What was the funeral like?" "Where was it held?" "Who officiated at the service?" "What can you remember about the eulogies?" "Who gave them?" "Did you say anything at the service?" "At the graveside?" "What was the casket like?" "What was the burial like for you?" "Were you satisfied with the service?"

Additional techniques for helping with reality of loss insights are as follows:

- Review the medical examiner's report*, death certificate*, or newspaper story.
- Look over funeral artifacts: guest book, condolence cards, memorabilia items, funeral expense invoice, and a catalog with a picture of the casket.
- Create a ritual on paper for a missed funeral; script the details from beginning to end.
- Create a guided imagery exercise* for recall of a loss event, funeral, memorial, or burial.

Identify Changes in Life

To help a grieving person to gain a sense of what has changed as a result of the loss, the following questions may be useful: "What is different in your life now?" "What do you miss the most?" "When is the worst time for you?" "In what way does your body feel different now?" "What are some next steps for you now?" "How has life been different since you lost your job (or changed jobs or survived the layoffs)?"

Summary of Task I

The reconnecting by various means of the grieving person with the reality factors associated with the loss may give rise to emotional release. These are normal and expected grief reactions, and the griever should be made to feel that this is acceptable and appropriate behavior.

Task II: Experiencing the Feelings of Grief

If you are a care provider seeing a grieving person for a counseling session, make sure that the room you are using is private, quiet, and soundproof. Have one or two boxes of tissues within easy reach. Allow ample time for the session so that you are not tempted to look at the clock or your watch—or be preoccupied with what time it is.

The goal of the care provider is to accept the grieving person at whatever level of emotional expression he or she is willing or able to express. To facilitate the further expression of grief, the care provider can make the following suggestions (see also Externalization):

- *Look at photos.* Photos are a good source of background information. Old photos can also provide opportunities for grieving people to talk about older losses and childhood messages received about the acceptability of expressing such feelings as sadness, anger, and fear.

- *Write letters.** Grieving people can be encouraged to write a letter to the deceased loved one, to "Death," to their cancer, to their loved ones, to the old job, to the old home, to the beloved pet, to their doctor, or to their body. The letter can be read aloud to the provider if desirable.

- *Write a history.* Some people have a better grasp of the reality of their loss after they put their loss in some kind of historical perspective. I have found that writing the history of a relationship that has ended or some other significant loss can help individuals express their feelings.

- *Write stories.** Written accounts of grief can be fictionalized by the grieving person as a way to elicit feelings. Some published stories can also be used to help a person express feelings of grief. A booklet I have used effectively in this way is *Love You Forever* (Munsch, 1986).

- *Drawings.** Artwork can be used as an alternative in the same way letters or stories are written. The technique is for people who are more comfortable expressing themselves with images than with words. If the care provider has no training in the interpretation of drawings, then the grieving person can be asked to talk about the drawing and how it feels to draw about the loss and to express grief feelings.

- *Create memory books.* Many grieving people want to collect photos, letters, travel, and other memorabilia pertaining to the loved one or loss. This task almost always involves others in the work of remembering and sharing feelings. Families can work on these together and share feelings while creating the album.

- *Read books about the expression of feelings.* Many books have been written for grieving people. One that I find especially useful is *When Going to Pieces Keeps You Together* (Miller, 1976), which demonstrates how people can heal if they allow themselves to express their most painful emotions.

Task III. Adjusting to a Life Changed: Creating New Meanings in the Post-loss World

Acknowledging the Changes

New meanings, self-pictures, and views of the world must be created for the post-loss life. Moving from couplehood to single status or parent to bereaved parent will require a reconfigured self-picture and a new way to be seen by others. Attig (2004) discusses grief as an active, engaging life process rather than passive. The assumptions and meanings of the pre-loss world need to be rewritten, and the provider can assist the grieving person with this reconstruction (Neimeyer, 2001). Grieving people will typically experience pain as they adjust to their new circumstances. To help grievers clarify the extent of their losses and gain insight into the cognitive restructuring that must be accomplished, care providers can suggest the following:

*Compile a loss book** that will describe the post-loss world. Include lists of:

1. "What's different now?"
2. "Who am I now?" . . . that I am no longer part of a couple, the mother of a newborn baby, a worker in my old job, able to walk or breathe without life support . . . the list can go on and on.
3. "What do I need to learn or get help with?" This list will help to identify new skills required for life in the post-loss world.
4. "How are others doing it?" Support groups made up of people with similar losses can provide a place of comfort, acceptance, and an opportunity to learn from others how to handle many of the concerns that are part of their new identity. Surrounded by people coping with similar challenges, grievers can feel a sense of normalcy and comfort. (See appendix B for a listing of support organizations.)

Care Provider as Coach and as Teacher in the Post-loss World

Care providers need to help grieving people to become functional in the post-loss world.

This might entail:

1. Explaining the nature of the grieving process to grieving people.*
2. Acknowledging and normalizing feelings and behaviors that take place in difficult situations. Widows, for instance, often report that they don't feel welcome when they are with married friends. People who have lost their jobs may withdraw from social situations to avoid painful and embarrassing questions and conversation.*
3. Providing decision-making support for newly widowed parents. For example, advising a widow on managing her teenagers, making decisions, maintaining, and relaxing certain limits. Other consultants, such as educators, clergy, and medical personnel may be useful as additional resources.*
4. Facilitating bereaved siblings to re-enter social activities. For example, encouraging a boy who has lost an older sibling to join a little league team, Boy Scout troop, and/or school club.
5. Supporting people who have lost a mate to begin socializing. For example, coaching a widowed man who wants to call a woman he knows and ask her for a date.

Grieving people who have lost a loved one may need the care provider's assistance as they develop a new picture of themselves in the post-loss world. Dennis Klass (2001) sees the development of a new way of being with other people as an important part of healing. Bereaved people may be very fearful and hesitant to leave their social safety net. When they do venture out into new settings, the care provider can help such persons by setting up "length-of-stay time limits" and a "back door" arrangement for easy departure if needed. For example, the care provider can suggest that a widow sit at the back of a religious service near an exit, or that she go to a party for only an hour, or take her own car so that she can leave when she wants to. *Remember to respect the person's own timing on beginning to reenter social life.*

I have counseled bereaved older widowed persons for several months before they were ready to join an adult community program. They usually become active participants in the program and sometimes become attached and remarry.

Care providers may also seek out other resources to help with the transition.

Some men and women desiring to reenter the social dating world may need fashion advice or information about activities or opportunities for meeting others. The road back to social functioning in the post-loss world may be slow with many stops, starts, and regressions. Grieving people are creating a new narrative for living—and this takes time. For many, a gradual reentry to outer society beyond the safety and comfort of their inner social support circle is the least threatening approach.

Additional Resources

- *Books* can be a great source of help for grieving people as they struggle with relearning the world and reinventing themselves. I particularly recommend *A Grief Observed* by C. S. Lewis (1961). This non-fictional account of untimely death recounts how the author and his wife were able to foresee his life without her and how he could bring their happiness together into his future after she died. In *When Bad Things Happen to Good People*, by Rabbi Harold Kushner (1981), the author tries to reconcile his earlier concepts of God with a new notion of God's role in tragedy. See appendix A for additional reading suggestions.

- *Drawings** can help a grieving person envision his or her new life. I suggest the "past, present, future" drawing. Ask the person to divide a piece of paper into thirds. Panel one depicts life *before* the loss occurred. Panel two depicts life now *since* the loss occurred. Panel three represents the life the person desires in the *future*. Another helpful activity is drawing what it will take to achieve the desired future state. Whatever form of artwork is used by the grieving person, it is useful to have the person describe what it is he or she has drawn, how they feel about the material, and how the drawings contribute to a sense of how they would like their life to be in the post-loss world.

- *Spiritual resources* that come from a grieving person's faith can help that person make sense of a tragic loss and carry these new meanings into the post-loss world. When appropriate, care providers can refer a grieving person to a member of the clergy or a spiritual director for additional help in understanding the loss.

- *Setting goals for the future* can help a grieving person focus on what's ahead rather than on what's behind. If a person is unable to generate goals, suggest meditation, relaxation, guided imagery, and story-making exercises, such as creating "a fairy tale of your own life." These techniques can help a griever visualize and regain a sense of life's possibilities.

- *Training and education* can help a grieving person who feels ready to move on. There are many workshops on grief, loss, trauma, and bereavement open to the public sponsored by such organizations as hospice, the Compassionate Friends, AARP, funeral establishments, the Red Cross, and other community organizations. Having an intellectual understanding of human grief can provide a grieving person with a sense of control and serve to demystify his or her own grief reaction.

Task IV: Reconfiguring and Relocating the Bond with the Lost Person or Other Loss

The goal of this task is to learn how to maintain a bond with a deceased loved one while reclaiming life in the post-loss world. The key lesson is to realize that the bond must be altered to fit the new reality, but that it can still exist. A grieving person needs to think, "Though the image of my loved one is always with me and while I hold on to the legacy of values we shared, I don't expect him or her to be physically present as a living bond-mate."

I suggest that people who are grieving need to create a new kind of bond with their deceased loved one—a *spiritual bond*—or one that creates a new image of the deceased loved one. This new bond should define the loved one as gone but still available to the grieving person in his or her thoughts. This can play an important role in providing continued connection to the loved one in the post-loss world. Care providers can help to facilitate this transition by the following:

1. *Ask questions** to uncover the grieving person's relationship to the ill or deceased loved one:
   - "How do you relate to your loved one now?"
   - "Do you ever find yourself talking to her or him?"
   - "When or under what circumstances do you talk to her or him?"
   - "How do you feel about doing this?"
   - "How does this affect your life?"
   - "What gets in the way of being able to have an inner conversation?"
2. *Deal with unfinished business** with the deceased loved one that may be preventing the formation of a continuing bond. The provider can assist with the recall of memories—both positive and negative concerning the deceased.

To elicit *positive memories*, use family photo albums, have the person write an autobiography, or create an annotated timeline highlighting key moments in the deceased person's life. Help the grieving person to verbalize what he or she wants to thank the loved one for, what legacy or values will be carried forward into the post-loss world.

Negative memory recall* may also need to surface for a sense of catharsis. What hurt or angry feelings, upsetting events, or sense of lack of attention is still unfinished from the relationship? This can be accomplished through writing a letter, making a list on a chalk board or flip chart, drawing a picture, talking out loud to the deceased, or in guided imagery.* Unpleasant memories associated with the deceased loved one may be traumatic for the grieving person. The care provider should be prepared for the possibility of a strong emotional release.

Care must be taken with individuals who are too fragile to handle traumatic memories. Some grieving people may need additional time to feel safe enough to engage in recall of negative memories and some may lack sufficient mental health to do this work. Individuals who show features of post-trauma stress should be seen by a professional who has experience with this level of anxiety disorder.

Care providers will need to be skilled in such externalization techniques* as the "empty chair," role-playing, or psychodrama. (The section on "Externalization of the Feelings of Emotional Pain" below provides further details.) They can also ask questions such as "What is still left over?" "If he or she were in that chair, what might you say to your loved one?" If the grieving person feels awkward about having a conversation with someone who is not there, the care provider can suggest that the person write a letter by asking, "What would you say to him or her in a letter?" "Would you feel comfortable sharing this letter with me?"

3. *Help the grieving person(s) say good-bye.** If a "good-bye" never took place or if it was insufficient, this lack of closure could block the formation of an altered (spiritual) bond with the loved one. (See "Saying Good-bye Exercise" below.)

4. *Discuss the ways that the loved one continues or could continue to be mentioned* in family rituals, conversations with family and friends, religious services, memorials, as well as memorialized through donations to charity.

5. *Help the grieving person envision the future through drawing.** Using the "past, present, future" drawing techniques, encourage the person to depict in the "future" panel the type of spiritual bond

he or she would like to establish with the deceased. When people have difficulty imagining such a bond, I sometimes simply ask the individual to "say whatever comes up about the deceased."*

Summary of Four Tasks of Mourning/Healing

The four tasks and the associated care provider actions listed above are a sample of what may be used to assist the grieving person's need to address each of the healing tasks. As noted, some of these require training in mental health skill areas such as in drawing interpretation, guided imagery, release of negative emotional material as unfinished business, or teaching about the human grief response. Questions and concerns regarding religious belief systems should be referred to members of the clergy and/or to a spiritual advisor. Physical concerns should be referred to medical and nursing care providers. The tasks clearly overlap and some of the strategies can be used for more than one task area. Worden's "four tasks" have been adapted for application to workplace change and grief (Jeffreys, 1995).

The work of addressing each of the four tasks may continue at varying levels of effort throughout life. Some people need far less of one area than another and typically may be addressing multiple areas simultaneously. When individuals seek and obtain grief counseling or grief therapy from a mental health professional, clinical tools exist that can be used as part of the practitioner's tool kit.

Clinical Tools for Mental Health Professionals*

Clinical interventions are behaviors that require (a) either technical training for volunteers from a sponsoring organization—hospice, hospital pastoral care department, community crisis center—or (b) professional provider training and/or continuing education programs for physicians, nurses, mental health professionals, funeral directors, or clergy. Clinical tools below* include methods for gathering needed information and techniques for trained care providers engaging in counseling or therapy. These can be used with individuals who are having difficulties with normal grieving and with complicated grief as well.

Grief Assessment*

Part of the information gathering process should include an assessment of the level and nature of grief. This can be done very informally by simply using the following questions in the grief assessment below.

Death Inquiry*

Learn the circumstances of the death:

- "Tell me what happened."
- "How did you find out?"
- "Was this death expected?"
- "Were you there at the time of death? Describe what that was like for you."
- "Tell me about the funeral. How was this for you?"
- "Did you get a chance to say anything before he or she died?"
- "Did you see the body? The burial? Cremains (cremation ashes)?"

History of the Relationship with the Deceased*

Determine the level of ambivalence and dependence the person had with the deceased:

- "How would you describe life with your loved one?" (Note how idealized the recall is.)
- "What was positive for you in this relationship? What was negative?"

Determine the nature and extent of unfinished business with the deceased:
"What is still left over for you about this relationship?"

Post-death History*

- "What has been happening since the death?"
- "How have things been between you and your family?"
- "How have people been reacting to you since the loss?"
- "How have things been at work, at school, at _____?"

Nature and Extent of the Current Grief*

- "How would you describe your grief?"
- "When is the hardest time?"
- "To what extent have you been able to return to usual activities?"
- "What physical symptoms are you experiencing?"
- "How have you been sleeping?"
- "What has your appetite been like?"
- "How has your energy level been?"
- "Have you been having any difficulty in concentrating?"

- "What helps you feel better?"
- "How has your attitude toward yourself been?"
- "Have you had any suicidal or homicidal thoughts?"

Available Support System and Resources

- "Who in your family or social network can you turn to?"
- "What organizations or community groups can you turn to for support?"
- "Do you have a religious or spiritual community to support you?"
- "In what way does your own belief system or life philosophy help you at this time?"

Cultural and Traditional Background Information

It is urgent for the care provider to learn as much as possible about the grieving person's religious, spiritual, and/or and cultural background so that the provider can minimize any behaviors that may be in conflict. Information about the family's traditions may be obtained during the assessment session and/or from family, friends, and neighbors.

Special Considerations Regarding Ethnicity, Religion, and Culture

- "Tell me about religious, ethnic, cultural beliefs or traditions and how these influence funeral, memorials, or burial/cremation rituals."
- "To what extent does your family observe these rituals?"
- "What are some reading resources you can provide me regarding the cultural requirements of your tradition?"
- "Who can I speak with to learn more about your traditions to facilitate our work together?"
- "What are your beliefs regarding an afterlife?"
- "How does this affect the way you maintain a continuing relationship with your loved one?"

Loss History*

- "What other losses have you thought about since you sustained this loss?"
- "Is there unfinished business or are there issues that need to be addressed from any of these previous losses?" "What are these issues?"
- "How did you and your family address each of these prior losses?"

- "May we make a list of these losses and any other issues in your past history?"

Suicide Risk Assessment*

Each care provider will usually develop his or her own individual methods for eliciting information on suicide risk. The goal is to determine the extent to which there is suicidal ideation and the existence of specific plans for self-destructive behavior. Does the survivor have a history of prior attempts or diagnosis of major depression? The existence of prior attempts and/or major depression can elevate the risk factor for suicide. (You can adapt the assessment items below to your own style of inquiry.) Take every comment related to killing self, not wanting to live, reunion ideation (wanting to die to be reunited with deceased loved one) seriously.

- Ask how often this thought comes up.
- Ask if they ever think about how they would do this.
- If they have no plan or ideas about methods, let them know that you take this very seriously and let the person know that it is important that they keep you informed about such ideas.
- If they indicate that this is a serious option, you can set up a contract regarding your being immediately notified should they feel that the impulse is strong enough to attempt suicide or harm themselves.
- If they refuse or if you doubt their sincerity, notify a family member.
- If the situation is such that you believe acting on suicidal impulse is likely, detain the person and call 911 or other pre-determined emergency support.
- Once a person has given some indication of suicidal ideation, the provider should keep current regarding any changes in the risk level.
- Determine to what extent the person is engaging in substance abuse because overdosing is frequently used as a method for suicide attempts.

Externalizing the Feelings of Emotional Pain*

Externalization Defined. Externalization is a process developed for use in workshops conducted by the former Elisabeth Kubler-Ross Center, is an expressive modality designed to facilitate the emotional release of stored unfinished business. It is a procedure provided for people who desire to release old or current feelings of grief. Generally, people externalize to the extent that they feel safe in their environment and with the provider facilitating this process.

Note: The externalization techniques used in the former Kubler-Ross workshops require specialized training by experienced facilitators. The process being described here is a limited version that can be done by trained mental health professionals.

The care provider needs to feel comfortable with the information expressed by the grieving person; otherwise, the grieving person will feel inhibited. Providers working with grieving or dying people and their families must pay attention to their own personal unfinished business to be able to attend to their griever's agenda rather than to their own. The grieving person needs to know that the provider can handle his or her anguish and won't be judgmental or flee from the distress of hearing the sound of emotional pain.

Care providers also need to keep in mind cultural variations that affect how comfortable a person may be when sharing intimate feelings. The provider should find out as much information regarding cultural norms *before* offering the grieving person an opportunity to externalize feelings. When in doubt, consult with a colleague or another resource person.

Grieving People Want to Be Heard.   They want to know that you know how hurt they are. They need to know it's okay to feel and express all of their thoughts to you, even the ones they consider "crazy." Your comfortable self, your good listener self, and your interest in their hurt and thoughts are the basis for a caring, safe, and healing environment.

Here are specific suggestions for helping grieving people release feelings of emotional pain:

- *Be self-aware*. Care providers need to be aware of their own Cowbells and be available to help the grieving person release his or her emotions. This communicates trust and safety.
- *Secure the environment*. Make sure that the work area is private, soundproof, and that the risk of interruptions is minimized. Cell phones and pagers should be turned off!
- *Establish confidentiality*. Assure the grieving person that what he or she says is private and confidential, and will not be released except in certain instances such as when there is a risk to the safety and/or life of the grieving person or of another person.
- *Time boundaries*. Clearly state the time boundaries of the session by saying at the outset, "We have 1 hour to be together this morning; if we need more time, we can schedule this." Avoid obvious checking of the clock or your watch.
- *Communicate permission to grieve*. Let the person know that this is a safe place and any feelings that come out are okay. "This is a place where people cry, express anger, and fears all the time." Make sure that tissue boxes and a waste can are placed within reach.

- *Be a skilled listener.* First listen—and then listen some more. Never interrupt the flow of feelings or thoughts. From time to time, paraphrase the content of what the person has said and then reflect back the *feelings* you hear: "What I hear you saying is. . . ." "It sounds like what this means to you is. . . ." "This is so very sad for you." "It sounds like you have so much pain." "I hear the pain behind those tears." This way, the person knows that he or she has been heard and feels acknowledged.
- *Going further.** Once the professional mental health care provider has established a good rapport with the grieving person, he or she can be offered an opportunity to express additional feelings by asking questions like, "What is still left over for you?" "What would you still like to tell your loved one?" If words fail, ask the person to do a drawing activity, put his or her thoughts into a letter to the deceased, and/or begin to keep a "feelings journal." Such a journal can record feelings throughout the week and be brought into the session to discuss with the care provider.

The use of some of the techniques of externalization as part of grief counseling can help with addressing Worden's Task II, which is concerned with the release of the emotional pain of grief. However, it is the combination of affective release and cognitive restructuring (making new meanings for the post-loss world) that provides the basis for healing grief.

Cognitive and Behavioral Approaches*

Once people begin to release their feelings through externalization, they need to address two critical cognitive issues in the grieving–healing process: the unfolding picture of self and the assumptions about the pre-loss world. In other words, they need to *reconfigure their sense of identity* and create *new meanings* and *new assumptions* for their new life. The process of reinventing self and relearning the world is a major step in the process of healing grief.

The point at which these cognitive issues are raised varies, and the care provider should take cues from the client's communication. When appropriate to the grieving client's need, it is useful to compare the realities of life before and after the loss. How the person made sense of the pre-loss world may not fit the post-loss world. The creation of a new self and new world meanings are usually not without some pain. For example, I worked with a bereaved mother who sobbed every time she took out the trash. "Am I going crazy?" she asked me. "All I'm doing is taking out the garbage, and I can't stop sobbing as I do this." I soon learned that this had been one of her dead son's chores. She wasn't going crazy. She was simply externalizing emotional pain while at the same time she was adapting to a new responsibility in her post-loss world.

When helping a grieving person adapt to the post-loss world by relearning his or her identity, the care provider can use the following questions:

"How are people reacting to you now?" "What is this like for you?" Focus on discussions of how the grieving person perceives other people's reaction to them. Locate the points of discomfort in the interactions. For example, friends and colleagues who are uncomfortable may change the topic, stay away, become very anxious and stumble for words, say hurtful things, press for too much information, or give unwanted and inappropriate advice. Assure the grieving person that such reactions are typical, and help him or her create some responses for use in several different scenarios or social situations, as well as how to avoid the situation. For example, if someone said to a widow or widower, "You should start dating," he or she can say, "Thanks, I'll think about that," or "I'll work on it," or "I know you're trying to help, but I'm just not there," or "I really can't talk now, see you another time." Some grieving people just walk away and firmly say, "That's not helpful!"

A care provider's questions about the details of social interactions can also help a widow/widower establish a new identity as a single person.

The new reality of who the grieving person is can unfold in conversations of how others react and how his or her new self-picture is being shaped by social interactions. People who have lost a life partner have a major investment in the identity of being part of a couple. What is it like to go to family and other social events as "a single and not part of a couple?" What is it like to attend a school function as the mother of a child whose father is dying? What is it like for a child whose parents are engulfed in caring for a dying sibling? When a significant relationship that helps us to define who we are is lost or is threatened, part of our self-picture is open to change.

To help in this process, care providers can ask:

- "Now that your husband is gone, what plans do you have for the house, the business, your daughter's wedding, or your family's vacation?"

- Ask the grieving person to talk about potential short-term and long-term changes. These questions can begin a process of thinking of what will be done in the new role of a bereaved person who must function without the loved one.
- "What's different for you now?" This question can initiate a discussion of how the *post-loss world is changed* and how the grieving person is adapting to some of the changes and not to others. All of these activities and discussions give the person an opportunity to hear him or her talk about the new circumstances. Naturally, emotional pain may accompany the intellectual discussions of the adaptation. One widow was calmly outlining the new skills she needed and the ways she would compensate for the emptiness she felt since her husband's death. Suddenly she began to sob and cried out, "No! No! I won't have him dead. I won't!" This is an opportunity for the care provider to facilitate additional emotional release.
- "*Who was I? Who am I now? Who will I be?*" The answers to these questions can be worked over a period of weeks through drawings (past, present, and future) or writing exercises ("My Goals for the Future"; "My Autobiography Five Years from Now"; "The Fairy Tale of My Life"). Wherever possible, ask the grieving persons to include any values and/or traits of the deceased loved one as they describe "Who Will I Be?" in any of these exercises. Often a discussion of the completed activities will help grieving people gain insight into the process of slowly adapting to the post-loss world and healing. A meeting of family members can be held to review a memory book, share feelings of grief, and discuss the deceased and the survivors' hopes for the future.

Assistance for Further Facing the Post-loss Reality

When grieving people are ready, they can be given various assignments that may help them to integrate their new understanding of what they have lost. Some appropriate assignments include visiting the gravesite, obtaining family photos since the death; listing items of the deceased to be given away to family and friends, creating a memory book, including funeral memorabilia, gathering notes about the deceased from friends and family, and making plans to modify the loved one's room or closets.

A care provider can also suggest the following cognitive/behavioral activities:

- Write a letter to yourself about who you are now.
- Find examples in films and novels of people who experienced a loss similar and study how they coped in their post-loss world.

- Create a list of ideal beliefs about yourself that you want to make a reality one day.
- Find a new hobby or activity that you enjoy that is not dependent on another person.
- Keep a record of positive experiences throughout the week.
- Where possible, schedule as many of the positive experiences listed.
- Make a list of tasks that must be accomplished, which were formerly the responsibility of the deceased. See how many of these tasks you can do.
- Develop a list of organizations and people who can help support completion of the four tasks of mourning.
- Rehearse responses to people who are unaware of the loss.
- Learn to use relaxation and meditation techniques.
- Compose a list of things that he or she is grateful for.

Dealing with Guilt

Elements of "guilt are typically present in each mourner's bereavement experience" (Rando, 1993, p. 479). Guilt is also a common feeling for family caregivers and other family and friends of ill and dying people. In certain situations, guilt may be especially intense and complex. Some manifestations of guilt are so debilitating for the grieving person that they contribute to a level of dysfunction that causes complications in the mourning process. This will be further addressed in chapter 9.

Often, bereavement guilt is related to the grieving person's caregiving role. We hear such statements as "I should have brought hospice in sooner and reduced his or her suffering," "I never should have put Mom in that nursing home," "We should have gotten another medical opinion," "I didn't visit her enough," "I wasn't there when he died," and "I didn't call 911 soon enough." Other comments about guilt relate to the relationship and/or activities taking place just prior to the death: "I wasn't such a good son," "I failed my parental job description," "I was so mean to my brother," "I never should have allowed her to go out that night," "We fought all the time and now. . . ."

Regrets, Recriminations, and Self-Condemnation.* Typically, regrets, recriminations, self-condemnation, and many "should haves and shouldn't haves" are part of the typical guilt conversations grieving people have. What they have in common is the feeling that "I didn't do it right; I wasn't good enough." Many times, guilt is a way of trying to extract some meaning from a situation that resists meaning making. By engaging in self-attacks for the perceived or real failures, the grieving person has a basis for explaining why this terrible thing happened. There are some mourners who feel strongly that the death or other loss is part of their own punishment for past misdeeds or sins. Some guilty feelings can arise simply because the grieving person survived while another person died.

> *The care provider* needs to be aware of the pervasiveness of guilty thoughts and comments and allow them to be presented at least initially without challenge. However, while guilty feelings should not be aggressively confronted, they should not be minimized or validated. I have found that guilt often dissipates over time and requires skilled listening and normalizing from the care provider. For example, "Guilt is something I hear a lot of the time. I hear what you are saying and want you to know that for many people this is part of the grieving process."

There are some situations in which the grieving person was actually involved in the cause of death through negligence or poor judgment (failure to adequately supervise a child, reckless driving, etc.). Grieving people suffering from guilt arising from these causes may need special help from a qualified mental health professional.

Here are some general guidelines for dealing with grieving people who feel guilty:

- *Listen and respect** the need for expressing these feelings. Obtain full expression of the guilt material.
- *Normalize** the feelings when appropriate.
- *Do a reality test** if guilt persists. To do this, ask the grieving person the following: "Do the medical facts support your beliefs? Does the police report support them? Does a review of the positive aspects of the relationship support your guilt?"
- *Use self-forgiveness** as a way of enabling a grieving person to acknowledge the imperfection of being human and provide a possibility of coexisting with the sad memories of the cause of death.
- *Offer the possibility of spiritual and religious guidance** in order to confess, do penance, and/or achieve atonement for perceived failings.

Forgiveness as a Healing Tool.*   Asking for and giving forgiveness is a useful activity for freeing the grieving person from negative material that has resisted release. The act of forgiveness is a way to alter the ties to a living or spiritual bond. It is an important part of saying good-bye and letting go of what was. Any unfinished business—resentments, frustrations, hurts, and other negative material—can be released like an "unfinished symphony" through the practice of forgiveness. According to Byock (1997), "The resolution of unfinished business can form the basis of new beginnings and a continued bond with the loved one" (p. 160).

The openness to and initiation of forgiveness does not condone the negative behavior that has caused pain and damage. Forgiveness is directed to the actor but not the act. Forgiveness often serves as the vehicle for releasing any old, unfinished business. Forgiveness can flow in each of three directions:

1. Forgiveness can be given to another person who has caused pain or injury.
2. Forgiveness can be requested from another to whom we may have caused pain or damage.
3. Forgiveness can be given to oneself.

The notion of forgiving oneself should not be overlooked. People who cling to guilt and are unable to heal can lighten their load by forgiving themselves. As the Hebrew sage Hillel said, "If I am not for myself, who will be for me? If I am only for myself, what am I?" The Buddha said, "There is no one in the universe more deserving of love than oneself." As Levine stated (1987, p. 90), "We ask for and offer forgiveness . . . because we no longer wish to carry the load of our resentments and guilts."

Saying Good-Bye as a Healing Tool*

Some grieving people may reject saying good-bye for their own reasons—they don't want to let go yet or simply feel it is unnecessary. This decision must be respected without any admonitions. Many people believe that the ideal time to say good-bye is while the dying person can still acknowledge his or her loved one. Some feel that good-bye is useful only before a loved one has died. There is no right way.

Following is a personal account.

> My friend had just slipped into a coma—he was dying after a long battle with lung cancer. His children were grown. His wife and children were sad and yet realistic about his imminent death. He had provided very well for them, both emotionally and financially, and they stood by his bedside waiting for him to stop breathing. About a half-hour later, his daughter arrived at the hospital after he lost consciousness. She was terribly upset to learn that she had "missed Dad."
>
> I suggested that she say, silently or out loud, whatever she wished she had been able to say to him before he lost consciousness. She hesitated, looked at me inquiringly, and I said, "You can assume that Dad can hear you." That was all she needed. About 15 minutes later, she left his room relieved that she had been able to say good-bye.

Since I had to leave, I stopped in my friend's room to say one more good-bye.

He lay on his back breathing with great effort. I told him silently that he had done a great job for his family and that, because of the way he had handled his end-of-life phase, they were in great shape—sad but okay. I said good-bye and told him that he didn't have to worry about his family and that he could leave anytime he needed to.

My office is 5 minutes from the hospital. As I came through the front door, the phone was ringing. His son-in-law told me my friend had just died.

There is no *one and only* time for saying good-bye. Good-byes can be said immediately after a person has been pronounced dead or a week, a month, or even years later. The uttering of the word "good-bye" directed to the loved one who has died is the mourner's way of taking a step into the grieving–healing journey.

Some grieving people reject the idea of saying *good-bye*. Care providers can let them know that any phrase (such as "so long for now") can be used instead. The care provider can also suggest, "Say anything you want your loved one to hear from you now as a form of good-bye, as a way of completion for now and/or of forgiveness. There may be other things to say to your loved one at another time.

Saying Good-Bye.* Saying "good-bye" can be a time to share what you have learned from the dying person and will use in your life. Remembering some pleasant times together and, if appropriate, a time to offer or request forgiveness. A time to clear and free the heart so that the dying person can leave less encumbered and the surviving person can continue life less encumbered. This can be done in person or through meditation or prayer when a loved one is many miles away.

Saying good-bye is especially useful when family or other intimates have come after the person has died and are feeling guilty and regretful at having missed the last opportunity to talk to the deceased. Byock (1997) suggests a four-part "good-bye" message that contains giving forgiveness, asking for forgiveness, expressing love, and saying good-bye. Saying "good-bye" is to begin or to continue a process of coping with the reality of the loss or imminent loss, and initiating a continuing connection to the loved one.

As discussed earlier, *care providers* can also help family members at this time by suggesting ways to say good-bye and ways to give permission to the dying loved one to leave. This is often difficult. Many times, the family doesn't want to let go, and dying people are reluctant to say good-bye even if they are in pain, for many want to stay and protect those who will be left behind. In situations where death is imminent, and the family is willing, care providers can help the family understand that they can assist the dying loved by saying things like, "It's all right to go whenever you are ready." "I love you and we'll be okay." Where the dying person has expressed guilt over leaving, such a statement by family members can ease the loved one's release and be a final gift.

Saying Good-Bye Exercise.* This is an activity that the reader can complete to experience saying good-bye in preparation for using it with people who have a loved one who is dying, has lapsed into a coma, or has already died. The activity itself can evoke strong emotions and is best done with another trusted person present. I usually recommend that students and trainees do as much as they are comfortable doing and note in their journal the areas of discomfort. These areas should be discussed or worked through as part of the "heart" dimension of the *exquisite witness* care provider.

Exercise 5. Saying Good-Bye

Directions: Write down the following:

1. Choose someone who you would want to say good-bye to if he or she were going to die, or someone who has already died that you would have wanted to say good-bye to.

2. Think of what legacy in values or ideals you have received from the person in terms of living life and what you would wish to say by way of thank you, of good-bye, or so long for now.

3. Think of what you can say to forgive him or her for any leftover negative material if appropriate.

4. Think of the forgiveness you may wish to ask for from this person if appropriate.

5. What else might you want to ask or say to this person?

6. In what way do you need to forgive yourself for any unfinished issues?

Take some time to sit and meditate with whatever has come up for you. Then do some journaling, listing areas of discomfort, unfinished material that may require additional attention—and material that brought a smile to your face. The more a care provider can be open to this personal material, the less energy will be used to hold it down. This frees the provider to be more available to grieving people and to living in general.

The Use of Rituals for Healing

Technically, " . . . a ritual is a specific behavior or activity that gives symbolic expression to certain feelings and thoughts . . . individually or as a group" (Rando, 1984, p. 105). Rituals are taking place all around us all the time. Rituals can be a one-time occurrence (a moment of silence) or a repeated event (memorial candle lighting). They provide a grieving person with an action to take at a time of feeling helpless. We tell grieving people *don't do nothing!* Doing nothing invites helplessness and despair.

Some death and mourning related rituals are already in place by virtue of our culture and religious traditions—such as procedures used by clergy, funeral directors, the military, and organizations such as unions, societies, and other groups. Ceremonial activities at funerals and memorials, and the burials and disposal of cremains may be pre-ordained by custom and religious requirement.

Some rituals can be as simple as the moment of silence before a meal or other social events. We frequently hear a wedding officiant acknowledge deceased individuals who will be "part of this special time as we bring them into our minds and hearts." At other times, we light a candle, plant a tree, place flowers at a grave, make a donation in someone's name, place a notice of remembrance in the newspaper, create a memorial foundation or scholarship fund, have a fundraiser for a special cause, organize a food drive, or have a benefit performance "in the name of. . . ."

All of the above are rituals designed to acknowledge and honor the death of a loved one, to maintain connection with them, and to give us a reason to undertake a useful action.

Holidays and Special Calendar Days.   Special days such as Mother's Day, Father's Day, and anniversaries are appropriate and natural times for bereaved people to acknowledge their lost loved ones and maintain their continued bonds. Care providers can help individuals and families to plan for some ritual or ceremonial observance of acknowledgment. Families can create artwork, letters of remembrance, memory albums, and collage posters.

When I was a child, Mother's Day was celebrated in part by dressing up in our best spring clothes and promenading on a broad avenue where we bought sweets from vendors. Adults wore a red carnation to signify that their mothers were still living.

Those people whose mothers were dead wore a white carnation. *Everyone* had a carnation to wear and everyone acknowledged his or her mother's existence. (I have suggested this simple ritual to people observing the first Mother's Day following their mother's death.)

A holiday like Thanksgiving offers many opportunities for remembrance.

Families can be encouraged to mention the name of their deceased loved one at family gatherings in some way. This may not be as difficult as it may seem at first. The first post-death Thanksgiving meal can be a time to start a new tradition. Prior to beginning the meal, the family can decide that all family members will have an opportunity to mention any blessings they are aware of and to name whomever they are missing. A deceased loved one's favorite food can be served, a candle can be lit in remembrance, and a vase of flowers can be placed on the table in honor of a deceased loved one. Sharing will help people recall the loved one's special role in the family. Remembrance, acknowledgment, and celebration of legacy are important ingredients in rituals. Each family will be able to create these to meet their own needs.

In addition to holidays, families have to cope with *life cycle events*— graduations, weddings, and birthdays. These can be very intimidating. Some grieving people commemorate these occasions by visiting the grave, urn, or site of scattered ashes; singing hymns and other meaningful songs; and recalling and reminiscing about the loved one.

Here is a personal story:

"Happy Steven's Birthday," I heard my son Ronald say into the telephone. His brother Steven would have been 35 years old today, October 23. His older sister, Deborah, called earlier. Each year on his birthday, my wife and our two surviving children make telephone or in-person contact to acknowledge the day. We repeat this ritual on November 23, the anniversary of his death. It's a simple ritual and serves our need to join in acknowledging that we are the family that lived through his illness and death. It makes me feel good to make this special connection on these important days.

However, some grieving people seek to avoid any overt rituals concerning their loved one. This is their decision and must be respected. The truth is that whether mentioned or not at a family meal, wedding, bar or bat mitzvah, confirmation, graduation, baby naming, baptism, or other life cycle event, the deceased loved one will be in the minds of those who are in attendance.

Some cultures revere and maintain contact with ancestors and bring the wisdom of those who went before into their lives. In this vein, we can acknowledge those values that have been received from the deceased loved one by means of a private meditation or prayer or through remembrances at a family gathering. Journal keepers can record this wisdom in their journals. None of these activities requires much time to plan or implement, yet they all maintain the continuing bond and bring the loved one into the post-loss world.

Spontaneous Rituals and Memorials.　These can be seen at locations where a vehicle crash has taken the life of someone's loved one. Crosses with flowers or ribbons dot highway median strips and roadways. Outpourings of flowers, cards, drawings, photos, covered the sides of fences, buildings, and sidewalks of the area in lower Manhattan where the World Trade Center towers were brought down by terrorists. The Royal Palace and many other areas in Britain were deluged with flowers after the death of Princess Diana.

The Vietnam Memorial is the site of many treasures and cards that are left at the base of the wall. The wall is visited every day, and on Memorial Day hundreds of people are present at the ceremonies. I was at the wall on one Memorial Day. The crowds were of mostly middle-aged men in various uniforms identifying their service and unit. Parents and wives, children and friends of the men and women whose names were on the wall were there in great numbers. Some silently moving through the post-ceremony throngs. Others, with red and tearing eyes, looked slightly dazed as they stared at the patterns of names on the black granite surface—a surface shining with death. Piled at the wall were flowers and assorted other items. I saw boots, medals, letters, poems, pictures, and other articles of clothing and battle gear. Many of the surviving veterans of "Nam" greeted each other, caught up on back home news, and parted with promises to "see you next year."

Just before the ceremony ended, our attention was directed to the bugler . . . this led me to write the poem below.

Taps at The Wall: A Ritual

Taps at The Wall
It tears into our hearts
And brings us into the memory.

I see men and women in various uniforms
With hands saluting the black granite tribute.
Gnarled, arthritic hands
And blotchy, wrinkled hands,
And young, sinewy hands,
Saluting the thousands who are not physically here.

But maybe, as we hear the final notes
Of that bugler's Taps,
I feel the Thousands from The Wall . . .
Saluting back.
November 11, 2002

©2002, J. Shep Jeffreys

☐ A Care Provider's Grief and Cowbells

Critical to the actions taken by a care provider is always his or her own unfinished business (Cowbells) or countertransference. A final consideration for care providers is their own stored loss material. They need to address this so that it doesn't distract them from hearing and being available to the people they are trying to help. A care provider's reaction to a grieving person's emotional pain has been called *compassion fatigue*, *secondary trauma*, *burnout*, and *countertransference*.

> I once worked with a woman in an abuse workshop who, as a child, had been repeatedly beaten by her mentally ill mother. In our session of work, she allowed herself to regress to that very young age and cried out, "Mommy, mommy, I didn't do anything." This caught me in the heart and throat, paralyzing me. Fighting back tears and the desire to cry, I helped the woman return to her present age, and, after drawing the session to a close, left the workshop area. As soon as I was

alone, I cried and cried without any clear idea why this was happening. As I began to calm down, her little child screams tore through me again. This time, I recognized those painful, shrieking cries. It was Steven's crying out in pain as he underwent a bone marrow aspiration or a particularly painful lumbar puncture. I had swallowed my cries at the time; and for all the intervening years they were crying for release. I could not have continued serving as a facilitator in that workshop if I had not been able to work with a colleague and let the stored, suppressed pain out.

The *exquisite witness* care provider must be aware of personal material that has the potential for drowning out the person being helped. So much of our stored, unfinished business lurks below our level of awareness and manifests itself in camouflaged ways. We may find ourselves unusually fatigued, sad, depressed, unmotivated, impatient, or irritable with others, reluctant to approach certain patients or make a home visit to certain families. When any of these conditions becomes apparent, the care provider must examine for the possibility of unfinished personal loss and grief business—and do something about it if it appears that Cowbells are ringing.

One of the best remedies is to seek out a colleague or another person who understands the work of providing care to bereaved, ill, or dying people, who can listen and be supportive. When I work with health care staff who are vulnerable to provider grief, I encourage them to have a staff "buddy"—someone who can be called when needed during or after the workday. Retreats, in-service workshops, and regularly scheduled support groups are other ways to help staff members cope with their inevitable Cowbells. Having a designated staff support person available on some regular basis for individual consultation is well worth the expenditure.

For 12 years I served as the consulting psychologist in the Johns Hopkins AIDS Service as a support to outpatient and inpatient staff providing care to patients and their families. We scheduled regular staff support groups, made individual staff consultation available, held quarterly memorial services for deceased patients, and held several retreats. People working in settings where there is continuous dying have their own denial systems penetrated repeatedly. Attending to their Cowbells becomes a matter of staff support that contributes directly to availability to patients as well as to staff well-being.

☐ Provider Self-Assessment: The Four Tasks of Healing Exercise

The exercise below will sample your awareness of any current effects of Cowbells in your life.

Exercise 6. Self-Assessment

Choose an important loss in your life, possibly one you listed in the Past Loss Survey in chapter 2. How would you assess your level of completion of each for the four tasks of grief (with regard to a personal loss)? Please place an **X** in the appropriate location between **10** and **0** to indicate the degree of completion. (This can be done on a separate sheet.)

Identify Loss:

1. How real does the loss feel to you now?

Very real	Still mostly
No doubt that it happened	unreal
10	0

2. To what extent have you expressed your feelings about this loss?

Many feelings	Little or no feelings have
have been expressed	been expressed
10	0

3. Rate your level of adjustment to life regarding the loss.

Pretty used to life	Not used to life without
without deceased	deceased (or other loss)
(or other loss)	
10	0

4. How much of your inner picture of the deceased or other loss object is still the way it was before the loss occurred?

My connection with deceased is	Still can't let go of him/her
continued as a new inner image	or other loss as it used to be;
or spiritual bond, and this fits	have difficulty forming
with my new life.	new interests in my life.
10	0

This exercise is a sample of what you feel about a particular loss now. It is not a clinical tool for diagnostic or any other clinical assessment purpose. It is a way of looking at self and beginning a process of thinking about what, if anything, is surfacing at a particular time about a specific loss. It can be used for opening a conversation with yourself or another person about your Cowbells, your unfinished loss material. Give it some time and journal whatever comes up. You can revisit the loss and your ratings on the self-assessment at a later time to see what changes, if any, have occurred.

☐ Conclusion

This chapter has provided the reader with an array of interventions to use with grieving people who require some form of assistance. These range from basic supportive interventions to those requiring clinical skills.

It is my desire that you, as care providers and providers-in-training, will use the suggested interventions above and adjust them to meet your needs or your grieving person's needs. Add to them and share them with your colleagues. With this repertoire of activities, you will be a comfort to those who need your help, and you will experience a satisfying level of comfort as you do this sacred work.

While presenting the keynote address at the National Convention of the Employee Assistance Professionals Association in Baltimore, W. Mitchell, author and motivational speaker, pointed to his wheelchair and said, "It's not what happens to you; it's what you do about it." A Chinese proverb tells us, "You cannot prevent the birds of sorrow from flying overhead, but you can prevent them from building nests in your hair." Your job as care providers is to help grieving people keep those nests out of their hair.

Sometimes, the grieving–healing process goes painfully off course. Care for people with special needs and those with significant grief complications will be addressed in chapter 9. This will be followed by a series of case studies for practical application of assessment and intervention skills in chapter 10.

Complications of the Human Grief Process

> *While this chapter is intended primarily for use by care providers with mental health training, all care providers can obtain some general benefit from the material for referral purposes, especially the section on the signs and symptoms suggesting complicated grief.*

☐ Introduction

Much of the human grief process follows broad but expected patterns of thinking, feeling, and behaving. People who are grieving a loss can be expected to cry and be sad, angry, frightened, confused, or apathetic. They talk about their loss, sigh often, and engage in various rituals connected to the loss. Grieving people can also be expected to be preoccupied with their distress during this period of being outside their "normal" or pre-loss life for variable lengths of time. With time, most grieving people gradually heal and reclaim life—not the same life but a reasonable and functional life.

Sadly though, not all grieving follows this pattern. Sometimes the grieving person is unable to engage in the usual and customary grieving process, and complicated grief occurs. This is not only true for individual loss and grief but also for the social groups of which the grieving person is a member. The ripples of grief reactions flow outward from the person and family to the community and sometimes to the national and international communities as well. Where communities have been impacted by disaster, natural or man-made, people who have witnessed the incident or have viewed media coverage may be at risk for complications of grief as well as for physical and psychiatric disorders (Zinner and Williams, 1998).

This chapter will discuss how care providers can identify and address the complications of grief. It will also describe the various syndromes or categories of complicated grief and consider those conditions and circumstances that are likely to result in complicated grief reactions. Additionally, psychiatric disorders that are associated with complicated grief will be identified, and considerations for people who are coping with such traumatic death as suicide and the death of a child will be discussed.

People experiencing complicated grief need to see a mental health professional for help. It is essential that *all* care providers be familiar with the signs and symptoms of complicated grief so that they can make appropriate referrals.

☐ Definition: What Is Complicated Grief?

Complicated grief refers to grief that escalates to problematic proportions; that is, it is extreme in one or more of the dimensions of typical grief—*severity* of symptoms, *duration* of severe symptoms, and *level of dysfunction* socially, occupationally, and with regard to activities of daily living. This requires treatment by a qualified mental health professional. While complicated grief occurs most often after the death of a person, I have counseled people who exhibited complicated grief due to loss of a career, their home, the realization that they would never have their own biological child, and loss due to separation or divorce.

Complicated grief is also called *complicated mourning, abnormal grief, pathologic grief, pathological bereavement, neurotic grief,* and more recently *traumatic grief.* We will use the term *complicated grief* as the designation for grief reactions that extend beyond the usual and expected behaviors for human grieving. Severe complications can become psychiatric disorders, which are discussed later in this chapter.

Bowlby (1980) identifies two forms of complication:

- Chronic or prolonged grieving and
- Absent or insufficient grieving.

Rando (1993) reiterates this formulation and writes that the person afflicted with complicated grief seeks one of two goals:

- To avoid aspects of the loss, its pain, and the full realization of its implications or
- To hold on to and avoid relinquishing the lost loved one.

The care provider can be most helpful to a grieving person when it is understood how a particular complication *serves* the person. For some, by avoiding the expression of the grief, the person avoids the terrible reality of the loss and subsequent pain. Others may hold on to the grief to maintain connection with the deceased or loss condition.

Signs and Symptoms Suggesting Possible Complications of Grief

How do we know when the ship of grief has been blown off course into *complicated* waters? While there are specific criteria for identifying and assessing complicated grief, in my experience the distinction between uncomplicated grief and complicated grief is not clear. Most signs and symptoms of complicated grief appear along a continuum from less severe to very severe (Bowlby, 1980). Levels of dysfunction and severity of symptoms can be used as markers to determine the degree of seriousness of the grief complication. *The only clear exception to this is the case in which an individual is judged to be a danger to self or to others.*

Grief, complicated or not, comes in waves, more severe at times and less at others. When the bad times exceed the better times, when the griever finds little relief from deep distress or continues to behave in ways that cause concern to family and friends, care providers can suspect complications in the grief process. It is also not uncommon for people who seek nongrief related help from a mental health professional to find that the emotional disorder of concern has its roots in or is being aggravated by complicated grief.

Danger Signals for Complicated Grief

I have compiled a list of the most commonly agreed on signs and symptoms of complicated grief from several sources (Horowitz, 1997; Jacobs, 1993, 1999; Parkes & Weiss, 1983; Prigerson & Frank, 1995; Raphael, 1983; Rando, 1993; Worden, 2002), as well as from my own clinical experience. When I see three or more of these signs, I am alerted to the strong possibility that there are complications of grief. Several of the individual items listed below are viewed as serious signs of the existence of problematic grief and are noted as *serious alerts*. The care provider should gather this information when taking a history, by observing first hand or from reports of family, and/or other providers.

Emotional Signals

- Continued irritability or outbursts of rage with violent implications *(serious alert)*.
- Deep feelings of guilt, regrets, and a self-picture significantly below the pre-death level *(serious alert)*.
- Episodes of severe emotional yearning, pining, and mental searching for the lost person.
- Intense acute grief triggered by visual cues, musical sounds, and even smells that recall the person or loss event.
- High anxiety about the safety, health, and possible death of self and loved ones.
- Feelings of despair, hopelessness, and apathy about the future, which are verbalized as "What's the use?" "Life will always be empty, meaningless, and lonely."
- High levels of stress and anxiety about day-to-day or future tasks.
- Frequent panic attacks and intensifying or expanding phobic reactions to leaving the house, having visitors, talking about the loss, or being with others who knew the lost loved one.
- Deep depression and inability to function in daily life.
- Lack of any emotional expression regarding the loss.
- Inability to express any sense of feelings.

Cognitive Signals

- Suicidal thoughts and/or plans to act upon the thoughts *(serious alert)*.
- Severe mental disorganization including inability to concentrate or learn new information and inability to recall previously known information *(serious alert)*.

- Intrusive, distressing memories and thoughts about the deceased or lost relationship.
- Avoidance of discussion of the loss and avoidance of all signs, symbols, and mention of death and death-associated activities.
- Rigid retention of lost person's space and all belongings, *or* immediate removal of all traces of the existence of the lost relationship.
- Feeling stunned, dazed, or disoriented.
- A sense of being dead or of not functioning.
- Major shift in personality style—introvert to extrovert or vice versa.
- Experience of ongoing numbness, alienation, and detachment from self and others.

Behavioral Signals

- Self-destructive behaviors including self-cutting, substance abuse, workplace failure, burning of social bridges, and constant self-defeating comments *(serious alert)*.
- Radical and sudden changes in lifestyle, shocking family and/or friends—relocating, changing jobs, dropping out of school, or divorcing *(serious alert)*.
- Compulsive sets of repeated behaviors that interfere with daily living.
- Imitating the speech, dress, and behaviors of the lost person.
- Engaging in compulsive post-loss caregiving and/or replacement relationships.

Physical Signals

- Physical symptoms that imitate those of the deceased *(serious alert)*.
- Chronic physical complaints, such as gastrointestinal disturbance, muscular aches, headaches.
- Major disturbances in sleeping and eating—too much or too little.

Summary of Serious Alerts

- Suicidal thoughts and/or plans to act upon the thoughts.
- Self-destructive behaviors including self-cutting, substance abuse, workplace failure, burning of social bridges, and constant self-defeating comments.
- Severe mental disorganization including inability to concentrate or learn new information and inability to recall previously known information.

- Deep feelings of guilt, regrets, and a very low self-picture.
- Continued irritability or outbursts of rage with violent implications.
- Radical and sudden changes in lifestyle, shocking family and/or friends—relocating, changing jobs, dropping out of school, or divorcing.
- Physical symptoms that imitate those of the deceased.

Determining the Presence of Complicated Grief

Problematic signals and symptoms alone may not necessarily indicate the presence of complicated grief. I have found that deeply distressing and immobilizing grief may be quite normal immediately after the traumatizing loss of a loved one or the diagnosis of a terminal illness. To make a determination of *when* grief is complicated, three measures must be applied to the grief reaction (Jacobs, 1999).

Three Measures for Determining Complicated Grief Reaction

1. The degree of *severe and devastating symptoms* reported by others or assessed by the survivor.
2. The *length of time* the symptoms have persisted.
3. The extent of profound and widespread *dysfunction* in the grieving person's life.

A mental health care provider typically makes this assessment. The answer to the questions how severe is too severe, how long is too long, and how dysfunctional is too dysfunctional is difficult to arrive at. This must be done weighing all factors that impinge on how a person grieves: cultural issues, personality features, nature of the loss, loss history, and mental status. Care providers should always seek consultation from another professional when there is any doubt as to whether an individual is dealing with grief complications.

The Severity of Symptoms.   There is no simple formula for determining when grief becomes complicated. Behavior can change back and forth between okay and not okay. "There are good days and bad days, and very bad days." Symptoms that are seen as crossing the boundary between the usual, expected grief, and complicated grief are as follows:

- Profound immobilization.
- Disorientation as to time, place, and person.

- Failure to eat or otherwise take the necessary steps for maintaining health.
- Persistent, unrelenting, and severely distressing intrusive thoughts about the loss.
- Active suicidal thoughts and plans for completing suicide.
- Homicidal ideation and/or actions or threats of violence to others.
- Psychotic episodes where the person is not in touch with reality.

The Duration of Severe Symptoms.   Severe symptoms alone do not necessarily indicate complicated grief. In some cases, signs and symptoms may persist for many months and even years as intermittent waves of acute grief triggered by internal memories or external cues and can be viewed as "normal" reactions. Over time, they appear less and less and stay for shorter periods of time. Waves of grief may be set off by anniversaries and other events that stimulate recall or may occur with no apparent explanations.

We can accept immobility, disorientation, lack of self-care, and even some psychotic features (hallucinations, delusions), as part of expected mourning for days and even some weeks after a loss has occurred. When these persist to a period of time where the individual requires the constant presence of another person to assure safety and well-being, then there is an indication of significant complicated grief and assessment for hospitalization should be made. The determination of what constitutes too long is really subjective and must be arrived at on an individual basis rather than a "one size fits all" formula for evaluation. The severity of grief reactions and their duration are viewed along with the extent and depth of dysfunction they impose on the grieving person's living.

The Extent of Dysfunction.   To what extent is the grieving person dysfunctional in his or her family and home life, workplace, community, and other social settings? If there is significant inability to return to an *acceptable* level of functioning, there is further cause to provide special help. Is the grieving person handling the customary activities of daily living, maintaining normal household routines, and functioning in his or her occupation and in other social settings? Of course, there can be multiple definitions of *acceptable*. Functioning can be great in the morning and deteriorate as the day progresses. There is no hard and fast rule, but the level of dysfunction plays a critical role in determining complications in the grief process.

☐ Complicated Grief Syndromes and Suggestions for the Care Provider

Complications of grief as originally discussed by Bowlby (1980), Lindemann (1944), Parkes and Weiss (1983), and Raphael (1983) are divided here into three syndromes or categories that are listed and described below. Suggestions for the care provider will follow the description of each category. Please note that these suggestions are intentionally generalized for each type of grief complication and should be modified to the unique needs of each grieving person. The reader is also referred to chapter 8 for additional clinical tools and interventions.

Syndromes of Complicated Grief Are:

- Chronic or prolonged grief,
- Delayed or inhibited grief, and
- Distorted grief.

Chronic or Prolonged Grief

My definition of *chronic* or *prolonged grief* is intense and persistent grief reactions that fail to reach some desired level of healing and adaptation to the post-loss world. This syndrome is characterized by sadness, ongoing sorrow, and preoccupation with and yearning for the lost person or condition, continued crying, depression, regrets, disorganized life, anxiety, inability to complete or address the process of saying good-bye, and a continuing sense that the loss has just occurred. People who have chronic grief reactions are unable to make any sense or meaning of the loss as it applies to their new post-loss life. They may be unwilling or unable to disconnect from the image of the lost loved one as a living and available human attachment. This keeps them in a pattern of intense grieving behavior that impedes their moving adaptively into the post-loss world. For some, the level of depression reaches a major affective disorder.

> A mother who had been grieving intensely for her son for over 2 years sought help in achieving some respite. She maintained that her acute grieving was her only connection to her son and that moving away from grieving would represent moving away from him. As she explained, "As long as the pain is there, so is he." Her agitated sad-

ness, anxiety-laden protesting, and searching behaviors were very problematic but she desperately needed this form of "contact."

Some people in prolonged grief exhibit agitated behaviors that are associated with the protest and searching reminiscent of early childhood attachment behavior (Bowlby, 1980). This can be characterized as a never-ending separation anxiety. The struggle to reunite with the lost person or condition (relationship, job, role) continues and dominates the life of the grieving person. The refusal to accept the reality of the loss or the recognition that the loss is irreversible causes the individual to remain in a state of agitation (Rando, 1993; Worden, 2002).

In some cases, chronic grief may be the product of a dependent and/or a possessive, *anxious–insecure* relationship that precludes the grieving person's ability to adapt to the post-loss world without the lost loved one. The anxious–insecure attachment style is characterized by distress and preoccupation with the pre-loss relationship (Fraley & Shaver, 1999). Fear of loss of the relationship, possessiveness, and dependency are also traits that I have found with people who have an anxious–insecure relationship. Prolonging grief maintains the attachment to the loved one and continues a familiar level of distress. Accompanying this can also be the fear on the part of the bereaved loved one that there will never be anyone else to be in a relationship with. (See chapter 2.)

A lack of adequate coping skills and resources for adaptive problem-solving may also contribute to the extended state of severe grief reactions. People who are limited in their general ability to cope with new situations, who lack confidence, and who have been emotionally unstable may find that healing into the post-loss world is a formidable task (Bonanno & Kaltman, 1999; W. Stroebe & Stroebe, 1987). Bonnano et al. (2002) suggest that people who have seen the world as a negative ("e.g., unjust or uncontrollable") place may find their loss "may confirm their negative world view and contribute to their spiraling distress" (p. 8).

The care provider should not be misled by the occurrence of ongoing grief reactions. These do not always represent complicated grief but rather a continuation of grieving that requires more time than is generally believed to be acceptable. This is particularly the case with bereaved parents who usually have more intense and continued grief that is not viewed as complicated but reflects the unique nature of parental grief (Klass, 1988). On the other hand, some people show no obvious signs of mourning behavior but do have other overwhelming issues that are masking their unresolved grief. This is discussed more fully in the section on "distorted grief" below.

Suggestions for the Care Provider for Chronic Grief

Reframing the Attachment Behavior

Help the grieving person find other ways to achieve the goal he or she now accomplishes through prolonged and profound grieving. For example, if the survivor is holding on to the deceased through mourning, he or she can be helped to reconfigure the bond with the deceased, that is, alter the inner image to form a spiritual and continuing bond. Rituals are surprisingly useful in constructing new ways of maintaining the connection. For example, mourners can plant a remembrance garden or tree; organize a memorial scholarship fund; take on or be involved in a cause that the loved one supported, such as a charity or medical research that is connected with his or her illness or other cause of death; donate money to an organization that the deceased was a member of; and/or create a memory album with collected memories from friends and family.

Other forms of acknowledgment besides continued mourning may assist the grieving person to move toward altering the internal picture of the loved one from alive-available to no longer alive but available in a symbolic or spiritual way. This new picture of the deceased can sufficiently liberate the grieving person to reclaim a life in the post-loss world.

Affective Release and Conflict Resolution

If the relationship was characterized by an anxious or ambivalent attachment, the grieving person can be helped to identify and process leftover ambivalent feelings from the relationship to move toward the goal of letting go of these feelings. The caregiver can suggest statements of closure such as "What do you need to say to your loved one as a way of letting go of unfinished business?" and "What can you say to her or him as a good-bye?" Care providers can suggest forgiveness exercises as a way to let go of negative material to assist with developing a continuing bond or relationship with the deceased that acknowledges him or her as part of a reclaimed life in the post-loss world.

Helping the grieving person to focus on ways to redefine him or herself in the post-loss world without the loved one's physical presence can also support separation from the deceased person as the only source of identity and validation. By identifying the positive characteristics and values of the deceased person he or she desires to carry forward into the post-loss life, the grieving person can form a new, continuing bond with the deceased and relinquish the need to hold on to grief as a chronic and disabling connection. A young man recalls or imagines sitting at his father's deathbed and is directed to say out loud his father's traits and values he admires and will use in his own life. A mother reflects on the courage and determination her son showed in the course of his illness and dying from AIDS. She tells herself that she will carry these attributes with her into the post-loss world. A man in the depths of chronic and disabling grief over his adult daughter's sudden death begins to view her gentle way of inter-acting as something of her that he will carry within in his new life.

Whenever possible, the grieving person should be helped to identify his or her own positive features and have these reinforced. Where the chronically grieving person can obtain further validation in other ways—from other friends and relatives, work, hobbies, community—the care provider should facilitate social activities that can accomplish this.

Some techniques that can help to facilitate new sources of validation include conversations about the relationship and reviewing both its posi-tive and negative features. In a similar way, journaling thoughts about the deceased or writing a letter to the lost loved one about what the grieving person seeks for self in the future, can help to alter the old internal self-image and create new objectives to be worked on. "Saying good-bye" and "forgiveness" exercises as well as the past, present, and future drawings described in chapter 8 can also be helpful in letting go of old pictures and seeing new possibilities. Activities can be repeated over time as needed and be given as homework or intermingled with other therapies.

Learning New Skills

Where a death or separation represents the loss of an extremely *dependent* relationship resulting in chronic grieving, the individual should be helped to identify the secondary consequences of the death and develop plans to adjust for the absence of the deceased loved one's functions. For example, where the lost loved one provided such tangible benefits as cooking, shopping, income, and/or home repairs, the grieving person can be helped to compensate for these roles by learning new skills or obtaining outside help. Where the deceased or separated loved one pro-vided a crucial source of identity and validation, counseling may be needed to proceed toward reconfiguring the individual's self picture as an autonomous being.

Resistance to Saying Good-Bye and/or Letting Go of the Way We Were

Care providers can use the "saying good-bye exercise" detailed in chap-ter 8 as a way to develop ways for the grieving person to say "good-bye" or "so long for now." If the mourner resists this activity, talk about the resistance: "I see that you don't want to do this. Let's take a few minutes to look at how your reluctance is serving you." "What do you think would happen if you *did* say goodbye?" Ask, "How else can you meet that goal? Let's make a list."

Co-Morbidity with a Psychiatric Disorder

I have found the following illnesses most likely to be present with complicated grief: borderline personality disorder, major depression, general anxiety disorder, post-traumatic stress disorder, agoraphobia, and substance abuse. The majority of my cases where there was co-morbidity were the diagnosis of both chronic grief and major depression. However, Melham et al. (2002) found that outpatients who presented with traumatic grief had co-morbid major depression and PTSD. Where the complication of chronic grief is a result of a pre-existing psychiatric problem such as pre-loss depression or anxiety disorder, treatment for the disorder, including anti-depressant or anti-anxiety medication, may be indicated before the grief issues are engaged. Borderline personality disordered individuals I have worked with who sustain a traumatic loss become very depressed and fall into a state of chronic mourning. They have require intensive treatment, typically need medication, and on occasion have to be hospitalized.

People with severe and chronic grief and a pre-loss history of major depression may already be under treatment for the depression. A thorough history should reveal patterns of affective disturbance, names of treating physicians, hospitalizations, and any medications taken. The pre-loss emotional disorder has a major impact on the course of the person's grief and vice versa. Each of these emotional difficulties aggravate the other and become further complicated should alcohol abuse be part of the mix of problems. I have found that the mood level must be raised before much therapeutic work on complicated grief can be accomplished. Nonphysician care providers must refer people with grief complications who show symptoms of clinical depression to a psychiatrist for a medication evaluation. (See section on associated psychiatric disorders for diagnostic criteria.)

Delayed or Inhibited Grief

Some grieving people appear to postpone the onset of their grief reaction for weeks, months, or years. In some cases, attention and energy is being absorbed by other more immediate requirements precluding personal grieving. For example, a man whose wife was killed in a car crash in which his son was severely injured spent months caring for the boy and arranging for educational placement. He was too preoccupied with caregiving and advocating for his son to allow himself to feel any grief. He was aware that his "time for grieving would come." For some grieving people, preoccupation with nongrieving activities serves as a socially acceptable means to avoid the expression of grief.

Other times, mourning is postponed because the individual does not feel safe enough or entitled to release his or her feelings of grief. This can be due to family pressure arising from "old childhood messages" (stiff upper lip), social pressure to "get on with life as quickly as possible," or the lack of social support for mourning. Some cultures encourage delaying or inhibiting grief. In these cases, some individuals express their grief privately when they are away from their families. Still other grieving persons may have physical conditions that preclude their grieving until such time as they are strong enough to mourn. This can be due to an accident in which a loved one was killed while the mourner survived but was seriously injured. This can also be the case in which an individual who succumbs to a psychiatric disorder that overwhelms and displaces any grief response until his or her state of mental health is restored.

Further, as indicated earlier, there is a growing literature attempting to identify and explain the basis for a minority of grievers who exhibit no typical signs or feelings of grief agitation or sadness. These "resilient" mourners may have some inner adaptive skills or other personality features that preclude usual grieving patterns. Some may have been viewed as having inhibited or delayed grief complications (Bonanno, 2004).

Finally, mourning can also be delayed when loved ones die during wars, terrorist attacks, or disasters, and especially in situations where there is no body to view and never will be.

Raphael (1983) states that grief is typically inhibited to "avoid the pain of the loss" (p. 60). Grief may be inhibited because the grieving person is unwilling to open up to the painful aspects of the relationship with the deceased and because it evokes negative feelings and terrible memories.

> A woman in a workshop I attended made it clear that she would never grieve the person she had selected to use in the "Saying Good-bye" exercise because "He was a terrible and hurtful person." "I mourned the positive parts of the relationship," she said "but since that constituted only a small part of who he was to me, I didn't have much grieving to do."

Where the death (AIDS, suicide, abortion) or the nature of the relationship to the deceased (gay partner, ex-spouse) or the status of the mourner (older people, children) are disenfranchised due to social stigma or lack of validation, social support may not be forthcoming and may result in insufficient or inhibited expression of grief. Without permission to grieve, the grief may be inhibited, stored, or can emerge in some other indirect or distorted way. Grief has to go somewhere, or it gets stored as unfinished business that can present itself as physical and/or psychiatric symptoms later.

Suggestions for the Care Provider for Delayed or Inhibited Grief

Lack of a Body or Other Physical Evidence of the Deceased

If the delay is related to lack of a body or other physical evidence (clothing or other effects of the missing loved one), then the care provider can suggest the gathering of evidence and data related to the circumstance of the death that will help grieving person be more informed regarding the facts of the loss. Memorial rituals, reviewing photographs of the accident or disaster site, newspaper accounts, and eyewitness statements can help to provide some closure for the bereaved person. Military families of missing-in-action loved ones have had burials with empty caskets at Arlington Cemetery as a way of obtaining completion and closure after many, many years of holding off the grieving with the hopes of recovering some remains.

Other Factors Delaying Grief Reaction

When other reasons for the delay are related to physical injury, illness, or emotional shock, the care provider can help the mourner accept the need for the delay and understand that grieving is a long-term process. The care provider can provide psychoeducational discussions to give the loved one a sense of how the human grief process unfolds over time.

Children frequently postpone active grieving for weeks and, in some cases, for months. This can alarm parents. A parent will sometimes seek a mental health consultation for a child who has lost the other parent or a sibling and who has not shown any evidence of grief. In private, away from the parent, these children frequently weep in my office and inform me that they do not do so "in front of mommy or daddy because it upsets them when I cry." Care providers can help parents and other adults in the child's life to understand the nature of children's grief and how it differs from adult grief.

Where the lack of grieving is a result of residual relational issues, the care provider can ask the griever to review the relationship with the deceased to determine the negative and positive aspects of the loss. The grieving person can be given the opportunity to say good-bye and forgive what was negative and unfinished, thus clearing the way for release of grief feelings.

Assistance help can be offered for the disenfranchised griever to develop permission to grieve. Begin the process by asking him or her to review and retell the story, review the consequences of the loss to him or her, and support any tears and feelings that come.

Providing a safe space and permission to grieve in small steps can assist the mourner who fears the pain and anguish of giving in to grief. Mourners can be assisted with grief expression by engaging in artwork, imagery, journaling incidents of grief, and describing what they fear might happen if they *did* allow the grief to come forward. A provider can ask the person to describe what he or she thinks might happen if the grief did come out.

Distorted Grief

The three most common forms of distorted grief are extreme anger, unremitting guilt, and the existence of continued problematic physical symptoms. Often, people suffering from distorted grief seek help for any of the above three conditions with no initial reference to grief at all. This underscores the need for care providers to take a comprehensive loss history with all clients.

In my experience, seldom do these distortions of underlying grief—rage, guilt, or psychosomatic symptoms originate solely with the issues of loss. Often they predate the loss event, are related to other life experiences, or are the result of the personality development and coping styles of the grieving person.

Here are three examples:

1. A bereaved father was in therapy for persistent rage and interpersonal conflicts. He reported that he was merely reacting to slights and hurts that he received. Eventually he realized that he was displacing the rage he felt toward himself for not being able to keep his child alive. He felt that he had failed his "parental job description." He was angry that his child was dead and grieved this loss with rage and bitterness. An older, buried issue regarding anger with his own father for being cold and distant surfaced during therapy. Subsequent treatment focused on his unfinished business with a father he felt had failed "his" parental job description. The clarification of anger to his father resulted in a softening of the attacks on himself and on other people in his life.

2. A woman who had been the family caregiver for her now deceased father presented with severe and unremitting guilt, remorse, and low self-picture. She also reported escalating family conflicts and significant symptoms of depression. She explained that she felt guilty that she had not been able to take better care of her dad who had suffered several strokes that left him unable to walk and to become increasingly demented. In spite of supportive and caring friends and the positive feedback she received regarding her truly excellent caregiving, she continued to feel depressed. Only when she began to talk about her earlier conflicted relationships with her parents and her older siblings did her depressive symptoms ease. The underlying issues were concerns regarding self-identity and entitlement in her family of origin.

3. A widower with two young school-aged children was referred by his physician for various physical complaints that the doctor believed to be stress related. His wife had died of cancer 6 months earlier. His outward expression of grief for his wife was limited. He was extremely preoccupied with other issues such as providing childcare for his children, his declining work performance, fears that he would lose his job, and particularly his preoccupation with various undiagnosed aches and pains. He was concerned that he had cancer and would be unable to care for his children. He read widely on tumors of internal organs and their accompanying symptoms.

   When one set of symptoms abated, another set arose. Though each medical test and examination proved negative, the man was concerned about the one-in-a million chance that he had cancer despite the medical facts. He was occasionally able to admit that his physical symptoms were related to the stress of providing care for his wife during the many months of her illness.

   Therapy was focused first on reducing his stress level using relaxation exercises and journaling episodes of anxiety. He was started on anti-anxiety medication and later explored several new childcare options as well as ways to improve his work output. When his anxiety stabilized, a review of his relationship with his deceased wife eventually led to focus on his mother who he described as a "nervous wreck."

   His mother had always been anxious about health issues, fearing she would die of cancer or some other terrible affliction. The man was able to use relaxation exercises, goal setting, and reconfiguration of his own self-picture in his therapy. He ultimately found a new job that was more interesting and closer to home.

He also indicated that he was thinking of dating. His physical symptoms were significantly diminished, but he planned to check in with his physician regularly—just in case.

Suggestions for the Care Provider for Distorted Grief

Initially, the care provider will need to focus on the presenting symptoms and complaints. These may require medical attention, especially if medication for depression, anxiety, and/or sleep disorder is indicated. To deal with rage and guilt, care providers can initially use relaxation techniques, hypnotherapy, and guided imagery. For some explosive rage disorders medication will need to be considered. Rage can also be reduced with regular physical exercise. Guilt can be eased through reality testing, that is, through confronting the actual events, facts, and information. (See chapter 8 for details on working with people experiencing problems with rage and guilt.)

Care providers can review the relationship with the deceased, especially during the period of illness, and examine the nature and duration of the caregiving role. Resentment during the period of caregiving needs to be normalized. The pre-illness relationship should also be explored and any unfinished business should be identified and processed through discussion, externalization of feelings, and the creation of a continuing or spiritual bond with the deceased loved one. Rituals, memorials, and creating eulogies can be useful in establishing a continuing bond.

It is always useful to determine the source of anger and assist the grieving person in externalizing this material. Where the anger cannot be reduced through review, processing, and/or reframing, the care provider can use "good-bye" and "forgiveness" exercises to help establish a sense of closure or partial completion for the grieving person.

To alleviate unremitting guilt and low self-concept, care providers can focus on the initial source of the person's sense of unworthiness. Other areas to explore are early attachment history and the "sense-of-self" in the relationship. The cognitive restructuring of self-picture can enable the grieving person to move into the post-loss world free from the sense of unworthiness that is typically associated with the distortions presented as guilt. The provider can reinforce positive self-statements and help the grieving person to see the loving role he or she had while serving as the loved one's caregiver. Counseling for developing and/or enhancing self-empowerment has been a major part of therapy for such individuals in my practice. Should the person slip into a depressive state, referral for antidepressant medication evaluation will be necessary.

☐ Predisposing Risk Factors: Circumstances and Conditions

There are four circumstances that potentially influence or affect a complicated grief reaction (Jacobs, 1999; Rando, 1993; Raphael, 1983; Worden, 2002). These are

- The nature of the death or other loss,
- The nature of the relationship to the deceased or separated person,
- The psychological characteristics of the grieving person, and
- Social issues associated with the death or other loss.

Depending on the negative characteristics of each of these four circumstances, the care provider may begin to suspect the presence of grief complications (or rule them out). After identifying the existence of potentially pre-disposing criteria, the care provider must carefully assess for the presence of complications in the grief process by applying the measures for determining complicated grief. Severity of the symptoms, length of time symptoms present, and extent of dysfunction. Additionally, the presence of the various "danger signals" detailed earlier in this chapter can also be helpful in determining the presence of grief complications.

Conditions That May Affect the Risk for Complicated Grief

The Nature of the Loss/Death Event

1. Sudden, unexpected, unprepared for death.
2. Violent, mutilating, or abusive homicide.
3. Suicide.
4. Occurrence of multiple deaths.
5. Death from a catastrophic disaster.
6. Death viewed as preventable.
7. Grieving person witnessed the violent death.
8. Grieving person played some role in cause of death.
9. No body or other evidence of death recovered.
10. Grieving person not informed of the death for some time and missed death-associated rituals.
11. Death of child.
12. Very lengthy illness.

The Nature of the Relationship with the Lost Loved One

1. An attachment disturbance in the form of an ambivalent, dependent, or otherwise insecure relationship.
2. A history of being sexually, physically, or emotionally abused by the deceased.
3. A preponderance of unfinished business at time of death.
4. Overidentification with the deceased.

Psychological Characteristics of the Grieving Person

1. Extremely dependent personality.
2. Severely limited ability to express feelings.
3. Intense feelings of inadequacy and guilt regarding relationship with deceased, especially during period of illness.
4. History of depressive illness and/or personality disorders.
5. History of past complicated grief reactions.
6. Loss of parents or other significant loss during childhood resulting in inadequate nurturing.
7. History of life crisis and unaccommodated multiple losses.
8. View of grief as the only way to maintain contact with deceased.

Social Issues Associated with the Death or Other Loss

1. Loss stigmatized by society such as suicide, AIDS, substance abuse, abortion, or criminal activity.
2. Grief feels disenfranchised by society; for example, the mourner is gay partner, elderly, or grieving a miscarriage. Lack of adequate social support for the grieving person and/or family may encourage a premature end to mourning.
3. Griever socially isolated and hesitant to express grief for fear of others' reactions.
4. Additional current major life crises: financial, occupational, physical, familial, or spiritual.

Grieving persons who meet any of the above conditions may develop into one or more of the syndromes of complicated grief. Some may also exhibit symptoms of a psychiatric disorder associated with problematic grief. Where these factors are present, care providers should assess the presence of complicated grief using the measures described earlier in this chapter.

☐ Psychiatric Disorders Associated with Complicated Grief

Death or other traumatic loss can result in a psychiatric condition or can aggravate an existing one. The following psychiatric disorders are associated with complications of the grief reaction.

Affective Disorders

Affective disorders are disturbances of mood and include major depression, bipolar disorder, and dysthymia. Affective disorders " . . . are the category most often diagnosed in individuals experiencing either uncomplicated or complicated mourning" (Rando, 1993, p. 199). It is believed that the psychiatric designation of depressive illness co-exists with many of the grief reactions we have described as complicated grief (Jacobs, 1999).

Care providers should assess for clinical depression when any features of complicated grief are present. Indicators of the presence of clinical depression include the presence and worsening of the following conditions: recurrent thoughts of death, suicidal ideation and/or plans, flat emotional expression, loss of energy and interests, guilt, feelings of worthlessness, sleep and eating disturbance, slowed down thinking and moving, difficulty in concentrating, and statements about feeling sad, hopeless, and discouraged (American Psychiatric Association, 1994, Diagnostic and Statistical Manual of Mental Disorders IV (DSM IV), p. 317.) Most of the people I have seen for help with continuing, severe, and painful grief fit this picture as well.

Chronic Grief and Depression

Differentiation of chronic grief from depression is unclear. It may be difficult to tease out an easy and simple formula for diagnosing depression in a chronically grieving person. Every set of criteria listed for clinical depression sounds and looks very much like people in deep grief over a death. The general consensus (Jacobs, 1999; Rando, 1993) is that it is hard to tell complicated or traumatic grief from depression but that there are some clinical impressions that may lead to a diagnosis of depression. According to Jacobs (1999), depression is distinguished by "pervasive, depressed mood disturbance, depressive cognitive schemata, and a disturbance of self-esteem . . . " (p. 37). Grief is more episodic and lacks the "feelings of worthlessness and pervasive feelings of guilt" associated with depression (p. 37). Rando (1993) cites the "damage to self-esteem created by depression as much greater, more global, and more associated with an unrealistic sense of worthlessness and guilt" (p. 204).

Extended duration of a depressed state for 6 months or more is seen as another indicator of depression. The co-morbidity of major depression and traumatic or complicated grief makes differentiation more difficult (Jacobs, 1999).

Most grieving people in my experience who develop a depressive disorder have had a history of depression prior to the loss or death event that is aggravated by the trauma of loss. A history of past treatment for depression and/or presence of depression in the family will further indicate the need for psychiatric support in order for grief therapy to proceed. Nonphysician care providers should refer clients to the primary care physician or to a psychiatrist for medication assessment and management when significant depression persists.

Demoralization

While this designation is not included in the official listing of psychiatric conditions (American Psychiatric Association, 1994), it is included here as a disorder experienced by many grieving people. This designation, first presented by Frank (1974) and later elaborated on by McHugh and Slavney (1998), describes a cluster of conditions characterized by the inability to meet expectations or "cope with some pressing problem" (Frank, 1974, p. 314). *Demoralized* persons have backed themselves into a psychological corner; they feel hopeless, helpless, isolated, and preoccupied with just trying to survive. Demoralization arises from such problematic life events as loss, grief, and relationship difficulties. The goal for treating such grieving people is to help them regain a sense of control and mastery of the future (McHugh & Slavney, 1998). If untreated, demoralization can lead to depression or anxiety disorders.

Anxiety Disorders

Anxiety is a common feature of acute grief. Those psychiatric disorders that are initiated by a death and/or other traumatic loss are more likely to fall into the anxiety disorders category. Post-traumatic stress disorder (PTSD), general anxiety, and panic disorders are typically found among people with complicated grief. If the death was traumatic—that is, sudden, violent or mutilating, suicide or homicide—the grieving person is at risk for PTSD. If the survivor witnessed or was involved in the events leading up to the death, there is a greater likelihood of PTSD developing (American Psychiatric Association, 1994, Diagnostic and Statistical Manual of Mental Disorders IV).

The role played by anxiety in the initial period of acute grief may alter the nature of the grief reaction. The agitated and distressing behaviors associated with separation anxiety—searching, yearning, pining, which are attachment behaviors—may be given full range of expression or controlled by using avoidance and denial strategies.

Other manifestations of anxiety disorders associated with complicated grief include (a) *general anxiety* regarding survival in the post-loss world—"How will I ever survive without her or him?"; (b) *social anxiety* associated with loss of a loved one that may take the form of agoraphobia or the fear of leaving the home, which is usually associated with fear of exposure to people, places, or signs that serve as memory triggers of the deceased or of the traumatic event; and (c) *panic disorders* as related to the physical health of themselves or of surviving loved ones.

Usually, anxiety needs to be treated before grief issues can be fully addressed. This may involve use of anti-anxiety medications, relaxation exercises, hypnotherapy, and cognitive/behavioral techniques. Treatment for PTSD symptoms—hyper-arousal reactions, sleep disturbance including nightmares, flashback memory of trauma event—associated with mourning may require a medical referral for antianxiety or sleep medication.

Adjustment Disorders

Depression, anxiety, or mixed depression and anxiety may present as transitory adjustment disorders "in response to a psychosocial stressor," that are not as severe as major depression or the anxiety disorders discussed above but exceed the expected reaction to a death or other loss (American Psychiatric Association, 1994, Diagnostic and Statistical Manual of Mental Disorders IV, p. 623). Many people suffering chronic grief are given a diagnosis of adjustment disorder with depression. This designation is justified on the basis that the depressive symptoms are related to a specific life stressor, that the condition is transitory, and that it has a negative impact on the quality of the grieving person's life. In cases where the death has resulted in ongoing medical, legal, financial issues, or family disruption (separation or divorce), the diagnosis for chronic adjustment disorder can be made (DSM IV, 1994).

☐ Traumatic Death

Extremely traumatic deaths such as violent, mutilating deaths, death of a child, war deaths, and death due to suicide or homicide result in survivors who are at high risk for complications of grief and associated psychiatric disorders. Traumatic deaths leave the mourner with post-traumatic stress and agitation. As indicated earlier, these include hyper-arousal, disturbed sleep, high anxiety, and disturbing intrusive images. This agitated and anxious state is diagnosed as post-traumatic stress disorder should it last more than a month (APA DSM IV, 1994).

Trauma symptoms require the attention of the mental health provider before focusing on loss sustained by the grieving person (Therese Rando, May 5, 2004, personal communication). The images, terror, anxiety, and agitated state will need to be processed, reviewed, desensitized, and softened before issues of loss and grief can be effectively addressed. We will discuss below suicide death and the death of a child as examples of traumatic death.

Suicide Death

" . . . the person who commits suicide puts their psychological skeletons in the survivors' emotional closet"

(Schneidman, 1972, p. x)

When a loved one has taken his or her own life, the survivors face difficult barriers to healing, including:

1. *Social stigmatization*—mourners are typically left with a legacy of shame, blame, and a desire to hide from the world. Grollman (1988) calls these grieving people *suicide victims*.
2. *Guilt*—Many mourners also feel guilty and plagued by failure because they feel that they should have prevented the suicide: "I should have known." "How did I miss the clues?"
3. *Anger*—This may take the form of blaming God, the physician, clergy, therapist, other family members, hospital staff, and self as well. Anger is often particularly strong when the person who committed suicide left children behind.
4. *Search for meaning*—Mourners struggle to make sense of the suicide asking, " Why? How do I make sense of this?" "How does this fit in with my sense of the world?" "*Nothing* makes sense anymore."

5. *Social awkwardness*—Many people simply do not know what to say to someone grieving a suicide. The griever may have to cope with intrusive and clumsy questions.
6. *Fears*—Some survivors of suicide become concerned that they or other loved ones will succumb to suicide.
7. *Emotional distress*—Suicide leaves many questions left unanswered, and grievers often suffer by having to deal with the deceased's unfinished business.
8. *Desire to deny the truth*—Mourners will frequently fail to tell the truth about the real cause of death, thus creating more tension in the family system.
9. *Medical, legal, and insurance investigations*—These necessary but intrusive processes may create additional stress and shame.
10. *Physical distress*—Mourners may feel like they are "going crazy" and experience somatic symptoms such as aches, pains, and psychosomatic illnesses.

In addition to the above, the "victim-survivors of suicide" may have complications in the form of inhibited grief and also are at risk for agitated depression.

The care provider should provide the survivors with information about the nature of grieving a suicide death and normalize their reactions of guilt, rage or profound despair. Grievers also need to be provided with opportunities to share their feelings with other family members to achieve a level of honesty with each other. Children in particular must have their questions answered and be included in discussions and family mourning activities to whatever extent is appropriate for their age. Various rituals, religious or nonreligious, can be used to help the family come together, share thoughts and feelings, and find ways to recall positive memories of the deceased loved one. Survivors should be urged to get proper rest, exercise, and regular meals. "Saying good-bye" exercises, forgiveness practices, and continued family discussions regarding the positives of the deceased loved one can begin the process of healing.

The care provider can also help friends of the family be supportive to families who are grieving a suicide death. Below are several suggestions for others who wish to be part of the family's healing process.

Supporting Suicide Survivors

- Sharing their own memories of the deceased
- Sharing what they learned from the deceased to use in their lives
- Accepting survivors' feelings without argument
- Inviting survivors to go on outings, for a walk, or shopping
- Sharing significant anniversaries and other dates
- Running errands for survivors
- Bringing food, cooking, and cleaning
- Inviting survivors over to their homes

There are many complex issues left behind for the mourners of someone who has died as a result of suicide. I have been at funerals for persons who completed suicide and heard eulogies filled with anger, questions, shame, and fear. Where families were able to view the life of the deceased loved one as having productive, loving, and even humorous aspects, the funeral served as a tribute, and the mourning proceeded toward a healing resolution. The suicide of a child places the parents and siblings at high risk for complications.

The Death of a Child and Complicated Grief

There are numerous factors that cause those who mourn the death of a child to be at high risk for complicated grief. These are:

1. *The nature of the attachment*. Parents see themselves in their child and view the child as part of them, their stake in the future. Thus, the death of a child is also the death of a part of the parent. It also severs parents' link to the future via this child. The loss looms as a catastrophic failure in the natural course of life and death.
2. *Tearing asunder of the parental identity*. Parents who experience loss of a child lose a major part of their personal identity. They also lose an important aspect of their social identity since a "parent" is a label of pride and status. After a child's death, they ask themselves: "Who am I now? I was his or her father or mother but now I am diminished."
3. *Failure*. Parents feel as if they have failed at their primary role of protecting their child. There may be no rational reasoning for this assessment. It is simply a part of parental bereavement behavior and adds to their stress and anxiety.

4. *Violation of assumptions*. The death of a child represents the end of an age of innocence. A new, post-loss world has come crashing down, and the shock waves are concussive. Families experiencing the death of a child will never be the same, and they grieve for this fact as well as for the loss of their child.

5. *Loss of a future caregiver and resource.* Older parents may also grieve not only the loss of a child but also the person they were counting on to provide care for them as they age. This is a theme heard frequently from older bereaved parents at Compassionate Friends support group meetings.

6. *Ambivalent social support*. Though you would think that society would be generous in its support of families that have lost a child, this is not always the case. Recall the "Safeway Samba" story in chapter 1 where the bereaved father noticed friends dodging him in the market aisles. Because the loss is so painful, others may need to keep away. Contact brings up their own fears of shattered assumptions about the world.

7. *Marital issues*. These issues take the form of incongruity of grieving styles and levels of healing attained. Every person grieves and heals differently—at his or her own rate. Each parent, for example, experiences unique secondary losses since each had a unique relationship with the child. Couples also may withhold their grief from each other in order to be protective; this creates communication shutdown. In addition, there may be conflict regarding when to resume sexual relations. If one partner seems unavailable or impatient, communication may further break down, and the relationship will begin to deteriorate. Marital distress is a secondary loss and requires special attention from a skilled mental health provider.

8. *Sibling issues*. The siblings of a deceased child are often forgotten during mourning. If the deceased child had a lingering illness, siblings may be overlooked even before the death occurred. Parents, in this case, may be so anguished over the health and survival of the ill child that the brothers or sisters receive little attention from them. After the death, the parents may be so grief stricken that the surviving siblings still get very little from them. They are at risk for acting out, becoming depressed, and physically ill. All of this adds to the mix of stress, anxiety, and complications of grief in the family.

9. *Suicide death of a child*. The death of a child by suicide raises the level of risk and the severity of grief complications for parents. Such grieving parents may have reactions that range from barely containable rage to uncontrollable anguish and anxiety.

A man whose son had died as a result of suicide was left with a vol-
cano of rage. To vent the rage, he bought second-hand china and
spent many hours at the county dump flinging the dishes into the
huge trash containers. He did this several times a week, and over several months his massive rage began to diminish. For many, the
release of parental or sibling rage and other feelings associated with a
child's suicide death represents an early phase of treatment. Once the
initial stage has been released, other grief issues can rise to the surface.

The care provider will need to explore relationship issues with the parents and siblings, to work on creating ways of understanding the suicide,
and gather positive aspects of the child's life that they can take with them
into their post-death world. Providers must help family members work on
forgiveness of the child and of themselves, and facilitate "saying good-
bye." Families can seek comfort in faith-based rituals where appropriate.

Behaviors That Signal Complicated Grief or Psychiatric Disorders in Bereaved Parents

To assist the care provider in further identifying and helping bereaved
parents, a list of signs and signals for complicated grief or psychiatric disorders follows. This section concludes with suggestions for care provider
interventions.

1. Rage and explosive episodes that are persistent and may erupt in
   violent attacks on others or create an angry, bitter, and unhappy
   person
2. A terrible sense of parental inadequacy, which affects other areas of
   life; statements of low self-worth, "I failed my job as parent";
3. Significant areas of dysfunction—in marriage, at work, with surviving other children, friends, in community organizations, and in
   their spiritual life—an expanding web of life difficulties;
4. Denial extremes—delusional thoughts and actions regarding the
   child still being alive; these thoughts and actions are beyond the
   expected use of linking objects and remembrance rituals;
5. Overidentification—frequently imitates dress, speech, and other
   behaviors of the dead child;
6. Histrionic and excessive overprotection of surviving children;
   obsessively watchful and smothering, protective behavior;
7. Phobias—avoids any reminders of child's death; flees any connection, and will not discuss any aspect of the child's life;

8. Signs and symptoms of major depression or of an anxiety disorder;
9. Continued disorientation, hallucinations, delusions, and dissociations;
10. Abandonment of family—parent takes no responsibility for other children or usual daily tasks of parenting or household requirements.

Care providers can help bereaved parents in the following ways:

- *Educate parents about the grief process and focus them on the needs of the surviving siblings and other family members.
- *Provide couples counseling to enhance their communication and help them respect different grieving styles.
- *Give them opportunities to tell their story and cry over and over again.
- *Work to alleviate guilt when possible.
- *Locate support groups such as the Compassionate Friends, Bereaved Parents USA, and Mothers Against Drunk Driving for social support. (See appendix B for additional resources.)
- *Assist them in addressing each of the four tasks of mourning and offer help as indicated under the appropriate complicated grief syndrome above.
- *Refer them for psychiatric assessment if depression or anxiety overwhelm the psychotherapy or if cognitive functioning rapidly deteriorates.
- *Refer them to their physician if physical complaints persist.

☐ An Emerging Clinical Entity: Traumatic Grief

Background

Earlier in this chapter three syndromes of complicated grief were presented. These complications in the grieving process describe responses of individuals with unusually distressing symptoms that fall between the natural, expected feelings, thoughts, and behaviors of normal grief, and those that can be diagnosed as a psychiatric disorder. As reviewed by Neimeyer (2004), a case has been made for the development and inclusion of a consolidated and distinct clinical entity called *complicated or traumatic grief* in the American Psychiatric Association's Diagnostic and Statistical Manual (Enright & Marwit, 2002; Horowitz et al., 1997; Jacobs, Mazure, & Prigerson, 2000; Prigerson, Frank, Kasl, Reynolds, & Anderson et al., 1995; Prigerson & Jacobs, 2001; Rando, 1993).

Studies have demonstrated that clusters of symptoms identified as complicated or traumatic grief are a clinical entity distinct from bereavement-related depression and anxiety disorders, and are also separate from normal grief (Boelen & van den Bout, 2003; Boelen, van den Bout, de Keijser, Hoijtink, 2003; Horowitz, 1997; Jacobs et al., 2000; Melham et al., 2002; Ogrodniczuk et al., 2003; Prigerson, et al., 1995; Prigerson et al., 1996; Prigerso et al., 1997; Prigerson et al., 1999; Prigerson & Frank et al., 1995). It was further determined that people with complicated or traumatic grief are at increased risk for cancer, cardiac disorders, alcohol and tobacco use and suicidal ideation (Ott, 2003; Prigerson et al., 1995).

Proposed Criteria

Jacobs et al. (2000) have presented a set of symptom criteria for diagnosing a person with traumatic grief disorder due to death that partly overlap with the Horowitz et al., (1997) criteria. Prigerson has indicated that these criteria may be adapted by clinicians for use with other traumatic loss events such as terminal diagnosis and other life-limiting medical conditions (H. Prigerson, personal communication, October 2, 2004).

Prigerson and her colleagues have determined two categories of symptoms: (a) *separation distress symptoms*—yearning, searching, and excessive loneliness, and (b) *traumatic distress symptoms*—intrusive thoughts and feelings, numbness, disbelief, and loss of trust.

The criteria (see following lists) include a 2-month duration of symptoms with no specific time relationship to time of death (Jacobs, 1999; Jacobs et al., 2000; Prigerson & Jacobs, 2001).

Proposed Criteria for Traumatic Grief

Criterion A

1. The person has experienced the death of a significant other.
2. The response involves intrusive, distressing preoccupation with the deceased person (e.g., yearning, longing, or searching).

Criterion B

In response to the death, the following symptom(s) is/are marked and persistent:

1. Frequent efforts to avoid reminders of the deceased (e.g., thoughts, feelings, activities, people, places).[1]

2. Purposelessness or feelings of futility about the future.
3. Subjective sense of numbness, detachment or absence of emotional responsiveness.
4. Feeling stunned, dazed or shocked.[1]
5. Difficulty acknowledging the death (e.g., disbelief).[1]
6. Feeling that life is empty, or meaningless.
7. Difficulty imagining a fulfilling life without the deceased.
8. Feeling that part of oneself has died.
9. Shattered worldview (e.g., lost sense of security, trust, or control).
10. Assumes symptoms or harmful behaviors of, or related to the death.
11. Excessive irritability, bitterness, or anger related to the death.

Criterion C

The duration of the disturbance (symptoms listed) is at least two months.[2]

Criterion D

The disturbance causes clinically significant impairment in social, occupational, or other important areas of functioning.

Source: Jacobs et al., 2000.
[1] Statistically low diagnostic probability (Prigerson & Jacobs, 2001, pp. 627-628).
[2] Duration changed to 6 months (H. Prigerson, personal communication, October 2, 2004).

Comments

Care providers have a responsibility to ensure that grieving people do not see their natural responses to loss as pathological. What may be normal and natural in terms of symptoms and their duration with some grieving circumstances may be seen as complicated or traumatic in others. On the other hand, it may also be fair to say that *all grief is complicated* because a life has been derailed and normal human functioning is distorted (Rubin & Malkinson, 2002). The continuing efforts to refine and legitimize the system for diagnosing people whose grief has taken a prolonged and unusually distressing direction is a welcome development.

☐ Conclusion

This chapter has provided a summarized version of the identification, nature and treatment of complicated grief and associated psychiatric disorders. The material, introduces very complex human issues that require careful attention to presenting symptoms. When there are questions, uncertainties, or doubts regarding the diagnosis of complicated grief, the reader is cautioned to make the necessary referrals to a mental health professional or to seek consultation with a colleague experienced with complications of grief and psychiatric disorders. I reiterate my caution to care providers. Unless there is profound and prolonged emotional distress with significant dysfunction in home, workplace, or other social settings, the behaviors of concern may be a part of "normal" or uncomplicated grief. A grief reaction observed for a particular individual with his or her unique personal history, cultural influences, and level of social support may be very much expected and within "normal" parameters.

That said, however, I offer yet another impression of "normal" grief and complicated grief. I approach all grief reactions as a complication in the life of the individual who seeks help with this human phenomenon. We travel life's roadway and suddenly, around the bend, the bridge is out. A death, a life threatening diagnosis, accident, layoff notice, or other traumatic change has painfully altered the course of our journey and requires a new way of looking at life. The process of grieving represents a disruption, a need for altering our direction, our plans, and how we identify ourselves in the post-loss/changed world. Normal grief presents many complications and deserves the help of a care provider who is an *exquisite witness*. People who are grieving deserve care at whatever level their situation requires whether we call it complicated or not. At all times, individual differences must be taken into consideration when determining how we as care providers will serve them.

In chapter 10 several case studies are presented that will provide the reader an opportunity to review, consider, and respond.

Case Studies

- ☐ Explanation of Case Studies
- ☐ Seven Case Studies
- ☐ Conclusion

Below are several case presentations that will give you an opportunity to do some assessment and indicate some possible interventions for immediate help in each of the situations involving grieving people.

> *Trainers/instructors* may wish to assign separate cases to small groups and have them compare responses in a general discussion. These can also be used in online, distance education programs, and as a pre- and post-assessment of theoretical and clinical learning. These cases can be developed more fully for clinical training purposes, either as written exercises or as role-play exercises.

☐ Explanation of Case Studies

The purpose of the following loss and grief case presentations is to give you an opportunity to:

- *Assess the needs* of the grieving individual(s),
- Determine what *additional information* may be necessary, and
- Provide some *initial help and recommendations* for long-term assistance.

We are not seeking in this activity to develop a comprehensive treatment plan in each situation but rather to help you get a sense of how to start the process of helping a grieving person. Several responses have been given for each of the cases as an example of what we are asking the reader to do for the sixth and seventh cases. Further, I have not provided a comprehensive response to each of the items. I invite you to add whatever else you feel you would want to know and do.

While all chapters in the book may provide guidance for responding to a particular case, the chapters that discuss material relevant to each case are indicated after each case title.

After reviewing the case material, think about what the person needs from you or someone else at that particular point in the process. Check the assessment material questions in chapter 8 for suggestions on what you may want to be looking for. Ask yourself:

- How can I be of most help right now?
- Can I do this alone or do I need somebody else to be part of the action?
- What family and other support people are available for the grieving person?
- What long-term assistance can I provide or refer to another provider?

☐ Seven Case Studies

Case 1. Perinatal Loss: When Dreams Are Crushed (Review Chapters 5 and 7.)

A young couple is in the hospital delivery room. This has been a difficult and disturbing pregnancy and the mother, who had spent much of the pregnancy in bed, has gone into premature labor. As the mother is being prepared for delivery, the doctor is unable to detect the baby's heartbeat. The physician listens again and again but to no avail. She has a colleague confirm her finding—the baby is dead. The man and woman are shocked and devastated, as are the doctors and nurses.

1. What do you see as the couple's immediate needs?
2. What additional information do you need? (spiritual/religious needs, support system, background)

3. What other steps would you take with the couple and/or with the nursing staff?
4. What additional recommendations do you have for them?
5. What (if anything) would you do additionally at this point?

Suggested Responses

1. The couple needs to be able to express their feelings. They may want to do this alone or with another person present. They can choose from several possibilities—family member, friend, chaplain staff, social worker, nurse, or personal clergy.
2. Information needed: physical/medical status of mother; pre-loss emotional functioning of husband and wife; identification of available support system, other losses or crises in their lives; spiritual/religious preferences.
3. Offer opportunities for them to hold and dress the baby, choose a name, take a picture, get a hand or footprint, say good-bye to the baby, and whatever else they need to say. Help them obtain whatever medical information from the doctors they may need in order to make some sense of what has happened. Get an okay from the nursing staff to let them remain in a room with the baby for awhile and even have some of their family with them.

   Facilitate the beginning of the notification process and any arrangements they wish to initiate regarding pastoral care, religious rituals, funeral, memorial, burial, cremation, and/or family gathering.
4. The couple or a supporting family member should be made aware of available resources, including the following: the Compassionate Friends self-help support groups, availability of reading material and other sources of medical information about neonatal loss, and where to get counseling should they desire it.
5. What (if anything) would you do additionally at this point?

Case 2. Advanced Cancer: Balancing Hope with Medical Reality (Review Chapters 7 and 8.)

A man with advanced cancer is seen at a pastoral counseling office at the insistence of his wife. She is concerned because he has unrealistic hopes for a new experimental chemotherapy. She and their young adult children know that there is very little possibility that he will benefit from any additional treatment. They do not discuss this with him for fear of dashing his hopes and upsetting him. He has made no arrangements about finances, or advanced directives, nor has he had any other discussions with the family.

1. What do you see as the family's immediate needs?
2. What additional information do you need?
3. What other steps would you take with the family?
4. What additional recommendations do you have for them?
5. What (if anything) would you do additionally at this point?

Suggested Responses

1. The family should have an opportunity to voice their concerns out loud both as individuals and as a group, and separately from the man in order to respect their desire not to upset him. It is important that the wife and children have the same up-to-date medical information and that relevant details have been provided. Where there is either very superficial information and/or information that is not current, a meeting with a medical provider should be arranged.

   A home visit can be very helpful to get an indication of how they communicate and how the man responds to them. A separate meeting should be held with the man to ascertain how much of the medical realities he really is aware. Also, he can be offered an opportunity to become updated by his oncologist. It is important that he get only as much information as he truly wants and not what he thinks you or the family want him to have. Gently inquire as to what he thinks he may need to do for and/or with his family in the event that the new treatment does not work out. You might ask what he may have done differently had the new chemotherapy not been available.

2. Additional information regarding the status of arrangements, financial, legal, advance health directives, and concerns about personal unfinished business should also be explored. Spiritual and/or religious resources and forms of external support should also be discussed. The emotional functioning of the wife and children should also be determined in the event that a mental health referral is required.

3. At the appropriate time, the family should be made aware of ongoing support groups in the community—widow support programs and general bereavement support groups for the children as well. Resources for obtaining future family or individual counseling should be provided. The family should also be given the opportunity to meet and determine how each person is faring emotionally in the face of the deterioration of their father/husband. Cancer support groups should be offered.

4. Discussion of the use of rituals and family activities to honor the man represents a way of looking ahead and taking positive action. Also, offer the possibility of thinking about how they would say

good-bye or what they would say to him at the very end. Any faith resources they might have can also be reinforced if desired. A clergy or spiritual advisor can be called in for this assistance.
5. What (if anything) would you do additionally at this point?

Case 3. Sudden Death of Young Child (Review Chapters 5, 8, and 9.)

A child was killed instantly when a car, being driven by his mother, slips on a wet surface and hits a tree. Both parents were moderately injured. They frequently express regret that they did not die in the accident. Father is depressed 6 months later and can't work. Mother keeps very busy. They are seen as a couple by a mental health professional because of husband's depression and its effect on their marriage and his work.

1. What do you see as the couple's immediate needs?
2. What additional information do you need?
3. What other steps would you take with the couple?
4. What additional recommendations do you have for them?
5. What (if anything) would you do additionally at this point?

Suggested Responses

1. The couple can be encouraged to express initially what they see as their needs from the care provider. This can form the basis of a plan for helping them. Unless they have an objection, they should be given an opportunity to tell the story of the tragic event and hear how this has been affecting each of them individually and as a couple. They need a safe place to release their feelings and especially their regrets if they desire to do so.
2. Additional information about the emotional functioning of each, both within and external to the relationship. How are they handling things with their older child? What support is available from family, friends, faith, or other community sources? Are they able to grieve together? How do they support each other? What are the details of workplace difficulties initially mentioned in the referral intake? Obtain a history and background on each of them and on their relationship.
3. Facilitate communication skill development and provide an understanding of the nature and differences of the human grief response. Also, coach them on understanding and dealing with the grief of their other child. At some later point help them to say good-bye to the deceased child and ask for his forgiveness.
4. Refer them to the local Compassionate Friends or Bereaved Parents of USA self-help group. Provide continued couple's sessions. Also,

assess the level of the husband's depression and determine the need for individual treatment and/or referral for anti-depressant medication evaluation. Offer them the opportunity to explore connection with their faith community or a spiritual advisor.

5. What (if anything) would you do additionally at this point?

Case 4. Eldergrief (Review Chapters 6, 8, and 9.)

A 75-year-old woman, newly widowed, has stopped coming to the senior center activities. She had attended intermittently for the month since her husband of 50 years died after a long battle with ALS ("Lou Gehrig's disease"). You are a trained volunteer from the Office of Aging who has met this woman in the past, has phoned her, and is now meeting with her at her home. The woman looked and sounded physically well but her energy appeared much lower than before. She says that since her husband died she feels lost and unsure of what to do and how to be. She has some friends and neighbors to talk with but she has "such an empty place in her body," and her home "suddenly feels so big and everything is scattered."

1. What does this woman need right now?
2. What other information do you want to obtain in order to help her?
3. What do you plan to do to help her in the short-term?
4. What long-term recommendations do you have for her?
5. What (if anything) would you do additionally at this point?

Suggested Responses

1. This woman needs some hope and a sense of self-worth in her strange, new post-loss world. She has lost her primary attachment figure and a productive, rewarding activity—her caregiving job—as well as her role as spouse. Initially, we want to hear all we can hear about what it was like to be a caregiver all that time and the difficulty of seeing your loved one literally "die by inches." We also want to encourage the telling of how it has been since he died.

   In addition, when a bereaved spouse can have some understanding of the multiplicity of his or her losses, the knowledge does give a sense of control to their situation. Not all persons want or can handle too much information; it must be done as an offer of clarification or why she feels as she does. If the offer is turned down, we want to continue to listen and then offer some action-oriented program possibilities.
2. Additional information in this case would be to determine the level of support from family, friends, and community resources—faith

community, neighbors, senior centers, widow support groups. Also, you would want to know how she learned how to be a home caregiver and what she liked about doing this work. As a fairly new widow living alone, you would also want to make some determination as to her self-destructive impulses. This is especially important if she has no family support and is seeking to withdraw from social contacts.

3. Offer her opportunities to attend the senior center's activities—even providing a "buddy" to pick her up so that they can attend together. There are other activity-oriented programs sponsored by faith communities, AARP, recreation departments, and other service organizations. If she rejects group activities, she may be interested in having a friend or family member visit her at home or call daily. If she wishes little or no contact, she may be content to have a family member check in on her at some agreed upon interval.

4. For a long-term recommendation, offer her a way to use her considerable home caregiving skills and knowledge. Many volunteer programs in nursing homes, hospitals, and other rehabilitation facilities would benefit from even a few hours a week from a person who has such caregiving experience. This would also benefit her in that she once again would feel productively engaged in a rewarding experience. The antidote to loneliness and depression often is found in providing care and service to others. Other possibilities could be connected to her spiritual pathway, and, if needed, individual mental health counseling. Also, offer her the opportunity to say good-bye or make any other statement she would like to have her husband hear from her.

5. What (if anything) would you do additionally at this point?

Case 5. Young Adult Suicide (Review Chapters 3, 5, 8, and 9.)

A 24-year-old single woman has been found dead in her apartment by her neighbor. She was taken by ambulance to the hospital emergency room and pronounced dead of an overdose of medications. No suicide note was found. The family has gathered in the hospital chapel. You are the on-call psychiatric resident and have been requested to meet with the family. When you enter, the mother is in shock, not speaking, and the father is barely controlling his rage. One brother and sister, both younger and still living at home, are quietly weeping. A chaplain's assistant is sitting silently near the parents and being an exquisite listener.

A police investigator is waiting outside to ask some routine questions. The emergency room supervisor has requested a psychiatric consultation because of the mother's state of shock and concern for the father's brimming rage.

1. What do you see as the family's immediate needs? (Psychiatric, medical, spiritual, or other support?)
2. What additional information do you need?
3. What other steps would you take for short-term help?
4. What additional longer-term mental health recommendations do you have for them?
5. What (if anything) would you do additionally at this point?

Suggested Responses

1. The concussive shock of a suicide is a devastatingly unique loss. No two situations are ever the same. People in shock need to be made to feel safe and able to say and ask whatever they need to. The chapel is a good place for them to be as long as others will not disturb the family. You would want to assess the emotional condition of each family member by informal observation and some casual questions: "How did you find out about this?" "What did you do then?" "Who besides the people here have you called?" The mother and father may need to scream, moan, and express their sorrow and rage they are feeling. This is the externalization of deep anguish, and, when it starts to come out, the care provider must be able to be there with this explosive material and allow it to flow. The parents must be kept safe and as an *exquisite witness* care provider, you are able to be with them and provide a sense of stability and security. When needed, medication for anxiety and distress can be provided.
2. It would also be useful to obtain the specific observations from the ER supervisor regarding the reasons for requesting the consultation, and also to have a few moments with the chaplain's assistant to get her impressions. In a situation which feels chaotic and out of control, providing some structure in the form of appropriate and innocuous questions can help to restore some sense of balance and caring. If they have many questions, take out a pad and write them all down and indicate that every effort will be made to get the answers. It is important that no emotion that comes up is judged as unacceptable or wrong.
3. The variety of reactions can also include self-destructive threats or threats to others. There should be a follow-up on such statements and an assessment made to determine the risk level for acting on such thoughts and the need for medical intervention and/or hospitalization. If this is not warranted, some form of very close observation by a family member or friend of the family should be arranged.

In some cases, the resident may prescribe medication for anxiety and/or for sleep.

Additionally, referral to an outpatient mental health resource may also be beneficial so that family members can feel the security of a safety net. The mother may simply be in shock, or she may have shut down to the point that she requires treatment. The father's barely controlled rage can be very appropriate to the situation, even if he releases it into the room. However, it can be indicative of other explosive issues and require professional help. You could also indicate that the chaplain's assistant is available for them right now as well. They should leave when they feel they are able to. Where it has been determined that family members are not safe to drive, transportation should be arranged.

The family should leave with phone numbers of whom they can call day or night should they feel out of control and in crisis. They should also be prepared for the routine questions the police may need to ask and any other required legal procedures. This is a difficult and sometimes time-consuming process, and at times results in delay in the releasing of the body.

4. For long-term recommendations, give the family the contact numbers for the Compassionate Friends and the SEASONS suicide support groups. If the topic of faith-based resources has come up, they should contact their clergy or spiritual adviser when they are ready to do so. If any of the family members were to be seen in therapy for any length of time, you could offer them the opportunity to say good-bye and forgive their deceased loved one and themselves. A follow-up call from a staff member is advised.

5. What would you do additionally at this point?

Your Turn to Respond

Case 6. Death of a Spouse (Review Chapters 2, 3, 8, and 9.)

A 59-year-old man has been widowed for 3 months after 35 years of marriage. He complains of concentration problems at work, difficulty sleeping, and finds himself drinking in excess of a six-pack of beer on weekends. The latter is unusual behavior for him. He admits to intermittent crying daily and calls his married daughter five to six times a week. Occasionally, he believes that he hears his wife calling him from some distant place in the house—usually at night. He admits to some anxiety regarding the possibility that he "is going crazy." He denies suicidal ideation but wonders if he will see her again "someday."

His daughter has suggested that he talk to his clergy about his questions regarding his bewilderment as to why his wife died so unexpectedly. The clergy has referred him to you for an assessment to decide whether he needs grief counseling.

1. What are some immediate suggestions that you can offer to give him some comfort and stability?

2. What additional information do you need in order to make an assessment?

3. What other steps would you take for short-term help?

4. What additional longer-term recommendations do you have for him?

Case 7. Dying Child and Siblings (Review Chapters 3, 4, 5.)

A 10-year-old girl is in her second round of chemotherapy for leukemia. She had been in remission for several months but is now weak, nauseous, and bald again. She has a younger sister, age 8, and an older brother, age 12. Her parents are heartsick over the reoccurrence of her tumor cells. The girl is very devoted to her parents and siblings and feels very badly that her illness has caused so much pain and disruption to their lives.

Her older brother has much ambivalence about his sick younger sister. He fears that she will die and yet makes angry comments about all of the attention she gets from Mom and Dad—especially Dad. People come to the house and all of their time is spent with his sister and she gets "so many cool things." When you talk to him alone, he says that he has a very bad sinus problem, "but I guess that's not bad enough." He "thinks" leukemia may be some kind of cancer but is "not sure how serious this is." He says that his parents do not talk much about his sister's illness, only about how tired they are and how "they can't do stuff with him anymore."

The younger sister idolizes her big sister and is not quite sure of how sick she is. She knows her parents are worried and always running to the doctor, the hospital, or the pharmacy. All of this frightens her, but no one will talk to her about her sister's illness.

The parents are dedicated to "beating this thing!" They get other medical opinions, search the Internet, and do everything they can to keep things "normal" in their home. They are asking for help because the school has reported that their son is acting out in school and his grades are falling. In addition, the younger sister's teacher has called with concerns that she is becoming increasingly withdrawn.

1. How can you be of most help right now?

2. Can you do this alone or do you need somebody else to be part of the action? (Who?)

3. What short-term external support can you suggest?

4. What long-term assistance can you provide or refer to another provider for?

☐ Conclusion

These accounts above represent just a sampling of cases that will come to your attention as a provider of service to grieving people. The amount of information supplied just scratches the surface of what you must obtain for any long-term help planning. Please add any ideas to those provided in response to the questions. Always seek the combined wisdom of colleagues whenever you can.

The epilogue that follows will provide an ending to our "heart," "head," and "hands" journey together. It is my hope that you will be an *exquisite witness* for the grieving people who so very much need you to be there to help when their tears are not enough.

Epilogue

"Two roads diverged in a wood, and I—
I took the one less traveled by,
And that has made all the difference."

Robert Frost

☐ Life, Loss, and Grief

And the painful losses I experienced have made more obvious the precious blessings I still retain in life.

As I conclude the writing of this book, I am more than ever convinced of the importance of communicating a simple message to all care providers and to all grieving people blessed by their care: Most grief is normal and needed for healing through loss. We need to learn to manage grief and to live with it side-by-side.

Imagine what the world might be like if all six billion people on this planet truly grasped the nature of normal grief and accepted without judgment, the variety of means for healing—using the griever's own time schedule. People may need to talk and talk and talk out grief, cry it out, scream it out, write it out, exercise it out, draw it out, creatively express it out, and find the means to somehow recreate self and life meanings in the post-loss world. Friends, family, and acquaintances must further accept that grieving people are subject to reoccurrences of grief reaction as life continues.

Author Gail Godwin, in her book, Father Melancholy's Daughter (Godwin, 2002), writes movingly of the way the thread of grief is woven into the fabric of the heroine's life (Her father has recently died and her mother has been dead for 16 years.):

> I could write a handbook on mourning: how it weaves in and out of the ordinary traffic of your days, for weeks and months (and maybe even years), sometimes diverting you with just a sharp little blip of a reminder, like the warning blips from . . . [a] siren ("Pull over to the side of whatever you are doing, and remember!"); other times bringing you to a full stop with a piercing, extended wail, requiring you to leave traffic altogether, turn your ignition off, put your head down on the steering wheel, let yourself be overwhelmed by the incredible words "Never Again," and wait for your breath to come back.
>
> You don't want the ache to go away, because as long as it's there, so are they. They make a place for themselves in the center of the ache, and you can go on living together that way for quite a while. They can go on living physically in you, as long as the ache is physically present (p. 319).

Additionally, those in the social world of people who grieve must also recognize the multiple effects of a person's loss and grief reaction on those around them. This includes the effect on care providers. Writing this book has been a healing, yet at times, painful experience for me. I continue to marvel at the grief that surfaces each time I write about my personal experience or when clinical work triggers a painful memory. Observations of this reality are reflected on below by Helane Jeffreys.

☐ Reflections of a Grief Psychologist's Wife

This is the story of the grief care provider as a front line soldier/hero,
Facing the assault of continuous, raw grief
And willing to be there and not turn away.
As a care provider, you are seeing sadness again and again.
It can and will eventually affect you.
When parents call you to ask for help because their child committed
   suicide,
Or when a television news report depicts a video footage of people
   crying after a

loved one was shot and killed,
And you get the phone call the next morning,
Or when your client feels nothing but pain and nothing you do seems
    to help,
Or when a school official refers a family whose child killed a best
    friend while
playing with a gun and the families are in indescribable pain,
I think of you in the same way as I think of the police, the firefighters,
the soldier, and all heroes.
You are vulnerable to the effects of the work you do—
the supporting, the helping, the being there.
Each time new grief announces itself you make yourself present
And are again challenged to take care of yourself.

©Helane Jeffreys, 2004

☐ Those Who Don't Turn Their Eyes Away

Writer Brad Lemley wrote a story for the *Washington Post Magazine* (1986) about his very sick newborn son. One day he observed the nurse try, yet again, to find an accessible vein for intravenous feeding. She found a vein and successfully inserted the needle. The nurse did not turn her eyes away from her task with this baby. There are so many other people in our society who do not turn their eyes away from jobs that most of us are happy to let them do—preparing bodies for viewings, emptying bedpans, recovering drowning victims, working the emergency rooms, and providing care to the dying, bereaved and very ill. All of these individuals do not, cannot, turn their eyes away from what has to be done to serve society's shadowy side.

Exquisite Witness grief care providers at all levels of training and experience will learn to stay focused on the task at hand, and this is facilitated by not turning their eyes away from their own current or old loss material.

As this book draws to a close, I want to assure you who are newly entering this work that while there are some tough and at times painful situations we face with grieving people, there are many gifts that we receive. Some of the treasures come in the form of being with sick and dying people who have reordered their priorities to such bottom line goals as being pain-free, being clean, and giving and receiving love. Other gifts come from the recognition of our own Cowbells, our personal unfinished grief which, when effectively managed, will not diminish our availability to those we are serving. Finally, while dying and death is a topic so many wish to turn their eyes away from, you as an *Exquisite Witness* provider will be shining your light into that darkness because you will not turn your eyes away. Your joy in this work will come from your confidence and comfort in knowing that you will be available to help grieving people heal "when tears are not enough."

May you always seek the "light" in your work.

Shep Jeffreys

Additional Readings

Spiritual and Cultural Considerations

Ashenburg, K. (2002). *The mourner's dance*. New York: North Point Press.

Berkus, R. (1984). *To heal again: Towards serenity and the resolution of grief*. Encino, CA: Red Rose.

Brener, A. (1993). *Mourning & mitzvah: A guided journal for walking the mourner's path through grief to healing*. Woodstock, VT: Jewish Lights.

Byock, I. (1997). *Dying well: The prospect for growth at the end of life*. New York: Riverhead Books.

Cox, G. R., Fundis, R. J. (Eds.). (1992). *Spiritual, ethical, and pastoral aspects of death and bereavement*. Amityville, NY: Baywood.

Doka, K. J., & Morgan, J. (Eds.). (1993). *Death and spirituality*. Amityville, NY: Baywood.

Doore, G. (Ed.). (1990). *What survives? Contemporary explorations of life after death*. Los Angeles: Tarcher.

Dossey, L. (1996). *Prayer is good medicine*. San Francisco: HarperCollins.

Hickman, M. W. (1994). *Healing after loss*, New York: Perennial/HarperCollins.

Irish, D.P ., Lundquist, K., Nelson, V. J. (Eds.). (1993). *Ethnic variations in dying, death, and grief*. New York: Taylor & Francis.

Koenig, B. A., & Gates-Williams, J. (1995). Understanding cultural differences in caring for dying patients, *West J Med, 163*, 244–249.

Kohner, N. & Henley, A. (1995). *When a baby dies: The experience of late miscarriage, stillbirth, and neonatal death*. San Francisco: HarperCollins.

Kramer, K. (1988). *The sacred art of dying: How world religions understand death*. New York: Paulist Press.

Kubler-Ross, E. (1975). *Death: Final stage of growth*. Englewood Cliffs, NJ: Prentice Hall.

Kubler-Ross, E. (1991). *On life after death*. Berkeley, CA: Celestial Arts.

Kushner, H. (1981). *When bad things happen to good people*. New York: Schocken.

Levine, S. (1982). *Who dies: An investigation of conscious living & conscious dying*. New York: Anchor Books.

Metrick, S.B. (1994). *Crossing the bridge: Creating ceremonies for grieving and healing.* Berkeley, CA: Celestial Arts.

McIntosh, D. C., Silver, R. C., & Wortman, C. B. (1993). Religion's role in adjustment to a negative life event: Coping with the loss of a child. *Journal of Personality and Social Psychology, 65,* 812–821.

Moody, R. A., Jr. (1975). *Life after life.* New York: Bantam.

Morse, M. (1990). *Closer to the light: Learnings from children's near-death experiences.* New York: Villard Books.

Murphy-Shigematsu, S. (2002). *Multicultural encounters: Case narratives from a counseling practice,* New York: Teachers College.

Putter, A. M. (Ed.) (1997). *The memorial rituals book for healing and hope,* Amityville, NY: Baywood.

Rinpoche, S. (1988). *The Tibetan book of living and dying.* New York: Crown.

Sarhill, N., Islambouli, R., Davis, M. P., & Walsh, D. (2001). The terminally ill Muslim: Death and dying from the Muslim perspective. *American Journal of Hospital Palliative Care, 18,* 251–255.

Talamantes, M. A. & Aranda, M. P. (2004). Cultural competency in working with Latino family caregivers. National Caregivers Alliance monograph. www.caregiver.org.

Weeks, O. D. (2004). Comfort and healing: Death ceremonies that work. *Illness, Crisis & Loss, 12,* 113–125.

Wicks, R. J. (1998). *Living a gentle and passionate life.* New York: Paulist Press.

Wicks, R. J. (1992). *Touching the holy.* Notre Dame, IN: Ave Maria Press.

Wicks, R. J. (2001). *Snow falling on snow.* New York: Paulist Press.

Wicks, R. J. (2003). *Riding the dragon.* Notre Dame, IN: Sorin Books.

Psychology of Human Grief

Attig, T. (2001). Relearning the world: Making and finding meanings. In R. A. Neimeyer (Ed.), *Meaning reconstruction & the experience of loss* (pp. 33–53). Washington, DC: American Psychological Association.

Becker, E. (1973). *The denial of death.* New York: Free Press.

Bloom-Feshbach, J., & Bloom-Feshbach, S. (1987). *The psychology of separation and loss.* San Francisco: Jossey-Bass.

Bonnano, G. A., Keltner, D., Holen, A., & Horowitz, M. J. (1995). When avoiding unpleasant emotions might not be such a bad thing: Verbal-autonomic response dissociation and midlife conjugal bereavement. *Journal of Personality and Social Psychology, 46,* 975–989.

Bonnano, G. A., & Kaltman, S. (1999). Toward an integrative perspective on bereavement. *Psychological Bulletin, 125,* 760–776.

Bonnano, G. A., Wortman, C. B., Lehman, D. R., Tweed, R .G., Haring, M., Sonnega, J., et al. (2002). Resilience to loss and chronic grief: A prospective study from pre-loss to 18 months post-loss. *Journal of Personality and Social Psychology, 83,* 1150–1164.

Cassidy, J. & Berlin, L. J. (1994). The insecure/ambivalent pattern of attachment: Theory and research. *Child Development, 65,* 971–991.

Cassidy, J., & Shaver, P. R. (Eds.). (1999). *Handbook of Attachment: Theory search and clinical applications.* New York: Guilford Press.

Doka, K. J. (Ed.). (1989). *Disenfranchised grief: Recognizing hidden sorrow.* Lexington, MA: Lexington.

Doka, K. J. (Ed.). (2002). *Disenfranchised grief: New direction, challenges, and strategies for practice.* Champaign, IL: Research Press.

Elison, J. & McGonigle, C. (2003). *Liberating losses: When death brings relief.* Cambridge, MA: Perseus.

Field, N. P., Nichols, D., Holen, A., & Horowitz, M. J. (1999). The relation of continuing attachment to adjustment in conjugal bereavement. *Journal of Consulting and Clinical Psychology, 67,* 212–218.

Figley, C. R., Bride, B. E., & Mazza, N. (Eds.). (1997). *Death and trauma: The traumatology of grieving*. Washington, DC: Taylor & Francis.

Harvey, J. H. (Ed.). (1998). *Perspectives on loss: A sourcebook*. Philadelphia: Brunner/Mazel.

Klass, D., Silverman, P. R., & Nickman, S. L. (Eds.), *Continuing bonds: New understanding of grief*. Washington, DC: Taylor & Francis.

Neimeyer, R. A. (1998). *Lessons of loss: A guide to coping*. New York: McGraw-Hill.

Neimeyer, R. A. (Ed.). (2001). *Meaning reconstruction & the experience of loss*. Washington, DC: American Psychological Association.

Neimeyer, R. A., Prigerson, H. G., & Davies, B. (2002). Mourning and meaning. *American Behavioral Scientist, 46*, 232–251.

Osterweis, M., Solomon, F., & Green, M. (1984). (Eds.), *Bereavement: Reactions, consequences, and care*. Washington, DC : National Academy Science.

Parkes, C. M. (1972). *Bereavement: Studies of grief in adult life*. Great Britain: Travistock.

Pennebaker, J. W., Mayne, T. J., & Francis, M. E. (1997). Linguistic predictors of adaptive behavior. *Journal of Personality and Social Psychology, 72*, 863–871.

Ponzetti, J. J., Jr. (1992). Bereaved families: A comparison of parents' and grandparents' reactions to the death of a child. *Omega, 25*, 63–71.

Rando, T. A. (Ed.). (1986). *Loss & anticipatory grief*. Lexington Books, Lexington.

Rando, T. A. (Ed.). (2000). *Clinical dimensions of anticipatory mourning: Theory and practice in working with the dying, their loved ones, and their caregivers*. Champaign, IL: Research Press.

Reite, M. & Field, T. (Eds.). (1985). *The psychobiology of attachment and separation*. New York: Academic Press.

Reite, M., & Field, T. (1985). The psychobiology of attunement in attachment. In M. Reite & T. Field (Eds.), *The psychobiology of attachment and separation* (pp. 177–189). Orlando, FL: Academic Press.

Stroebe, M. S., Hansson, R. O., Stroebe, W., & Schut, H. (Eds.). (2001). *Handbook of bereavement research: Consequences, coping, and care*. Washington, DC: American Psychological Association.

Stroebe, M. S., Strobe, W., & Hansson, R. (Eds.). (1993). *Handbook of bereavement: Theory, research and intervention*. New York: Cambridge University Press.

Viorst, J. (1986). *Necessary losses*. New York: Fawcett Gold Medal.

General and Self-Help

Aiken, L. R. (2001). *Dying, death, and bereavement* (4th ed.). Mahwah, NJ: Erlbaum.

Berkus, R. (1984). *To heal again: Towards serenity and the resolution of grief*. Encino, CA: Red Rose Press.

Clough, S. L. (2001). *When you don't know what to say: Encouraging words for the hurting heart*. Eugene, OR: Harvest House.

Cook, A. S., & Dworkin, D. S. (1992). *Helping the bereaved*. Amityville, NY: Baywood.

Doka, K. J., & Davidson, J. D. (Eds.). (1998). *Living with grief: Who we are, how we grieve*. Washington, DC: Hospice Foundation of America.

Donnelley, N. H. (1987). *I never know what to say*. New York: Ballantine/Epiphany.

Frankl, V. E. (1977/1987). *Man's search for meaning (Rev. ed.)*. London: Hodder and Sloughton.

Grollman, E. (1997). *Living when a loved one has died*. Boston: Beacon.

Harvey, J. H. (Ed.) (1998). *Perspectives on loss: A sourcebook*. New York: Taylor & Francis.

Hickman, M. W. (1994). *Healing after loss*. New York: Perennial/HarperCollins.

Jeffreys, J. (1995). *Coping with workplace change: Dealing with loss and grief*. Mason, OH: (Crisp) Thomson Learning.

Koppelman, K. L. (1994). *The fall of a sparrow: Of death and dreams and healing*. Amityville, NY: Baywood.

Kubler-Ross, E. (1974). *Questions and answers on death and dying*. New York: Macmillan.

Levine, S. (1979). *A gradual awakening*. New York: Anchor Books.

Lewis, C.S. (1976). *A grief observed*. New York: Bantam books.

Lord, J. H. (1987). *No time for goodbyes*. Ventura, CA: Pathfinder Publications.

Miller, W. A. (1976). *When going to pieces holds you together*. Minneapolis, MN: Augsburg Publishing.

Moffat, M. J. (Ed.). (1982). *In the midst of winter: Selections from the literature of mourning*. New York: Vintage Books.

Schaefer, D. & Lyons, C. (1986). *How do we tell the children?* New York: Newmarket Press.

Schiff, H. S. (1986). *Living through mourning: Finding comfort and hope when a loved one has died*. New York: Penguin Books.

Siegel, B. (1986). *Love, medicine, and miracles*. New York: Harper & Row.

Smith, H. I. (2002). *Friend grief: An absence called presence*. Amityville, NY: Baywood.

Stearns, A. K. (1985). *Living through personal crisis*. New York: Ballantine Books.

Stearns, A. K. (1995). *Living through job loss*. New York: Fireside/Simon & Schuster.

Whitaker, A. (Ed.). (1984). *All in the end is harvest: An anthology for those who grieve*. London: Darton, Longman & Todd.

Wolfelt, A. D. (1998). *Healing the grieving heart: 100 practical ideas for families, friends & caregivers*. Fort Collins, CO: Companion Press.

End of Life, Illness, and Family Caregivers

Albom, M. (1997). *Tuesdays with Morrie: An old man, a young man, and life's greatest lesson*. New York: Doubleday.

Callanan, M., & Kelley, P. (1992). *Final gifts: Understanding the special awareness, needs, and communications of the dying*. New York: Bantam.

Davy, J., & Ellis, S. (2000). *Counseling skills in palliative care*. Buckingham, England: Open University Press.

Doka, K. J. (1993). *Living with life-threatening illness: A guide for patients, their families, and caregivers*. New York: Lexington Books.

Field, M. J., & Cassel, C. K. (Eds.). (1997). *Approaching death: Improving care at the end of life*. Washington, DC: National Academy Press.

Field, M., & Duda, D. (1987). *Coming home: A guide to dying at home with dignity*. New York: Aurora Press.

Foley, K. M. & Gelband, H. (Eds.). (1997). *Improving palliative care for cancer: Summary and recommendations*. National Academy Press: Washington, DC.

Kubler-Ross, E. (1978). *To live until we say goodbye*. Englewood Cliffs, NJ: Prentice Hall.

Laungani, P. Therapeutic strategies for coping with a life-threatening illness: A personal testament, *Illness, Crisis and Loss. 11*, 162–182.

Levine, C. (Ed.). (2000). *Always on call: When illness turns families into caregivers*. New York: United Hospital Fund.

Levine, S. (1984). *Meetings at the edge: Dialogues with the grieving & dying, the healing and the healed*. New York: Anchor Books.

Lynn, J., & Harrold, J. (1999). *Handbook for mortals: Guidance for people facing serious illness*. New York: Oxford University Press.

McLeod, B. W. (1999). *Caregiving: The spiritual journey of love, loss, and renewal*. New York: Wiley.

McLeod, B. W. (2002). *And thou shalt honor: The caregivers companion*. Wiland-Bell Productions, www.RODALESTORE.com.

Morgan, J. D. (Ed.). (1996). *Ethical issues in the care of the dying and bereaved aged*. Amityville, NY: Baywood.

Nuland, S. B. (1993). *How we die: Reflections on life's final chapter*. New York: Vintage Books.

Rosenblum, D. (1993). *A time to hear: A time to help: Listening to people with cancer*. New York: Lexington Books.

Tobin, D. (1999). *Peaceful dying: The step-by-step guide to preserving your dignity, your choice, and your inner peace at the end of life.* Reading, MA: Perseus.

Family, Bereaved Parents, and Elders in Grief

Caserta, M. S., & Lund, D. A. (1992). Bereavement stress and coping among older adults: Expectations versus the actual experience. *Omega, 25,* 33–45.

DeFrain, J., Ernst, L., Jakub, D., & Taylor, J. (1991). *Sudden infant death: Enduring the loss,* Lexington, MA: Lexington Books.

DeMaso, D. R., Myer, E. C., & Beasley, P. J. (1997). What do I say to my surviving children? *Journal of the Academy of Child and Adolescent Psychiatry, 36,* 1299–1302.

Depaola, S. J., Griffin, M., Young, J. R., & Neimeyer, R. A. (2003). Death anxiety and attitudes toward the elderly among older adults: The role of gender and ethnicity. *Death Studies, 27,* 335–354.

Figley, C. R. (1989). *Helping traumatized families.* San Francisco: Jossey-Bass.

Hagemeister, A. K. & Rosenblatt, P. C. (1997). Grief and the sexual relationship of couples who have experienced a child's death. *Death Studies, 21,* 231–253.

Kohner, N. & Henley, A. (1995). *When a baby dies,* New York: HarperCollins.

Mandel, E. (1981). *The art of aging.* Minneapolis, MN: Winston.

McGoldrick, M., & Walsh, F. (Eds.). (1991). *Living beyond loss: Death in the family.* New York: Norton.

Pincus, L. (1974). *Death and the family: The importance of mourning.* London: Faber & Faber.

Rando, T. (Ed.). (1986). *Parental loss of a child.* Champaign, IL: Research Press.

Rosenblatt, P. C. (2000). *Help your marriage survive the death of a child.* Philadelphia: Temple University Press.

Rosof, B. D. (1994). *The worst loss: How families heal from the death of a child.* New York: Holt.

Rothman, J. C. (1997). *The bereaved parents guide.* New York: Continuum.

Sharkin, B. S. & Knox, D. (2003). Pet loss: Issues and implications for the psychologist. *Professional Psychology: Research and Practice, 34,* 414–421.

Smith, H. I. (2002). *Friend grief: An absence called presence.* Amityville, NY: Baywood.

Walsh, F. & McGoldrick, M. (1998). A family systems perspective on loss, recovery, and resilience. In P. Sutcliffe, G. Tufnell, & U. Cornish, *Working with the dying and bereaved: Systemic approaches to therapeutic work* (pp. 1–26). New York: Routledge.

Weaver, J., & Koenig, H. G. (1996). Elderly suicide, mental health professionals, and the clergy: A need for clinical collaboration, training, and research. *Death Studies, 20,* 498–508.

For Children, Adolescents, and Their Adults

Alexander-Greene, A. (1999). *Sunflowers & rainbows for Tia: Saying goodbye to Daddy.* Omaha, NE: Centering corporation.

Bode, J. (1993). *Death is hard to live with.* New York: Bantam/Doubleday/Dell.

Brown, L. K., & Brown, M. (1996). *When dinosaurs die: A guide to understanding death.* United States: Little, Brown, and Company.

Buscaglia, L. (1982). *The fall of Freddie the leaf: A story of life for all ages.* Thorofare, NJ: Slack.

Clifton, L. (1983). *Everett Anderson's goodbye.* New York: Henry Holt.

Curry, C. (2003). *I remember you today: An interactive picturebook for children dealing with loss and grief.* Annapolis, MD: Annapolis Publishing.

The Dougy Center for Grieving Children. (1999). *35 ways to help a grieving child.* Portland, OR: Author.

The Dougy Center for Grieving Children. (1999). *Helping teens cope with death.* Portland, OR: Author.

Farber, N. (1979). *How does it feel to be old?* New York: Dutton.

Fogerty, J. (2000). *The magical thoughts of grieving children.* Amityville, NY: Baywood.

Goldman, L. (1996). *Breaking the silence: A guide to help children with complicated grief—suicide, homicide, AIDS, violence, and abuse.* Washington, DC: Taylor & Francis.

Goldman, L. (1998). *Bart speaks out: An interactive storybook for young children on suicide.* Los Angeles: Western Psychological Services.

Gootman, M. (1994). *When a friend dies.* Minneapolis, MN: Free Spirit.

Grollman, E. (1990). *Talking about death: A dialogue between parent and child.* Boston: Beacon Press.

Grollman, E. (1993). *Straight talk about death for teenagers.* Boston: Beacon Press.

Grollman, E. (Ed.). (1995). *Bereaved children and teens.* Boston: Beacon Press.

Heeguard, M. (1988). *When someone very special dies.* Minneapolis, MN: Woodland Press.

Jordan, M. (1989). *Losing Uncle Tim.* Niles, IL: Albert Whitman.

Keating, P. (1995). *After the funeral.* New York: Paulist Press.

Kohner, N., & Henley, A. (1995). *When a baby dies: The experience of late miscarriage, stillbirth, and neonatal death.* San Francisco: Pandora.

Kubler-Ross, E. (1983). *On children and death.* New York: Macmillan. Boston: Beacon Press.

McCracken, A., & Semel, M. (1998). *A broken heart still beats after your child dies.* Center City, MN: Hazelden.

Mellonie, B., & Ingpen, R. (1983). *Lifetimes: The beautiful way to explain death to children.* Toronto: Bantam Books.

Mundy, M. (1998). *Sad isn't bad: A good-grief guidebook for kids dealing with loss.* St. Meinrad, IN: Abby Press.

Munsch, R. (1986). *Love You Forever.* Willowdale, Ontario, Canada: Firefly Books.

Rando, T. A. (Ed.). (1986). *Parental loss of a child.* Champaign, IL: Research Press.

Romain, T. (1999). *What on earth do you do when someone dies.* Minneapolis, MN: Free Spirit.

Schafer, D., & Lyons, C. (1986). *How do we tell the children?* New York: Newmarket Press.

Schatz, W. (1984). *Healing a father's grief.* Redmond, WA: Medic Publishing.

Scherago, M. (1987). *Sibling grief: How parents can help the child whose brother or sister has died.* Redmond, WA: Medic Publishing.

Schiff, H. S. (1977). *The bereaved parent.* New York: Penguin Books.

Simon, N. (1986). *The saddest time.* Morton Grove, IL: Albert Whitman.

Sims, A. M. (1986). *Am I still a sister?* Blue Springs, MO: Starline Printing/Big A & Company.

Stein, S. B. (1974). *About dying.* New York: Walker & Company.

Stickney, D. (1982). *Waterbugs and dragonflies.* New York: Pilgrim Press.

Teakle, H. (1992). *My daddy died: Supporting your children in grief.* North Blackburn Victoria, Australia: Collins Dove.

Thomas, M. S. (1988). *Saying goodbye to Grandma.* New York: Clarion.

Varley, S. (1984). *Badger's parting gifts.* New York: Mulberry books.

Viorst, J. (1971). *The tenth good thing about Barney.* New York: Simon & Schuster.

Wackenshaw, M. (2002). *Caring for your grieving child: Engaging in activities for dealing with loss and transition.* Oakland, CA: New Harbinger Publications.

Wilhelm, H. (1988). *I'll always love you.* New York: Random House.

Winsch, J. L. (1995). *After the funeral.* New York: Paulist Press.

Wolfelt, A. D. (1991). *A child's view of grief.* Fort Collins, CO: Center for Loss and Life Transition.

Wolfelt, A. D. (1996). *Healing the bereaved child.* Fort Collins, CO: Center for Loss and Life Transition.

Worden, J. W. (1996). *Children and grief: When a parent dies.* New York: Guilford.

Care Provider Interventions; Complicated Grief

Figley, C. R. (Ed.). (1995). *Compassion fatigue: Coping with secondary traumatic stress disorder in those who treat the traumatized.* New York: Brunner/Mazel.

Jacobs, S. (1993). *Pathologic grief: Maladaption to loss*. Washington, DC: American Psychiatric Press.

Jacobs, S. (1999). *Traumatic grief: Diagnosis, treatment, and prevention*. New York: Brunner Mazel/Taylor & Francis.

Lendrum, S. & Syme, G. (1992). *Gift of tears: A practical approach to loss and bereavement counseling*. London: Brunner/Routledge.

Lindemann, E. (1979). The symptomology and management of acute grief. *American Journal of Psychiatry, 101*, 141–148. (Original work published in 1944).

Maltsberger, J. & Goldblatt, M. (Eds.). (1996). *Essential papers on suicide*. New York: New York University Press.

Marwit, S. J. (1996). Reliability of diagnosing complicated grief: A preliminary investigation. *Journal of Clinical and Consulting Psychology, 64*, 563–568.

Neimeyer, R. A. (2000). Searching for the meaning of meaning: Grief therapy and the process of reconstruction. *Death Studies, 24*, 541–558.

Rando, T. A. (1993). *Treatment of complicated mourning*. Champaign, IL: Research Press.

Worden, J. W. (2002). *Grief counseling and grief therapy*. New York: Springer.

Zinner, E. S., & Williams, M. B. (Eds.). (1999). *When a community weeps: Case studies in group survivorship*. Philadelphia: Brunner/Mazel.

APPENDIX

B

Organization Resources

AARP
American Association of Retired Persons
601 E Street, NW
Washington, DC 20049
202-434-2277
www.aarp.org

Alzheimer's Association
919 North Michigan Avenue, Suite 1000
Chicago, IL 60611-1676
800-272-3900
www.alz.org

American Academy of Hospice and Palliative Medicine
http://www.aahpm.org

American Association of Suicidology
4201 Connecticut Avenue, NW, Suite 310
Washington, DC 20008
www.suicidology.org

ARCH National Respite Network
800 Eastowne Drive, Suite 105
Chapel Hill, NC 27514
www.archrespite.org

Bereaved Parents of USA
P.O. Box 95
Park Forest, IL 60466
president@bereavedparentsusa.org
www.bereavedparentsusa.org

Candlelighters Childhood Cancer Foundation
7910 Woodmont Avenue, Suite 460
Bethesda, MD 20814
301-657-8401
800-366-2223
www.candlelighters.org

Compassionate Friends
P.O. Box 3696
Oak Brook, IL 60522-3696
630-990-0010
www.compassionatefriends.org

The Dougy Center for Grieving Children
3909 S. E. 52nd Street Avenue
P.O. Box 86852
Portland, OR 97286
1-503-775-5683 (Ext. 27)
www.dougy.org

Eldercare Locator (1-800-677-1116)
Family Caregivers Alliance
690 Market Street, Suite 600
San Francisco, CA 94104
415-434-3388
800-445-8106
www.caregiver.org

Funeral Consumers Alliance
info@funerals.org
www.funerals.org
GriefNetwww.kidsaid.com

Helping Grieving People
J. Shep Jeffreys
GriefCareProvider.com

Hospice Foundation of America
1-800-854-3402
www.hospicefoundation.org

Living Wills (Advance Directive)
http://www.mindspring.com

Mothers Against Drunk Driving
511 E. Carpenter Freeway, Suite 700
Irving, TX 75062
800-GET-MADD (438-6233)
www.madd.org

National Alliance for Caregiving
4720 Montgomery Lane, 5th Floor
Bethesda, MD 20814
www.caregiving.org

National Association of Professional Geriatric Care Managers
1604 N. Country Club Road
Tucson, AZ 85716-3102
520-881-8008

National Cancer Institute, National Institutes of Health
31 Center Drive, MSC 2590
Bethesda, MD 20892-2580
www.nci.nih.gov

The National Center for Post-Traumatic Stress Disorder (PTSD)
United States Department of Veterans Affairs
802-296-6300
www.ncptsd.org

National Council on Disability
1331 F St., NW, Suite 850
Washington, DC 20004
202-272-2004 TTY: 202-272-2074
www.ncd.gov

National Family Caregivers Association
10400 Connecticut Avenue, #500
Kensington, MD 20895-3944
1-800-896-3650 (Bereavement Kit available)
www.nfcacares.org

National Hospice Organization
901 North Moore Street, Suite 901
Arlington, VA 22209
703-243-5900
http://www.nhpco.org

National Sudden Infant Death Syndrome Alliance
1314 Bedford Avenue, Suite 210
Baltimore, MD 21208
410-653-8226
http://www.sidsalliance.org

National SIDS Resource Center
http://www.sidscenter.org

Parents of Murdered Children, Inc.
100 East 8th Street
Cincinnati, OH 45202
888-818-POMC
www.pomc.org
Red Cross
www.redcross.org

SEASONS: Suicide Bereavement
P.O. Box 187
Oak Brook, IL 60522
http://suicidehotlines.com

Tragedy Assistance Program for Survivors
2001 S Street, NW, Suite 300
Washington, DC 20009
800-959-TAPS
http://www.taps.org

Advance Medical Directive

Norman L. Cantor
Rutgers Law School

☐ Part I: Introduction

The following material is designed to guide my medical treatment after I have become incompetent—that is, unable to understand the nature and consequences of important medical decisions. The object is to appoint a decision maker on my behalf (to be known as my health care representative) and to instruct that decision maker concerning the level of deterioration that would warrant ending life-sustaining medical intervention. I assume that comfort care (care intended to keep me pain free, clean, and comfortable) will always be provided.

☐ Part II: Designation of a Health Care Representative

A. Primary Designation

I, _____ , hereby designate the following individual as my health care representative to act on my behalf, in the event of my incompetence, with respect to any and all health care decisions. These include decisions to provide, withhold, or withdraw life-sustaining measures, to hire and fire health care providers, or to transfer my care to another physician or institution.

Primary Health Care Representative:

Name _____

Address _____

City _____ State _____

Telephone _____

B. Alternate Designation(s) (Naming of Alternate(s) Is Recommended, but Not Required)

In the event the individual named above is unavailable, or is unable or unwilling to serve as my health care representative, I hereby designate the following individual(s) to act as alternate(s):

First Alternate:

Name _____

Address _____

City _____ State _____

Telephone _____

Second Alternate:

Name _____

Address _____

City _____ State _____

Telephone _____

C. Consultation

To the extent feasible in the circumstances, I direct my health care representative to confer with the following individuals prior to making any health care decisions on my behalf. These individuals may provide advice to be considered by the health care representative, but they shall not have veto power over the health care representative's decisions. (Check all that apply, and provide names and telephone numbers if not specified above):

_____ a) Family member(s):
_____ b) My physician or physicians:
_____ c) My attorney:
_____ d) My priest, minister, rabbi, or other clergy person:
_____ e) Others:

☐ Part III: General Instructions for Care

To inform those responsible for my care, I declare that there are circumstances in which I would not want my life to be prolonged by further medical treatment. In such circumstances (as described below), life-sustaining measures should not be initiated and, if they have been initiated, they should be discontinued. I recognize that this is likely to hasten my death.

If I become stricken with a serious illness or condition, with no reasonable expectation of cure or recovery to a competent state, I do not want life-sustaining treatment to be provided or continued after my health care representative determines that the burdens of my continued existence outweigh the benefits or that my condition has permanently deteriorated to a point of intolerable indignity. In making these judgments, I want my health care representative to consider my suffering and my diminished quality of life, with particular attention to the elements of indignity noted in my values profile in Part IV. In the event my wishes are not clear, or if a situation arises that I did not anticipate, my health care representative is authorized to use his/her best judgment about what I would want done, keeping in mind my conceptions of indignity sketched in Part IV.

☐ Part IV: Values Profile Introduction

Like many people, I am concerned about medical prolongation of my life upon reaching an intolerably deteriorated condition. Below I have given my reactions to various factors which many people consider important in shaping postcompetence medical care. To the extent that I am concerned about such factors, I have indicated conditions that, for me, are intolerable.

A. Pain and Suffering

1. In my postcompetency state, I am concerned about extreme pain and would expect to receive pain medication to make me as comfortable as possible. My attitude toward being in a permanent condition in which pain can be controlled only by substances that leave me unconscious all or most of the time:
   ___ intolerable; I prefer to be allowed to die, even if that means withholding or withdrawal of artificial nutrition and hydration in my unconscious condition.
   ___ intolerable; I prefer to be allowed to die, but I want artificial nutrition and hydration.
   ___ a very negative factor, to be weighed with other factors in determining intolerable indignity.
   ___ unimportant; I prefer that I be kept alive even if pain medication leaves me unconscious.

2. My attitude toward being in a permanent condition in which pain or suffering can be controlled only by substances that leave me disoriented and confused all or most of the time:
   ___ intolerable; I prefer to be allowed to die, even if that means withholding or withdrawal of artificial nutrition and hydration in my disoriented condition.
   ___ intolerable; I prefer to be allowed to die, but I want artificial nutrition and hydration.
   ___ a very negative factor, to be weighed with other factors in determining intolerable indignity.
   ___ unimportant; I prefer that I be kept alive even if pain medication leaves me disoriented.

B. Mental Incapacity

1. In my postcompetency state, I am concerned about the level of my mental deterioration to the following extent:
   ___ a very critical factor
   ___ important, but not determinative by itself; a factor to be weighed with other factors in determining intolerable indignity
   ___ unimportant

2. My attitude toward a permanently unconscious state, confirmed by up-to-date medical tests, showing no hope of ever regaining connsciousness:
   ___ intolerable; I prefer death
   ___ tolerable
   ___ tolerable, so long as insurance or other nonfamily sources are paying the bills

3. My reaction to profound dementia to the point where I can no longer recognize my loved ones and interact with them in a coherent fashion:
   ___ intolerable; I prefer death
   ___ a very negative factor, to be weighed with other factors in determining intolerable indignity
   ___ tolerable

4. My reaction to dementia to the point where I can no longer read and understand written material such as a newspaper:
   ___ intolerable; I prefer death
   ___ a very negative factor, to be weighed with other factors in determining intolerable indignity
   ___ tolerable

5. My reaction to moderate dementia (such as Alzheimer's disease) characterized by frequent confusion and loss of short-term memory, though I am still able to experience pleasant feelings and emotions and to interact with people:
   ___ intolerable; I prefer to be allowed to die, even if this means nontreatment of curable conditions such as pneumonia or infections
   ___ a very negative factor, to be weighed with other factors in determining intolerable indignity
   ___ tolerable

C. Physical Immobility

1. In my incompetent state, I am concerned about physical immobility to the following extent:
   ___ important
   ___ unimportant

2. My reaction to being permanently bed-ridden:
   ___ intolerable; I prefer death
   ___ a very negative factor, to be weighed with other factors in determining intolerable indignity
   ___ tolerable

3. My reaction to being nonambulatory, meaning that I can leave my bed but can only move around if others transport me in a wheelchair:
   ___ intolerable; I prefer death
   ___ a very negative factor, to be weighed with other factors in determining intolerable indignity
   ___ tolerable

D. Physical Helplessness

1. In my incompetent state, I am concerned about my independence and ability to tend to my own physical needs to the following extent:
   ___ important
   ___ unimportant

2. My reaction to being incapable of feeding myself:
   ___ intolerable; I prefer death
   ___ a very negative factor, to be weighed with other factors in determining intolerable indignity
   ___ tolerable

3. My reaction to being incapable of dressing myself:
   ___ intolerable; I prefer death
   ___ a very negative factor, to be weighed with other factors in determining intolerable indignity
   ___ tolerable

4. My reaction to being incontinent:
   ___ intolerable; I prefer death
   ___ a very negative factor, to be weighed with other factors in determining intolerable indignity
   ___ tolerable

E. Interests of Loved Ones

1. In my incompetent state, the emotional and financial burdens imposed on my loved ones are of concern to the following extent:
   ___ a critical factor
   ___ an important factor, depending on degree of burden
   ___ unimportant

2. My reaction to emotional strain posed for my spouse or other loved ones surrounding me during my incompetency:
   ___ an important factor
   ___ a somewhat important factor
   ___ unimportant; although I care about my loved ones, I want my treatment decisions to be based on my own circumstances

3. My reaction to a heavy financial burden being imposed on my spouse or other loved ones:
   ___ an important factor
   ___ a somewhat important factor
   ___ unimportant; although I care about my loved ones, I want my treatment decisions to be based on my own circumstances

4. My reaction to my assets being depleted by heavy medical expenses for my care:
   ___ an important factor
   ___ unimportant

F. Living Arrangements

1. In my incompetent state, I am concerned about my living arrangements to the following extent:
   ___ not important; I want my care to be determined by my personal condition rather than the surroundings
   ___ some living arrangements would be intolerable (if so, proceed to the next question)

2. I would find any of the following living arrangements intolerable, so that if there were no alternative I would prefer cessation or withdrawal of life-sustaining medical care:

___ living at home, but with need for full-time help

___ living permanently in the home of one of my children or other relative

___ living permanently in a nursing home or other long-term care facility

___ being confined to a hospital with little or no hope of ever leaving

G. Types of Medical Intervention

1. My attitude toward artificially provided fluids and nutrition, such as feeding tubes or intravenous infusion:

___ to be handled in the same way as other medical interventions (guided by my instructions above)

___ to be provided at all times, regardless of my condition

2. I understand decisions as to all types of medical intervention will be governed by my instructions as indicated in this document. However, I feel an especially strong aversion to certain form(s) of intervention. (*Indicate here any special aversions, such as to a respirator, a blood transfusion, or CPR*):

_____

_____

_____

3. My attitude toward hand- or spoon-feeding in the event that I have reached a level of deterioration that I have defined as intolerably undignified:

___ I wish to receive oral nutrition only so long as I am willingly taking what is offered, and I do not want to be force-fed or to receive artificial nutrition or hydration in the event I am resisting oral nutrition.

___ I wish to receive oral nutrition only so long as I am willingly taking what is offered, but I would expect artificial nutrition or hydration in the event I am resisting oral nutrition.

☐ Part V: Signature and Witnesses

A. Signature

By writing this directive, I intend to ease the burdens of decision making on those entrusted with my health care decisions. I understand the purpose and effect of this document and sign it knowingly, voluntarily, and after careful deliberation.

Signed this _____ day of _____, 20____

Printed Name _____

Address _____

City _____ State _____

Signature _____

B. Signature of Witnesses

I declare that the person who signed this document, or asked another to sign this document on his or her behalf, did so in my presence, that he or she is personally known to me, and that he or she appears to be of sound mind and free of duress or undue influence. I am 18 years of age or older and am not designated by this or any other document as the person's health care representative, nor as an alternate health care representative.

Witness's Printed Name _____

Address _____

City _____ State _____

Signature _____

Witness's Printed Name _____

Address _____

City _____ State _____

Signature _____

C. Signature of Health Care Representatives and Alternates (Optional, but Strongly Encouraged)

I have read this document and agree to act as health care representative, or as an alternate health care representative.

_____

Signature of Primary Health Care Representative

_____

Signature of First Alternate

_____

Signature of Second Alternate

D. Periodic Review

**You may cancel or change this document at any time. You should review it every so often. Each time you review it, place your initials and the date here:

Cantor, N. L. (1998). Making advanced directives meaningful. _Psychology, Public Policy and Law, 4,_ 629–652.

References

Addington-Hall, J. (2002). Researach sensitivities to palliative care patients. *Euro. Journal Cancer Care, 11,* 220–224.

Ainsworth, M. D. S., Blehar, M. C., Waters, E., & Wall, S. (1978). *Patterns of attachment: A psychological study of the strange situation.* Hillsdale, NJ: Erlbaum.

Ainsworth, M. D. S., & Bowlby, J. (1991). An ethological approach to personality development. *American Psychologist, 45,* 333–341.

Albom, M. (1997). *Tuesdays with Morrie.* New York: Doubleday.

American Cancer Society. (1999). *Cancer facts and figures, 1999, selected cancers.* Retrieved August 5, 2004 from www.cancer.org/statisticscff99selectedcancers.html

American Psychiatric Association. (1994). *Diagnostic and statistical manual of mental disorders* (4th ed.). Washington, DC: Author.

American Psychological Association. (2003). Guidelines on multicultural education, training, research, practice, and organizational change for psychologists. *American Psycholologist, 58,* 377–402. adapted. Washington, DC: Author.

Archer, J. (1999). *The nature of grief: The evolution and psychology of reactions to loss.* London: Routledge.

Arno, P., *Economic value of informal caregiving,* presented at the American Association of Geriatric Psychiatry, February 24, 2002. Retrieved August 25, 2004 from http://www.caregiver.org/caregiver/jsp/home.jsp

Arno, P .S., Levine, D., & Memmott, M. M. (1999). The economic value of informal caregiving, *Health Affairs, 2,* 182–188.

Ashenburg, K. (2002). *The mourner's dance.* New York: North Point Press.

Attig, T. (1996). *How we grieve: Relearning the world.* New York: Oxford University Press.

Attig, T. (2000). *The heart of grief: Death and the search for lasting love.* New York: Oxford University Press.

Attig, T. (2001). Relearning the world: Making and finding meanings. In R. A. Neimeyer (Ed). *Meaning reconstruction & the experience of loss* (pp. 33–53). Washington, DC: American Psychological Association.

Attig, T. (2004). Meanings of death seen through the lens of grieving. *Death Studies, 28,* 341–360.

Beery, L. D., Prigerson, H. G., Bierhals, A. J., Santucci, L. M., Newsom, J. T., Maciejewski, P. K., et al. (1997). Traumatic grief, depression and caregiving in elderly spouses of the terminally ill. *Omega, 35,* 261–279.

Bernstein, P. P., & Gavin, L.A. (1996). The death of a child: Implications for marital and family therapy. In J. Lonsdale, *The Hatherleigh guide to marriage and family therapy* (pp. 147–167). New York: Hatherleigh Press.

Bloombaum, M., Yamamoto, J., & James, Q. (1968). Cultural stereotyping among psychotherapists. *Journal of Consulting and Clinical Psychology, 32,* 99.

Boelen, P.A. & de Keijser, J. (2003). Traumatic grief as a disorder distinct from bereavement-related depression and anxiety: A replication study with bereaved mental health care patients. *American Journal of Psychiatry, 160,* 1399–1341.

Boelen, P.A., van den Bout, J., de Keijser, J., & Hoijtink, H. (2003). Reliability and validity of the dutch version of the Inventory of Traumatic Grief (ITG). *Death Studies, 27,* 227–247.

Bonanno, G. (2004). Loss, trauma and human resiliency. *American Psychologist, 59,* 2–28.

Bonanno, G. & Kaltman, S. (1999). Toward an integrative perspective on bereavement. *Psychological Bulletin, 125,* 760–776.

Bonanno, G., Wortman, C., Lehman, D., Tweed, R., Haring, M., Sonnega, J., et al. (2002). Resilience to loss and chronic grief: A prospective study from preloss to 18 months postloss. *Journal of Personality and Social Psychology, 83,* 1150–1164.

Boss, P. (2004) Ambiguous loss. In F. Walsh & M. McGoldrick, (Eds.), *Living beyond loss: Death in the family* (2nd Ed) (pp. 237–246). New York: Norton.

Bowen, M. (1991). Family reactions to death. In F. Walsh & M. McGoldrick (Eds.), *Living beyond loss: Death in the family* (pp. 79–92). New York: Norton.

Bowlby, J. (1969). *Attachment and loss, Vol. 1. Attachment.* New York: Basic Books.

Bowlby, J. (1973). *Attachment and loss, Vol. 2. Separation: Anxiety and anger.* New York: Basic Books.

Bowlby, J. (1979). *The making and breaking of affectional bonds.* London: Tavistock.

Bowlby, J. (1980). *Attachment and loss, Vol. 3. Loss: Sadness and depression:* New York: Basic Books.

Brain Injury Association of America (n.d.). *What is brain injury:Statistics.* Retrieved June, 21, 2004 from http://www.biausa.org/Pages/What_is_brain_injury.html

Byock, I. (1997). *Dying well: The prospect for growth at the end of life.* New York: Riverhead Books.

Byrne, G. J. A., & Raphael, B. (1997). The psychological symptoms of conjugal bereavement in elderly men over the first 13 months. *International Journal of Geriatric Psychiatry, 12,* 241–251.

Cantor, N. L. (1998). Making advanced directives meaningful. *Psychology, Public Policy, and Law, 4,* 629–652.

Carter, B. (1991). Death in the therapist's own family. In F. Walsh & M. McGoldrick (Eds.), *Living beyond loss: Death in the family* (pp. 273–283). New York: Norton.

Centers For Disease Control. (2001). *TBI in the US: A report to Congress.* Retrieved January 16, 2001 from http://www.cdc.gov/ncipc/pub-res/tbicongress.htm

Centers For Disease Control. (2001). *SafeUSA—What you should know about spinal cord injury.* Retrieved January 16, 2001 from http://www.cdc.gov/safeusahome/home/sci.htm

Centers For Disease Control. (2001). HIV/AIDS surveillance report, US HIV and AIDS cases reported through December 1999, *Year End Edition, 2.* Retrieved January 16, 2001 from http://www.cdc.gov/hiv/stats/hasr1102.pdf

Centers For Disease Control. (2004). Deaths: Preliminmary data for 2002, *National Vital Statistics Reports, 52,* 1–48.

Cohen, R. (2004). *Blindsided: A reluctant memoir.* New York: HarperCollins.

Compassionate Friends, Inc. (1999). When a child dies: A survery of bereaved parents. *The Forum Newsletter, Association for Death Education and Counseling, 25,* 1/10–11.

Davies, B., Gudmundsottir, M., Worden, W., Orloff, S., Sumner, L., & Brenner, P. (2004). "Living in the dragon's shadow" Fathers' experience of a child's life-limiting illness. *Death Studies, 28,* 111–135.

Davis, C. G., Nolen-Hoeksema, S., & Larson, J. (1998). Making sense of loss and benefiting from the experience: Two contruals of meaning. *Journal of Personality and Social Psychology, 75,* 561–574.

Doka, K. J. (Ed.). (1989). *Disenfranchised grief: Recognizing hidden sorrow.* Lexington, MA: Lexington.

Doka, K. J. (Ed.). (2002). *Disenfranchised grief: New direction, challenges and strategies for practice.* Champaign, Ill: Research Press.

Doka, K. J. (2002). How could God?: Loss and the spiritual assumptive world. In J. Kauffman (Ed.). *Loss of the assumptive world: A theory of traumatic loss.* (pp. 49–54). New York.: Brunner-Routledge/Taylor & Francis.

Duncan, I., (1927). *My life.* New York: Boni and Liverright.

Enright, B. P. & Marwit, S. J., (2002). Diagnosing complicated grief: A closer look, *Journal of Clinical Psychology, 58,* 747–757.

Family Caregivers Association, (2000). Random Sample Survey of 1000 Adults, Funded by CareThere.com, Summer, 2000.

Fanos, J. H. (1996). *Sibling loss.* Mahwah, NJ: Lawrence Erlbaum.

Fears, D. (2002, July 15). America—the sweet hereafter: Tradition minded Asians bring ancerstors ashes to U.S. *The Washington Post,* p. A1.

Feeney, J. A. (1998). Adult attachment and relationship-centered anxiety: Responses to physical and emotional distancing. In J. A. Simpson & W. S. Rholes (Eds.), *Attachment theory and close relationships* (pp. 189–218). New York: Guilford.

Fenchuk, G. W., (Ed.), (1994). *Timeless wisdom* (p. 2). Midlothian, VA: Cake Eaters, Inc.

Field, T. (1985). Attachment as psychobiological attunement: Being on the same wavelength. In M. Reite & T. Field (Eds.), *The Psychobiology of Attachment and Separation* (pp. 415–454) New York: Academic Press.

Fraley, R. C. (2002). Attachment stability from infancy to adulthood: Meta-analysis and dynamic modeling of developmental mechanisms. *Personality and Social Psychology Review, 6,* 123–151.

Fraley, R. C., Davis, K. E., & Shaver, P. R. (1998). Dismissing-avoidance and the defensive organization of emotion, cognition, and behavior. In J. A. Simpson & W. S. Rhodes (Eds.), *Attachment theory and close relationships* (pp. 249–279). New York: Guilford.

Fraley, R C., & Shaver, P. R. (1999). Loss and bereavement: Attachment theory and recent controversies concerning "grief work" and the nature of detachment. In J. Cassidy &. P. R. Shaver (Eds.), *Handbook of attachment: Theory, research, and clinical applications* (pp. 735–759). New York: Guilford.

Frank, J. D. (1974). *Persuasion and healing.* Baltimore: The Johns Hopkins University Press.

Frankl, U. E. (1977). *Man's search for meaning.* New York: Pocket Books.

Freud, S. (1957). Mourning and melancholia. In J. Strachey (Ed.. and Trans.), *The standard edition of the complete psychological works of Sigmund Freud* (Vol. 14). London: Hogarth. (Original work published 1917).

Galinsky, N. (2003, January/February). The death of a grandchild: A complex grief. *The Forum Newsletter, Association for Death Education and Counseling, 29,* 6–7.

Gjerdingen, D. K., Neff, J. A., Wang, M., & Chaloner, K. (1999). Older persons' opinions about life-sustaining procedures in the face of dementia. *Archives of Family Medicine, 8,* 21–425.

Godwin, G. (2002). *Father melancholy's daughter.* New York: William Morrow.

Goldman, L. (1996). We can help children grieve: A child-oriented model for memorializing, *Young Children, 51,* 69–73.

Goldman, L. (2000). *Life and loss: A guide to help grieving children* (2nd ed.). New York: Taylor & Francis.

Goldman, L. (2002). The assumptive world of children. In J. Kauffman (Ed.), *Loss of the assumptive world: A theory of traumatic loss. The series in trauma and loss* (pp. 193–202). New York: Brunner-Routledge.

Goodman, K.W. (1998). End-of-life algorithms. *Psychology, Public Policy, and Law, 4,* 719–727.

Grollman, E. A. (1988). *Suicide: Prevention, intervention postvention* (2nd Edition). Boston: Beacon Press.

Hall, C. I. (1997). Cultural malpractice: The growing obsolescence of psychology with the changing U.S. population. *American Psychologist, 52,* 642–651.

Hazen, C., & Shaver, P. (1990). Love and work: An attachment-theoretical perspective. *Journal of Personality and Social Psychology, 59,* 270–280.

Hogan, N. S., & DeSantis, L. D. (1996). Adolescent sibling bereavement: Toward a new theory. In C. Corr & D. B. Balk (Eds.), *Helping adolescents cope with death and bereavement* (pp. 173–195). Philadelphia: Springer.

Horowitz, M. J., Siegel, B., Holen, A., Bonanno, G.A., Milbrath, C. & Stinson, C.H. (1997). Diagnostic criteria for complicated grief disorder, *American Journal of Psychiatry, 157,* 904–910.

Insel T. R. (2000). Toward a neurobiology of attachment. *Review of General Psychology, 4,* 176–185.

Institute of Medicine (1997). *Approaching death: Improving care at the end of life.* M. J. Field & C. K. Cassel (Eds.). Washington, DC: National Academy Press.

Institute of Medicine (2001). *Improving palliative care for cancer.* K.M. Foley & H. Gelband, (Eds.), Washington, DC: The National Academy Press.

Irish, D. P. (1993). Introduction: Multiculturalism and the majority population. In D. Irish, K. Lundquist, & V. Nelsen (Eds.), *Ethnic variations in dying, death, and grief: diversity in universality* (pp. 1–10). Philadelphia: Taylor & Francis.

Jacobs, S. (1999). *Traumatic grief: Diagnosis, treatment, and prevention.* Philadelphia: Brunner/Mazel.

Jacobs, S., Mazur, C., & Prigerson, H. (2000). Diagnostic criteria for traumatic grief. *Death Studies, 24,* 185–199.

Jeffreys, J. S. (1995). *Coping with workplace change: Dealing with loss and grief.* Menlo Park, CA: Crisp/Thomson Learning.

Johnson, S. E. (1987). *After a child dies: Counseling bereaved families.* New York: Springer.

Kissane, D. W., Bloch, S., Onghena, P., McKenzie, D. P., Snyder, R. D., & Dowe, D. L. (1996). The Melbourne family grief study, II: Psychosocial morbidity and grief in bereaved families. *American Journal of Psychiatry, 153,* 659–666.

Klass, D. (1988). *Parental grief: Solace and resolution.* New York: Springer.

Klass, D. (1996). The deceased child in the psychic and social worlds of bereaved parents during the resolution of grief. In D. Klass, P. R. Silverman, & S. L. Nickman (Eds.), *Continuing bonds: New understanding of grief* (pp. 199–215). Washington, DC: Taylor & Francis.

Klass, D. (1997). The deceased child in the psychic and social worlds of bereaved parents during the resolution of grief. *Death Studies, 21,* 147–175.

Klass, D. (1999). *Spiritual lives of bereaved parents.* Philadelphia: Brunner/Mazel.

Klass, D. (2001). The inner representation of the dead child in the psychic and social narratives of bereaved parents (pp. 77–94). In R. Neimeyer (Ed.), *Meaning reconstruction and the experience of loss.* Washington, DC: American Psychological Association.

Klerman, G. L., & Clayton, P. (1984). Epidemiologic perspectives on the health consequences of bereavement. In M. Osterweis, F. Solomon, & M. Green (Eds.), *Bereavement: Reactions, consequences, and care* (pp. 15–44). Washington, DC: National Academy Press.

Koenig, B. A. (1997). Cultural diversity in decision-making about care at the end of life. In M. Field & C. Cassel, (Eds.), *Approaching death: Improving care at the end of life* (pp. 362–382). Washington, DC: National Academy Press.

Koenig, B. A., & Gates-Williams, J. (1995). Understanding cultural differences in caring for dying patients, *Western Journal of Medicine, 163,* 244–249.

Kubler-Ross, E. (1969). *On death and dying: What the dying have to teach doctors, nurses, clergy and their own families.* New York: Macmillan Publishing.

Kubler-Ross, E. (1978). *To live until we say goodbye.* Englewood Cliffs, NJ: Prentice-Hall.

Kubler-Ross, E. (1981). *Living with death and dying.* New York: Macmillan Publishing.

Kushner, H. (1981). *When bad things happen to good people.* New York: Schocken books.

Leon, I. G. (1992). Perinatal loss: Choreographing grief on the obstetric unit. *American Journal of Orthopsychiatry, 62,* 7.

Levine, S. (1987). *Healing into life and death.* New York: Doubleday.

Lewis, C. S. (1961). *A grief observed.* San Francisco: Harper.

Lindemann, E. (1944). Symptomology and management of acute grief, *American Journal of Psychiatry, 101,* 141–148.

Lund, D. A., & Caserta, M. S. (1992). Older bereaved spouses participation in self-help groups. *Omega, 25,* 47–61.

MacLean, P. D. (1952). Some psychiatric implications of physiological studies on frontotemporal portions of limbic system ("visceral brain"). *Electroencephalography & Clinical Neurophysiology, 4,* 407–418.

MacLean, P. D. (1955a). The limbic system ("visceral brain") in relation to central gray and reticulum of the brain stem; evidence in emotional process. *Psychosomatic Medicine, 17,* 355–366.

MacLean, P. D. (1955b). The limbic system ("visceral brain") and emotional behavior. *Archives of Neurology & Psychiatry (Chicago), 73,* 130–134.

MacLean, P. D. and Pribram, K.H. (1953). The neuronographic analysis of medial and basil-cerebral cortex. *Journal of Neurophysiology, 16,* 312–323.

MacLean, P. D. (1973). *A triune concept of the brain and behavior.* University of Toronto Press.

MacLean, P. D. (1985). Brain evolution relating to family, play, and the separation call. *Archives of General Psychiatry, 42,* 405–417.

Marshall, V. W. (1996). Death, bereavement, and the social psychology of aging and dying. In J. D. Morgan (Ed.), *The ethical issues in the care of the dying and bereaved aged* (pp. 57–73). Amityville, NY: Baywood.

McGoldrick, M. (1991). Echoes from the past: Helping families mourn their losses. In F. Walsh & M. McGoldrick (Eds.), *Living beyond loss: Death in the family* (pp. 50–78). New York: Norton.

McGoldrick, M., & Gerson, R. (1985). *Genograms in family assessment.* New York: Norton.

McGoldrick, M., & Walsh, F. (1991). A time to mourn: Death and the family life cycle. In F. Walsh & M. McGoldrick (Eds.), *Living beyond loss: Death in the family* (pp. 30–49). New York: Norton.

McGoldrick, M., & Walsh, F. (1991). Loss and the family: A systemic perspective. In F. Walsh & M. McGoldrick (Eds.), *Living beyond loss: Death in the family* (pp. 2–29). New York: Norton.

McHugh, P. & Slavney, P. (1998). *The perspectives of psychiatry (2nd Edition).* Baltimore: The Johns Hopkins University Press.

McIntosh, D. N., Silver, R. C., & Wortman, C. B. (1993). Religion's role in adjustment to a negative life event: Coping with the loss of a child. *Journal of Personality and Social Psychology, 65,* 812–821.

McLeod, B.W. (1999). *Caregiving: The spiritual journey of love, loss and renewal.* New York: John Wiley & Sons.

McLeod, B.W. (Ed.). (2002). *And thou shalt honor: The caregiver's companion.* Rodale: Rodalestore.com.

Melham, N.M., Rosales, C., Karageorge, J., Reynolds, C., Frank, E. & Shear, M. (2001). Comorbidity of Axis I disorders in patients with traumatic grief. *Journal of Clinical Psychiatry, 62,* 884–887.

Miller, J. S., Segal, D. L., & Coolidge, F. L. (2001). The comparison of suicidal thinking and reasons for living among younger and older adults. *Death Studies, 25,* 357–365.

Miller, W. (1976). *When going to pieces holds you together.* Minneapolis, MN: Augsburg Publications.

Mitford, J. (1963). *American way of death.* NY: Simon & Schuster.

Morgan, J. D. (1995). Living our dying and our grieving: Historical and cultural attitudes. In H. Wass & R. A. Neimeyer (Eds.), *Dying: Facing the facts* (pp. 25–45). Washington, DC: Taylor & Francis.

Moss, M. S., Moss, S. Z., & Hansson, R. O. (2001). Bereavement and old age. In M. S. Stroebe, R. O. Hansson, W. Strobe, & H. Schut, (Eds.), *Handbook of bereavement research: Consequences, coping, and care* (pp. 241–260). Washington, DC: American Psychological Association.

Multiple Sclerosis Society. (2001). *MS, the disease.* Retrieved January 16, 2001 from http://www.msaa.com

Munsch, R. (1986). *Love you forever.* Willowdale, Ontario, Canada: Firefly Books.

Nadeau, J. W. (2001). Meaning making in family bereavement: A family systems approach. In M. S. Stroebe, R. O. Hansson, W. Stroebe, and & H. Schut (Eds.), *Handbook of bereavement research: Consequences, coping, and care* (pp. 329–347). Washington, DC: American Psychological Association.

National Cancer Institute: Office of Education and Special Initiatives (2003). Palliative care: A review of the literature. *Special report to Office of Special Initiatives* No. 263-01-D-0174.

National Institutes of Health (2002). *Symptom management in cancer: Pain, depression, and fatigue.* State-of-the-science conference statement, October 26, 2002.

National Vital Statistics System. (2001). Births, marriages, and deaths: Provisional data for January-December 2000. *National vital statistics reports.* *49,* (6).

National Vital Statistics System. (1997). Births and deaths: Preliminary data for 1997. *National vital statistics reports,* 47, (4).

National Vital Statistics System. (1995). Births and deaths: Uniited States, 1995. *Monthly vital statistics report.* *45,* (3).

Neimeyer, R. A. (1998). *Lessons of loss: A guide to coping.* New York: McGraw-Hill.

Neimeyer, R. A. (2001). The language of loss: Grief therapy as a process of meaning reconstruction. In R. A. Neimeyer (Ed.), *Meaning reconstruction & the experience of loss.* pp. 261–292. Washington, DC: American Psychological Association.

Neimeyer, R. A. (2003). Death anxiety and attitudes toward the elderly among older adults: The role of gender and ethnicity. *Death Studies, 27,* 335–354.

Neimeyer, R. A. (2004). Research on grief and bereavement: Evolution and revolution. *Death Studies, 28,* 529–530.

Neville, K. (2003). In D. A. Miserando's *Celebrity Café Interview.* Retrieved October 20, 2003 from http://www.thecelebritycafe.com

Newman, J. (1997/2002). At your disposal: The funeral industry prepares for boom times. In G.E. Dickinson & M. R. Leming (Eds.), *Dying, death and bereavement* (6th ed. pp.18–27) Guilford, CT: McGraw-Hill/Dushkin. (Original in Harpers, November, 1997).

Nickerson, K., Helms, J., & Terrell, F. (1994). Culture mistrust, opinions about mental illness, and black student attitudes toward seeking psychological help from white counselors. *Journal of Counseling Psychology, 41,* 378–385.

Nouwen, H. (1972). *The wounded healer: Ministry in contemporary society.* New York: Doubleday & Company.

Ogrodniczuk, J.S., Piper, W.E., Joyce, A.S., Weidman, R., McCallum, M., Azim, H., et al., (2003). Differentiating symptoms of complicated grief and depression among Psychiatric outpatients. *Canadian Journal of Psychiatry, 48,* 87–93.

Oliver, L. E. (1999). Effects of a child's death on the marital relationship: A review. *Omega, 39,* 197–227.

Ortega y Casset, J. (1957). *The revolt of the masses.* New York: Norton.

Ott, C.H. (2003). The impact of complicated grief on mental and physical health at various points in the bereavement process. *Death Studies, 27,* 249–272.

Parkes, C. M., & Weiss, R. S. (1993). *Recovery from bereavement* (softcover ed., 1995) Northvale: NJ: Jason Aronson.

Parkes, C. M., Laungani, P., & Young, B. (Eds.). (1997). *Death and bereavement across cultures.* London: Routledge.

Ponzetti, J. (1992). Bereaved families: A comparison of parents' and grandparents' reactions to the death of a child. *Omega, 25,* 63–71.

Prigerson, H. G., Bierhals, A.J., Kasl, S.V., Reynolds, C.F. III, Shear, M.K., Day, N., Beery, et al. (1997). Traumatic grief as a risk factor for mental and physical morbidity. *American Journal of Psychiatry, 154,* 616–623.

Prigerson, H. G., Frank, E., Kasl, S. V., Reynolds, C. F. III, Zubenko, Houck, G., P. R., et al. (1995). Traumatic grief and bereaved-related depression as distinct disorders: Preliminary empiracle validation in elderly bereaved spouses, *American Journal of Psychiatrey, 152,* 22–30.

Prigerson, H. G. & Jacobs, S. C. (2001). Traumatic grief as a distinct disorder: A rationale, consensus criteria, and a preliminary empiracle test. In M. S. Stroebe, R. O. Hansson, W. Stroebe, & H. Schut (Eds.), *Handbook of bereavement research: Consequences, coping, and care* (pp. 613–637). Washington, DC: American Psychological Association.

Prigerson, H. G., Maciejewski, P. K., Newsome, J., Reynolds, C. F. III, Frank, E., Bierhals, E. J., et al, (1995). The inventory of complicated grief: A scale to measure certain maldaptive symptoms of loss, *Psychiatry Research, 59,* 65–79.

Prigerson, H. G., Shear, M. K., Jacobs, S. C., Reynolds, C. F. III, Maciejewski, P. K., Davidson, J.R.T., et al. (1999). Consenus criteria for traumatic grief: A preliminary empirical test. *British Journal of Psychiatry, 174,* 67–73.

Prigerson, H. G., Shear, M.K., Newsom, J.T., Frank, E., Reynolds, C.F., III, Maciejewski, P.K., et al. (1996). Anxiety among widowed elders: Is it distinct from depression and grief? *Anxiety, 2,* 1–12.

Rando, T. A. (1993). The increasing prevalence of complicated mourning: The onslaught is just beginning. *Omega, 26*, 43–59.

Rando, T. A. (1993). The treatment of complicted mourning. Champaign, IL: Research Press.

Rando, T. A. (1986). The unique issues and impact of the death of a child. In T.A. Rando (Ed.), *Parental loss of a child* (pp. 5–43). Champaign, IL: Research Press.

Rando, T. A. (1984). *Grief, dying and death: Clinical interventions for caregivers*. Champaign, IL: Research Press.

Raphael, B. (1983). *The anatomy of bereavement*. New York: Basic Books

Raphael, B., Minkov, C., & Dobson, M. (2001). Psychotherapeutic and pharmacological intervention for bereaved persons. In M. S. Stroebe, R. O. Hansson, W. Strobe, & H. Schut (Eds.), *Handbook of bereavement research: Consequences, coping, and care* (pp. 587–612). Washington, DC: American Psychological Association.

Reed, M. L. (2003, January/February). Grandparents' grief—Who is listening? *The Forum Newsletter, Association for Death Education and Counseling, 29*, 1–3.

Repole, M. J. (1996). The death of a sibling: Theories of attachment and loss. *Dissertation Abstracts Internatonal: Section B: The Sciences & Engineering, 57* (3-B), 2181. US: University Microfilms International.

Rosen, E. (1990). *Families facing death: Family dynamics of terminal illness*. Lexington, MA: Lexington Books.

Rosenblatt, P. C. (1993). Cross-cultural variation in the experience, expression, and understanding of grief. In D. Irish, K. Lundquist, & V. Nelsen (Eds.), *Ethnic variations in dying, death, and grief: Diversity in universality* (pp. 13–19). Philadelphia: Taylor & Francis.

Rosenblatt, P. C. (2000a). *Help your marriage survive the death of a child*. Philadelphia: Temple University Press.

Rosenblatt, P.C. (2000b). *Parent grief: Narratives of loss and relationship*. Philadelphia: Brunner/ Mazel.

Rothman, J. C. (1997). The bereaved parents survival guide. New York: Contiuum.

Rubin, S. (1996). The wounded family: Bereaved parents and the impact of adult child loss. In D. Klass, P. R. Silverman, & S. Nickman (Eds.), *Continuing bonds: Understanding the resolution of grief* (pp. 217–232). Washington, DC: Taylor & Francis.

Rubin, S., & Malkinson, R. (2001). Parental response to child loss across the life cycle: Clinical and research perspectives. In M. S. Stroebe, R. O. Hansson, W. Stroebe, & H. Schut (Eds.), *Handbook of bereavement research: Consequences, coping, and care* (pp. 219– 240). Washington, DC: American Psychological Association.

Sakalauskas, P. (1992). Understanding the spiritual and cultural influences on the attitudes of the bereaved. In G. R. Cox & R. J. Fundis (Eds.), *Spiritual, ethical and pastoral aspects of death and bereavement* (pp. 81–91). Amityville, NY: Baywood.

Saunders, C. (2002). The philosophy of hospice. In N. Thompson (Ed.), *Loss and grief: A guide for human services practitioners* (pp. 23–33). New York: Palgrave.

Scherago, M. (1987). *Sibling grief*. Redmond, WA: Medic Publishing Company.

Schwab, R. (1998). A child's death and divorce: Dispelling the myth. *Death Studies, 22*, 445–468.

Shneidman, E. S. (1972). Forward. In A. C. Cain (Ed.), *Survivors of suicide* (pp. ix–xi). Springfield, IL: Thomas.

Simpson, J.A., & Rholes, W.S. (1998). Attachment in adulthood. In J. A. Simpson & W. S. Rholes (Eds.), *Attachment theory and close relationships*. New York: Guilford.

Smilansky, S. (1987). On death: Helping children understand and cope. New York: Peter Lang.

Smith, S. A. (2002). *Hospice concepts: A guide to palliative care in terminal illness*. Champaign, IL: Research Press.

Solsberry, M. S. W. (1984). Reacting to particular types of bereavement: Death of a child. In M. Osterweis, F. Solomon & M. Green (Eds.), *Bereavement: Reactions, consequences, and care* (pp. 47–68). Washington, DC: National Academy Press.

Spiritual care work group of the international work group on death, dying and bereavement. (1990). *Death Studies, 14*, 75–81.

Stroebe, M. S., & Henk, S. (2001). Models of coping with bereavement: A review. In M. S. Stroebe, R. O. Hansson, W. Stroebe, and H. Schut (Eds.), *Handbook of bereavement research: Consequences, coping, and care* (pp. 375–403). Washington, DC: American Psychological Association.

Stroebe, M. S., & Schut, H. (2001). Meaning making in the dual process model of coping with bereavement. In R. A. Neimeyer (Ed.), *Meaning reconstruction & the experience of loss* (55–73). Washington, DC: American Psychological Association.

Stroebe, M. S., & Stroebe, W. (1991). Does "griefwork" work? *Journal of Consulting and Clinical Psychology, 59,* 479–482.

Stroebe, W., & Stroebe, M. (1987). *Bereavement and health.* N.Y.: Cambridge University Press.

Sue, S. W., & Sue, D. (2003). *Counseling the culturally diverse: Theory and practice* (4th ed.). New York: Wiley.

Sue, D. (2004). Whiteness and ethnocentric monoculturalism: Making the "invisible" visible. *American Psychologist, 59,* 761–769.

Talamantes, M. A. & Aranda, M. P. (2004). Cultural competency in working with Latino family caregivers. National Cargivers Alliance monograph. Retrieved August 12, 2004 from http://www.caregiver.org.

Teno, J. M., et al., (2004). Family perspectives on end-of-life care at the last place of care. *Journal of the American Medical Association, 291,* 88–93.

U.S. Department of Health and Human Services, (1998). Family caregiver alliance fact sheet

Walsh, F. (2004). Sprituality, death and loss. In F. Walsh, & M. McGoldrick, (Eds.) *Living beyond loss: Death in the family,* (2nd ed. pp. 182–210). New York: Norton

Walsh, F. & McGoldrick, M. (1991). Loss and the family: A systemic perspective. In F. Walsh & M. McGoldrick (Eds.), *Living beyond loss: Death in the family* (pp.1–29). New York: Norton.

Walsh, F., & McGoldrick, M. (1998). A family systems perspective on loss, recovery and resilience. In P. Sutcliffe, G. Tufnell, & U. Cornish, *Working with the dying and bereaved: Systemic approaches to therapeutic work* (pp. 1–26). New York: Routledge.

Wayment, H. A., & Vierthaler, J. (2002). Attachment style and bereavement reactions. *Journal of Loss and Trauma, 7,* 129–149.

Weaver, A. J. & Koenig, H. G. (1996). Elderly suicide, mental health professionals and the clergy. *Death Studies, 20,* 495–508.

Weeks, O. D. (2004). Comfort and healing death ceremonies that work. *Illness, Crisis & Loss, 12,* 113–125.

Wicks, R. J. (1995). *Seeds of sensitivity.* Notre Dame, IN: Ave Maria Press.

Worden, J. W. (1996). *Children and grief.* New York: The Guilford.

Worden, J. W. (2002). *Grief counseling and grief therapy: A handbook for the mental health practitioner* (3rd ed.). New York: Springer.

Wortman, C. B., & Silver, R. C. (1989). The myths of coping with loss. *Journal of Consulting and Clinical Psychology, 57,* 349–357.

Wudel, P. (2002). *When you sit at the bedside of someone is who dying.* Washington, DC: Joseph's House Hospice. Unpublished manuscript.

Zinner, E. S. (2002). Incorporating disenfranchised grief in the death education classroom. In K. J. Doka (Ed.), *Disenfranchised grief: New direction, challenges and strategies for practice* (pp. 389–404). Champaign, Il: Research Press.

Zinner, E. S. & Williams, M.B. (1999). *When a community weeps.* New York: Brunner/Mazel.

Index